Social Influences on Information and Communication Technology Innovations

Arthur Tatnall
Victoria University, Australia

Managing Director: Lindsay Johnston
Senior Editorial Director: Heather A. Probst
Book Production Manager: Sean Woznicki
Development Manager: Joel Gamon
Development Editor: Development Editor
Acquisitions Editor: Erika Gallagher
Typesetter: Jen McHugh
Cover Design: Nick Newcomer, Lisandro Gonzalez

Published in the United States of America by
Information Science Reference (an imprint of IGI Global)
701 E. Chocolate Avenue
Hershey PA 17033
Tel: 717-533-8845
Fax: 717-533-8661
E-mail: cust@igi-global.com
Web site: http://www.igi-global.com

Library of Congress Cataloging-in-Publication Data

Social influence on information and communication technology innovations /
Arthur Tatnall, editor.
p. cm.
Includes bibliographical references and index.
Summary: "This book discusses in great detail the use of actor-network theory in offering explanations for socio-technical phenomena, focusing heavily on information communication technologies"--Provided by publisher.
ISBN 978-1-4666-1559-5 (hbk.) -- ISBN 978-1-4666-1560-1 (ebook) -- ISBN 978-1-4666-1561-8 (print & perpetual access) 1. Diffusion of innovations--Social aspects. 2. Information technology--Social aspects. 3. Technological innovation--Social aspects. 4. Actor-network theory. I. Tatnall, Arthur.
HM846.S58 2012
303.48'33--dc23

2012002109

British Cataloguing in Publication Data
A Cataloguing in Publication record for this book is available from the British Library.

Table of Contents

Detailed Table of Contents

In the current climate of global competitiveness, many organisations are increasingly dependent on their IT strategy – either to increase their competitiveness, or often just to survive. Yet little is known about the non-technical influencing factors (such as people) and their impact on the development and implementation of IT strategy. There would therefore seem to be prima facie evidence that there is a need for a new approach to examining the relationships between social factors, technology and the organisation with respect to the development and implementation of IT strategy. This article seeks to make a contribution in this regard. Structuration Theory and Actor-Network Theory were employed to analyse how non-technical factors influence IT strategy. Structuration Theory holds that human actions are enabled and constrained by structures. Structures are rules and resources that do not exist independently of human action, nor are they material entities. Giddens describes them as 'traces in the mind' and argues that they exist only through the action of human beings. Actor Network Theory (ANT) provides a fresh perspective on the importance of relationships between actors that are both human and non-human. By their very presence, actors work to establish, maintain and revise the construction of organisational networks of aligned interests and gradually form stable actor-networks. ANT emphasises the heterogeneous nature of actor-networks which consist of and link together both technical and non-technical elements.

Recent work on information systems has discussed the nature and the complexity of the Information Infrastructures (II) concept. This research has mainly focused on two aspects: studying the process that both shapes and stabilizes information infrastructures, and studying the role played by information infrastructure in leveraging business performance. Using the ideas proposed by the Actor Network Theory (ANT), this article suggests a new way to conceptualise the nature of II, that is, its ontology. Using ANT as an ontological foundation to analyse the relations among actors, the article proposes the concept of information infrastructures in action to highlight their dynamic nature. This leads us to consider information infrastructures not as stable entities, but rather as entities performed in, by, and through relations. The aim of this work is to overcome the limitations associated with studying information infrastructures that rely on stability and manageability assumptions. Conceiving information infrastructures in terms of performative forces that evolve dynamically, this work provides a framework to examine information infrastructure in terms of dynamic relationships by looking at the process that shapes these relationships. The article suggests that information infrastructures should not be studied retrospectively to understand how they are established, but rather should be studied focussing on the process of making. Here we study the action of making rather than the processes that made.

ICT has been used in medical General Practice throughout Australia now for some years, but although most General Practices make use of ICT for administrative purposes such as billing, prescribing and medical records, many individual General Practitioners themselves do not make full use of these ICT systems for clinical purposes. The decisions taken in the adoption of ICT in general practice are very complex, and involve many actors, both human and non-human. This means that actor-network theory offers a most suitable framework for its analysis. This article investigates how GPs in a rural Division of General Practice not far from Melbourne considered the adoption and use of ICT. The study reported in the article shows that, rather than characteristics of the technology itself, it is often seemingly unimportant human issues that determine if and how ICT is used in General Practice.

This article explores issues associated with giving non-human actors a voice of their own in actor-network theory based research. What issues arise in doing so? Does doing so increase understanding of the issue to hand, bring to life and make more accessible and interesting the stories of these actors? Or does this anthropomorphism detract from the issues at hand? The authors discuss these broader issues and then present findings from an ANT field study which investigated the implementation of institutional repositories and their relations with the spread of open access to scholarly publishing. This paper experiments with allowing some of the non-human actors to speak for themselves. The authors conclude with a discussion which opens the debate: does giving voice to non-human actors bring them to life and make them better understood as intimately entangled with each other and human actors in the socio-material practices of the everyday? And what are the challenges in doing so?

Despite the rampant growth in technology-based service delivery options, the implementation of these contemporary forms of service channels continues to be risky and problematic for organisations. Current conceptualisations of IS implementation is rather narrow and highlights only particular aspects of this phenomenon. This paper adopts a socio-technical lens to enhance our understanding of the implementation of an Internet-based self-service technology (ISST) at a major South African healthcare insurance firm. Actor-Network theory's (ANT) key conceptual elements of inscription and translation are used to describe how the design and use of this self-service technology emerged from the co-entanglement between the technological and social. Drawing from a field study, this paper demonstrates the complex interdependencies and interactions among contrasting social, political, economic and technological issues and therefore advances implementation theory for these contemporary service channels in yet another important way.

Research involved with Actor-Network Theory (ANT) application in engineering domains often crosses through its fundamentals. In fact, exploring trends that envisage ANT as a paradigm that can prove valid in the engineering design field, researchers sometimes enrol in discussions that drive them to its roots. Obligatory Passage Points (OPP) and Immutable Mobiles (IM) are two of the fundamental concepts that need to be revisited. These concepts are critical to understanding innovation in Actor-Networks, especially for the part of IMs. In the pursuit of that understanding, the authors opt to entangle ANT and engineering design and explore a framework based on Programs of Action where actors are represented as taxonomies of competences. These actors are hybrids but, when human, they are mainly engineers engaged in the scope planning and resource management in engineering design projects or processes. This article exercises and develops a constructive process towards a methodology to approach innovation in engineering design. This research is useful for the first stages of the project design process and, in a broader way, to the full cycle of the engineering design process.

This article examines the role of actors in a Social Network Sites and also the triggers and challenges they represent to social networking between today's communities and businesses. A Social Network Sites is the product of the evolution of social liaisons and the emergence of online communities of people who are interested in exploring the concerns and activities of others. A social network is the assembly of direct or indirect contacts; a network is the product of interactions with the actors (individuals, families, enterprises, etc.) enabled by means of the structural design of web 2.0. Social Network Sites bring people together to interact through chat rooms, and share personal information and ideas around any topics via personal homepage publishing tools. This article is intended to be a trigger to deeply and more intensely explore potential roles of actor-network theory in the Social Network Sites context, in today's and tomorrow's world.

Using an ANT approach based on Programs of Action the authors explore the description of innovation cases to discover internal referents that conveys their meaning. This paper revisits some old and well

Preface

WHY IS ANT A USEFUL FRAMEWORK FOR INVESTIGATING TECHNOLOGICAL INNOVATION?

ABSTRACT

This preface discusses Actor-Network Theory (ANT), and in particular Innovation Translation – its approach to innovation adoption and its value as an analytical framework for theorising technological innovation. It begins by noting the controversy with the name: actor-network theory (ANT), and whether this should be changed to something like "actant-rhyzome ontology" of "the sociology of translation." It then makes use of a number of early classic papers by Latour, Callon, and Law to show why ANT provides a useful framework for handling socio-technical situations without privileging the social over the technical or vice-versa. A process of technological innovation making use of an approach involving the four moments of Innovation Translation is illustrated and an argument made for its value in other socio-technical situations involving technological innovation.

WHAT'S IN A NAME?

Actor-network theory can be rather daunting for someone beginning to approach it: a superficial understanding of the idea of human and non-human actors is easy, but coming to a better idea of what this all means is not so straightforward. Actor-network theory (ANT) has been around since the mid-1980s and was developed by Bruno Latour, Michel Callon, and John Law in an attempt to give a significant voice to technological artefacts as they considered that both social and technical determinism are flawed. ANT was designed to instead give a socio-technical account in which neither social nor technical positions are privileged.

In 1999 Latour remarked that that there were four things wrong with actor-network theory: "*the word actor, the word network, the word 'theory' and the hyphen*" (Latour, 1999). Later he changed this view and notes that:

"I was ready to drop this label for more elaborate ones like 'sociology of translation', 'actant-rhyzome ontology', 'sociology of innovation', and so on, until someone pointed out to me that the acronym A.N.T. was perfectly fit for a blind, myopic, workaholic, trail-sniffing and collective traveller. An ant writing for other ants, this fits my project very well!" (Latour, 2005:9).

This preface will use discussion of some of the early classic ANT papers (and also some more recent ones) to investigate why actor-network theory provides a useful approach to theorising technological innovation, and one that provides insights that other approaches do not.

Electric Vehicles and Problematisation

In a classic ANT paper from the mid-1980s Michel Callon (1986a) tells the story of the attempted development by Electricité de France (EDF) of its electric vehicle (VEL – véhicule électrique) in the early 1970s. He notes that EDF's plan for the VEL *"not only determined the precise characteristics of the vehicle it wished to promote, but also the social universe in which the vehicle would function."* (Callon, 1986a:21). A group of engineers from EDF outlined their ideas for creating a new market for VEL in publications and funding applications. They went to great pains to make a case for an electric vehicle that would overcome the place in society of the traditional motorcar. The engineers believed that both the techno-scientific and the social issues that could lead to this change could be solved.

Callon describes how EDF drew a picture of the internal combustion engine car as 19th century industrial revolution technology, responsible for most of the noise and pollution in our cities. They suggested that their plan would turn the car into a simple useful object without these problems. The EDF identified the CGE (Compagnie Génèrale d'Electricité) as the company to develop the electric motor and the batteries, while Renault would manufacture the car body. Callon identifies the human entities responsible for all this, but also points out that these are not alone in exerting an influence, so setting the scene for ANT's treatment of human and non-human actors.

"Up to this point, the entities are ones familiar to the sociologist. There are consumers, social movements and ministries. But it would be wrong to limit the inventory. There are also accumulators, fuel cells, electrodes, electrons, catalysts and electrolytes. For, if the electrons do not play their part or the catalysts become contaminated, the result would be no less disastrous than if the users rejected the new vehicle, the new regulations were not enforced, or Renault stubbornly decided to develop the R5. In the world defined and built by the EDF, at least three new and essential entities must be added: zinc/air accumulators, lead accumulators, and fuel cells with their cohort of associated elements (catalysts, electrons etc.)." (Callon, 1986a:23).

HUMAN AND NON-HUMAN ACTORS: ACTOR-NETWORK THEORY

Actor-network theory considers both social and technical determinism to be flawed and proposes instead a socio-technical account (Callon & Latour, 1981; Latour, 1986; Law & Callon, 1988) in which neither social nor technical positions are privileged. In this socio-technical order nothing is purely social and nothing is purely technical (Law, 1991). What seems, on the surface, to be social is partly technical, and what may appear to be only technical is partly social. ANT deals with the social-technical divide by denying that purely technical or purely social relations are possible. It offers the notion of heterogeneity to describe projects such as the use of a programming language, database management system, barcode scanner, human programmer, and operator in the construction of a computer system for use in stock control in a supermarket. The utilisation of heterogeneous entities (Bijker, Hughes, & Pinch, 1987) then avoids questions of: "is it social?" or "is it technical?" as missing the point, which should be: *"is this association stronger or weaker than that one?*" (Latour, 1988:27). This can be done after identification of both human and non-human actors – as was the case with the VEL.

To address the need to treat both human and non-human actors fairly and in the same way, actor-network theory is based upon three principles: agnosticism, generalised symmetry, and free association (Callon, 1986b). In summary, under these principles, actor-network theory attempts impartiality towards all actors in consideration, whether human or non-human, and makes no distinction in approach between the social, the natural and the technological. As Callon puts it:

"The rule which we must respect is not to change registers when we move from the technical to the social aspects of the problem studied." (Callon, 1986b:200).

"It makes sense to treat natural and social adversaries in terms of the same analytical vocabulary. Rather than treating, for instance, the social in one way and the scientific in another, one seeks instead to follow the fortunes of the network in question and consider its problems, the obduracy of the elements involved in those problems, and the response of the network as it seeks to solve them." (Law, 1987:4).

In actor-network theory an actor is any human or non-human entity that is able to make its presence *individually felt* (Law, 1987) by the other actors. An actor is made up *only* of its interactions with these other actors (de Vries, 1995; Law, 1992), and Law (1992) notes that an actor thus consists of an association of heterogeneous elements constituting a network. Callon (1986a) argues that an actor can also be considered, at times, as a black box, as we do not always need to see the details of the network of interactions that is inside it. The concept of a network is an important one in actor-network theory.

ANT also attempts to do away with binaries like far/close, macro/micro, and inside/outside (Latour, 1997) as it claims that it is not whether or not the various elements of a network are in close physical proximity that matters. What does matter is their interconnectedness. In considering macro/micro distinctions, Latour (1997) maintains that one network is never "bigger" than another, but simply "longer" or more intensely connected and that concepts like outside or inside make no sense as a network is made up only of interconnections. What is important is whether or not a connection has been established between elements. In ANT the passage of time also loses much of its importance and becomes just a consequence of the formation of alliances between actors rather than a fixed explanatory framework (Latour, 1991).

Latour argues that for every "socio-technical imbroglio" (Latour, 1988) two things are necessarily involved in the formation of its definition. Firstly, we need to determine the number of people who are convinced that it can be considered as a simple single entity (a black box), and secondly, what sorts of changes it must undergo to convince still more people of this. But the formation of a network is not the end of the story as networks are always unreliable and can become unstable. Callon (1987) further proposes that entities become strong and stable by gathering a "mass of silent others" to give them greater strength and credibility. A network becomes durable partly due to the durability of the bonds that hold it together, but also because it is itself composed of a number of durable and simplified networks.

"The solidity of the whole results from an architecture in which every point is at the intersection of two networks: one that it simplifies and another that simplifies it." (Callon, 1987:97).

Actor-network theory, or the "sociology of translations" (Callon, 1986b; Law, 1992), is concerned with studying the mechanics of power as this occurs through the construction and maintenance of networks made up of both human and non-human actors. It is concerned with tracing the transformation of these heterogeneous networks (Law, 1991) that are made up of people, organisations, agents, machines, and many other objects. It explores the ways that the networks of relations are composed, how they emerge and come into being, how they are constructed and maintained, how they compete with other networks, and how they are made more durable over time. It examines how actors enlist other actors into their world and how they bestow qualities, desires, visions, and motivations on these actors (Latour, 1996). Law and Callon put it this way:

"Our object, then, is to trace the interconnections built up by technologists as they propose projects and then seek the resources required to bring these projects to fruition." (Law & Callon, 1988:285).

ARAMIS: A COMPLEX INNOVATION

Latour's book (1996) tells the story of a revolutionary "guided-transportation" system intended to be part of the Parisian public transportation system in the 1970s. It was intended for the Petite Ceinture district in Paris. Work on the system commenced in 1969 and was abandoned in 1987. Apart from its allusion to The Three Musketeers, **Aramis** is an acronym for *Agencement en Rames Automatisées de Modules Indépendants dans les Stations* (Arrangement in Automated Trains of Independent Modules in Stations). The idea was to produce a system that combined the flexibility of a car with the efficiency of a railway. The book tells of Aramis' conception, development, and ultimate failure in the form of a detective story, and tells it simultaneously from several different perspectives using a number of different voices. A young engineer and the sociologist, Norbert, conducting the investigation carry the storyline. The engineers and administrators who worked on Aramis speak through both interviews and documents. The "author" interjects from time to time to provide a sociological commentary, and later, Aramis speaks on its own behalf, bewailing its fate. In the book, each voice, or reality (Wertheim, 1997) is identified by the use of a different typography. This style of writing provides an interesting and novel approach. The young engineer describes the technique used by Norbert to organise "*meetings and confrontations*" (Latour, 1996:6) in the evenings after the interviews to discuss the events of the day and to determine which actor to follow next. The sources of data used in Aramis are principally interviews and documents.

Like most new technology, this innovative Parisian transport project was not seen as being *real* at the beginning of its development (Tatnall, 2005). In common with other technological projects it could not possibly be real at the beginning as it did not then exist for people to see and to evaluate whether it might be something they could use. The problem was that Aramis never did succeed in becoming real and hence eventually died. Latour describes Aramis as "*merely realizable*" and "*not yet real*" (Latour, 1996:85) and notes that Aramis should have taken on reality by degrees.

The story of Aramis shows how an innovative project like this can involve a great deal of complexity that can easily be overlooked. Aramis made use of non-material couplings between carriages to facilitate fast coupling and uncoupling of the independent modules. Technical issue with these couplings presented a good deal of trouble, and a simplistic investigation of the story of Aramis could easily conclude that this was the reason for its failure. The real story is, however, much more complex!

ANT and Complexity

A major issue in any research dealing with technological innovation is how to understand and handle the complexities of this technology. A common method of handling complexity in all subject areas lies in simplification, but in this case, the danger with simplification is that it runs the risk of removing just those things that constitute the description wanted by concealing the parts played by many actors (Suchman, 1987). It can be argued that without this detail, any understanding of technological innovation tends to be superficial and lacks the necessary detail that would allow a more holistic account. Of course some simplification is necessary in order to represent the infinite possibilities of any complex situation and all research methodologies offer ways of simplifying complex social phenomena. The question here is which details to include and which to leave out, and who is to decide. ANT attempts to resist any attempt at the process of explanation by labelling, and Law notes that any attempt at naming does analytical work and "*strains to perform simplicity*" (1997). In this respect, an appropriate research approach needs to ensure that complexities are not lost "*in the process of labelling*" (Law, 1999:9).

An actor is not just a point object but an association of heterogeneous elements themselves constituting a network, so each actor is also a simplified network (Law, 1992). An actor can, however, in many ways also be considered as a black box, and when we open the lid of the box to look inside it will be seen to constitute a whole network of other, perhaps complex, associations (Callon, 1986a). In many cases, details of what constitutes an actor – details of its network – are a complication we can avoid having to deal with all the time. We can usually consider the entity just as an actor, but when doing this though it must be remembered that behind each actor there hide other actors that it has, more of less effectively, drawn together (Callon, 1987). This means that any changes affect not just this actor, but also the networks it simplifies (Callon, 1987). It is, likewise, often also possible to "punctualise" (Law, 1992) a stable network and so consider it in the form of a single actor. Whenever possible, it is useful to simplify, to an actor, a network that acts as a single block or a black box to make it easier to deal with. An actor then:

"... can be compared to a black-box that contains a network of black-boxes that depend on one another both for their proper functioning and for the proper functioning of the network." (Callon, 1987:95)

The important thing to note about the use of black-boxing for simplification is that the complexity is not just put into the black box and lost as it is always possible, and indeed necessary, to periodically reopen the black box to investigate its contents. The complexity is punctualised (Law, 1992:385), but not lost, and the *messy reality* (Hughes, 1983) is retained.

It is a feature of actor-network theory that the extent of a network is determined by actors that are able to make their presence individually felt (Law, 1987) by other actors. The definition of an actor requires this and means that, in practice, actors limit their associations to affect only a relatively small number of entities whose attributes are well defined within the network (Callon, 1987). This simplification is only possible if no new entities appear to complicate things, as the actor-network is the context in which the significance and limitations of each simplified entity is defined (Callon, 1986a). If a new element is added, or if one is removed, then some of the other associations may be changed as it is the juxtaposition of actors within the network that is all-important.

"The simplifications are only possible if elements are juxtaposed in a network of relations, but the juxtaposition of elements conversely requires that they be simplified" (Callon, 1987:95).

Latour (1997) notes that actor-network theory is not about *traced* networks, but about the activity of network *tracing*. He maintains that a network cannot exist independently of the act of tracing it, and that it should be thought of not so much as a thing, but as the recorded movement of a thing. He contends that there is no difference between the explanation of some project, and telling the story of how a heterogeneous engineer (Law, 1987) mobilises actors, and a network subsequently surrounds itself with new resources. Of networks, he notes that: "... by their very growth they become more and more of an explanation of themselves" (Latour, 1997:8).

Portuguese Navigation, Jet Planes, Scallops, and Fishermen

Looking at the expansion of Portuguese sea trade routes to India, Law (1986b, 1987) suggests that the process that led to the Portuguese domination of the Indian Ocean can be explained through system building or heterogeneous engineering. Law suggests that Portuguese king Henry the Navigator was the heterogeneous engineer who made this happen. The actors he identifies include: the boats used, need for a large crew to row and hence need to stop often to replenish supplies, masters of the vessels, Cape Bojador (point of no return), ocean currents, et cetera. (A shift in focus from Henry to the master of the vessel would bring a further network of sailors, spars, and stores into focus.) The galleys initially used were essentially war vessels needing to undergo several translations to become suitable for their new task. Law suggests three necessary technological innovations needed to be engineered: the improved sailing ship, the magnetic compass, and better knowledge of the Atlantic currents.

"... the stability and form of artifacts should be seen as a function of the interaction of heterogeneous elements as these are shaped and assimilated into a network." (Law, 1987:3)

An early paper on technological innovation by Law and Callon outlines the TSR2 military aircraft project in the UK in the late 1950s and early 1960s (Law & Callon, 1988, 1992). It describes how it was conceived, designed, and developed. It also looks at the various technical, political, and bureaucratic difficulties that led to its demise. The prototype aircraft flew well and were well liked by their pilots, but cost overruns and various political decisions following a general election led to its cancellation. This is seen as another example of a situation where an examination of either the technical or the social alone would not have revealed the true picture.

Innovations are of no value unless they are adopted and used, and in another classic ANT paper, Callon tells of domestication of the scallops and fishermen in St Brieuc Bay in France (Callon, 1986b). The population of scallops in St Brieuc bay was in decline and the story describes the attempts of three marine biologists to develop a conservation strategy to halt this decline. Actors are soon determines to be the scallops, the fishermen and the marine biologists. It was clear that changes would need to be made to the way the scallops developed and to the methods used by the fishermen. Callon explains how this was achieved in terms of the four moments of translation which are discussed in the next section.

Innovation Translation

The model of translation as proposed in actor-network theory thus proceeds from a quite different set of assumptions to those used in Innovation Diffusion (Rogers, 1995, 2003) or the Technology Acceptance Model (Davis, 1989). Latour (1986) argues that the mere possession of power by an actor does not automatically confer the ability to cause change unless other actors can be *persuaded* to perform the appropriate actions for this to occur. The notion that power is an attribute that can be *possessed* by an actor is an essentialist one, and Latour contends that rather than this it is the number of other people who enter into the situation that indicate the amount of power that has been exercised (Latour, 1986). He maintains that in an Innovation Translation model, informed by actor-network theory, the movement of an innovation through time and space is in the hands of people, each of whom may react to it in different ways. They may accept it, modify it, deflect it, betray it, add to it, appropriate it, or let it drop (Latour, 1986). He adds that this is true for the spread of anything from goods and artefacts to claims and ideas. In this case the adoption of an innovation comes as a consequence of the actions of everyone in the chain of actors who has anything to do with it. Furthermore, each of these actors shapes the innovation to their own ends, but if no one takes up the innovation then its movement simply stops; inertia cannot account for its spread. Instead of a process of transmission we have a process of continuous transformation (Latour, 1996) where faithful acceptance involving no changes is a rarity requiring explanation.

"Instead of the transmission of the same token – simply deflected or slowed down by friction – you get ... the continuous transformation of the token." (Latour, 1986:286)

McMaster *et al.* (1997) add that innovations do not wait passively to be invented or discovered, but are instead created:

"... from chains of weaker to stronger associations of human and non-human alliances. ... Each actant translates and contributes its own resources to the shape and ultimate form of the emerging black box." (McMaster, et al., 1997:4).

The key to innovation is the creation of a powerful enough consortium of actors to carry it through, and when an innovation fails to be taken up, this can be considered to reflect on the inability of those involved to construct the necessary network of alliances amongst the other actors (McMaster, et al., 1997). Getting an innovation accepted calls for strategies aimed at the enrolment of others in order to ensure the creation of the black box. Latour (1986) maintains that this is done by interesting others and then getting them to follow our interests, so becoming indispensable to them. This process is facilitated if other possibilities are first blocked off.

"The work of generating interest consists in constructing these long chains of reasons that are irresistible, even though their logical forms may be debatable" (Latour, 1996:33).

An actor-network is configured (Grint & Woolgar, 1997) by the enrolment of both human and non-human allies, and this is done by means of a series of negotiations in a process of re-definition in which one set of actors seeks to impose definitions and roles on others (Callon, 1986b). Translation can be regarded as a means of obliging some entity to consent to a detour (Callon, 1986a) that takes it along a path determined by some other entity. Law (1987) uses the term *heterogeneous engineer* to describe the entity that designs and creates these detours. A heterogeneous engineer is then able to speak on behalf of other actors enrolled in the network. The process of translation has four aspects or moments (Callon, 1986b):

a. In **Problematisation** a group of one or more key actors attempts to define the nature of the problem and the roles of other actors so that these key actors are seen as having the answer, and being indispensable to the solution of the problem (McMaster, et al., 1997).

In the case of VEL, problematisation of the petrol driven motorcar as noisy and polluting set the scene for the need for an electric vehicle. For the scallops in St Brieuc Bay:

"... the problematization describes a system of alliances, or associations, between entities, thereby defining the identity and what they want" (Callon, 1986b:206).

"They also show that the interests of these actors lie in admitting the proposed research programme. The argument which they develop in their paper is constantly repeated: if the scallops want to survive (no matter what mechanisms explain this impulse), if their scientific colleagues hope to advance knowledge on this subject (whatever their motivations be), if the fishermen hope to preserve their long term economic interests (whatever their reasons) they must: 1) know the answer to the question: how do scallops anchor?, and 2) recognize that their alliance around this question can benefit each of them." (Callon, 1986b:205)

b. **Interessement** is a series of processes which attempt to impose the identities and roles defined in the problematisation on the other actors. It means interesting and attracting an entity by coming between it and some other entity (Law, 1986a). "To be interested is to be in between (inter-esse), to be interposed." (Callon, 1986b :208). In the case of the scallops of St Brieuc Bay, Callon suggests that each entity can submit to being integrated into the plan or refuse by defining its identity and interests in another manner:

"Interessement is the group of actions by which an entity (here the three researchers) attempts to impose and stabilize the identity of the other actors it defines through its problematization." (Callon, 1986b:207).

c. **Enrolment** then follows through a process of coercion, seduction, or consent (Grint & Woolgar, 1997), leading to the establishment of a solid, stable network of alliances.
d. **Mobilisation** occurs as the solution gains wider acceptance (McMaster, et al., 1997) and an even larger network of absent entities is created (Grint & Woolgar, 1997) through some actors acting as spokespersons for others.

To define the relationship between themselves, many actors make use of intermediaries such as texts, technical artefacts, humans with specific skills, and money (Callon, 1991). These intermediaries then constitute the form and substance (Callon, 1992) of the interactions. A network becomes durable when actors feel no need to spend time opening and looking inside black boxes, but just accept these as given.

CONCLUSION

Many other situations involving technological innovation have resulted in ANT papers, including a number in the *International Journal of Actor-Network Theory and Technological Innovation*. Apart from these, however, there have been many ANT papers covering diverse topics including: the UK Cervical Screening Programme, the 19th century Luddite rebellion, the introduction and use of computers in schools, how university students build expert systems, medical school curricula, hospitals and other things medical, projects in museums, car parking systems, the achievements of Louis Pasteur, and the simultaneous invention of the Kodak camera and the mass market for amateur photography. Topics of other papers include: how changes occur in regional economies, the formation of attitudes by farmers and "field-level bureaucrats" on issues of farm pollution, the globalisation of coffee marketing, and a description of the failure of the IT Department in a UK City Council to adopt a structured systems design methodology.

Technological innovations are adopted for a variety of reasons, but these are often not the reasons proposed by the instigators and promoters of these technologies. The processes by which they are adopted are also often not entirely rational. Most of the various approaches to theorising the processes involved in innovation describe reasons for adoption based on a potential user's interpretation of the characteristics or usefulness of the technology, but do not really offer any good explanation for partial adoptions. In this respect Innovation Translation provides useful in allowing for people and organisations often not just accepting technological artefacts in their entirety in the form offered, but translating then into a form that contains just those aspects or applications of the technology that fill their real needs.

Arthur Tatnall
Victoria University, Australia

REFERENCES

Bijker, W. E., Hughes, T. P., & Pinch, T. J. (Eds.). (1987). *The social construction of technological systems: New directions in the sociology and history of technology*. Cambridge, MA: MIT Press.

Callon, M. (1986a). The sociology of an actor-network: The case of the electric vehicle . In Callon, M., Law, J., & Rip, A. (Eds.), *Mapping the dynamics of science and technology* (pp. 19–34). London, UK: Macmillan Press.

Callon, M. (1986b). Some elements of a sociology of translation: Domestication of the scallops and the fishermen of St Brieuc Bay . In Law, J. (Ed.), *Power, action & belief: A new sociology of knowledge?* (pp. 196–229). London, UK: Routledge & Kegan Paul.

Callon, M. (1987). Society in the making: The study of technology as a tool for sociological analysis . In Bijker, W. E., Hughes, T. P., & Pinch, T. P. (Eds.), *The social construction of technological systems* (pp. 85–103). Cambridge, MA: The MIT Press.

Callon, M. (1991). Techno-economic networks and irreversibility . In Law, J. (Ed.), *A sociology of monsters. Essays on power, technology and domination* (pp. 132–164). London, UK: Routledge.

Callon, M. (1992). The dynamics of techno-economic networks . In Coombs, R., Saviotti, P., & Walsh, V. (Eds.), *Technological change and company strategies* (pp. 72–102). London, UK: Hartcourt Brace Jovanovich.

Callon, M., & Latour, B. (1981). Unscrewing the Big Leviathan: How actors macro-structure reality and how sociologists help them to do so . In Knorr-Cetina, K., & Cicourel, A. V. (Eds.), *Advances in social theory and methodology. Toward an integration of micro and macro-sociologies* (pp. 277–303). London, UK: Routledge & Kegan Paul.

Davis, F. (1989). Perceived usefulness, perceived ease of use, and user acceptance of Information Technology. *Management Information Systems Quarterly, 13*(3), 318–340. doi:10.2307/249008

de Vries, G. (1995). Should we send Collins and Latour to Dayton, Ohio? *EASST Review, 14*(4).

Grint, K., & Woolgar, S. (1997). *The machine at work - Technology, work and organisation*. Cambridge, UK: Polity Press.

Hughes, T. P. (1983). *Networks of power: Electrification in Western society, 1880-1930*. Baltimore, MD: Johns Hopkins University Press.

Latour, B. (1986). The powers of association . In Law, J. (Ed.), *Power, action and belief. A new sociology of knowledge? Sociological Review monograph 32* (pp. 264–280). London, UK: Routledge & Kegan Paul.

Latour, B. (1988). The prince for machines as well as for machinations . In Elliott, B. (Ed.), *Technology and social process* (pp. 20–43). Edinburgh, UK: Edinburgh University Press.

Latour, B. (1991). Technology is society made durable . In Law, J. (Ed.), *A sociology of monsters. Essays on power, technology and domination* (pp. 103–131). London, UK: Routledge.

Latour, B. (1996). *Aramis or the love of technology*. Cambridge, MA: Harvard University Press.

Latour, B. (1997). *On actor-network theory. A few clarifications.*

Latour, B. (1999). On recalling ANT . In Law, J., & Hassard, J. (Eds.), *Actor network theory and after* (pp. 15–25). Oxford, UK: Blackwell Publishers.

Latour, B. (2005). *Reassembling the social: An introduction to actor-network theory*. Oxford, UK: Oxford University Press.

Law, J. (1986a). The heterogeneity of texts . In Callon, M., Law, J., & Rip, A. (Eds.), *Mapping the dynamics of science and technology* (pp. 67–83). UK: Macmillan Press.

Law, J. (1986b). On the methods of long distance control: Vessels, navigation and the Portuguese route to India . In Law, J. (Ed.), *Power, action and belief: A new sociology of knowledge?* (pp. 234–263). London, UK: Routledge & Kegan Paul.

Law, J. (1987). Technology and heterogeneous engineering: The case of Portuguese expansion . In Bijker, W. E., Hughes, T. P., & Pinch, T. J. (Eds.), *The social construction of technological systems: New directions in the sociology and history of technology* (pp. 111–134). Cambridge, MA: MIT Press.

Law, J. (1991). Introduction: Monsters, machines and sociotechnical relations . In Law, J. (Ed.), *A sociology of monsters: Essays on power, technology and domination*. London, UK: Routledge.

Law, J. (1992). Notes on the theory of the actor-network: Ordering, strategy, and heterogeneity. *Systems Practice*, *5*(4), 379–393. doi:10.1007/BF01059830

Law, J. (1997). *Topology and the naming of complexity* [Draft Web publication].

Law, J. (1999). After ANT: Complexity, naming and topology . In Law, J., & Hassard, J. (Eds.), *Actor network theory and after* (pp. 1–14). Oxford, UK: Blackwell Publishers.

Law, J., & Callon, M. (1988). Engineering and sociology in a military aircraft project: A network analysis of technological change. *Social Problems*, *35*(3), 284–297. doi:10.1525/sp.1988.35.3.03a00060

Law, J., & Callon, M. (1992). The life and death of an aircraft: A network analysis of technical change . In Bijker, W., & Law, J. (Eds.), *Shaping technology/building society: Studies in sociological change* (pp. 21–52). Cambridge, MA: MIT Press.

McMaster, T., Vidgen, R. T., & Wastell, D. G. (1997, 9-12 August, 1997). *Towards an understanding of technology in transition. Two conflicting theories.* Paper presented at the Information Systems Research in Scandinavia, IRIS20 Conference, Hanko, Norway.

Rogers, E. M. (1995). *Diffusion of innovations* (4th ed.). New York, NY: The Free Press.

Rogers, E. M. (2003). *Diffusion of innovations* (5th ed.). New York, NY: The Free Press.

Suchman, L. A. (1987). *Plans and situated actions. The problem of human-machine communication.* Cambridge, UK: Cambridge University Press.

Tatnall, A. (2005). In real-life learning, What is meant by 'real . In van Weert, T., & Tatnall, A. (Eds.), *Information and communication technologies and real-life learning - New education for the knowledge society* (pp. 143–150). New York, NY: Springer/IFIP. doi:10.1007/0-387-25997-X_16

Wertheim, M. (1997). The love of technology bites back. *21-C, 1-97,* 80-81.

Chapter 1
The Use of Structuration Theory and Actor Network Theory for Analysis:
Case Study of a Financial Institution in South Africa

Tiko Iyamu
Tshwane University of Technology, South Africa

Dewald Roode
University of Cape Town, South Africa

ABSTRACT

In the current climate of global competitiveness, many organisations are increasingly dependent on their IT strategy – either to increase their competitiveness, or often just to survive. Yet little is known about the non-technical influencing factors (such as people) and their impact on the development and implementation of IT strategy. There would therefore seem to be prima facie evidence that there is a need for a new approach to examining the relationships between social factors, technology and the organisation with respect to the development and implementation of IT strategy. This article seeks to make a contribution in this regard. Structuration Theory and Actor-Network Theory were employed to analyse how non-technical factors influence IT strategy. Structuration Theory holds that human actions are enabled and constrained by structures. Structures are rules and resources that do not exist independently of human action, nor are they material entities. Giddens describes them as 'traces in the mind' and argues that they exist only through the action of human beings. Actor Network Theory (ANT) provides a fresh perspective on the importance of relationships between actors that are both human and non-human. By their very presence, actors work to establish, maintain and revise the construction of organisational networks of aligned interests and gradually form stable actor-networks. ANT emphasises the heterogeneous nature of actor-networks which consist of and link together both technical and non-technical elements.

DOI: 10.4018/978-1-4666-1559-5.ch001

INTRODUCTION

The primary aim of the study was to address the question: what are the socio-technical factors influencing the development and implementation of information technology (IT) strategy in the organisation?

IT virtually affects every aspect of any organisation that deploys it (Cats-Baril and Thompson, 1997). IT strategy helps to set direction (Straub & Wetherbe, 1989), comprehension and focus on the future in the wake of change in the organisation that it supports. Undoubtedly, IT has been the greatest agent of change in the last century and promises to play this role even more dramatically in the coming decades (Kling, 2000). However, IT strategy often focuses almost exclusively on the technology, the non-human aspect of the strategy (Boar, 1998), and either by oversight or ignorance pays less attention to the people aspect, which more often than not, turns out to be the deciding variable of strategy success. Orlikowski (1993) argued that organisational politics has an important influence on the degree to which IT, through its strategy, can be used.

There is no conflict or contradiction in the combined use of both Structuration Theory (ST) and Actor-Network Theory (ANT) in the research on which this article is based. The aim is not to compare and contrast ST and ANT, but to highlight their importance and complementary usefulness in the research, which is the primary objective and strength of this article.

A combination of Structuration Theory and Actor-Network has been used by Brooks and Atkinson (2003), who interpreted ST and ANT into a 'new' theory which they call StructurAN-Tion Theory. In this study, the theories are used separately and complementary in the analysis of the case study in order to focus on different, if complementing issues. They helped us to gain an understanding of the enabling and constraining influences of the technical and non-technical components in the development and implementation of IT strategy.

The contribution of ST is that it provides a means for understanding how social institutions are produced and re-produced over time (Rose, 1998). Giddens (1984) defines social systems as visibly patterned interdependent networks of actions, where change in one part results in change in another. The Theory of Structuration suggests that human actions simultaneously condition and are conditioned by organisational properties in social contexts.

ANT does not distinguish between human and non-human agents and rejects distinctions between the technical and the non-technical (Latour, 1987, 1996; Callon & Law, 1989). Its focus can be on the micro, meso or macro level of the establishment of heterogeneous networks of aligned interests, and its use in this study was to provide a vehicle for understanding the impact of organisational politics on IT strategy development and implementation, with the latter seen as the institutionalised result of the establishment of a network of aligned interests.

The different theoretical concepts of ST and ANT emphasise different social contexts and facilitate different types of explanations.

ST does not allow for the examination of relationships between people and technology, and, for example, how power and values are embedded in the use of technology. Monteiro and Hanseth (1996) argued that ST simply does not provide a fine grained analysis of the interaction between individuals and technology.

An interrogation of the relationship between individuals and technology, which ST lacks, is complemented by ANT. ANT is concerned with the interactions between technology and individuals (Law, 1992), and contains a wealth of concepts for understanding the relationship between technology and individuals. The combination and complementary use of ST and ANT allowed a more complete analysis of how IT strategy development and implementation are affected by non-technical factors.

RESEARCH APPROACH

The research approach, including the data collection was guided by the research question: what are the socio-technical factors influencing the development and implementation of IT strategy in the organisation?

The organisation used in the case study is a financial institution in South Africa. It has one of the largest IT departments in the country, with over four hundred and fifty employees. There were many departments and units, including architecture, application development, and network and support in the computing environment.

The representatives of the different units within the computing environment constitute the governing body of its IT department, which is headed by the CIO. The governing body was referred to as the IT Exco (IT Executive Committee). As illustrated in Figure 1 below.

The roles of the various IT managers are briefly described as follows:

1. The Chief Information Officer (CIO) was the head of the IT department. The CIO was responsible and accountable for all IT-related issues in the organisation.
2. The Chief Technology Office (CTO) was responsible for the IT architectural issues and technology management. The architectural issues included design, standards, principles and governance of the technology.
3. The Platform Manager covers all products (applications) supported by the computing environment.
4. The Risk Manager was responsible for all IT risk issues relating to computing and business processes.
5. The Service Manager was responsible and accountable for contracts and services provided to the business units by the IT department.
6. The Application Manager was the head of the business application development unit. The unit responsibilities included design, building support for, and maintenance of the applications within the organisation.
7. The Finance Manager is responsible for technology expenditure within the department. This includes hardware, software and services.

The case study approach was selected primarily because it enables in-depth exploration of complex issues. According to Yin (1994), the

Figure 1. Organisational structure

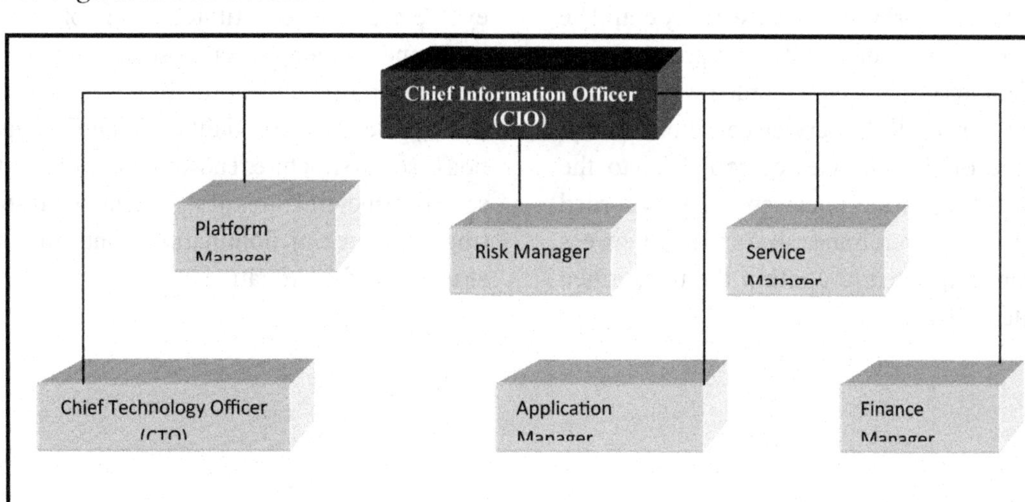

case study approach allows an investigation to retain the holistic and meaningful characteristics of real-life events such as individual life cycles, organisation and managerial processes, change, and the maturation of industries.

An interpretive research approach (Walsham, 1995) was adopted and data was collected through semi-structured interviews conducted in the organisation, as well as from relevant documentation provided by the organisation. The data collected were relevant to the development and implementation of IT strategy. The case study took cognisance of the fact that actors can be part of many networks at the same time, manifesting themselves differently within a particular network and further that actors play decisive roles in the construction of the networks that they are part of. Data collection was performed in the following order:

1. Documentation concerning IT strategy, governance and policy were collected.
2. Based on the information and literature reviewed, and the research questions, a set of questions was formulated. This set of questions was used to conduct the interviews in the case study.
3. Structured interviews were conducted with identified key employees in the organisation. A formulated checklist was used as a guiding principle during the interview process so that uniformity and consistency could be assured in the data collection process.
4. The interviews were recorded with the permission of the interviewees. Fortunately, none of the interviewees objected to the recording of the interviews. The recorded interviews were transcribed and interviewees were requested to confirm the transcribed interviews.

METHODOLOGY

The underpinning theories, ST and ANT were drawn to gain an understanding of the socio-technical factors influencing the development and implementation of IT strategy in the organisation. The study uses the concepts of *duality of structure* and *moments of translation* from ST and ANT, respectively, to analyse the data collected in the case study.

Duality of Structure

The word 'structure' must not be confused with its obvious connotation of organisational hierarchy in the English language. Structure in Structuration Theory are rules and resources, instantiated in recurrent social practice (Giddens, 1984). Giddens defines structural properties as both the medium for and the outcome of the conduct it recursively organises. According Giddens (1984), one of Structuration Theory's contributions relates to the "reciprocal, mutually reinforcing, nature of agents and structure interaction. Conceptualising structure as flexible and recognising that rules and resource control mechanisms are continually reinforced and or redefined through agent action, enables a dynamic view of ethics within the organisation. The duality of structure focuses on the processes through which legitimating structures evolve and are reconstituted by action".

Human action is composed of structures of meaning, power and moral frameworks. Giddens (1984) offers three modalities that link human action to social structure. These include interpretative schemes (the structures of signification), resources (the structures of domination), and norms (the structures of legitimation):

1. **Interpretative schemes:** standardised and shared stocks of knowledge that people use to interpret behaviour and events, and thereby achieve meaningful interaction.
2. **Resources:** either authoritative or allocative, they are the means for exercising power, accomplishing goals, realising intentions.
3. **Norms:** rules for sanctioned or appropriate conduct, defining the legitimacy of interaction within a setting's moral order (Orlikowski & Robey, 1991).

No organisation has total power to determine what the choice(s) of an actor will be in a particular circumstance. Giddens (1984) advocates an action and structure duality; the actor by virtue of interaction with the organisation being both constrained by and, in a sense, (re)creating the structure(s) of the organisation. This results from modalities that link particular types of interaction with particular structural elements Giddens (1984). The three key types of modalities are *interpretative scheme*, *facility* and *norm*. This is diagrammatically shown in Figure 2 above.

The duality of structure helps in understanding the contextual dynamics within which ethical dilemmas are resolved. Structures embody the ethical norms, which influence actions. Actions by agents may lead to changes in how rules and resources influence interactions and to the reinforcement of the norms upon which these interactions are based. Once in place, the new processes foster further changes through interacting modalities.

Moments of Translation

ANT focuses on how people and objects are brought together in stable, heterogeneous networks of aligned interests through processes of translations and negotiations (Callon, 1986; Law, 1991; and Callon & Law, 1989). According to Callon (1986), the translation process follows four stages. Figure 3 below depicts the four stages of the process of translation and indicates the possibility of repeat cycles upon unsuccessful moments of translation:

1. **Problematisation or how to become indispensable:** This is the first stage of the translation process. In this stage, the focal actor problematises an issue. The focal actor analyses, defines and proposes a solution for the problematised issue. The idea of problematisation is to foster relationships, and to allocate and reallocate power between

Figure 2. Dimensions of the duality of structure (Giddens, 1984)

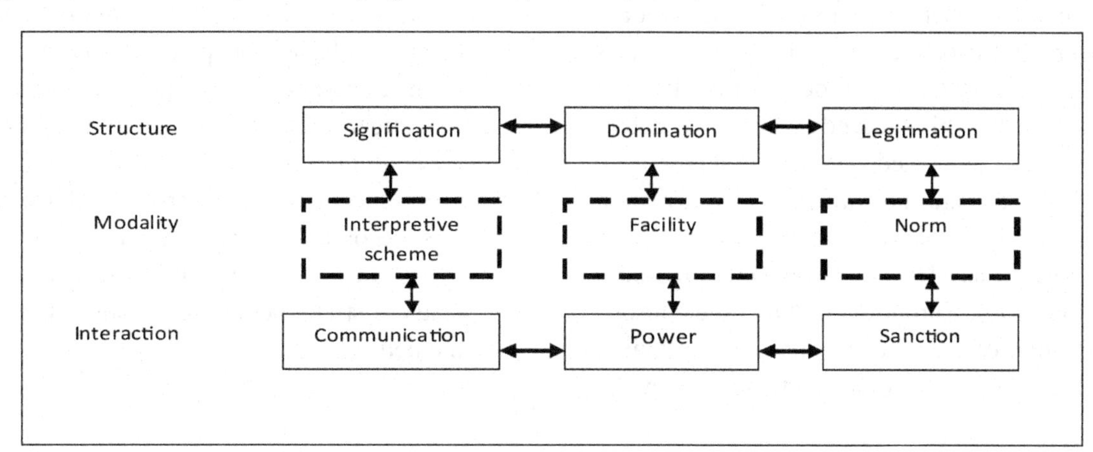

Figure 3. Four moments of translation (Callon, 1986)

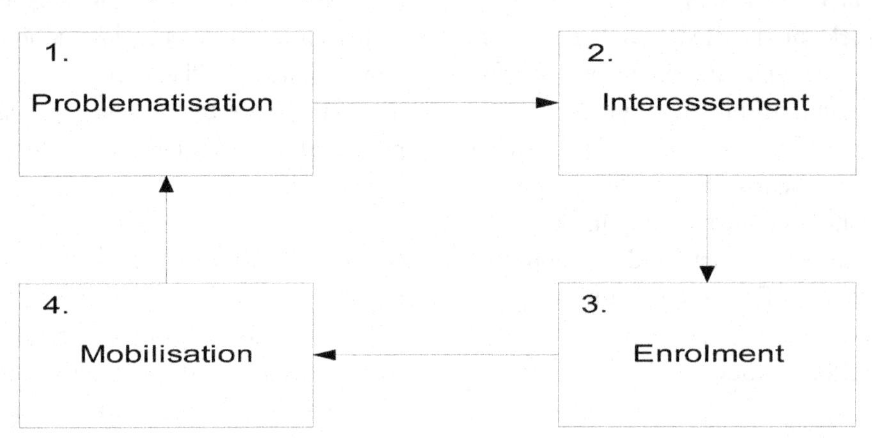

involved actors. Callon (1986) refers to an Obligatory Passage Point (OPP) as a situation that has to occur in order for all the actors to satisfy the interests that have been attributed to them by the focal actor. The focal actor defines the OPP through which the other actors must pass and by which the focal actor becomes indispensable.

2. **'Interessement' or how the allies are locked into place:** Interessement is the set of actions by which an actor attempts to impose and stabilise the identity of other actors in the same network for the cause of problematisation. As described by Callon (1986), it involves a process of convincing other actors to accept the solution proposed by the focal actor. The initiator(s) seek to lock the other actors into the roles that are proposed for them. In other words, actors are engaged in the process of confirming the OPP. This succeeds when other actors become interested in the solution proposed. They change their affiliation to a certain group in favour of the new actor.
3. **Enrolment: How to define and coordinate the roles:** Enrolment involves the consolidation of the alliances through bargaining and mutual concessions. As defined by the focal actor, the solution is accepted as a new concept through the process of negotiation. A new network of interests is created or generated. Actors accept the roles defined for them when enrolling in the network (Callon, 1986). ANT proposes that enrolling allies creates aligned interests and the translation of their interests must be such that participation will lead to the network's impact. Enrolment can be seen as a successful outcome of the *'problematisation'* and the *'interessement'* processes.
4. **The Mobilisation of allies: The spokespersons as representatives:** In this (the last) stage, a set of methods is used to represent the group effectively. "Who speaks in the name of whom?" (Callon, 1986). Some actors are used as (new) initiators. They become delegates or spokespersons for the focal actor. The new network starts to operate in a target oriented approach to implement the solution proposed. According to Callon (1986), through mobilisation of allies, actors become legitimate spokespersons of the groups they claim to represent. This leads to strengthening and stabilisation of the network.

ANALYSIS

The Case as Viewed Through Structuration Theory

The organisation's computing environment is structured as a hierarchical system, within which activities take place and are managed by individuals and groups (units) of employees. Responsibilities are accorded on the basis of the organisation's rules and regulations. Within the IT department, there are rules, regulations, processes and procedures, which are enforced through organisational structures. The IT Executive Committee (IT Exco) formulates these policies, which are binding and all employees including the managers are expected to adhere to them.

In the computing environment, there are various agents, some involved in the development of IT strategy while others are not. Agents are intimately connected with rules and available resources. Within these rules, the available resources are applied. The employees involved in the development of the IT strategy included the Chief Information officer (CIO), IT managers and IT architects.

The employees that are involved or responsible for the development of the IT strategy are not necessarily the ones who are involved in its implementation of the IT strategy. The implementers of the IT strategy include employees such as IT managers, IT architects, IT technical staff and users (employees). According to the mandate accorded to these IT managers, they make the final decisions within their various units in the computing environment of the organisation. The CIO of the organisation has a mandate to decide on any unclear instances in the development and implementation of the IT strategy. The CIO delegates responsibilities for the various components of the IT strategy to the IT managers who report directly to him. The responsibilities include exploitation of resources and execution of policies.

These agents do not act in a vacuum but within a structure (rules and resources). Structure and agency, according to Giddens (1984), are a duality that cannot be conceived separately from one another.

In conjunction with available resources, the organisation has rules and regulations within which IT strategy is developed as well as implemented. The resources for achieving the development and implementation of the IT strategy in the organisation include technical and non-technical factors, such as technology and people, respectively. The organisation has rules and regulations through which the development and implementation including resources are managed. However, there is a period of consultation with IT managers, but the decision is essentially a top-down one, taken on the basis that the organisation must have an IT strategy to support and enable the organisational processes and activities.

The CIO, in accordance with the organisation's mandate to him, defines the rules within which the IT strategy is developed and allocates tasks to the different IT managers. The management practices of the development of the IT strategy are recognised by the IT managers, and there are effective practices for making changes to the IT strategy. The CIO's approval of the developed IT strategy leads to its implementation. There is a gap between those who develop and those who implement IT strategy in the organisation, mainly because many of those implementing IT strategy are not involved in the development. Also, the computing environment does not have complete and necessary structures for implementing the IT strategy. There are no defined rules and processes within which the IT strategy can be implemented. The implementers tend to work around the information that is laboriously provided by individual managers, rather than follow their information needs and requirements. As a result, there are no effective practices.

Based on the organisation's rules, the CIO is mandated to allocate the available resources for the development and implementation of the IT strategy. On another level, the organisation's rules permits the IT managers to make decisions concerning different resources. While development of the IT strategy in the organisation is undertaken by the CIO and his direct reporting line of IT managers, each of the IT managers is allocated part of the IT strategy to be implemented. The CIO instructs the IT managers to enforce performance contracts for the implementation of the IT strategy.

The results of the analysis of the mutual dependency of agency and structure, and their link via modalities within the computing environment of the organisation are discussed below. The discussion should be read together with the tables that follow to get a full appreciation of the duality of structure during IT strategy development and implementation, respectively.

Dimensions of the Duality of Structure

The dimensions of the duality of structure as it applied in the development and implementation of IT strategy in the organisation are captured in tables 1 and 2 below. For the purpose of analysis, social structures and human interactions in the development as well as in the implementation of IT strategy are divided into Giddens' three dimensions and the recursive character of these dimensions is illustrated by the linking modalities.

The structures and interactions that take place during the development of IT strategy are not necessarily the same during the implementation of IT strategy.

Duality of Structure: Signification and Communication

During the development of IT strategy, decisions are reached through the IT Exco meetings and processes. Based on the rules and regulations of the organisation, employees do not necessarily have the right and privilege to contribute to those decisions, and not every employee is allowed to participate in the development of the IT strategy.

IT strategy plays an important role in the organisation by supporting and enabling its business processes and activities. The employees believe that IT strategy is the platform upon which to set goals and use the scarce resources to satisfy the business needs. The general opinion is that IT strategy is very important and thus it must be aligned with the business strategy.

After the development of IT strategy, it is communicated to all employees through their various managers, including the organisation's intranet site, and there is a presentation by the CIO to the wider audience of the computing environment in the organisation. IT strategy is communicated for the sole purpose of implementation. The means through which the implementation is carried out is also presented and communicated to all employees in the computing environment including business managers who receive the services of the IT department.

For awareness and implementation purposes, the managers of the various units within the IT department present only that part of the IT strategy that concerns their unit to their employees: The CTO presents the architectural strategy aspect of the IT strategy to the architects; The IT manager for application presents the business applications strategy aspect of IT strategy to employees within the application unit.

In implementing IT strategy, each unit is allocated a task and each unit further allocates part of its task to individual employees. Deadlines are set for the individual tasks. During task allocation and deadline fixture, negotiation takes place between the managers and the employees involved. When consensus is reached between the employee and the manager, the performance contract is signed, listing the various tasks and timeframe within which duties will be carried out and completed. At this point of agreement between both parties, the performance contract is enforced.

The implementation of IT strategy in the organisation is critical in order for objectives to be achieved. However, there are problems. Implementing IT strategy is largely dependent on the employees, who have widely differing levels of interest and technical skills. Some are interested and eager to carry out (implement) their allocated tasks. Others don't see any personal value in it and simply regard it as an extra burden in their already complicated activities in the computing environment. Deadlines come and go, and many of the tasks are not completed.

Collective choice is involved in defining the needs and allocation of resources in the development of IT strategy to meet the business strategy needs. Debate, discussion, pressure and protest are all part of the process of collective action, which determines which needs should be met or at least each need's priority, and the distribution of resources.

The employees are not merely workers of the organisation, but are a part of the organisation, and it is through their input to the implementation of IT strategy that they contribute to the organisation. Some employees are very experienced and others are technically skilful. IT managers and their various subordinates (employees) engage in interactions in terms of the performance contracts to achieve the objectives of the IT strategy.

The technical component of IT strategy is given more priority than the non-technical factors in the development and implementation. No doubt, the development as well as the implementation of IT strategy has primary technical activities. In the computing environment, non-technical factors are regarded as secondary issues. Ironically, these components make the rules and regulations of development and implementation of IT strategy effective or defective. One of the employees explained this as follows: *"Our IT strategy implementation often goes along technical lines and is very technically oriented and not necessarily aligned with the strategy; so you have the people who make the decisions at a much lower level, at an operational level will make technology choices which are because of the technology not because they match with a particular strategy."*

Employees feel they are neglected in the development and as such, they lack the interest to try and gain an understanding of IT strategy. The different levels of interests and understanding make communication difficult. In this situation, achieving the necessary cooperation of the employees can potentially be quite difficult. As a result, the rules, regulations and resources to implement IT strategy are not appropriately adhered to.

In addition, some of the employees are of the opinion that there is poor communication in the IT department and that the poor communication contributes to the different levels of interest.

It became clear from discussions with interviewees that conflict exists between the employees and IT managers across the different 'units' in the computing environment. While the latter can be seen to encapsulate the positive qualities of management and superiority as they strive to provide quality service to the business needs, the former encompasses the more negative aspects.

Duality of Structure: Legitimation and Sanction

IT strategy is important to the organisation. As such, the responsibility and accountability for IT strategy, including the development and implementation, is mandated to the highest authority, which is the office of the CIO. In developing IT strategy, the CIO applies the mandate accorded to him by the organisation to ensure that the managers reporting to him abide by the rules and regulations within which IT strategy is developed. An employee related the boundary of the rules of responsibilities as follows: *"the CIO is responsible for the IT strategy, the CTO, Risk Manager are responsible for executing parts of the strategy and it filters down to other employees"*

In the development as well as implementation of IT strategy in the organisation, the CIO presents mandatory rules and regulations to which IT managers and the rest of the employees abide. These rules and regulations are seen and accepted as an obligation within which IT strategy is developed and implemented in the organisation. The rules and regulations allow for how the tasks of developing and implementing of IT strategy are allocated to the employees. The allocated tasks are treated as non-negotiable and built into individual performance contracts of each employee.

Though mandatory rules and regulations exist with respect to the development and the implementation of IT strategy in the computing environment of the organisation, getting buy-in from the employees is still very necessary and vital. The mandatory rules and regulations without buy-in remind us of the adage that says 'you can drag a horse to the river but you cannot force it to drink the water'.

As a result of the imposed rules and regulations, some of the employees are proactive participants and others are reluctant or antagonistic in the development as well as in the implementation of IT strategy in the organisation. Some of the employees at the junior level are interested in more active roles in the development of IT strategy. Unfortunately, the rules of the organisation do not allow their participation in the development of IT strategy.

Employees do not have an option. They have to accept the rules and regulations, as provided by the computing environment, which guide the development and implementation of IT strategy in the organisation. However, some employees feel left out and think they have ideas that could contribute, particularly to the development of IT strategy. As a result, there are mixed reactions from the employees.

The employees were aware of the criticality of their roles, particularly in the implementation of IT strategy. They felt that the managers do not realise or are ignorant of the difference that they, the employees, could make to the implementation of IT strategy as a result of their stock of knowledge about the organisation.

Duality of Structure: Domination and Power

The organisational rules and regulations bind the IT department, which is managed by the CIO. The CIO and the IT Exco manage and control the broad strategic decision-making of IT strategy. The CIO makes the final decision on all matters relating to IT strategy in the organisation.

The IT managers have lesser authority (as compared to the CIO), which they use to respond to conflicting demands of the employees. The CIO has maximum authority to demand from his employees the deliverables for the development and implementation of IT strategy in the organisation.

Within their level of management, the IT managers do not have equal power to contribute and make decisions in the development and implementation of the IT strategy in the organisation. Some IT managers are directly involved in the development of IT strategy and others are not. IT managers such as the Chief Technology Officer (CTO) and Risk Manager are specifically mentioned by many of the interviewees. They are seen and regarded as more popular and powerful than others. This is due to the extent of their involvement in IT strategy. There are about thirty IT managers on the same level in the computing environment of the organisation.

As a result of unequal power and popularity on the management level within the computing environment of the organisation, IT managers are struggling to attain power, influence and control. This was evident in the interviews. Some of the power struggles are a manifestation of racial acts. This was experienced at the senior level, as a result of the replacement of a white male CIO with a black male CIO.

Similarly, the employees share unequal power in the implementation of the IT strategy. Some of the employees are seen and considered to have more privilege than others. This is perceived to relate to technical skills, stocks of knowledge or an established relationship with the IT manager and or other employees concerned in the particular implementation.

The control of activities in IT strategy is evidently unequal in the two fields of development and implementation. The CIO and the senior IT managers (the managers who report directly to the CIO) are more in control of the development of IT strategy, while implementation issues are often controlled by employees at lower levels.

IT strategy is regarded as a critical tool for the enabling and support of the business processes and activities in the organisation. As such, interpretation and sense making of IT strategy in the computing environment are vital. Also very important is how the strategy is communicated to the employees who are involved in the development and implementation.

The development and implementation of the IT strategy is done through allocation of tasks and all employees in the computing environment are involved, but at different levels. Employees at the senior levels carry out the development and the rest of the employees are largely involved in the implementation of IT strategy. All employees accept their individual and group tasks as defined by their performance contracts.

The rules and regulations dictate 'power' through the allocation and control of resources during the development and implementation of IT strategy. Another important factor is how employees, including managers, applied resources within their reach and control. Managers dominated according to the resources they have at their disposal.

In this analysis, some of the difficulties of IT strategy are exposed, including the autonomy of the managers and the varying degrees of interests of employees within the units headed by the managers. It is evident that employees (non-managers) are marginalised in the development of IT strategy. It is also evident that rules and regulations are very important factors in the development as well as the implementation of IT strategy in the organisation.

Using the duality of structure from Structuration Theory, we were able to analyse the recursive relationship between structure and human actions in the development and implementation of IT strategy.

During development of the IT strategy, the CIO and his direct line of reporting IT managers are in full control, as mandated by the organisation. Communication is restricted to intra group communication, excluding the rest of the employees. These communicative actions reproduce the structures of signification that says that development of the IT strategy would be undertaken by the CIO and his team. Using the power bestowed on him by the organisation, the CIO takes responsibility for the development of the IT strategy and assembles an elite group – those IT managers reporting directly to him – to develop the IT strategy. These actions produce and reproduce the structures of domination which put all decisions regarding the development of the IT strategy in the hands of the CIO and his team. Finally, when the CIO and IT Exco approve the developed strategy, it is filtered through to the rest of the employees as an accomplished fact, reproducing the structure of legitimation which recognises the CIO as being solely responsible and accountable for the IT strategy.

During implementation of the developed IT strategy, employees are mobilised by their managers to undertake the implementation of aspects of the IT strategy by allocating these as tasks to them. Communication is one-way, from employees to the IT managers, and focuses mainly on technical issues. These communicative actions reproduce structures of significance, which are that technical aspects receive priority due to the technical interests of employees, regardless of their actual match with the developed IT strategy. Employees and managers use their technical abilities and information to protect their own interests, reproducing the structures of domination, based on technical skills and knowledge of the organisation, respectively. Finally, employees work according to their individual performance contracts without full understanding of the developed IT strategy. Their work is affected by politics of rivalries which create an environment of non-cooperation during implementation. All of this reproduces the structure of legitimation that employees at lower levels, who have not been involved in the development of the strategy, will implement the strategy.

In Tables 1 and 2, the ST analyses of the organisation's computing environment as presented above are summarised for development and implementation, respectively.

Tables 1 and 2 are discussed in detail below. Analysis through Actor-Network Theory is now undertaken.

The Case Study as Viewed Through ANT

This section analyses the case study from an Actor-Network Theory (ANT) perspective by drawing upon the sociology of translation as described in the section on research methodology. The focus is on how 'the actor-network' grows, changes and possibly stabilises during development and implementation of IT strategy within the computing environment of the organisation. The case study is analysed on the basis of the four moments of translation, namely, *problematisation*, *interessement*, *enrolment* and *mobilisation*.

The main goal and objective of IT strategy is to align it with the business strategy of the organisation. To achieve this, a set of requirements is formulated. The requirements are problematised by the CIO for the employees. IT strategy is developed and implemented as a solution for these requirements. The most important actors which were involved in the actor-network, and their interests, are first described. This is followed by the analysis, using the four moments of translation.

The business managers develop the business strategy on behalf of the organisation, with which the IT strategy is aligned. The business managers present the organisation's business goals and objectives to the computing environment through the Chief Information Officer (CIO). The CIO is responsible and accountable for IT strategy including its related issues in the organisation. The CIO is the main interface between the IT department and the rest of the organisation. The CIO is the head of the IT Executive committee (IT Exco) in the IT department of the organisation. The Chief Technology Officer (CTO) is a member of the IT Exco and reports directly to the CIO. The CTO is responsible and accountable for the architectural component of IT strategy, including technology management within the computing environment. In addition, on behalf of the organisation, the CTO investigates and researches the technology trends in the industry and their alignment to the business goals and objectives of the organisation. Other actors include IT managers, architects and employees.

The IT managers referred to here are those reporting directly to the CIO. Together with the CIO, they are responsible for the development of IT strategy in the organisation. The IT managers are also responsible for the day-to-day tasks, such as the implementation of IT strategy operations within the computing environment of the organisation. These operations include both technical and non-technical resources. The architects, together with the CTO, develop the architectural component of IT strategy. They are also responsible for the governance of the technologies based on the principles and standards as set by them within the IT strategy mandate. Each architect has an area (domain) of responsibility such as software, hardware and processes. IT employees, excluding the managers, are largely responsible for implementing and applying the principles and standards as dictated by IT strategy in the organisation. IT employees are divided across the units of the IT department, which includes application design and development, network configuration and storage management.

The key non-human actors included technology, performance contracts and skills-set. The technology includes hardware and software, which are selected in the development and implementation of IT strategy. The manner in which the different hardware and software were selected during development and how they were implemented was critical for the IT strategy. Tasks are allocated and managed during the development and implementation of IT strategy in the organisation in accordance with performance contracts

Table 1. IT strategy development: Duality of structure during IT strategy development

Signification	Domination	Legitimation
Since IT strategy is as important as the business strategy in the organisation, development remains with the senior employees. This includes the CIO, Exco and architects.	The CIO and his direct line of reporting IT managers are quite autonomous despite the nominal hierarchical structure within the IT department. Employees cannot make decisions on issues around the development of IT strategy.	The CIO is responsible and accountable for the IT strategy of the organisation.
Interpretative scheme	**Facility**	**Norms**
IT strategy is the platform upon which to set goals and use the scarce resources to satisfy the business needs. As such, both (IT and Business) strategies must be aligned with each other. The responsibility for this has been mandated to the CIO.	The CIO has the authority to allocate resources to the development of the IT strategy.	There are mandatory rules and regulations of the organisation.
Communication	**Power**	**Sanctions**
There is little communication between the CIO and his direct line of reporting IT managers, who together are responsible for the development of IT strategy, and the rest of the IT managers and employees.	The CIO uses his mandate to assemble an elite group to develop the IT strategy.	IT strategy is developed and approved by the CIO and IT Exco, and then filtered through to the rest of the employees.

Table 2. IT stategy implementation: Duality of structure during IT strategy implementation

Signification	Domination	Legitimation
Technical aspects receive priority due to the technical interests of lower level decision makers, not because they match with a particular aspect of the IT strategy.	Implementation is dictated more by what can be done, than by what should be done.	IT strategy implementation is carried out by employees at lower levels who have not been involved in the development of the strategy.
Interpretative scheme	**Facility**	**Norms**
Employees rely on technical abilities and understanding when interpreting their implementation tasks.	Use of available skills and capacities are often preferred above recruitment of required skills.	Implementation of IT strategy is done according to individual performance contracts.
Communication	**Power**	**Sanctions**
There is a one-way, high-level communication from the CIO and the IT managers to the rest of the employees to move from development to implementation. During work on implementation, there is a one-way, technical level communication from the employees to the IT managers and from IT managers to the CIO.	The IT managers including employees use individual authority and information within their reach and technical ability to protect their individual interests.	Employees accept their individual tasks to implement IT strategy without full understanding of the developed strategy. Politics of rivalries affect the workload and create an environment of non-cooperation for work to be done.

with various individuals, teams and groups. All employees in the computing environment have a performance contract, through which individual activities are controlled and managed. The employees have different technical skills sets. Also, some of the employees are more highly skilled than others. The skills sets are considered in the allocation of tasks to the employees.

ANT Translation: Problematisation

The business managers present the CIO with the organisation's strategy, with which he must align IT strategy. The CIO introduces the business strategy to his executive (IT Exco) team, which includes the Chief Technology Officer (CTO) and certain IT managers (Risk and Strategic Manager, Application Development Manager and Service Delivery Manager). The IT Exco is requested to develop the IT strategy for the organisation and ensure that it aligns with the business strategy.

For the purpose of development, the IT Exco splits IT strategy into components such as architecture, application and infrastructure. IT strategy components are allocated to the appropriate authority as defined by IT Exco. The individual heads of the units are responsible and accountable for the various components that are allocated to his or her unit.

All IT-based solutions in the organisation are dictated by the IT strategy of the organisation. All issues and matters relating to the IT strategy are addressed through appropriate channels (units) such as architecture, application and hardware as defined by the IT Exco. The head of each of these units has a mandate to approve/disapprove decisions pertaining to issues relevant to their individual unit. The CIO makes the final decision within the computing environment of the organisation.

Development and implementation of the IT strategy is done through allocation of tasks, responsibilities and human resources to employees in the organisation. For example, all architectural works in the organisation are approved and certified by the architecture department for approval.

The performance contract is engaged to ensure that each employee performs his/her individual tasks in the development and implementation of the IT strategy. The IT managers manage the performance contract of individual employees under their auspices. Similarly, the CIO manages the performance contract of the IT managers.

During this stage, the CIO uses the main goal and objective of IT strategy, namely, to align with the business strategy of the organisation, and hence to formulate a set of requirements. These requirements are problematised by the CIO, and under his leadership, the development and implementation of IT strategy is presented as a solution to the problematised issue. The processes of development and implementation of the IT strategy are defined as the Obligatory Passage Points (OPP) through the implementation of individual performance contracts in which agreed upon tasks related to the development and implementation of the IT strategy are assigned to all employees.

ANT Translation: Interessement

At the organisation, the IT strategy is currently developed and reviewed annually. Sometimes, the implementation is not completed until the following year. The performance contract, which is instituted by the organisation, is used to carry out tasks in the development and implementation of IT strategy in the computing environment. The outcome of individual performance contracts is used to determined employees' annual salary increases and financial bonuses. As a result, some employees become interested in the development as well as implementation of IT strategy.

With regard to the development and implementation of the IT strategy, employees are required to have a performance contract. To a certain extent, negotiation is allowed but it is highly restricted. This process involves every team, unit and individual including the CIO and the IT managers in the computing environment of the organisation.

The various interests in IT strategy are either individual or team based. Individual interests are mostly based on 'stocks of knowledge', which make the employee concerned more comfortable in carrying out his/her tasks. The team interest is according to roles, responsibilities and skills-set. In all cases, however, the performance contract and its outcome, with attached possible salary increases and financial bonuses, could be seen as a major driver of the interest of employees.

ANT Translation: Enrolment

The participation of employees in the development and implementation of IT strategy is key in achieving its aims and objectives. The CIO and the IT Exco use the performance contract as a system which enables them to persuade and convince employees at all levels to engage in the development and implementation of IT strategy in the organisation.

Development and implementation of IT strategy in the organisation is done through allocation of tasks to employees and managed by IT managers. The task allocation is done in accordance with individual and team roles and responsibilities within the computing environment. This is based on performance contracts as outlined by the rules and regulations.

Heads of the different teams in the computing environment report the activities and progress of events of the teams to their immediate managers and the IT Exco. The activities and progress reports include the allocated tasks in the development and implementation of IT strategy. This is done in order to assess elements such as risks and gaps, including participation levels of employees in the development as well as in the implementation of IT strategy in the organisation.

However, some of the employees still do not or only reluctantly participate in the development and the implementation of IT strategy. Some employees attribute reasons for their lack of participation in the development and implementation of IT strategy to a lack of opportunity to participate - often caused by racial prejudices. Other employees, mostly on the senior level, admitted that there were factors and circumstances that sometimes prevented individuals from participating in IT strategy in the organisation.

In addition, some employees at times get mixed messages from different sources in the development and implementation of IT strategy in the organisation. These messages are attributed to personal interests. Also, there are some instances in which decisions are not reached by the parties (stakeholders) involved in the different tasks of development and implementation of IT strategy. In such cases, the action and reaction of the employee or managers responsible becomes a matter of individual choice.

The majority of employees at the lower levels do not have a full understanding of how IT strategy is developed, yet they enrol in the implementation. The high level of enrolment and participation are due to the performance contract, which forces every employee to enrol accordingly and complete the allocated tasks in the development and implementation of the IT strategy. The low level of commitment, however, causes division and the pursuit of individual interests among the employees.

ANT Translation: Mobilisation

The realisation of the annual salary increase, including financial incentives, motivates many employees to be committed to the IT strategy in the organisation. Also, IT managers in the various units are tasked to encourage employees in their various units to be committed to the development and implementation of IT strategy. The tasks are linked to the performance contract. As a result of the potential impact of the performance contract, the IT managers speak positively on behalf of their superior (CIO) and the IT department on the need, aims and objectives of IT strategy in the organisation.

Employees in the organisation understand the development and implementation of IT strategy differently. Some of the employees think it is too complex and therefore will not meet its goals and objectives. Others, who are believed to be more experienced, consider the development and implementation of the IT strategy to be in order and excellent.

Even though understanding is at different levels/stages, employees are encouraged to participate in IT strategy development and implementation. The IT managers perform the allocation task on a one-on-one basis and in the group meetings with their employees. This process gives the IT managers the opportunity to persuade each of the employees twice. This leads to increased employee participation in IT strategy. For example, the employees (particularly the technical specialists) who did not understand how decisions about IT strategy were made in the organisation are now knowledgeable about it. Each IT manager represents their unit or group at the management level in the development and implementation of IT strategy.

The rules of the organisation, through the performance contract, enable the IT managers to mobilise employees in the implementation of the IT strategy. Also, some employees are able to mobilise their colleagues based on their stock of knowledge. The mobilisation is, however, more around the attainment of performance contract outcomes than about the IT strategy as such. In other words, the actor-network mobilises around loosely coupled individual and/or group targets more than around the solution proposed during problematisation.

It could also be argued that the solution and the OPP proposed during problematisation had within it the seeds of such a fragmented mobilisation: a holistic IT strategy, properly communicated to all levels, was not put forward as the solution to be attained; rather, with the development of the IT strategy done "behind closed doors", this was poorly communicated to the different levels with the emphasis then shifting to the implementation. More specifically, the processes of implementation (the OPP) became the solution to the problematised issue of supporting the business strategy. This meant, *a priori*, that the focus of individuals and groups would be on their tasks within the relative process (es), without necessarily paying attention to the broader picture (which they did not have) and their role therein. Added to this the performance contract and individually negotiated targets meant even more that individual interests and rivalries between managers and groups led to a fragmented mobilisation of the network.

From the point of view of the focal actor, the CIO, this was not a problem, as the network would indeed operate relatively stable and in a target oriented manner to implement the solution proposed. This does not mean, however, that a coherent and holistic IT strategy would be the result of the implementation process.

FINDINGS

The results of the case study revealed some factors that were analysed and shown to be problems during the development and implementation of the IT strategy in the organisation:

1. First was the relationship issue between actors involved in the development and implementation of IT strategy in the organisation. The relationship issue was critical in the process of development and implementation of IT strategy. It influences how development and implementation of IT strategy is interpreted and affects the way tasks were allocated and carried out. For example, some employees were selective on who they associate or work with. A senior employee explained as follows: *"Some people don't like working with other people. My case is an example. Some people do not like working with me. The reasons are partly a power struggle, partly ignorance, personal and staff capabilities."*

2. Secondly, the analysis revealed how employees responded to the structures within the computing environment in the process of development and implementation of IT strategy in the organisation. These actions or responses include how the development and implementation of IT strategy was then interpreted, how the various involved tasks were allocated, how these tasks were sanctioned and carried out.

The research established that the rules, regulations and available resources of the organisation were used as guiding principles in the development and implementation of IT strategy. In some instances, the rules, regulations and available resources were used for personal interests, which were sometimes to the detriment of the organisation as they are promulgated. Personal interests of the employees were prevalent influencing factors in the case study. These included acts of racism, and the use of stocks of knowledge about the organisation. The proposition used was that the implementation of IT strategy was influenced by the knowledge of users which manifested itself in the form of key concepts that represented the basic criteria for the implementation of the IT strategy in the organisation. The factors were construed to be manifestations of organisational politics.

The research also revealed that the non-technical factors were as important as the technical factors when it came to influencing the development and implementation of IT strategy in the computing environment of the organisation. The research explored these non-technical factors, specifically with respect to the implementation of IT strategy. This included exploring the organisational view, personal views, perceptions among the employees, and personal experiences during implementation of IT strategy.

The structures in the computing environment, within which the IT strategy was developed and implemented, were manoeuvred by employees when they were enacted. Most of these manoeuvres resulted from personal interests which influenced their interpretation of the structures. These manoeuvres manifested themselves as organisational politics.

A satisfactory account of the interwoven relationship between IT management and employees within the computing environment was lacking in the process of development and implementation of IT strategy in the organisation. The researchers were more interested in how this interplay works, not only *that* it exists. The results of the analysis should be of interest to the Human Resource department of the organisation. They could gain a better understanding of issues such as racial divisions and transformation, affecting employees in the computing environment. As revealed in the analysis and interpretation of the case study, the actors in the computing environment are concerned with factors such as job security, resource control and domination during the implementation of IT strategy.

The study revealed that non-technical factors are very influential in the implementation of IT strategy. These include how tasks are allocated, the effect of domination by some employees and why certain processes and activities are, or are not sanctioned. Typically, there is more focus on the technical factors than on non-technical factors in the implementation of IT strategy. This finding of the research has the potential to change the way that IT strategy is currently developed and implemented.

Using the duality of structure from Structuration Theory, the focus in the case study was on the recursive relationship between structure and human actions during the development and implementation of IT strategy. Development of IT strategy was in the case study fully controlled, as mandated by the organisation, by the top management team of the computing environments. Communication was restricted to intra group communication, excluding the rest of the employees. These communicative actions reproduce the structures of signification that says that development of the IT strategy should be undertaken by the top IT management team. Using the power bestowed on them by the organisation, the top IT management team takes responsibility for the development of the IT strategy. These actions produce and reproduce the structures of domination which put all decisions regarding the development of the IT strategy in the hands of the top IT management team. Finally, when the team approves the developed strategy, it is presented to the rest of the employees as an accomplished fact, reproducing the structure of legitimation which recognises the team as being solely responsible and accountable for the IT strategy.

The analysis based on ANT showed that a relatively stable network of aligned interests failed to establish itself. While the problematisation phase could be regarded as successful, the same cannot be said of the subsequent phases. Sufficient interest was not built amongst the rest of the employees, beyond the top IT management teams, who were responsible for the development of the IT strategy. This could be ascribed to the poor top-down communication, coupled with issues of mistrust and private technical interests which were not focused on the broader interest of the organisation. Enrolment depended on coercion, coupled with performance related incentives, and in many cases employees only reluctantly accepted their tasks and roles in the implementation process. It was therefore not surprising that mobilisation was fragmented and unsuccessful, with little or no signs of third level initiators mobilising other employees. All of this added up to an unsuccessful translation and alignment of interests with no expectation of a stabilised network.

CONCLUSION

The empirical findings of this study contribute to the understanding of the impact of non-technical factors on IT strategy in the computing environment of the organisation. The study also contributes to a better understanding of the roles of actors, structures and the individuals and groups of individuals involved in the implementation of IT strategy.

The complementary use of Structuration Theory and Actor-Network Theory as lenses through which the analysis was undertaken, revealed a rich context that otherwise would not have been observed. It enabled the explanation of the interaction between technology, human action and organisational structure, affecting the strategic IT direction of the organisation. This represents a contribution to Information Systems Research methodology. We believe that this approach could, in many cases, be used to conduct more in-depth analyses of the social aspects that so often lead to failures of information system projects.

REFERENCES

Boar, B. H. (1998). *Information Technology Strategy as Commitment*. RCG Information Technology. Available: http://www.rcgit.com/Default.aspx. Accessed 02 December 2004

Brooks, L., & Atkinson, C. (2003). STRUCTURANTION in Research and Practice: Representing Actor Networks, Their Structurated Orders and Translations. In B. Kaplan, D. Truex, D. Wastell, T. Wood-Harper, & J. I. DeGross (Eds.), *Information Systems Research: Relevant Theory and Informed Practice* (pp. 389-409). Boston: Kluwer Academic Publishers.

Callon, M. (1986). Some elements of the sociology of translation: Domestication of the scallops and the fisherman of St Brieuc Bay. In J. Law (Ed.), *A New Sociology of Knowledge, power, action and belief* (pp.196–233). London, Routledge.

Callon, M. (1991). Techno-economic networks and irreversibility. In J. Law (Ed.), *A sociology of monsters. Essays on power, technology and domination* (pp. 132-164). London; Routledge.

Callon, M., & Law, J. (1989). On the Construction of Sociotechnical Networks: Content and Context Revisited. *Knowledge and Society: Studies in the Sociology of Science Past and Present* (Vol. 8) (pp. 57-83).

Cats-Baril, W., & Thompson, R. (1997). *Information Technology and Management*. Chicago: Irwin Press.

Giddens, A. (1984). *The Constitution of Society: Outline of the Theory of Structuration*. Cambridge, UK: Polity Press.

Jones, M. (1999). Structuration Theory. In W. L. Currie & R. D. Galliers (Eds.), *Rethinking Management Information Systems* (pp. 103-134). UK: Oxford University Press.

Kling, R. (2000). Learning About Information Technologies and Social Change: The Contribution of Social Informatics. *The Information Society*, *16*(3), 217–232. doi:10.1080/01972240050133661doi:10.1080/01972240050133661

Latour, B. (1987). *Science in Action: How to follow Scientists and Engineers through Society.* Cambridge, Massachusetts: Harvard University Press.

Latour, (1996). Social Theory and the Study of Computerised Work Sites, In W. J. Orlikowski, G. Walsham, M. R. Jones, & J. I. DeGross, (Eds.), *Information Technology and Changes in Organizational Work* (pp. 295-307). London: Chapman & Hall.

Law, J. (1991). Monsters, Machines and Sociotechnical Relations. In J. Law (Ed.), *A Sociology of Monsters: Essays on Power, Technology and Domination* (pp. 1-23). London: Routledge.

Law, J. (1992). Notes on the theory of the actor-network: ordering, strategy, and heterogeneity. *Systems Practice*, *5*(4), 379–393. doi:10.1007/BF01059830doi:10.1007/BF01059830

Monteiro, & Hanseth, O. (1996). Social Shaping of Information Infrastructure: On Being Specific about the Technology, In W. J. Orlikowski, G. Walsham, M. R. Jones & J. I. DeGross, (Eds.), *Information Technology and Changes in Organizational Work* (pp. 325-343). London: Chapman and Hall.

Orlikowski, W. (1993). CASE tools as organisational change: Investigating incremental and radical changes in systems development. *MIS Quarterly*, *17*(3), 1–28. doi:10.2307/249774doi:10.2307/249774

Orlikowski, W., & Robey, D. (1991). Information Technology and the Structuring of Organizations. *Information Systems Research*, *2*(2), 143–169. doi:10.1287/isre.2.2.143doi:10.1287/isre.2.2.143

Rose, R. (1998). Evaluating the contribution of Structuration Theory to the Information Systems discipline. In *Proceedings of the 6th European Conference on Information Systems (ECIS), Aix-en-Provence*, France.

Straub, W. D., & Wetherbe, C. J. (1989). Information Technologies for the 1990s: And Organisational Impact Perspective. *Communications of the ACM*, *32*(11). doi:10.1145/68814.68818doi:10.1145/68814.68818

Walsham, G. (1995). The Emergence of Interpretivism in IS Research. *Information Systems Research*, *6*(4), 376–394. doi:10.1287/isre.6.4.376doi:10.1287/isre.6.4.376

Walsham, G. (1997). Actor Network Theory and IS Research: Current Status and Future Prospects. In A. S. Lee, J. Liebenau, & J. I. DeGross, (Eds.), Information Systems and Qualitative Research. London: Chapman & Hall.

This work was previously published in International Journal of Actor-Network Theory and Technological Innovation, Volume 2, Issue 1, edited by Arthur Tatnall, pp. 1-26, copyright 2010 by IGI Publishing (an imprint of IGI Global).

Chapter 2
Information Infrastructure:
An Actor-Network Perspective

Antonio Cordella
London School of Economics, UK

ABSTRACT

Recent work on information systems has discussed the nature and the complexity of the Information Infrastructures (II) concept. This research has mainly focused on two aspects: studying the process that both shapes and stabilizes information infrastructures, and studying the role played by information infrastructure in leveraging business performance. Using the ideas proposed by the Actor Network Theory (ANT), this article suggests a new way to conceptualise the nature of II, that is, its ontology. Using ANT as an ontological foundation to analyse the relations among actors, the article proposes the concept of information infrastructures in action to highlight their dynamic nature. This leads us to consider information infrastructures not as stable entities, but rather as entities performed in, by, and through relations. The aim of this work is to overcome the limitations associated with studying information infrastructures that rely on stability and manageability assumptions. Conceiving information infrastructures in terms of performative forces that evolve dynamically, this work provides a framework to examine information infrastructure in terms of dynamic relationships by looking at the process that shapes these relationships. The article suggests that information infrastructures should not be studied retrospectively to understand how they are established, but rather should be studied focussing on the process of making. Here we study the action of making rather than the processes that made.

INTRODUCTION

Since the introduction of computers in the middle of the twentieth century, the potential of Information Technology (IT) to transform organizations has been a constant subject of analysis for both organization studies and information systems research. Each new generation of technology and every major technological innovation has been followed by strong claims that organizations, businesses, and society in general, would have to be radically and fundamentally transformed to take into account the new opportunities offered by the innovations in technological capabilities.

DOI: 10.4018/978-1-4666-1559-5.ch002

The changes brought about by technologies in organizations have been discussed examining how technology can help to reorganize work activities or improve their management. A very similar debate characterises the dispute on the role of information infrastructures in supporting economic activities in contemporary society. As a result of the increased diffusion of information technologies in organizations and in society, the level of interdependence among single information systems is escalating such that today, it is very difficult to think about independent information systems as opposed to Information Infrastructures (IIs) (Hanseth, 2004b). In fact, information infrastructures are characterised by the intricate interplay of the set of interconnected hardware, software, and procedural configurations. These artefacts are commonly deployed to support and enact pre-determined paths of behaviour in organizations and among users.

This article aims to contribute to this area of research by questioning the nature of information infrastructures which try to partially fill the gap identified by Orlikowski and Iacono (2001) in the theoretical conception of IT and hence information infrastructures. In making this contribution, this article discusses how the traditional distinction between technology and organization, and the analyses based on these distinctions, are not sufficient to explain the problem associated with information infrastructure design, deployment, and management. This article focuses on information infrastructures looking at the interplay between technologies and the organizations using them, responding to Lee's (2001) claim that "research in the information systems field examines more than just the technological system, or just the social system, or even the two systems side by side; in addition, it investigates the phenomena that emerge when the two interact". This interplay is regarded as the main force that shapes information infrastructures, and hence it is the most important fact to be considered in order to understand the complexity of these systems.

Actor network theory (ANT) provides the interpretative framework of analysis underpinning this study. ANT recognises that technology and people are not distinct pre-existing actors which influence each other through their relationships. Instead, they are considered as the constitutive elements of these relationships and, at the same time, the output of these same relationships. Following this ontology, information infrastructures are considered to be phenomena in action: IIs are the outcome of the relational status that continuously shapes and reshapes their characteristics. This relational status of shaping and reshaping reveals information infrastructures are the output of the recursive dynamic interaction between technology and people, and are not, following the more traditional assumption of II, the stable set of underlying functionalities that standardize organizational actions as the foundation of organizational activities (Broadbent & Weill, 1999; Hammer & Champy, 1993; Weill & Broadbent, 1998). Deploying this general framework, this article contributes to the debate by discussing, in depth, the nature of information infrastructures building upon concepts and ideas borrowed from the Social Studies of Science and Technology (SSST), in particular ANT. The building upon these concepts and ideas has led to the study of information infrastructures as emergent phenomena that are dynamically and continuously defined and re-defined within their use – rather than simply looking at the planned consequences of adopting a specific technology, or the result of planned actions by users and organizations.

The relational dimension of information infrastructure is studied as the outcome of the existing intricacy and interdependence among various technologies and applications (Hanseth, 2004b), and as a result of the adoption and use of these technologies and applications by organizational agents.

Thus, the basic argument underpinning the overall work in this article is that technology and its users co-define their trajectories in a dynamic interplay that is constantly reshaped by its output. This interplay is what defines IIs as emergent phenomena in a state of permanent action rather than being a stable, static organizational foundation.

To study this interplay, the article proposes using ANT as an ontological stance to offer a possible new definition of what an II is.

BACKGROUND

When IT was first introduced to organizations, it was mainly considered as an agent of automation similar to the machines introduced by manufacturing firms during the industrial revolution. Following the characteristic and dominant understanding of technology that was typical of the industrial revolution, information technology was considered as a mechanical means of substituting human actions with more efficient, regulated, and standardized processes. In this context, the new technology was used to provide better production infrastructure by improving efficiency through the automation of human activities within work processes; the problem of its interplay with the organization was neglected: the organization will align with the technology that embeds optimal production sequences. From this perspective, IT is regarded essentially as an *industrial* technology (Curley & Pyburn, 1982). It views technology as a "fixed set of functionalities" (Lee, 1999) whose purpose is self-evident. Thus, there is little uncertainty about the procedures and consequences of information technology implementation: it is under control, its consequences are planned, and problems are related only to technical issues concerning the automation of tasks.

A broader and better understanding of the complexity associated with the adoption of IT in organizational contexts emerges when information technology is recognised as an *intellectual* technology (Curley & Pyburn, 1982), i.e. a technology that defines its characteristics in the interaction with the humans who use it. Following similar arguments, Zuboff (1988) claims that IT has two different impacts on organization: computers can either *automate* work or *informate* work. In the former case, technology can be considered as an *industrial* technology. In the latter, computers change the quality and quantity of available information because they not only provide more data or other capabilities for dealing with it, but also because they modify the context in which the information is used. As a consequence, the skills needed to perform a specific activity are qualitatively different from those required for doing the same work before the information technology was introduced.

IT implementations and their impact on an organization are therefore not completely predictable and under control, as they change the complex contextual environment where an II is deployed. This makes it more difficult, if not impossible, to completely plan the consequences of its adoption. Similarly, Lee (1999) argues that "an information system and its organizational context each have transformation effects on the other. They are more like the reagents that react to and change each other's properties in a chemical compound than the inert elements that retain their respective properties in a chemical mixture" (Lee, 1999). Given that we want to explain these mutual effects in the analysis of the relationship between technology and its users, we have to change the focus of the investigation from the evaluation of the effects, to the study of the process that produces these same effects. This means that the dynamic interplay between organizations and information technology is the condition that has to be analysed in order to gain a better understanding of the effects of information technology adoption in organizational settings.

Information infrastructures are embedded in, and defined by, this interplay and lead to the exploration here of the concept of *information infrastructure in action*. As indicated earlier, in terms of infrastructure, the core proposition is that the role, effects, and implications of information technologies cannot be defined if they are not considered in terms of the emergent phenomenon, the outcome of the contingent and contextual interplay between information technology and its users in the organization.

Traditionally, the role of technological systems in organizational settings is often envisioned as either a technological problem or an organizational one. In describing the tension between technologies and social settings, Markus and Robey (1988) refer to an *emergent* perspective that focuses on the interaction between organizations and technology as a response to both technological determinism and social determinism. Similarly, Barley (1986) suggests structuration theory (Giddens, 1984) to describe the ongoing and recursive effects between an organization's institutional settings and behaviours, and the new technologies. Likewise, Orlikowski (1992) discusses technology as a soft structural property of organizations, arguing that technology is "experienced differently by different individuals" (Orlikowski, 2000); in practice, technologies are defined "to refer to the specific structure routinely enacted as we use specific machines, techniques, devices, gadgets in recurrent ways in our daily activities" (Orlikowski, 2000). Orlikowski's assertion prepared the ground for the growing body of research in the IS field that approaches the analysis of this interplay from a *structurational* perspective (Ngwenyama, 1998; Orlikowski, 1992, 2000; Orlikowski & Robey, 1991; Walsham, 1993), which is grounded in the analysis of the course of human action. Therefore, it is useful to explain the emergence of diverse uses of the same technology in different contexts (Orlikowski, 2000). Nevertheless, this approach principally takes into consideration only one of the aspects of the interplay, namely the process of the social construction of technology. The approach neglects the importance of the role played by technologies and their characteristics in the understanding of their deployment, use, and adoption in social contexts (Hanseth, 2004a) by arguing that technology only exists in our minds; technology "exists only in and through our descriptions and practices" (Grint & Woolgar, 1995). Therefore, Orlikowski's assertion fails to recognise that the characteristic of the object/technology is also an essential element to be considered when we try to understand the possible ways the object/technology can be shaped (J Law, 1992).

Technology's importance in understanding the configuration of an organization is not new. It has been recognized since Woodward's seminal work (1965) in the late fifties, Thompson's (1967) in the late sixties and, in general, by technology studies of organization which considered technology an essential determinant of organizational structure. Consequently, technology has often been considered the material cause that determines organization structure (Orlikowski & Barley, 2001). In this understanding, technology develops independently from social contexts - but directly affects society.

Both the techno-deterministic and socio-deterministic approaches underestimate the importance of the interaction between technology and organization, and the process that mutually shapes the two: one does not deterministically shape the other. Rather, it is the dynamic interaction between the two that shapes the ongoing configuration of technology and organization: one does not pre-exist the other. ANT is chosen to explain this dynamic interaction because it focuses on the relationships between human and non-human entities, the actors interact dynamically in circularity, and share "mutual constituency" in the process (Latour, 1999a; Suchman, 1987). This perspective indicates that an information infrastructure cannot be considered as the invisible background to other kinds of work (Star, 2002): II has to be conceptualised as an emergent phenomenon that cannot be understood from the stability and form of artefacts; it must be understood as the output of the "interaction of heterogeneous elements that are shaped and assimilated into an open ended network" (J Law, 1990) of relationships.

It seems that the conventional models of analysis, which draw on the consideration technology's effect on people or vice-versa, tend to be more linear and neat than the reality that emerges from the analysis of the constitutive relational interplay between technology and its users.

Based on these observations, this article reframes the problem of information infrastructures in terms of action and dynamic interplay. We thus claim here that IIs emerge – they only exist when they are used in and by the organization. Grounded in the ontological assumption of ANT, this stance argues that information infrastructures are the intricate combination of the information systems used and the organization's practices and routines. Consequently, IIs do not ontologically pre-exist the organization and users that employ them.

INFORMATION INFRASTRUCTURE IN ACTION

Information infrastructures can be conceived as a negotiation process outcome among different information systems, work practices, and routines in the daily activities of organizations, but also as the context within which this negotiation takes place.

Information infrastructures emerge out of this negotiation, but the negotiation itself defines the actors involved in it and the context where it takes place. By discussing the more recent literature on II, it is possible to depict these dynamics and provide a substantial argument in favour of the idea underpinning this work, in which IIs are dynamic phenomena that evolve and change over time.

As argued by Weill and Broadbent (1998), information infrastructures get implemented to foster business strategies and to improve the competitive capabilities of firms. Implementations of IIs can thus be considered strategic responses to external market forces that pressure companies in competitive markets. At the same time, these implementations define and re-define the market forces within which companies compete. In the late nineties, for example, IBM largely reorganized the infrastructure around a CRM system to better position the company in the global market and to survive increased industry competition (Ciborra & Failla, 2000). Implementing a CRM, IBM aimed at speeding up the sequence of activities needed to complete a negotiation cycle: starting with the identification of business opportunities, continuing through to making an offer, writing the contract, and delivering the solution, and ending with the monitoring of customer satisfaction. This implementation, however, changed the competitive environment where IBM competed. As discussed by Bakos and Treacy (1986), strategic investment in ICT influences industry forces which themselves have a direct effect on firm performance.

Information infrastructures are not only deployed to respond to competitive needs, but also to comply with technological innovations that reshape a company's IT domain. New industry standards push the organization infrastructure to change so that it is interoperable with widely adopted standards, for example the large investment to make systems Y2K compliant. The tension between standardization and flexibility characterises all infrastructural standards (Hanseth, Monteiro, & Hatling, 1996a) and pushes for continuous changes and adaptations in the information infrastructure. This tension becomes the main force that reshapes the information infrastructure. But at the same time, the adoption of standards reinforces *de facto* standards, shaping the technological domain companies operate in. Hanseth and Braa (2000) show how standards played a major role in the process that shaped the II at Norsk Hydro. In this case, the Bridge standard deeply affected the development path of the overall company infrastructure. Bridge was the initial standard the company developed its information infrastructure. Because of this initial choice, every change in the II had to comply with the Bridge standard. This made Bridge the platform every development had to be deployed on.

Bridge has hence evolved and adapted to make growth possible of the infrastructure itself. This process, however, has led to a reinforcement of the Bridge platform, making it impossible to develop solutions that, for standardization reasons, are not compliant with the Bridge standard.

For the same reason, a new infrastructure calls for changes and adaptations in the existing information infrastructure. These changes can be both technological and organizational. New standards have to be designed to guarantee the interoperability of the new infrastructure with all systems in place (installed base). Changes in standards and the development of technological gateways increase the complexity of the technological systems and make future changes and adaptations more difficult and demanding (Hanseth & Braa, 2000). Once again, the installed base gets reinforced and becomes more difficult to change.

Similarly, the implementation of an information infrastructure calls for changes in the internal organization of processes and organizational routines. New IIs facilitate the re-organization of work processes and routines because the technological architecture redistributes and re-organizes the information flow, and thus the interdependence among pre-existing organization departments and functions (Kallinikos, 2006). Contextually, the new II defines these organizational information flows and interdependence. II can in fact prescribe a set of organizational protocols and procedures that constrain organization action in specific circumstances (Timmermans & Berg, 1997).

Every change in technology or in the organization of work activities produces side effects. Groups of users as well as technologies are always affected by changes in the information infrastructure, but they are also forces that produce these changes. These effects can be either negative, so that changes leave "angry orphans" (Hanseth, 1996), or positive, making these actors reinforce their interests in the information infrastructures. Whether the effects are negative or positive, both cases generate forces that shape the II. Organization agents can align their interest with a specific technology thus reinforcing the role of this technology in the organization, but technology itself can align different interests and lead to unexpected outcomes, betraying the initial supporters (Hanseth & Braa, 1998). Returning once again to the deployment of the Norsk Hydro II, Hanseth and Braa (1998) highlight how the II gets shaped by the alignment of interests in the infrastructure and, at the same time, how the same infrastructure gets shaped by the resistance of other actors against it. The SAP implementation at Norsk Hydro shows that an infrastructure designed and controlled by managers and IT personnel can also be an actor shaping both its environment and its own future. The technology builds alliances with others and gets shaped by these alliances. However, the alliances can change over time. At Norsk Hydro, SAP was first allied with top management, playing the role as a powerful change agent. Later on, SAP allied with local managers and users, helping them to bring the change process under their influence and in the direction they preferred. Finally, SAP changed its role as it got integrated into a larger corporate infrastructure. To summarize, it became everybody's enemy by resisting all organizational change and reinforcing the installed base.

Moreover, IIs designed and implemented to reduce information flow complexity in an organization can be the reason why, instead of decreasing the information flow, the organization increases it and the costs of managing it (A. Cordella, 2006; Kallinikos, 2006), leading to a redefinition of the organization's boundaries, procedures, and routines. Kallinikos (2006) largely discusses how the interconnection between information growth, and information and communication technologies, leads to a redefinition of an organization's boundaries. New organization forms and organization structures are hence emerging because of the effects of II on the access and distribution of information. Distributed work and network organization can be discussed as organizations' responses to the information growth associated with the deployment of II. The unexpected outcomes and trends shaping IIs are calling for interventions to decide on how to handle the existing information infrastructures shaken by these outcomes. These interventions are, however, also the reason why changes in infrastructure are needed. Adaptations, ad hoc interventions, and bricolage are needed to keep the infrastructure alive, but they take time to be devised and implemented. "This causes a main phenomenon: technologies and processes drift, so what one obtains at the end of the implementation process is not what the system was designed for originally" (Ciborra, 2004).

Drift leads to the emergence of a new infrastructure, with characteristics that result from interactions among different information systems, work practices, and routines in the daily activities of organizations within the context the organization acts in. However, this drifting infrastructure becomes a new infrastructure that, for the organization, endogenously implements new, constant tensions among different information systems, work practices, and routines in the daily activities of organizations. This effect generates a circular loop that explains why IIs are always dynamically in action, changing over time and never becoming monolithically stabilised.

These dynamics can be described by figure 1.

Circularity, as described by actor network theory, seems to be the essential characteristic of IIs. Circularity is a relationship where every actor network affects and is affected by the characteristics of the actors, and where emergent characteristics of the actors affect and are affected by the characteristics of the actor network. These characteristics have been discussed here looking at how II is affected and affects information systems, work practices, and routines in the daily activities of organizations within the context the organizations operate in.

Figure 1.

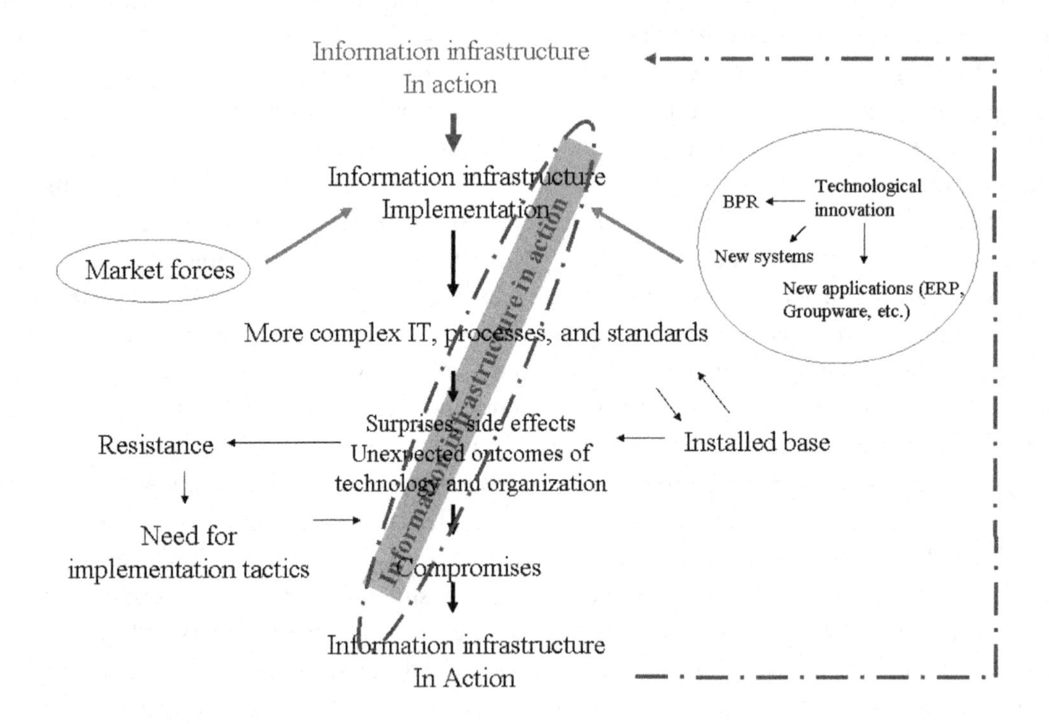

The information infrastructure in action argument proposed here is grounded both on the analysis of the existing literature in the field of IIs and in the theoretical framework provided by the actor network theory. Next, we will discuss the background of this argument and propose a detailed analysis of actor network theory to support the theoretical argument in favour of the concept of information infrastructure in action.

RELATED RESEARCH

Organizations are increasingly dealing with the development of technological solutions which have to interact with existing technological systems, thus multiplying the number of existing systems, the need for interaction among them, and their intricacy (Hanseth, 2004b). One obvious consequence of this new stage of development for information systems in organizations is that it is no longer possible to focus on the study of the individual IS without considering the infrastructure within which it is deployed and that it defines. Information systems are increasingly interconnected and intertwined in complex information infrastructures, such that the notion of IIs and their study has witnessed growing interest in information systems research.

The study of information infrastructure in organizational settings is therefore not new. However, the last decade has presented an increasing interest in the study of the socio-technical dimension of information infrastructure and hence actor network theory. These studies have helped to highlight the importance of the interplay between the technologies and the social context using them.

The theoretical need for defining IIs from a socio-technical perspective reflects the attempt to supersede the limitation of studies on II that recognised too much agency on behalf of either humans or technology (Quattrone & Hopper, 2006), neglecting the intertwined effects of the two in shaping the nature of IIs.

Traditionally, the concept of IIs has been associated with standardization projects for corporate information systems and data throughout a corporation (Weill & Broadbent, 1998). This vision has been strengthened by the diffusion of ERP systems and by the attempts to re-engineer the corporation. IIs have thus been conceived, within the techno-deterministic stance, as instruments to foster the achievement of these goals. Accordingly, the borders of II and the organization using it are clearly defined by the infrastructure's scope and range (Keen, 1991). Management's task is to deploy the proper infrastructure to gain a competitive advantage for the firm. Infrastructure can play different strategic roles (Broadbent, Weill, & St. Clair, 1999) to support and leverage business strategies. The strategic alignment of the business strategy and the II is the managerial challenge that, according to Weill and Broadbent (Weill & Broadbent, 1998), can be solved following proper methodology designed to guide managerial choices in this challenging task.

A different conceptualisation of II emerges from the studies that have conceived it from a socio-technical stance.

These studies have discussed different problems related to II taking a similar approach to the one we take in this work. However, these studies have focused on the discussion of the relational dimension of IIs, but not directly dealt with the problem of defining what an II is. The II relational dimension is taken here as a point of departure to attempt to redefine the concept of II along the ontological argument proposed by ANT.

Hanseth and Monteiro (1996a) have examined the increased level of interdependency within information systems and the need to develop standards to make both the integration among information systems and the development of IIs possible. Hanseth (1996), has discussed IIs as layers of technologies and how these different layers shape the development of the II. Similarly, Hanseth and Monteiro (1996b) discuss the nature of technical standards by studying the different level of inscriptions embedded in technology. These studies, in line with what we discuss and argue here, show that the deployment and implementation of IIs is not a linear process that follows a predefined path of action. It is rather the outcome of the tension among different forces. While discussing the deployment and implementation of a new II to support medical work between two Norwegian hospitals, Aenestad and Hanseth (2000) show how the ideas of II deployment, that perceive this process as linear and definable *ex-ante*, are far from useful for discussing the dynamic that takes place during the deployment of IIs. As we argue in this work, their study clearly illustrates that IIs are defined within the dynamics associated with their daily use. Events, circumstances, and unpredictable courses of action shape the deployment trajectory of an II. And thus stands the background upon which we build our claim in favour of a reflection on the nature of II.

Research cited thus far has used ANT largely to discuss the dynamics that take place when IIs and standards are deployed in organization settings. It must however be noted that this research has mainly used ANT as an analytical lens and not as an ontological perspective to explore the essential nature of technology and hence II (A Cordella & Shaikh, 2003). In this article, we propose the use of ANT as an ontology (A Cordella & Shaikh, 2003; Quattrone & Hopper, 2006) to develop a possible analytical framework to better understand how technology and its users co-define their trajectories in a dynamic interplay that is constantly reshaped by its output.

As argued by Star and Ruhleder (1996), there is a need to find a perspective that supports the development of a more precise understanding of the complex and dynamic set of relationships that intertwine work-practices, organizational agents' actions, and technology. An infrastructure should be viewed as something that emerges from people, their daily actions, and technologies (Star & Ruhleder, 1996). Accordingly, an II is more than and distinct from the sum of different information technologies; rather it is a dynamic socio-technical network which connects to and lives within, above, and below existing organizational arrangements (Hanseth, 2000). These ideas of infrastructure move the focus from what the technology is that makes the infrastructure to what defines an infrastructure, highlighting the role of the socio-technical tensions as the force that shapes the infrastructure (Star & Ruhleder, 1996).

This contribution tries to enrich the emerging debate regarding the notion of II, providing a new theoretical foundation to it.

EMERGING CONCEPTUALIZATION OF INFORMATION INFRASTRUCTURE

In his philosophical reflection about the nature and role of IIs in contemporary society, Dahlbom (2000) argues against using the notion of infrastructure when we refer to information technology as a productive foundation. In his vision, information technology "rather than being a productive foundation, is a flexible means of communication, by which social structures are formed, re-formed, and dissolved, in a continuous process of networking" (Dahlbom, 2000). He calls for switching the study of II towards his view that contemporary society, the information society, is a society without a specific infrastructure, without a traditional, stable set of artefacts that characterised the industrial society. In his understanding, the information society infrastructure is now defined by a dynamic and unstable set of relationships, summarised in the idea of "networking", here conceived as a configuration of communication activities (Dahlbom, 2000). In his visualization, the underlying foundation of this communication activities concept cannot be conceived as a monolithic, stable, and cumbersome set of machines, cables, and standards, but rather as a dynamic, light, and malleable set of relationships. The traditional view of a fixed infrastructure is therefore opposite to his conceptualisation of interaction in a network, that is the light, dynamic foundation making the interaction among agents possible.

However, what about the fixed foundation – the machines, cables, and cumbersome technological artefacts needed to provide the interactive settings?

Once again, the understanding of technology and people as a dichotomy has been proposed to explain their interaction. In this specific case, it is the dynamic set of relationships that explains, and gives meaning to, the complex phenomenon of the interaction between people and technology.

Nevertheless, the "heavy" set of technical objects (computers, cables, standards, etc.) cannot be separated from the light, dynamic set of relationships – they cannot be considered without the "activities" they enable, and neither can these activities be conceived separately from the machines and cables. Using Orlikowski's (1992) argument, information technology both enables and constrains relationships, but it is also shaped and constrained by them. However, framing this problem in this manner considers technology and society as two entities that pre-exist the relationships, and the analysis focuses upon who or what is in command of the action.

Following Latour's (1999b) argument, a different conceptualisation of the problem is proposed here, where neither technology nor people are assumed in command of the action. This view suggests that analytical frameworks based on constructivism and technological determinism do not suit research for this relational status.

As discussed earlier, such limitations have led to the need for a reformulation of the problem in terms of dynamic action, where object and subject are both defined in a dynamic process, in which events, circumstances, and complex heterogeneous networks co-define what the infrastructure is – IT is not the object that enables the subject's action. In this re-conceptualisation, the infrastructure is no longer considered a static underlying foundation, but the outcome of dynamic action. Whether public or private, open or closed, technology is not the foundation that enables different kinds of actions and communications such that it can be relegated to the background of our analysis in order to better focus on the activities that are supported by it. The artificial distinction between technology (objects) and society is thereby reconstructed as an action that takes place in this dynamic setting. This supersedes the dichotomist distinction of reality that leads to socio- and techno-deterministic studies of technology (Latour, 1999b).

SO, WHAT IS AN INFORMATION INFRASTRUCTURE?

Analysis of the literature suggests both a lack of consistency in the debate around the concept, nature, and effects of the information "infrastructure" on an organization, and suggests a failure to answer the question: "what is an infrastructure?" (Star & Ruhleder, 1996)

Etymologically, "infrastructure" is the combination of the Latin prefix "*infra*" meaning below, underneath, and the suffix "*structura*" meaning "the way in which an edifice, machine, implement, etc. is made or put together" (OED, 2001). This etymology recalls the context in which the word was used primarily to describe an aspect of the construction of buildings, roads, etc., i.e. "parts of an undertaking; substructure, foundation" (OED, 2001). In this context, the infrastructure is the fixed, unchanging foundation upon which the building is constructed. It is the long-term and permanent installation that is by definition stable and unchangeable because it provides the basis for further development of the construction.

As outlined earlier, this concept of a fixed foundation has been employed to explain the role of information technology as the stable foundation upon which organizational activities are established and exploited (Broadbent, Weill, & Clair, 1995; Edwards, 2003; Hammer & Champy, 1993). This understanding indicates why information technologies, and in particular standards, have been considered as a solution that can make data throughout a corporation stable over time and space. Hypothetically, this is achieved by homogenizing the organization's information system architecture in order to support further development upon a well-defined set of technologies and associated organizational procedures. Standards have been considered to play a crucial role at the point when technology acquires momentum, when competing or complementary components are being added to what is becoming information infrastructure (Edwards, 2003; Hughes, 1993). Standards are then seen as the solution that homogenises large-scale integrations so that they can be stable integrated infrastructures (Fomin, 2003) and provide solid ground for integrated business strategy development. Information infrastructures can in fact be seen as an investment made to achieve specific objectives, such as a strategic solution to save cost via economies of scale; or as a way to benefit from the life of the current strategy, or as a strategic solution to enable current and future flexibility (Broadbent et al., 1995).

This way of looking at an organization's information infrastructure is powerful, and in line with an objectivistic approach to analyse the use and implementation of IT in organizations, because it does not consider the complexity of the phenomena that characterize the daily dynamics of the organization's infrastructure, such as the effects of users' reactions, the pre-existing installed base, etc (Ciborra, 2000). However, these dynamics are a fundamental characteristic of IIs (Ciborra, 2000). As previously discussed, research in the area of information systems has already recognised these peculiarities and discussed their implication for the study of IIs (Aenestad & Hanseth, 2000; Hanseth & Braa, 2001; Star & Ruhleder, 1996).

In line with these thoughts, in this article we do not conceive an infrastructure as a simple tool used to pursue predefined goals. We discuss its embeddedness, its being the sum total of the dynamic processes of an organizations' actions that shape - and are shaped by - the continuous influence exercised by humans over technologies, and vice versa. Information infrastructures are hence considered more than the outcome of a dynamic set of relationships. We go beyond this definition and claim that IIs are in action, meaning they are not stable but *performed* in, by, and through relations.

Accordingly, we have to change our notion of infrastructure from a concept of stability, typical of the construction-industrial era, towards a more flexible conception open to the dynamism needed to meet the challenges of the information society. As in the cases previously discussed, organization IIs emerge and continuously change through a complex, dynamic, and open-ended network of relationships. Paraphrasing Law (1992), infrastructures are what they are because they are a patterned network of heterogeneous relations of heterogeneous materials. They are not defined by one or more entities in isolation from each other, and neither are they defined over time and space. They are emergent phenomena that are dynamically generated and regenerated in open-ended relationships. To study the action of this interplay, we ground our research on the ideas proposed by actor network theory and suggest a framework that defines what an infrastructure is once it is considered within the relationships that shape it.

Actor Network Theory has already been largely used in information system research. Below, we will present a short analysis of the existing research in the discipline that has been informed by ANT. Building upon this research, we discuss the ontological dimension of ANT and we show how this dimension can be useful in sustaining the argument favouring the notion of information infrastructure in action.

ACTOR NETWORK THEORY IN INFORMATION INFRASTRUCTURE RESEARCH

A strong distinction between the social and the technological dimensions characterised the first studies on the diffusion of computer-based technologies in society (Dahlbom & Mathiassen, 1993; Walsham, 1997). When changes in technologies and their uses made it more difficult to clearly identify the distinction between technology and its users (Dahlbom, 1997), as with the case of networked-based technologies, a new interest in studying the interplay between the two emerged.

The first phase was mainly characterised by research in optimal models for managing IIs (Dahlbom, 1997). The second phase focuses more on analysing the relations between technology and society, where the "symbolic boundary between people and information technology is in a constant state of flux across a wide spectrum of contemporary work and leisure activities" (Walsham, 1997). ANT breaks this symbolic boundary, addressing the problem with a different insight. Information technology and users are not defined outside their relationship because they are a set of relational networks.

The significance of the interplay between technology and society is not new in IS literature, nor is ANT the only theory to address this issue. In the 1990s, structurational models of technology addressed the interplay problem between technology and users (Orlikowski, 2000); the same can be said for hermeneutics (Lee, 1994) and phenomenological studies of information systems (Boland, 1985). In these contexts, the interpretivist approach has been growing in strength in the IS field since the mid-1990s (Klein & Myers, 1999; Lee, Liebenau, & De Gross, 1997; Walsham, 1993, 1995). Such interpretivist approaches within IS research acknowledge that, although information systems have a physical component that permits their technical operation, they are designed and used by people operating in a complex social context (Doolin, 1998). Thus, an information system is understood (constructed) differently by different individuals, and is given meaning by the shared understanding of such phenomena. This understanding arises out of social interaction and not from the essential characteristics of the technology: "Events, persons, objects are indeed tangible entities. The meanings and wholeness derived from or ascribed to these tangible phenomena in order to make sense of them, organize them, or recognize a belief system, however, are *constructed realities*" (Lincoln & Guba, 1985). The interpretive epistemology thus considers knowledge within a constructivistic ontology, and the use, design, and study of information systems in organizations is thought of as a hermeneutic process of reading and interpreting this construction as a text (Walsham, 1993).

In this context, actor network theory is proposed as another constructivist approach (Orlikowski, 2000) that moves "one step further towards a more detailed understanding of the relationships between information technology and its use" (Hanseth & Monteiro, 2002).

A large number of IS studies based on actor network theory focus their attention on the relationships between information technology and its user. The ANT analytical lens allows different approaches to study these relationships while looking at IIs. They are, for example, studied looking at how specific inscribed characteristics of actors affect a chosen actor-network, where inscription is defined following Akrich's (1992) socio-constructivistic explanation: the activity of "designers" who define "actors with specific tastes, competences, motives, aspirations, political prejudices, and the rest, and assumes that morality, technology, science, and economy will evolve in particular ways". In this tradition, Monteiro and Hanseth (1996) discuss the role of standards in the shaping of large IIs. The same authors (1995) examine the effects of standards on the achievement of flexibility in the actor-network that shaped the TCP/IP protocol. Timmermans and

Berg (1997) analyse how medical protocols affect the contingent practices of medical intervention, and Bowker and Star (1994) discuss the effect of using the International Classification of Diseases within different actor-networks.

However, an alternative use of actor network theory can be undertaken to analyse the process that shapes and possibly, but not necessarily, stabilizes an actor-network. In this case, using ANT ontological stances, the focus is not on the study of the effects that specific actors have on the black-boxing of inscriptions in a specific actor-network, but on the interplay analysis taking place in the actor-network that can, but not necessarily, result in a black-boxed relationship. According to Lanzara (1999), rather than "opening the black-box" to study the process that made it stable, this formulation of the problem "tracks the process *before the box actually gets closed"* if it indeed ever gets closed. We want to study IIs in the making, rather than in their hypothetical crystallised forms. Kallinikos (2002) similarly argues that human-computer interaction must be analysed by considering the complexity of the forces that are involved. He states they "must be analyzed with reference to the constitutive properties of technology and the distinctive forms by which various technologies invite or admit human participation". Indeed, the focus is on the relational process that can eventually be resolved in specific and contingent settings where black-boxed hybrids are created.

As discussed above, actor network theory has analysed in detail the effects of black-boxed hybrids in the development of specific settled arrangements in actor networks (Bowker & Star, 1996). However, following Bowker and Star (1996), we are "advocating a development of the theory that pays more attention to the work that allows for hybrids to be manufactured and so explores the terrain of the politics of science in action" (Bowker & Star, 1996). Here we propose to use ANT as an ontological foundation to inform the research of the process that dynamically shapes and reshapes information infrastructures. In the next section, we will discuss ANT and highlight this ontological foundation.

ACTORS, NETWORKS, DYNAMIC RELATIONSHIPS: ACTOR NETWORK THEORY

Latour (1987) argues that science and technology have to be studied in action and that we have to focus on the dynamics of their interaction, rather than on the stability of their relationships. The analytical framework provided by ANT offers the theoretical and methodological underpinning for the study of II deployment in terms of these dynamic relationships. It permits infrastructure to be conceived as a phenomenon in action that both emerges from and affects the interplay of different actors participating in open network relationships. This means that the framework proposed here provides the necessary foundations to study the constitutive characteristics of an information infrastructure: its "being in action". The theory is thus positioned in the middle of the debate between the extremes of technologically-deterministic and constructivist studies. On one extreme, these alternative approaches assume that all outcomes of technological change are attributable to the 'technological' rather than the 'social' (Grint & Woolgar, 1995). At the other extreme, social determinism argues that relatively stable social categories can be used to explain technical change, and concentrates on the investigation of social interactions, relegating technology to something that can be forgotten. This bundling means that fixed and unproblematic properties, or 'essences' can then be assigned to the technology and used in any explanation of change.

Actor network theory contributes to this debate from an intermediary position that systematically avoids the dualism between technology and society (Bloomfield & Vurdubakis, 1997) by focusing on the processes through which socio-technical networks are created. As Law (1999) puts it, "entities take their form and acquire their attributes as a result of their relations with other entities"(John Law, 1999). In the same way, Law (1992) argues that society, organizations, agents and technological artefacts are all effects generated in patterned networks of diverse materials.

These considerations move the focus of the analysis from the actor - either technology or society - towards the more complex and less-defined phenomenon that is the interaction. This change in focus not only affects the analysis of the phenomenon, but also affects the assumptions about the nature of the entities that constitute it. ANT incites us to reconsider socio-technical relationships as an open-ended set of interactions where the actors of the socio-technical interplay do not pre-exist the relationship. Instead, the actor has a "relational materiality" (John Law, 1999) that is generated *in* and *by* these relationships, i.e. actors achieve their form and attributes as a consequence of their relations with other actors. This reflects an aversion to accepting *apriori* the pre-existence of social structures and differences as somehow intrinsically given in the order of things. There are no distinctions between social and technical subsystems. It is the relationship that produces the emergence of actors from the very interplay among different human and non-human entities. There is no case of a local or global dimension here, only a relational one[1] (Latour, 1999a).

This is clearly a claim against the dualistic distinction between technology and organizations. Technology and people do not have *apriori* different and defined effects on their relational interplay. Both participate in, and mediate, the relational networks - but they are also the outcome of the same relationships. The concepts of subjectivity and objectivity themselves do not exist other than in the context of the relationships. Thus, Latour (1999a) proposes the redefinition of the concepts in terms of "intersubjectivity" and "interobjectivity" to emphasise the relational dimensions of the two.

The relationships developed in a network that dynamically shape and re-shape the actors also recursively define the characteristics of the involved actors. The actor can thus be defined as one output of the relationship in a network, where Callon (1993) defines a network as a "group of unspecified relationships among entities of which the nature itself is undetermined".

However, and this is where the complexity and power of the theory emerges, the actors that are part of the network are also the constitutive elements of the network. This is the foundation of the concept of an actor network: actor and network are concatenated and one cannot be defined without the other. "The actor network is reducible neither to an actor alone nor to a network...an actor network is simultaneously an actor whose activity is networking heterogeneous elements and a network that is able to redefine and transform what it is made of" (Callon, 1987).

In ANT, actors are not defined and analysed in a static set of relationships. It is the researcher who artificially defines the analytical range of the study to see "what the various actors in a setting are doing to one another" (Akrich & Latour, 1992). By limiting the level or focus of the investigation, it is possible to study and understand some of the relationships that are shaping both actors and the relational networks. However, it must be understood that actors and actor networks are naturally *embedded* in open ranges of relationships that cannot be artificially limited by the scope of any particular analysis. Actor networks are *open-ended* and can be only artificially (but usefully) closed and isolated from the broad and natural openness of relationships.

The complexity of the relational pattern in an actor network is enhanced by the fact that not all the actors embody the same level of flexibility. Actors embody various characteristics that are the outcome of their relationships with "heterogeneous elements, animate and inanimate, that have been linked to one another for a certain period of time" (Callon, 1987). These characteristics are renegotiated in the interplay with other actors. An actor-network embodies these characteristics so that the outcome is the result of "a set of diverse forces"(Akrich, 1992) that affects and defines the inter-networked relational settings. These forces can be considered by the actors as an embodiment of "prescriptions", defined as "what a device allows or forbids from the actors - humans and non-humans - that it anticipates; it is the morality of a setting both negative (what it prescribes) and positive (what it permits)" (Akrich & Latour, 1992). An actor analysed in isolation (taken out of the network) is seen to embody specific inscribed characteristics that may strongly affect the configuration of the contextual relational network under analysis. However, the settlement of the actor network is not defined *a priori*. It emerges from the complex, open set of relations and from the characteristics of the elements that are both part of, and constitute, the actor-network. People and technology "are never located in bodies and bodies alone, but rather that an actor is a patterned network of heterogeneous relations, or an effect produced by such a network" (J Law, 1992). As a consequence, actors do not embody action or *actantiality* (potential for action); it is their relational dimension that generates instances of action (Latour, 1999a; J Law, 1992). The actantiality is generated in a circular and recursive process of negotiation, which is the course that defines and redefines actors in their multiple contexts. Since actors are in action and, as a consequence, in a continuous state of mutation, their continuous relational interplay is the *performative* characteristic of actor networks, where actors are in fact "*performed* in, by, and through relations" (John Law, 1999). The diverse configurations of actors in an actor network, and the process of stabilization of the relationships, are the outcomes of the alignment of different actors that results from the outcome of the interplay between different forces.

Thus, actors and actor networks reflect a process of multiple trajectories that can become either stable, as a dynamic equilibrium, or reflect unstable misaligned relationships. While actors emerge and retreat from the interplay in the actor networks, they also define the characteristics of the interplay via their embodiment of relationships in other actor networks. Therefore, the actors are not neutral to the relational context: they are influenced by the network and, in turn, they influence that network. Actors in their interplay within the actor network negotiate their forces in a process of *translation*. "By translation we understand all the negotiations, intrigues, calculations, acts of persuasion and violence thanks to which an actor or force takes, or causes to be conferred to itself, authority to speak or act on behalf of another actor or force" (Callon & Latour, 1981). Translation is the circular process of "interpretation" or, as Callon (1991) puts it, the "definition" that every actor makes of other actors in the actor network.

The dynamics of translation reflect different levels of actor inscription and alignment rigidity achieved in the actor network. When actors translate each other, they try to enrol the other to "support" or believe in them (Latour, 1987). The less-prescribed actors get more easily translated and reconfigured into the interests of others than those with more strongly inscribed and rigidly prescribed trajectories. If the process of translation does not result in an alignment of interests, it is considered misaligned. In this case, the actors are configured in "separate spaces with no common measure" (Callon, 1991). A misaligned actor network does not produce a set of relationships that can be analysed as a stable and configured output of the relational interplay in the actor network. This means that the actor network cannot be *black-boxed* and thus considered as an element produced by many elements acting as one (Latour, 1987). Most actor networks are of this type.

Finally, recalling the concept of circularity of actor network relationships, it is clear that every actor network affects – and is affected by – the characteristics of the actors, and then by the different interests the actors bring to the actor network. Every actor can bring characteristics that have emerged from other actor networks to which it belongs because an actor can, and usually does, belong simultaneously to more than one actor network at a time. Recursively, new, emergent characteristics are re-proposed back into the other actor-networks. This circularity explains the action that is endogenous to the relational interplay analysed by actor network theory.

CONCLUSION

This article provides the theoretical background to discuss and support the explanation of the ideas underpinning the concepts of information infrastructure in action. The work covers the theoretical and philosophical assumptions that are used to frame this concept, and contextualises this work within information systems literature and ANT to provide the answer to the question: *What is an information infrastructure?*

This article proposes to frame information infrastructures in action as the outcome of the process of negotiation among different information systems, work practices, and routines in the daily activities of organizations. Conceiving information infrastructures as performative forces that dynamically evolve *in fieri*[2], this work supersedes the limitation of studying information infrastructure by only looking at what has happened and how it has happened. Rather, it proposes to shed light on what is happening and how it is happening. Information infrastructures should not be studied retrospectively to understand how they get shaped but rather how the actions shaped them. Here we claim we have to study the action of making rather than the processes that made it. This claim is a consequence of the limitation that we have found in literature regarding the definition of what an information infrastructure is. To overcome this limitation, we propose a theoretical framework based on ANT that directly addresses the ontological problem of defining what an information infrastructure is.

REFERENCES

Aenestad, M., & Hanseth, O. (2000). *Implementing open network technologies in complex work practices. A case from telemedicine.* Paper presented at the IFIP WG 8.2 International Conference. The Social and Organizational Perspective on Research and Practice in Information Technology, Aalborg, Denmark.

Akrich, M. (1992). The de-scription of technical objects. In W. E. Bijker & J. Law (Eds.), *Shaping technology / building society: studies in sociotechnical change* (pp. 205-224). Cambridge Ma: The MIT Press.

Akrich, M., & Latour, B. (1992). A summary of a convenient vocabulary for the semiotics of human and non-human assemblies. In W. E. Bijker & J. Law (Eds.), *Shaping technology / building society: studies in sociotechnical change* (pp. 259-264). Cambridge, Ma: The MIT Press.

Bakos, J. Y., & Treacy, M. E. (1986). Information technology and corporate strategy: a research perspective. *MIS Quarterly, 10*(2), 107–119. doi:10.2307/249029

Barley, S. R. (1986). Technology as an occasion for structuring: evidence from observations of CT scanners and the social order of radiology departments. *Administrative Science Quarterly, 31*(1), 78–108. doi:10.2307/2392767

Bloomfield, B., & Vurdubakis, T. (1997). Paper traces: inscribing organization and information technology. In B. Bloomfield, R. Coombs, D. Knights, & D. Littler (Eds.), *Information Technology and Organization*. Oxford: Oxford University Press.

Boland, R. J. (1985). Phenomenology: A Preferred Approach to Research in Information Systems. In E. Mumford, R. Hirschheim, G. Fitzgerald, & T. Wood Harper (Eds.), *Research Methods in Information Systems*. Amsterdam: NorthHolland.

Bowker, G., & Star, S. L. (1994). Knowledge and Infrastructure in international information management: Problems of classification and coding. In L. Bud-Frierman (Ed.), *Information acumen: The understanding and use of knowledge in modern business* (pp. 187-216). London: Routledge.

Bowker, G., & Star, S. L. (1996). How things (actor-net)work: Classification, magic and the ubiquity of standards. *Available at,* http://weber.ucsd.edu/~gbowker/actnet.html.

Broadbent, M., Weill, M., & Clair, D. (1995). *The role of information technology infrastructure in business process redesign.* Unpublished manuscript, Center for information systems research, Sloan School of Management.

Broadbent, M., Weill, M., & St. Clair, D. (1999). The Implications of Information Technology Infrastructure for Business Process Redesign. *MIS Quarterly, 23*(2). doi:10.2307/249750

Broadbent, M., & Weill, P. (1999). The implication of information technology Infrastructure for business process redesign. *MIS Quarterly, 23*(3).

Callon, M. (1987). Society in the Making: The Study of Technology as a Tool for Sociological Analysis. In W. E. Bijker, T. P. Hughes, & T. J. Pinch (Eds.), *The Social Construction of Technological Systems. New Directions in the Sociology and History of Technology.* Cambridge, MA: MIT press.

Callon, M. (1991). Techno-economic networks and irreversibility. In J. Law (Ed.), *A sociology of monsters: essays on power, technology and domination* (pp. 132-161). London: Routledge.

Callon, M. (1993). Variety and Irreversibility in Networks of Technique Conception and Adoption. In D. Foray & C. Freemann (Eds.), *Technology and the Wealth of Nations: Dynamics of Constructed Advantage* (pp. 232-268). London, New York: Pinter.

Callon, M., & Latour, B. (1981). Unscrewing the Big Leviathan: How Actors Macro-Structure Reality and How Sociologist Help Them To Do So. In K. Knorr-Cetina & A. V. Cicouvel (Eds.), *Advances in Social Theory and Methodology: Towards an Integration of Micro and Macro-Sociology* (pp. 277-303). Boston, MA; London: Routledge.

Ciborra, C. U. (Ed.). (2000). *From Control to Drift.* Oxford: Oxford University Press.

Ciborra, C. U. (2004). *Digital Technologies and the Duality of Risk.* Retrieved from http://www.lse.ac.uk/collections/CARR/pdf/Disspaper27.pdf

Ciborra, C. U., & Failla, A. (2000). Infrastructure as a process: the case of CRM in IBM. In C. U. Ciborra (Ed.), *From Control to Drift: the Dynamics of Corporate Information Infrastructures* (pp. 105-124). Oxford: Oxford University Press.

Cordella, A. (2006). Transaction costs and information systems: does IT add up? *Journal of Information Technology, 21*(3), 195–202. doi:10.1057/palgrave.jit.2000066

Cordella, A., & Shaikh, M. (2003). *Actor Network Theory and After: What's new for Information Systems research* Paper presented at the European Conference on Information systems, ECIS, Naples, Italy.

Curley, K. F., & Pyburn, P. J. (1982). "Intellectual" Technologies: The key to Improving White-Collar Productivity. *Sloan Management Review, 24*, 31–39.

Dahlbom, B. (1997). The new informatics. *Scandinavian Journal of information System, 8*(2).

Dahlbom, B. (2000). Postface: from infrastructure to networking. In C. U. Ciborra (Ed.), *From Control to Drift.* Oxford: Oxford University Press.

Dahlbom, B., & Mathiassen, L. (1993). *Computer in Context.* Cambridge, Massachusetts: Blackwell.

Doolin, B. (1998). Information Technology as Disciplinary Technology: Being Critical in Interpretive Research on Information Systems. *Journal of Information Technology, 14*(4), 301–311. doi:10.1057/jit.1998.8

Edwards, P. N. (2003). Infrastructure and Modernity: Force, Time, and Social Organization in the History of Sociotechnical Systems. In T. J. Misa (Eds.), *Modernity and Technology*. Cambridge, MA: MIT Press.

Fomin, V. (2003). *The role of standards in information infrastructure development, revisited.* Paper presented at the Standard Making: A Critical Research Frontier for Information Systems MISQ Special Issue Workshop, Seattle.

Giddens, A. (1984). *The constitution of society: outline of the theory of structuration*. Cambridge Cambridgeshire: Polity Press.

Grint, K., & Woolgar, S. (1995). On Some failures of nerve in the construction of feminist analyses of technology. *Science, Technology & Human Values, 20*(3), 286–310. doi:10.1177/016224399502000302

Hammer, M., & Champy, J. (1993). *Reengineering the corporation: a manifesto for business revolution* (1st ed.). New York, NY: HarperBusiness.

Hanseth, O. (1996). *Information technology as Infrastructure.* Unpublished Ph.D Thesis, School of Economics and Commercial Law, Goteborg University, Goteborg.

Hanseth, O. (2000). Infrastructures: From Systems to Infrastructures. In K. Braa, C. Sørensen & B. Dahlbom (Eds.), *Planet Internet.* Lund, Sweden: Studentlitteratur.

Hanseth, O. (2004a). Actor network theory and information systems: What's so special. *Information Technology & People, 17*(2), 116–123. doi:10.1108/09593840410542466

Hanseth, O. (2004b). *From systems and tools to networks and infrastructures - from design to cultivation. Towards a theory of ICT solutions and its design methodology implications.* Unpublished manuscript.

Hanseth, O., & Braa, K. (1998). *Technology as a Traitor: Emergent SAP Infrastructure in a Global Organisation.* Paper presented at the Proceedings of the Nineteenth International Conference on Information systems, ICIS'98, Helsinki.

Hanseth, O., & Braa, K. (2000). Who is in control? Designers, managers – or technology? In C. U. Ciborra (Ed.), *From Control to Drift: The Dynamics of Corporate Information Infrastructures*. Oxford: Oxford University Press.

Hanseth, O., & Braa, K. (2001). Hunting for the treasure at the end of the rainbow. Standardizing corporate IT infrastructure. *Computer Supported Cooperative Work (CSCW). The Journal of Collaborative Computing, 10*(3-4), 261–292. doi:10.1023/A:1012637309336

Hanseth, O., & Monteiro, E. (2002). *Understanding Information Infrastructure*: Manuscript.

Hanseth, O., Monteiro, E., & Hatling, M. (1996a). Developing information infrastructure: The tension between standardization and flexibility. *Science, Technology & Human Values, 21*(4), 407–426. doi:10.1177/016224399602100402

Hanseth, O., Monteiro, E., & Hatling, M. (1996b). Inscribing behaviour in information infrastructure standards. *Accounting, Management and Information System.*

Hughes, T. P. (1993). The Evolution of Large Technological Systems. In T. P. Bijker, T. P. Hughes & T. J. Pinch (Eds.), *The social construction of technological systems: New directions in the sociology and history of technology*. Cambridge: MIT Press

Kallinikos, J. (2002). *Re-opening the Black Box of Technology.* Paper presented at the EGOS 2002, Barcelona.

Kallinikos, J. (2006). *The Consequences of Information: Institutional Implications of Technological Change*. Cheltenham: Edward Elgar.

Keen, P. W. (1991). *Shaping the future: Business Redesign through information technologies* Boston: Harvard Business School Press.

Klein, H. K., & Myers, M. D. (1999). A set of principles for conducting and evaluating interpretive field studies in information systems. *MIS Quarterly, 23*(1), 67–93. doi:10.2307/249410

Lanzara, G. F. (1999). Designing Systems In-Action: between transient constructs and permanent structures. Copenhagen: Keynote Speech, European Confrence of Information Systems.

Latour, B. (1987). *Science in action: how to follow scientists and engineers through society.* Cambridge, MA: Harvard University Press.

Latour, B. (1999a). On Recalling ANT. In J. Law & J. Hassard (Eds.), *Actor Network Theory and After* (pp. 15-25). Oxford: Blackwell Publishers / The Sociological Review.

Latour, B. (1999b). *Pandora's hope*. Cambridge, Massachusetts: Harvard University Press.

Law, J. (1990). Technology and heterogeneous engineering: The case of Portuguese expansion. In W. E. Bijker, T. P. Hughes & T. J. Pinch (Eds.), *The social construction of technological systems: New directions in the sociology and history of technology* (pp. 111-134). Cambridge, Mass. and London: MIT Press.

Law, J. (1992). Notes on The Theory of the Actor Network: Ordering, Strategy and Heterogeneity. *Systems Practice, 5*(4). doi:10.1007/BF01059830

Law, J. (1999). After ANT: complexity, naming and topology. In J. Law & J. Hassard (Eds.), *Actor Network Theory and After* (pp. 1-14). Oxford: Blackwell Publishers / The Sociological Review.

Lee, A. S. (1994). Electronic Mail as a Medium for Rich Communication: An Empirical Investigation Using Hermeneutic Interpretation. *MIS Quarterly, 19*(2), 143–157. doi:10.2307/249762

Lee, A. S. (1999). Researching MIS. In W. L. Currie & R. D. Galliers (Eds.), *Rethinking Management Information Systems*. Oxford: Oxford University Press.

Lee, A. S. (2001). Editorial. *MIS Quarterly, 25*(1).

Lee, A. S., Liebenau, J., & De Gross, J. I. (Eds.). (1997). *Information Systems and Qualitative Research*. London: Chapman and Hall.

Lincoln, Y. S., & Guba, E. G. (1985). *Naturalistic Inquiry*. Beverly Hills: Sage Publications.

Markus, M. L., & Robey, D. (1988). Information Technology and Organizational Change: Causal Structure in theory and Research. *Management Science, 34*(5). doi:10.1287/mnsc.34.5.583

Monteiro, E., & Hanseth, O. (1995). Social shaping of information infrastructure: on being specific about the technology. In W. J. Orlikowski, J. Walsham, M. R. Jones & J. I. De Gross (Eds.), *Information Technology and Changes in Organizational Work* (pp. 325-343). London: Chapman a& Hall.

Monteiro, E., & Hanseth, O. (1996). Social shaping of Information Infrastructure: on being specific about technology. In W. J. Orlikowski, G. Walsham, R. Jones & J. I. De Gross (Eds.), *Information technology and changes in organizational work*. London: Chapman & Hall.

Ngwenyama, O. K. (1998). Groupware, social action and organizational emergence: on the process dynamics of computer mediated distributed work. *Accounting, Management and Information Technologies,* (8), 127-146.

OED. (2001). *Oxford English Dictionary*. Retrieved from www.oed.com.

Orlikowski, W. J. (1992). The duality of technology: Rethinking the concept of technology in organizations. *Information Systems Research*, *3*(3).

Orlikowski, W. J. (2000). Using Technology and Constituting Structures: A Practical Lens for Studying Technology in Organizations. *Organization Science*, *11*(4), 404–428. doi:10.1287/orsc.11.4.404.14600

Orlikowski, W. J., & Barley, R. B. (2001). Technology and Institutions: What can research on information technology and research on organization learn from each other? *MIS Quarterly*, *25*(2), 145–165. doi:10.2307/3250927

Orlikowski, W. J., & Iacono, S. (2001). Research commentary: desperately seeking the "IT" in IT research - a call for theorizing the IT artifact. *Information Systems Research*, *10*(2).

Orlikowski, W. J., & Robey, D. (1991). Information technology and the structuring of the organizations. *Information Systems Research*, *2*(2). doi:10.1287/isre.2.2.143

Quattrone, P., & Hopper, T. (2006). What is IT? SAP, Accounting, and Visibility in a Multinational Organisation. *Information and Organization*, (16): 212–250. doi:10.1016/j.infoandorg.2006.06.001

Star, S., & Ruhleder, k. (1996). Steps toward an Ecology of Infrastructure: Design, Access for Large Information Space. *Information Systems Research*, *7*(1), 111–134. doi:10.1287/isre.7.1.111

Star, S. (2002). Got Infrastructure? How Standards, Categories and Other Aspects of Infrastructure Influence Communication. The 2nd Social Study of IT: LSE workshop on ICT and Globalization.

Suchman, L. (1987). *Plan and situated actions: the problem of human machine communication*. Cambridge: Cambridge University Press.

Thompson, J. D. (1967). *Organizations in action; social science bases of administrative theory*. New York: McGraw-Hill.

Timmermans, S., & Berg, M. (1997). Standardization in action: Achieving universalism and localisation through medical protocols. *Social Studies of Science*, *27*(1), 111–134.

Walsham, G. (1993). *Interpreting Information Systems in Organizations*. New York: John Wiley.

Walsham, G. (1995). Interpretive case studies in IS research: nature and method. *European Journal of Information Systems*, *4*, 74–81. doi:10.1057/ejis.1995.9

Walsham, G. (1997). Actor-Network Theory and IS research: Current status and future prospects. In A. S. Lee, J. Liebenau & J. I. DeGross (Eds.), *Information systems and qualitative research* (pp. 466-480). London: Chapman and Hall.

Weill, P., & Broadbent, M. (1998). *Leveraging the new infrastructure: how market leaders capitalize on information technology*. Boston, Mass.: Harvard Business School Press.

Woodward, J. (1965). *Industrial organization: theory and practice*. London, New York: Oxford University Press.

Zuboff, S. (1988). *In the Age of the Smart Machine*. New York: Basic Books, Inc.

ENDNOTES

1. Obviously, the analysis of the relational dimension can be more focused on the study of local or global relationships.
2. From Latin: in the course of execution; a thing commenced but not completed

This work was previously published in International Journal of Actor-Network Theory and Technological Innovation, Volume 2, Issue 1, edited by Arthur Tatnall, pp. 27-53, copyright 2010 by IGI Publishing (an imprint of IGI Global).

Chapter 3
Adoption of ICT in Rural Medical General Practices in Australia:
An Actor-Network Study

Patricia Deering
National Health Workforce Task Force, Australia

Arthur Tatnall
Victoria University, Australia

Stephen Burgess
Victoria University, Australia

ABSTRACT

ICT has been used in medical General Practice throughout Australia now for some years, but although most General Practices make use of ICT for administrative purposes such as billing, prescribing and medical records, many individual General Practitioners themselves do not make full use of these ICT systems for clinical purposes. The decisions taken in the adoption of ICT in general practice are very complex, and involve many actors, both human and non-human. This means that actor-network theory offers a most suitable framework for its analysis. This article investigates how GPs in a rural Division of General Practice not far from Melbourne considered the adoption and use of ICT. The study reported in the article shows that, rather than characteristics of the technology itself, it is often seemingly unimportant human issues that determine if and how ICT is used in General Practice.

DOI: 10.4018/978-1-4666-1559-5.ch003

INTRODUCTION

Most medical practices in Australia make good use of many aspects of Information and Communications Technology (ICT) for administrative purposes, but it is not the case that as many individual medical general practitioners (GP) also do so for clinical purposes. The study reported in this article found that it is important to note the difference between the adoption of ICT by *general practice* (the organisation) and its adoption and use by *general practitioners* (the individuals). The adoption process in each case is complex, and many stakeholders have grappled with issues such as the cost of computerisation, the rapid changes in technology, the lack of agreed standards and the problems of introducing technological solutions into the daily work place of general practice.

While there are generally pockets of high uptake and use of ICT in different parts of Australia, there are differences in the details of adoption from one practice to another and even within practices. There are also differences in adoption in terms of the acceptance of the idea (of using ICT) versus doing something practical with it.

Some rural areas in Australia are extremely remote, but the study reported in this article examined use of ICT in the Central Highlands Division of General Practice [1] (CHDGP), based in a rural area not very far from the outskirts of Melbourne (the State capital). GPs in rural areas, even those that are not extremely remote, face special challenges in relation to their use of ICT. A major consideration relates to resources and geographical distance: the further you are away from the resources of a large city, the longer it takes and the more it costs to gain access to them. This is particularly the case with hardware and software purchases, training and support for ICT use (Burgess 2002).

This study investigated how GPs in CHDGP considered the adoption of ICT. CHDGP is one of 111 nationally funded divisions of general practice in Australia (along with 8 state-based entities) that have been charged with the task of linking General Practitioners with each other and with linking GPs with their communities to improve health outcomes. The study investigated and modelled the socio-technical factors that acted to enable, and to inhibit uptake and use of ICT by GPs in this region. After an initial survey of the use of ICT by GPs, the research reported in this article details case studies of two representative practices from the 43 existing within the study area.

Research on the use of ICT in 1190 medical general practices in Australia by Henderson, Britt and Miller (2006) indicated that all but 79 had a computer available for medical use. Figure 1 gives an indication of the availability of ICT in medical practices.

It is important to note that this Figure shows reported availability and not actual use by individual GPs. Research has shown, however, that in the study area individual GPs continue to use ICT mainly for administrative and some clinical functions but that much less use is made of online functions and to assist with diagnosis (NHIMAC 1999; GPCG 2001; Henderson et al. 2006).

Figure 1. Computer availability at medical practices (adapted from Henderson et al. (2006))

A computer is *available* for:	Number of practices	Proportion of all practices
Billing	1050	79.6%
Prescribing	1101	83.5%
Medical records	934	70.8%
Other administrative tasks	974	73.8%
Internet/e-mail	888	67.3%

As many ICT products have now been developed to support medical general practitioners in all aspects of their work, and much research and development has been done in this area, it should now be questioned why GPs are not making as much use of these systems as they could (Deering and Tatnall 2008). Research had shown that there is still reluctance, in particular from many rural general practitioners, to fully implement ICT in primary health care in Australia (Everitt and Tatnall 2003).

MODELLING ICT AND GENERAL PRACTITIONERS AS AN ACTOR-NETWORK

There are many complex factors and entities involved in determining how GPs adopt and use ICT, and any research approach that ignores the inherent complexity of this socio-technical situation is unlikely to produce useful answers. This research project initially set out to compare two different approaches to modelling the adoption of ICT by rural GPs: Innovation Diffusion (Rogers 2003) and Innovation Translation, informed by Actor-Network Theory (ANT) (Callon 1986b; Latour 1986; Latour 1996). It was soon decided, however, that the socio-technical nature of the situation strongly suggested that Innovation Diffusion would not provide as rich a framework as Actor-Network Theory, which allows for the views of all the subjects to be fully documented and explained (Tatnall 2009b). This approach was necessary because the complexity of health delivery in Australia has increased the need to manage information in medical practices, leading to a multi-stakeholder environment involving both human and non-human entities (Deering and Tatnall 2008). ANT, as the reader will be aware, allows the researcher to adopt the position of not privileging the explanatory power of one type of actor over another (Tatnall 2009a) and allows the inherent complexity of a situation like this to be handled appropriately.

One way in which ANT handles complexity is in its use of black boxes (Callon 1986b) used to temporarily hide this complexity. In complex situations where the individual details of actors and the network of interactions within a particular group do not need to be considered at this time, this group can be considered to form a black box (Callon 1986b) and handled as if they constituted a single actor. At some later time the black box of networked actors can be opened and its contents reconsidered.

A key notion of ANT is associated with the translation of ICT from a stage of non-adoption to one of adoption. These stages of translation (Callon 1986b), referred to later in the article, are:

- **Problematisation:** where key actors attempt to define the nature of the problem at hand and the roles of other actors so that they are seen to have the answer and be indispensable to the solution of the problem.
- **Interessement:** the processes which attempt to impose the identities and roles defined in problematisation on other actors – to lock other actors into their proposed roles and replace existing networks with those created by the enrollers.
- **Enrolment:** occurs if interessement is successful. This leads to the establishment of a solid, reliable network of alliances, but does require roles to be adopted through coercion, seduction or consent.
- **Mobilisation:** occurs as the proposed solution gains wider acceptance.

ACTOR-NETWORK THEORY AND GP ADOPTION OF ICT

The concept of an *actor* underlies ANT. This term is used to represent any physical entity whose presence makes a difference, and Callon (1991:140) describes an actor as "any entity able to associate texts, humans, non-humans and money". Latour notes that "when an actor simply exerts power nothing happens and s/he is powerless: when, on the other hand, an actor exerts power it is others who perform the action" (Latour 1986:264). The main advice on method suggested by the proponents of actor-network theory is to "follow the actors" (Callon 1986a; Callon 1991; Latour 1996) and to let them set the framework and limits of the study themselves (Tatnall 2007). In this research this means that actors influence or enrol other actors in their network, and are influenced in turn. It also means that people and things pick up an idea, technique or process as they see it, which is not necessarily the same as that originally intended. Of course, in the attempt to move from interessement to mobilisation the idea, techniques or process may be rejected; actors do not have to be successful.

Enrolling others actors can simply be seen as an act of negotiation through which one actor becomes indispensable to another as part of an alliance. Completely successful network enrolment then, involves interessement (Callon 1986b), an entanglement of sorts whereby all in the network will speak as if of one voice. A successful enrolment or translation (Callon 1986b) therefore does not depend on any initial impetus, but rather on what each person involved in the network does with the idea or artefact, for they have a choice as to what they will do. Interessement means that their chosen uses have become close to identical. The first task in undertaking a research project like this then is to identify as many of the actors as possible, and to look in some detail at their contributions and how they interact with each other.

The following sections identify important actors that have played a significant role in the adoption of ICT by GPs in Australia, and specifically in CHDGP. Much of the material for this section is a result of interviews conducted with key stakeholders in these groups and a review of archival records.

Royal Australian College of General Practitioners

One important actor to quickly emerge at a national level was the Royal Australian College of General Practitioners (RACGP) which began to investigate the use of ICT over 20 years ago when it joined with MedRecord Computers Systems and jointly launched the Computer Assistance Practice Project. The National Computer Committee of the RACGP was formed in 1986 as an advisory body to the RACGP council on all matters relating to medical computing. This organisational structure was successful mainly because it attracted a younger group of GPs who were the first computer literate graduates to enter the profession and become fellows of the College. By 1992 RACGP, the Australian Medical Association (AMA) and the Australian Commonwealth Government negotiated a strategy to address problems affecting general practice, and it was at this time that the issues involved in ICT were flagged: the RACGP had enrolled some new allies to the cause of computerising General Practice – the AMA and the Commonwealth Government.

To understand that computerisation in the Central Highlands Division of General Practice could not have happened without the influence of the RACGP it is important to examine the role that the RACGP played in the national adoption process and then how that spun off into the research area. The influence of the College can initially be seen through its actions in the creation of standards for general practice. Standards are generally agreed by the membership and then set by the College as a black box. In unpacking the layers of the black box of the College it is important to acknowledge the role of setting standards (which set effective and clear pathways for GPs to follow).

Fuchs (1992) suggests that what is accepted as a black box is defined largely through collegiate control and that membership of such a collegiate involves the assessment and attainment of appropriate qualifications. It follows from this that a professional group such as the RACGP can be put down to successful networks that have created black boxes. Latour (1986) has described this process of a network (read RACGP) becoming an actor that can be applied to the computerisation of general practice. From its position of being an accepted black box in general practice it has had influence in the process.

General Practice Computing Group

Another significant actor that now appears, also at a national level, is the General Practice Computing Group (GPCG). The role of the GPCG, formed in 1997, was to support the acceleration of computerisation and the use of computers in general practice. It was never the primary goal of this group to have *general practitioners* use computers as it considered that this would happen in the future with the use of clinical decision making tools, broadband and a secure Internet. The General Practice Computing Group was quickly accepted as the peak body for medical informatics in Australian General Practice.

The GPCG was formed because there was a need for coordination of, and a much sharper focus in, general practice information technology (Mott 2001). At this time it was generally accepted that uptake of computers was not occurring quickly enough and the profession needed to address this (Interview – GPCG, 2005). The role of the GPCG as an actor was confirmed when it was officially recognised by the Royal Australian College of General Practitioners and a multi-partnership was created between the Australian College of Rural and Remote Medicine, Australian Divisions of General Practice, Australian Medical Association (AMA), Consumers Health Forum, Medical Software Industry Association, the Rural Doctors Association of Australia, the consumer health forum, and various government agencies. The national prescribing service was an observer to the GPCG. With such a network there can be little doubt that it has been one of the main public instigators of the adoption of computers in general practice in Australia.

Parallel to lobbying for the formation of the GPCG, the RACGP was also lobbying for a redefinition of the Better Practice Program (- this voluntary program was another national Government initiative designed to provide financial recognition for general practices that focussed on patient needs and providing continuing, comprehensive 'whole of patient' care), resulting in this becoming broader based and not only supporting clinical development, but also supporting the profession financially by balancing the difference between sectors in fee for service payments. This, it was argued, would support better service to patients.

The Practice Incentives Program

Archival records at RACGP show how it joined forces with the AMA to produce a joint position statement in regard to the implementation of ICT. These records suggest that, based on the belief that Australian GPs will purchase and use computers when they see that ICT can generates direct benefits for patient care at a cost that represents a worthwhile business investment, a strategic approach to implementation is needed. They point out that if ICT only provides benefits to governments, other funding agents, researchers, planners and other sectors of the health care system, GPs will not consider the investment to put them in their surgeries as being worthwhile.

The Practice Incentives Program (PIP), which replaced the Better Practice Program in 1998, was established nationally to financially reward GPs and practices for, amongst other things, adopting computers. Evidence from this research suggests that the PIP payments dramatically increased the adoption of computers in general practice in the study area.

There can be little doubt that without the GPCG the inclusion of computer use in PIP payments would not have occurred. It is thus clear that the building of networks and the political activity of the GPCG increased the level of adoption of computers in general practice. It is, however, also clear that the level of adoption varied around the country. The interplay of computers, the requirements from the PIP and the aspirations of the doctors are all linked in a complex network of relationships that play a part in the process and level of adoption. So despite the incentives offered by the PIP and the activities of the GPCG, the adoption of computers and the way that they are used by GPs and practices within the study area is still incomplete and so this research looked for further explanations as to why this was the case.

The IT/IM Officer

Another important actor, this time at a local level, was the Information Technology/ Information Management (IT/IM) Officer in each of the Divisions of General Practice. It was the role of this person to assist both the Division itself, and local General Practices in their adoption and use of ICT. This officer's role was pivotal to the establishment of computerisation in CHDGP, however the achievements did not come without difficulties which in themselves created barriers to adoption of IT/IM in this Division. The position description of the IT/IM Officer indicated that this person's task would be to lead the implementation of IT/IM in the division and to deliver high quality, timely, cost effective ICT solutions to CHDGP member practices. They were to work in partnership with key stakeholders to maximise the contribution of information management and technology to high quality healthcare and an efficient health system. This IT/IM Officer was to have primary responsibility for leading, guiding, coaching and supporting staff across the diverse range of practice in the division.

However, according to the IT/IM officer (Interview, 2004) appointed at CHDGP the challenges that she faced were as follows:

- Unrealistic expectations of the professions, government and industry.
- Inadequate change management procedures, including social and organisational informatics issues.
- Lack of information system standards and benchmarks.
- Fragmented political and legislative approaches and support.
- Fragmented financial approaches and support, including an unfilled need for clear business models with which to engage the clinical software industry.

In an Interview (2004) she indicated that: "My first thoughts about the job were that I was there to assist in bringing about some behavioural change. I thought this was a bit amazing as when I first started I came to this job thinking that the GPs would be enthusiastic to change because of the benefits that the technology would bring to them. I was mostly wrong about this, many of the GPs did not want to have anything to do with ICT but they did see that it would help the practice deliver a better service."

Small Business Aspects of General Practices

Rural GPs, however, operate very much in the mode of small business (Burgess and Trethowan 2002) and this is another factor to be considered. The similarities between general practice and small businesses are evident, with concerns about having the resources, (especially time and money) to devote to ICT, lack of ICT expertise, poor support and technical assistance, and a struggle to see the benefits of ICT usage (GPSRG 1998). GPs' actual usage of ICT reflects the patterns of small business usage and GPs, like small businesses, generally have fewer resources available to devote to ICT projects and have less formalised planning and control procedures (such as evaluation and review). Often, the small business owner/manager (who in this case is likely to be the GP, but many practices are shifting towards a corporate model of ownership) does not have the time, resources or expertise necessary for such tasks (GPCG 2001; Burgess 2002). In addition to these problems, GPs face added problems in relation to privacy and confidentiality, and are concerned that having a computer on their desk may interfere with their patient consultations (GPSRG 1998). This all means that factors affecting the adoption and use of ICT by small businesses made a more than useful ancillary point for examining such uses of ICT by GPs in this study.

There exists a dichotomy for rural GPs in the study area (CHDGP); whereas on the one hand they function as small businesses, on the other they are juxtaposed by the way that they were inculcated into the persona of carer. This is in contrast to what GPs say they want and what they are required to do in acting as a small business. The perception of themselves as gatekeepers of health and as independent practitioners that most GPs still generally have, along with a need for autonomy, a lack of business training, and the rapidly changing health care system all come together to provide barriers to the adoption and fuller use of ICT in general practice in the study area. Case study interviews revealed that older GPs typically did not view themselves as business people, nor as employees. Younger GPs, or those who trained in other countries, however, are more likely to see themselves this way, particularly if they are women.

An ANT analysis of small business aspects of GPs' adoption of ICT provides a platform to show how structures, agents and policy become an entangled and consolidated whole. Some of the key factors shaping the uptake of ICT are perceptions of the usefulness of the technology, GPs' feelings of anxiety or trepidation surrounding computer use, decision making processes in general practice, a change from solo practices to larger and corporate practices, the age of the practitioners and access to support. It is also clear that a new actor has emerged: the Practice Manager, who has typically taken over the role of choosing, operating and managing the ICT used in the practice.

Practice Manager

Each practice in CHDGP has a Practice Manager whose job it is to manage the business side of the practice. They are employed to do administrative tasks like hiring reception staff, organising the purchase of equipment, and doing the accounts. The Practice Manager is typically someone with business and managerial expertise who does not necessarily have any background in medicine (except in one case where a retired GP had taken on this role). In many ways the Practice Manager acts as a gatekeeper to the practice as they see their role as protecting the medical staff from outside interruptions. As their job involves determining the *best* way for the practice to be run, they often support the introduction of ICT. The role of the Practice Manager expanded dramatically with the introduction of IT/IM payments within the PIP.

Healthcare Computer Systems

A whole group of non-human actors could be black-boxed under the heading 'Healthcare Computer Systems'. These would include the GPs computers, the office computers, the backup files, the computer furniture, the broadband network connections and the healthcare software packages. A number of different healthcare software packages are in use around Australia, but the most commonly used is one called Medical Director. Healthcare software packages are probably the most important actors within the Healthcare Computer Systems group as it is these actors that the individual GPs have to learn about and use. If they do not want to have anything to do with maintaining the computers or broadband connections there is probably someone else in the Practice who can handle this, but if they are to make any significant use of the systems at all, they must learn about and use one of the software packages. Each of these packages, however, operates in a rather different way and can affect the operation of the practice and the way that individual GPs work as suggested by the following quote from a Practice Manager: "*This practice uses the Genie medical software. We do not use Medical Director as it causes problems with the way that we have our system networked here at the practice.*" (Interview 35 2005). While this group of actors is a most important one, as they have little relevance to the two case studies presented in this article, we will here regard them simply as a black box.

Other Actors

There are many other human and non-human actors involved in the adoption of ICT in general practice, but the main additional actors include the GPs themselves, the Practice Principal (the senior GP), the Practices (where their needs and outlook are different to that of either the GPs or the Practice Manager), the patients, the buildings, the medical technology, the Federal Government (for funding) and the pharmaceutical companies. Space in this article does not, however, permit a full actor-network analysis of these other actors, and they also have little relevance to the two case studies presented here.

RESEARCH METHOD

As Yin (1994) points out, case studies are valuable where policy change is occurring in messy real world settings, and when it is important to understand why such interventions succeed or fail. The study was undertaken through case studies and extended interviews, and revealed a number of interesting findings. The process of selecting sites for study was central to the case study approach and a number of selection strategies were used. Because resources for this case study work were limited, it was necessary to design a 'purposive' sample that was typical of the phenomenon being investigated. Expert advice from staff at Central Highlands Division of General Practice, and the coordinator of the Practice Managers group, herself a Practice Manager, was used in developing this sample which in the end involved intensive case studies of four practices. The research originally planned to undertake simple case studies of 32 practices, but this turned out not to be possible and instead intensive case studies of four of the practices were undertaken. In addition, interviews were conducted with several key actors (or those associated with key actors) and the content of relevant archival documents. The data collection for the project occurred from 2003-2007.

The early fieldwork for this research used structured interviews and observation of meetings in the hope of generating data that could be used to identify and refine specific research questions inductively. This type of design, in which detailed research questions emerge during the course of the study, has been advocated for general use in the study of the impact of government policies in the health system. Silverman (1993) claims that in some ways it is similar to the way in which clinical consultations are conducted. These involve initial exploration followed by progress over time towards a diagnosis inferred from the available data. From the point of view of Actor Network the patient is enrolled in the process of diagnosis, the doctor guides the process and then may enrol the use of the internet via the computer on the desk to assist in the diagnosis. Thus a diagnosis is arrived at and the short term network is dissolved when the patient leaves the consultation room. In the case of the adoption of computers in the practice the network established is much longer term but in the scheme of time still short term, so will endear itself to the case study approach of Actor Network.

Semi-structured interviews were conducted on the basis of a looser structure consisting of open-ended questions that define the area to be explored, at least initially, and from which the interviewer or interviewee may diverge in order to pursue an idea or response in more detail. Depth interviews, which were less structured than this, were also undertaken. These covered only one or two issues, but in much greater detail. Such an interview began with the interviewer saying, "*This research study is about how GPs use computers. Can you tell me about your own use and experiences with computers?*" Further questions would be based on what the interviewee said, and consisted mostly of clarification and probing for details.

TWO GENERAL PRACTICE CASE STUDIES

To illustrate how some of the decision making was undertaken at a local level we now present an analysis of two practices. The first practice had seven full-time and several part-time GPs, two job sharing practice nurses, seven part-time receptionists and one full-time Practice Manager. There were nine computers with one on each doctor's desk and three laptop computers for use by GPs in training. The practice had access to e-mail and the Internet via broadband and made use of clinical practice management software. The practice was well advanced in its use of ICT at the time of the study, but had initially been very slow in adoption. It turned out that far from having anything to do with the technology itself, the initial slowness was because the father of the present Practice Principal was not comfortable with ICT. As he was not far off retirement, but still practicing at the time, no one wanted to make him feel uncomfortable by introducing technology with which he was not familiar.

The practice had long recognised the need to use computers – "look it was years ago, about 1990 that we talked about the use of computers in this practice, I think after some of us had been to a conference in Melbourne at the RACGP, but we decided the cost was too great for the benefits we thought we would get out of it. We also thought that we were too busy to take the time to learn about how to use them." (Interview of Practice Principal, 2005) A dramatisation, based on interview material, of the internal factors influencing the decision making involved in putting off adoption of ICT can be outlined as follows in Figure 2.

This case study clearly illustrates the human side to adoption decisions. In this case the decision to delay adoption had nothing to do with any perception that the software might be immature or that the patients would not accept it. It had nothing to do with any need for training by the staff, but everything to do with the respect for one particular doctor.

In a different practice within the Division another dramatisation (also based on interview material) shows how the role of the IT/IM Officer can be used to influence ICT adoption decisions.

In this case the computer systems, hardware, broadband connections and software were much better understood, and the advantages of using these systems for administrative purposes well appreciated. There was, however, little or no discussion about using ICT for clinical purposes.

CONCLUSION

The adoption and use of ICT in General Practice is most important as it offers potential improvements both in efficiency and in the quality of healthcare. It is clear, however, that although most General Practices make use of ICT for administrative purposes such as billing, prescribing and medical records, many General Practitioners themselves do not make full use of these ICT systems. Adoption decisions in an area such as this are very complex, and involve many actors. This means that actor-network theory offers a very suitable framework for analysis.

Whereas an analysis approach based on Innovation Diffusion (Rogers 2003), the Technology Acceptance Model (TAM) (Davis 1986; Davis

Figure 2.

Problematisation Said the Practice Manager to the Principal of the practice: *"The conference was very interesting and it would be good to get us on computers as soon as we can. It would probably save us a lot of work. I suppose that is the way that this practice has to go."*

Interessement Said the Practice Manager to the Practice Principal's father. *"What do you think of this idea about computers? I think they are probably good but I'm worried about you."*

The Practice Principal's father in reply to the practice manager: *"Don't worry about me. I will probably retire when we have to go to computers. I don't want to just yet, but there you go I don't think I could cope with computers at my age."*

Interessement and Translation

Said the Practice Manager to the Principal of the practice: *"I'm worried about a few things; one of them is the reaction of this practice when we computerise. You know they all think the world of your father and if we computerise we will lose him from the practice as I think he will retire. Most of the patients would not want that to happen. We would not want to lose the skills he has before he has finished passing them on."*

"Will you have a talk to him about it and see if we can work this out? He is too good a doctor to lose; we all love him very much. Maybe we can think of a way around this?"

Enrolment Said the Practice Manager to the Principal of the practice: *"Have you had a chance to talk to your father?"* "Yes." *"What was the outcome?"* "He will retire if we computerise right now – maybe we should wait for a while." *"Well that's probably good thinking because I have been talking to the other staff members and I think that we will lose other staff if he goes. That would be a problem that we did not know we had."*

"Maybe we could set your father the task of finding out about computers for the practice, and get the other staff to find out information too. We could get them to form a development group for us and report at a staff meeting about the progress that they are making."

Said the Practice Manager to the Practice Principal's father *"Dad, I wonder if you could help me with this computerisation thing. We will have to computerise at some time, but I can see that this is not the right time for any of us. So I wonder if you would be able to help us to make the time right. We need a wise head in this because it will be a big commitment and needs to happen the way we all want."*

Said by the Practice Manager to the staff members: *"We have decided to put off the process of computerising the practice. We have decided that we want a team approach to this thing and that we would like to have a few people involved. We have got Father on board to head up the investigation for us but we need other wise heads to make sure we get all the information together. So I am calling for volunteers."*

Mobilisation Practice Manager in staff meeting: *"I am sure that the computerisation of this practice will cause a lot of changes. They will have to be managed and I am prepared to take a lot of responsibility for that."*

1989) or similar approaches would typically suggest that characteristics of the technology itself were the driving factors, the analysis of stories in ANT leads to a better understanding of the establishment and the evolution of power relationships, because all the fluctuations that occur are preserved in these histories. In ANT, translation is the mechanism by which the networks progressively take form, resulting in a situation where certain entities control others.

This study has shown that it is sometimes these seemingly unimportant human issues that determine if and how ICT is used in General Practice. The roles of actors such as the RACGP, GPCG, and the IT/IM Officer have been important in the acceleration of the adoption process. It can also be seen from individual practice case studies that the roles played by particular individuals, such as the Practice Manager or the Practice Principal, as well as certain GPs are crucial to adoption decisions. Various non-human actors also play an important role. In each of the reported case studies it can be observed that the technology was seen as rather intimidating and this reduced the likelihood of its adoption. No matter how good the technology is, it must be adopted by people before it can be used.

ACKNOWLEDGMENT

This research was partly funded by a grant from the Australian Research Council (ARC).

REFERENCES

Burgess, S. (2002). Information Technology in Small Business: Issues and Challenges. In S. Burgess (Ed.), *Information Technology and Small Business: Issues and Challenges* (pp. 1-17). Hershey, Pennsylvania, USA: IGI Global.

Burgess, S., & Trethowan, P. (2002). *GPs and their Web sites in Australia: Doctors as Small Businesses*. IS OneWorld, Las Vegas.

Callon, M. (1986a). The Sociology of an Actor-Network: The Case of the Electric Vehicle. In M. Callon, J. Law, & A. Rip (Eds.), *Mapping the Dynamics of Science and Technology* (pp. 19-34). London, Macmillan Press.

Callon, M. (1986b). Some Elements of a Sociology of Translation: Domestication of the Scallops and the Fishermen of St Brieuc Bay. In J. Law (Ed.), *Power, Action & Belief. A New Sociology of Knowledge?* (pp. 196-229). London, Routledge & Kegan Paul.

Callon, M. (1991). Techno-Economic Networks and Irreversibility. In J. Law (Ed.), *A Sociology of Monsters. Essays on Power, Technology and Domination* (pp. 132-164). London, Routledge.

Davis, F. D. (1986). *A Technology Acceptance Model for Empirically Testing New End-User Information Systems: Theory and Results.* Boston, MIT. Doctor of Philosophy.

Davis, F. D. (1989). Perceived Usefulness, Perceived Ease of Use, and User Acceptance of Information Technology. *MIS Quarterly, 13*(3), 318–340. doi:10.2307/249008

Deering, P., & Tatnall, A. (2008). Adoption of ICT in an Australian Rural Division of General Practice. In N. Wickramasinghe & E. Geisler (Eds.), *Encyclopaedia of Healthcare Information Systems, 1*, 23-29. Hershey, PA: IGI Global.

Everitt, P., & Tatnall, A. (2003). *Investigating the Adoption and Use of Information Technology by General Practitioners in Rural Australia and Why This is Less Than it Might Be*. ACIS 2003, Perth, ACIS.

GPCG. (2001). *Measuring IT Use in Australian General Practice. Brisbane, General Practice Computing Group.* University of Queensland.

GPSRG. (1998). *Changing the Future Through Partnerships. Canberra, Commonwealth Department of Health and Family Services.* General Practice Strategy Review Group.

Henderson, J., Britt, H., & Miller, G. (2006). Extent and utilisation of computerisation in Australian general practice. *The Medical Journal of Australia, 185*(2), 84–87.

Latour, B. (1986). The Powers of Association. In J. Law (Ed.), *Power, Action and Belief. A New Sociology of Knowledge? Sociological Review monograph* (pp. 264-280). London, Routledge & Kegan Paul.

Latour, B. (1996). *Aramis or the Love of Technology*. Cambridge, MA: Harvard University Press.

Mott, K. (2001). GP Corporatisation - The Consumer Perspective. *The Medical Journal of Australia, 175*, 75–76.

NHIMAC. (1999). *Health On-Line: A Health Information Action Plan for Australia.* Canberra, NHIMAC.

Rogers, E. M. (2003). *Diffusion of Innovations*. New York: The Free Press.

Silverman, D. (1993). *Interpreting qualitative data: methods for analysing talk, text and interaction*. London: Sage.

Tatnall, A. (2007). *Innovation Translation in a University Curriculum*. Melbourne: Heidelberg Press.

Tatnall, A. (2009a). Information Systems, Technology Adoption and Innovation Translation. *International Journal of Actor-Network Theory and Technological Innovation, 1*(1), 59–74.

Tatnall, A. (2009b). Innovation Translation and Innovation Diffusion: A Comparison of Two Different Approaches to Theorising Technological Innovation. *International Journal of Actor-Network Theory and Technological Innovation, 1*(2), 67–74.

Yin, R. K. (1994). *Case Study Research, Design and Methods*. Newbury Park: Sage Publications.

ENDNOTE

[1] This was the title of this organisation at the time of this research project, but it has now changed to Central Highlands General Practice Network (CHGPN).

This work was previously published in International Journal of Actor-Network Theory and Technological Innovation, Volume 2, Issue 1, edited by Arthur Tatnall, pp. 54-69, copyright 2010 by IGI Publishing (an imprint of IGI Global).

Chapter 4
Having a Say:
Voices for all the Actors in ANT Research?

Mary Anne Kennan
Charles Sturt University, Australia

Dubravka Cecez-Kecmanovic
University of New South Wales, Australia

Jim Underwood
University of Technology Sydney, Australia

ABSTRACT

This article explores issues associated with giving non-human actors a voice of their own in actor-network theory based research. What issues arise in doing so? Does doing so increase understanding of the issue to hand, bring to life and make more accessible and interesting the stories of these actors? Or does this anthropomorphism detract from the issues at hand? The authors discuss these broader issues and then present findings from an ANT field study which investigated the implementation of institutional repositories and their relations with the spread of open access to scholarly publishing. This paper experiments with allowing some of the non-human actors to speak for themselves. The authors conclude with a discussion which opens the debate: does giving voice to non-human actors bring them to life and make them better understood as intimately entangled with each other and human actors in the socio-material practices of the everyday? And what are the challenges in doing so?

INTRODUCTION

Interpretive research endorses and legitimises the voices of people, the human subjects we study in the field. We hear what they think and feel what they feel. But what about non-humans we study, such as Information System (IS), databases, organisations, and other non-humans? In interpretive studies authors let human subjects speak about themselves and the non-humans in their world, make sense of them, and interpret them. As human subjects and researchers have specific goals and intentions and speak from the perspective of their particular situation, they often attribute different meanings to IS or certain types of technology, hence the concept of "interpretive flexibility"

DOI: 10.4018/978-1-4666-1559-5.ch004

(Orlikowski, 1992). The non-humans have no say. In the world of separated subjects (humans) and objects (non-humans), assumed in interpretive studies, our examination and understanding is subject-centered.

In the world of social materiality (Dale, 2005) where subjects and objects are seen as mutually enacting and co-producing, the gaze is changing. It is not the subject's perspective that is privileged but instead the world is seen as a flat constellation of relations among subjects, material objects such as technologies, and conceptual objects such as ideas. Rather than focusing on the impacts of technology on people and organizations, or the interaction of people and technology, the sociomaterial approach focuses on the subjects-objects and the social-material intertwining and co-enacting in practice (Orlikowski & Scott, 2008; Suchman, 2007). Objects are not passive things without agency. Instead they are seen as actors capable of action and affecting others through relations. The agency of actors, both human and non-human, emerges in their mutual relations through ongoing co-production and co-enactment (Cecez-Kecmanovic & Nagm, 2009). So, the question arises: How do we present objects' acting and how can objects have voice in our understanding and reporting from the field?

We aim to examine this question by adopting Actor-Network Theory (ANT) - one of the most vocal and perhaps most influential theoretical developments in the realm of sociomateriality. ANT was conceived by Latour and Woolgar (1986) while studying the work of scientists in the Salk Institute of Medical Research, and is deliberately agnostic about distinctions between 'social' and 'natural'. Instead ANT theorises the growth of 'hybrids', networks of people, tools and concepts held together by (sometimes unwilling) collaboration (Latour, 1993). ANT has generally been adopted by researchers keen to avoid the subject/object, nature/society dualisms (Vidgen & McMaster, 1996) and thus avoid both technological and social determinism. By proposing a symmetrical treatment of human and non-human actors ANT has a significant potential to contribute to better understanding of technology and information systems in organisations and life in all its rich complexity (Tatnall & Gilding, 1999).

In this paper we propose a conceptual and methodological extension of ANT to allow non-humans to have a voice. We aim first to show that humans and non-humans are co-acting and thereby co-creating each other in actor-networks. Actor-networks are brought together by relations among actors, attempting to enrol each other to enact desired scripts and achieve goals. To investigate the intentions and goals of human actors and their understanding of the emerging network, researchers often rely on interviews and texts (such as e-mails and documents) produced by the humans. This is how we identify and present voices of humans and let them tell their story. But this is only a partial story. The story of non-humans is missing.

On the one hand the humans realise their intentions by acting and interacting through material objects (e.g., technology) which simultaneously shape humans' agency and the ways their intentions are achieved. A non-human or object may be inscribed by the intentions of humans (oriented toward a goal) but such object inscription never acts alone and exactly as intended and continues to act beyond the intended domain and timeframe. The force of non-humans is thus felt everywhere: in a business process enabled by an ERP system, in a paper submission to an institutional repository, which can accept or reject it, when a virus invades your computer. The problem in an ANT study is to let them, the non-humans, speak, let them represent themselves and have a say. But how to do it, how to allow them to speak, is not well explained or practiced in ANT studies. In this paper we present and illustrate a technique of actors' speaking that was used to represent non-human actors (including software, processes and concepts) during a large study of the development of (possibly open access) institutional repositories

(IR) in universities (Kennan, 2008). By letting all actors, humans and non-humans tell a story, and specifically by allowing non-humans to relate their own experiences in the network and to express their struggles 'while coming into being', we gain new insights into why the actors interact in the way that they do and why the realities are produced the way they did.

In the following section we discuss previous work on the representation of non-human actors. This is followed by a brief history of, and motivation for, IR and open access. We then introduce our case study, our research method, and a chronological narrative of the development of the repository. In the penultimate section we show how, with a little imagination, the non-humans can speak. Finally we explain how this technique has helped us to further understanding of the ever changing network, and discuss further questions that are raised by our use of this method.

REPRESENTING NON-HUMAN ACTORS

'How are non-humans to be represented? How are they to be articulated? How do non-humans speak? How can I be assured that I reliably report what they are saying (Pouloudi & Whitley, 2000, p. 341)? Using IR as an example, we show how by giving, literally, a voice to non-human actors such as 'peer review', 'open access' and repository software, we can clarify our understanding of the place of these actors in the network, and the way they form alliances (or not) with other actors to enable the repository to come into being.

We suggest that non-human objects have agency in the actor-networks by enabling or disabling certain relations: by making some actions by other actors effective, legitimate, ethical, (or otherwise), for example, as well as influencing yet other actors to take particular actions. For instance journal ranking lists influence academics' selection of publishing outlets; a journal policy that allows post-print open access IR depositing makes it legitimate and ethical for an academic to post a published paper in an IR; IR technology that assists academics in posting their papers through a user-friendly interface and efficient back-office processing may encourage IR depositing (academics actions). In each of these cases, it is human beings that create or transform these non-human actors (journal rankings; journal policy; IR technology) and enrol them in a network to achieve a particular aim.

Studying and understanding the agency of non-human actors however is not easy. It requires different strategies to find out, typically by observing or experiencing human interaction with them in different situations and how they change over time. Such strategy needs to be sensitive to the changes and stories of both the non-human and human actors but most importantly to the dynamics of their relations. In other words, the strategies suggested here should not privilege the human perspective but focus on the intertwining and entanglement of human and non-human actors from both perspectives. For example, journal ranking lists influence academics' selection of publishing outlets; a journal policy that allows post-print open access (OA) depositing into repositories makes it legitimate and ethical for an academic to post a published paper on an institutional repository; IR technology that assists academics in posting their papers through a user-friendly interface and efficient back-office processing may encourage IR self-depositing (academics actions). In each of these cases, it is human beings that create or transform these non-human actors, but how a non-human actually acts only partially depends on the intentions, objectives and interests of the human creators (which are 'inscribed' more or less reliably into the non-human actor). The agency of the non-human actor is occasioned in its relations with other actors (e.g., academics) and therefore also depends on the actors' intentions, objectives and interests. ANT brings to the open the intertwining and entanglement of human and non-human actors involved in relations in the dynamic actor-networks.

When reporting on human actors, researchers usually use extensive quotes from human actors to ground their interpretation and add strength to their arguments. But they always interpret, filter, summarise, and synthesise the data available, running the risk of excluding something critical (to the humans studied), misinterpreting something informants say, and drawing conclusions different from those other researchers with access to the same material may draw (Pouloudi & Whitley, 2000). This is based on the assumption that there isn't a single 'correct' interpretation. As this is accepted for humans, we question why not also for non-humans? Some authors go beyond reporting and interpreting human actions and articulations. Boland, for example, fictionally places human actors into a room where the limits of language in doing systems work is discussed using their imaginary voices. Boland (2000) explains that he has 'spent some time thinking' about the characters before setting them into a conversation to see what happens. It is obvious that he is deeply familiar with the characters' writing and has immersed himself in their words and the relationship of those words to the issue discussed. He takes this performative approach of putting words into particular actors' mouths to 'make the ideas ... come alive just a bit more' (Boland, 2000, p. 48) - and he succeeds. The imaginary dialogue creates an intensely readable and animated work which encourages the reader to think about the issues to hand and perhaps learn something and find paths for future investigation. In this paper we extend Boland's approach by putting words into the 'mouths' of non-human actors in the same way, to compensate for their ability to 'answer back' directly. This does not mean that a researcher is assuming a "god-like" position, as some might suggest. On the contrary, a researcher gets into the position of an object, a non-human in an actor-network, and attempts to see and experience the world subjectively from within.

Generally ANT researchers speak in the third person about non-humans as actors with agency e.g. 'visual basic mounted a challenge', 'Visual basic enrolled ...' (Tatnall, 2000), 'the groom is on strike' (Latour, 1992); or we encourage other actors to speak on their behalf. In doing so, however, it is our contention that we lose something. Like Boland (2000) we wanted the actors to 'come alive a bit more', so we thought to experiment with not just talking about the agency of non-human actors but by in a sense anthropomorphising them – giving them a voice of their own. Non-human actors do not have the ability of independent articulation but we can come to know them in other ways, for example by interaction with them, from articulations by human actors about non-human actors and by watching them interact with other actors (Hosein, 2003). Porsander (2005) further develops the idea by giving a voice to an information system so that it may tell its own story. Like Latour (1992) we perceive the non-human actors as constructed or co-opted by humans, substituting for the actions of humans and shaping human action by their affordances and therefore deserving to be represented as richly and fully as possible. Here we experiment with method assemblage, crafting and bundling (Law, 2004) what we have learned about and from actors into depictions which aim to make them come alive.

SCHOLARLY PUBLISHING, OPEN ACCESS AND INSTITUTIONAL REPOSITORIES

Publishing means to 'make public' so it can be read by others, and it is argued that at present the primary form of scholarly communication is via articles formally published in journals and book chapters, or disseminated at conferences. Different actors have different roles within the scholarly publishing environment. Academics and scholars write the articles and are also the main targets as readers of those same articles; they also provide certification through peer review. Journals provide the registration of a work. Multiple organisations provide awareness and accessibility, from the journal publishers themselves to commercial indexing and abstracting organisations and libraries. Libraries also provide archiving and access to wider readerships. Profits are invariably made directly only by the publishers, although one may argue that academics and scholars profit indirectly, through increased reputation, grants, tenure, promotion and so on (Kling & Callahan, 2003).

ICT developments have created high expectations for improvements in scholarly communications and scholarly publishing. From the 1990s it was envisaged that electronic publication would make materials available to readers in all locations 24 hours a day, ensure that costs would be lower, make publication timelier, and enable a wide variety of document and data formats and other media to be included. This would lead to participation in scholarly publishing being more open and democratic and the papers being available to a wider audience (Harnad, 1999; Willinsky, 2006). Against these expectations, with the development of electronic publishing the costs for scholars, universities and other institutions accessing these journals are steadily rising, often faster than the rate of inflation (Van Orsdel & Born, 2008). The new technology has emphasised the tensions between researchers who use publishing to advance enquiry, share findings, influence others and generate impact, and publishers who profit from the sales of subscriptions to libraries, aggregators and individuals (Clarke & Kingsley, 2008).

In response to this tension an 'Open Access' (OA) movement has formed, primarily driven by scholars and librarians and the Internet and the World Wide Web (WWW), to promote the open access vision to scholarly works, enabling scholars and other interested readers to 'read, download, copy, distribute, print, search or link' (Budapest Open Access Initiative, 2002) to the full text of works, without financial, legal or technical barriers. As the OA vision spreads it attracts other actors into its vision of freely available research: research funders, software developers, disciplinary communities, research institutions and even publishers. OA does not have a single organisation or society promoting or supporting it. There is a loose cluster of advocacy and activists, organisations and individuals, which we refer to loosely as the OA movement.

One way to provide OA is the institutional repository (IR). Many studies have found that increasingly universities around the world are implementing OA IR (Lynch & Lippincott, 2005), but actual growth in content has been very slow (McDowell, 2007). The case studies on which this paper is based were undertaken for just this reason - to understand why the number of contributions to a repository in a particular institution was growing much slower than expected.

ASSEMBLING ALLIES FOR REPOSITORIES: THE CASES

The Institutions and the Repositories

The research was undertaken in a leading Australian university (Janus) with around 40,000 students, 6,000 staff, and a library with over two million items. A second Australian university (Jupiter) of similar size was included in the original study, because its IR implementation was more advanced and researchers were familiar with using it, and with the ideal of open access. At the beginning of the study Janus University was in the early stages of IR implementation, one of many of the 39 Australian Universities that were implementing or were considering implementing institutional repositories. Once the project had been set up development and implementation was expected to take three years, but Table 1 shows Janus's original plan was highly optimistic.

Jupiter had an even more optimistic plan, to implement an OA IR in the space of one year. The project was implemented within its time frame. Take up of the system was slow at first, only 425 items in the first 12 months; however, in 2007 nearly 4,000 items were deposited. Table 2 below presents the timeline for the Jupiter University IR implementation.

Data Collection and Analysis

This large research project started with an investigation of OA and IR in general, and the two case studies were seen as an example with which to illuminate the general relationships of IR and OA. The lead author conducted the study in both universities. The Janus IR project was traced from

Table 1. Janus University IR implementation timeline

Phase	**Dates**	**Planned activity**	**Actual Activity**
Phase 0	August 2003 October 2003 January 2004		Bid submitted Bid accepted Appointment of Consortium Project Manager
Phase1	January 2004 – December 2004	Demonstrate	**June 2004** Notification of software choices Appointment of Janus University Project Manager **June 2004 – March 2006** Janus Project Manager seeks researchers and Schools to contribute, and harvests from university web pages, working papers, technical reports etc.
Phase 2	January 2005 - December 2005	Deploy	Merged demonstration and deployment **May 2006** Project Manager 2 appointed. Demonstration and some deployment. **June 2007** Project Manager 3 appointed
Phase 3	January 2006 – December 2006	Distribute	**December 2007+** Distribute – soft launch announced at Academic Board.
Postscript	2008+		Actual distribution **January 2008+** Outreach librarians promote to researchers. As at October 17 2008 2,425 deposits.

Table 2. Jupiter University IR implementation timeline

Phase	Dates	Planned activity	Actual Activity
Phase 0	**2002**		DVC's previous interest in scholarly communication and OA culminates in resolve to implement an OA institutional repository
Phase1	**2003**	Implementation of policy for deposit in IR Implementation of IR	**May 2003** – Draft policy for deposit policy presented to research and development Committee **September 2003** – Policy endorsed by Academic Board **June 2003** – Repository Project Manager appointed, OSS software selected June – November 2003 – Project manager collects "low hanging fruit" and begins to enrol researchers.
Phase 2	**2003-2004**	Deployment and distribution of IR and (mandate) deposit policy	**November 2003** – IR launched **January 2004** – Policy takes effect **January 2004+** Strong recruitment program, emphasising the benefits to individuals, the university and scholarship, continuing and ongoing

its early stages throughout its implementation and testing. The study of Jupiter University IR began after implementation, so historical information about the implementation and current usage data were collected. The ANT approach led to following the actors, not just through the local implementation in a university, but through to the more global relations in publishing practices. Investigation of the emergence and reconfiguration of actor-networks led to further actors, human and non-human, who needed to tell their story.

Stories were collected via interviews, documents, observations of actors and interaction with IR. Interviews were conducted with 32 human actors from Janus and 20 from Jupiter. At first the interviews and other texts were analysed in the usual way – following the actors, understanding their interests and actions, and thus revealing emergent, complex networks of relations. As research progressed, human and non-human actors formed and changed alliances, such as those among OA activists, researchers, journals, OA IR and, research papers, thus creating and reconfiguring actor-networks. Description of these actors, their actions and their relations tended to be from the viewpoint of human actors, similar to most ANT studies. Despite an explicit attempt in most ANT studies to treat human and non-human actors equally, non-human actors were not represented as richly and as authentically as human actors. The problem was to present all actors as if from their perspective, to let them speak using their own voice and tell a story that is true to them. To do this we use a technique of actors' speaking (Kennan, 2008) that we describe in the next section.

When describing the interactions in the network we felt that there was no suitable way to represent non-human actors as richly as the humans were represented through extracts from interviews and texts, so we had to (re)invent one. Following Porsander (2005) we give non-human actors a voice of their own, that they may "tell" their own story. Using example from our scholarly publishing case we meet the actors, many of whom appear in both cases. We experiment with an "assemblage", crafting and bundling (Law, 2004) what we learned in our field study about and from the actors into stories that generate their presence and give them a voice. In the following section we give examples of this, and then discuss the advantages and possible application of this method. Our aim is to present an interesting and lively story, informed by our observations, and interactions with the actors which will assist in increasing understanding without implying "correctness".

THE ACTORS SPEAK

Using Boland's (2000) terminology we have 'spent some time thinking' about the non-human characters in this story. Further, we spent some time being with them, interacting with them. We craft what we have learned from hearing other actors talk about their relations with them in interviews and texts, from interrogating them ourselves, and from observing them interact in their relations with other actors in the story. From these experiences we imagine articulation from their point of view, for them to state their positions, so we can try to hear what they could tell us, had they the power of speech.

A Research Paper

I can take many different forms. I may be a journal article, conference paper, book chapter. I may be written on paper or in electronic form or both. I may be MS Word, LaTex, pdf or HTML or other. I am born from the writing up of research and the thinking and theorising of my authors. I may be distributed in journals, books, proceedings, via the Internet, e-mail, weblogs, repositories, in pre-print, post-print, re-print. I am written by scholars, for scholars in a way that is inaccessible to practitioners or patients or other 'outsiders'. I am written to enable the sharing of knowledge within a scholarly community. My authors give me away to journals to publish.

My value is increased by being read, by being published, so authors give me away for free, even though my birth may not be easy. I am a child given up to the adoptive parents of a journal so that my life and my authors' life may be better. Sometimes the journal I am published in has a very small readership. I then have less chance of being found and read by potential readers. If my authors deposited me in an open access IR as well as publishing me, I would have more chance of being read. I do not understand why they do not deposit me in an IR, when the journal or conference they publish me in permits this, which as of the 28th May 2009, 60% of publishers permit (http://www.sherpa.ac.uk/romeo.php?stats=yes).

I can also experience difficulties in getting published. Sometimes my content is cross disciplinary or in a new and emerging field and no specific journal is right for me. My authors struggle to find me a journal parent. Sometimes I am published in high impact journals, sometimes in a lesser one; sometimes in a local journal for a small but specific audience, sometimes an international journal aimed at a wide audience. Sometimes I am something on the way to being something else: a conference paper on the way to being a journal article, a journal article on the way to being a thesis or a book. My authors and readers sometimes rank me according to where and how I appear rather than for my own content and contribution to knowledge.

Sometimes I am very unlucky and I don't get published at all. I remain stillborn as a pre-print or working paper, unpublished, and unloved – sadly because my whole purpose is to be published and to be read, to add to the scholarly corpus, to be cited and not to languish in the dark.

Peer Review

I am peer review. I am also sometimes called refereeing. I have the power to decide which papers get into journals, conference proceedings and research books. I am usually performed by a group of experts, called reviewers, who read papers and perform a supposedly impartial review of them, their method and contribution. I am considered to be essential to ensuring that published papers reach standards of academic rigor and quality. Reviewers are typically anonymous and independent. There is a perception that when I am performed blind or especially double blind the paper is more likely to receive an unbiased and serious review. Authors appreciate the quid pro quo nature of refereeing and being refereed and the feedback I provide them when I am in a good mood – an honest, fair and constructive report that enables paper improvement.

There is a tension in my identity. I am not always one. There are tensions within me. Sometimes I can be in a bad mood and then I am not without my critics. This can make me overly harsh and critical of the papers I review. Sometimes I band with friends who think the same way I do and we form cliques and hierarchies that are difficult to break into or overcome. Although reviews are 'double blind' often I can recognize an author by the nature of their contribution. Where review is not double blind the temptation to allow my own ideas and mood to influence my judgment sometimes overrides my natural good sense. Sometimes too, I can make a mistake, or miss one, rejecting a new, unusual or innovative paper or allowing a paper to go through that perhaps should not.

To increase my transparency sometimes I practice "open review". In fields where preprints are deposited in open access repositories authors are inevitably known to reviewers, and some journals accept this, and even encourage the search for good papers from preprint repositories. Despite, or because of, the open nature of the review I can be fair and constructive in my feedback to authors. I don't think OA will compromise my role as some claim, merely change the detail of how I am performed.

A Chorus of Journals

We are scholarly journals. We publish papers that are peer reviewed and relate to a particular academic discipline, field or sub-field. We have many similarities, we also have many differences. Here we talk about the things we have in common but you, the reader, need to be aware that differences also apply between those of us from different disciplines, countries or cultures. Authors submit their papers to us. Editors read them to see if the paper warrants further peer review or refereeing to assess whether it meets our criteria. In most fields we are ranked sometimes formally, sometimes informally. Our quality and impact are also assessed, sometimes quantitatively, sometimes qualitatively. Researchers can be very strategic about selecting those of us in which to publish their work. Established authors understand the complex relations between we journals in their field, and the differentiations of ranking and reputation in our highly stratified society.

Each of us aims for a different audience of readers and authors. We battle with each other to keep and improve our audience and our reputation. Our audiences may be researchers' academic peers, specific fields and sub-fields within disciplines, practitioners, students, even the interested lay-person. We depend on peer review and on the papers submitted for publishing. We seek high quality papers and allocate the task of selecting good papers to peer review.

We try to serve two masters, the academic community of authors and readers, editors and reviewers who wish to widely distribute their research and knowledge (and build their reputations) and the commercial and learned-society publishers who want us to make them a profit. It is difficult and we are torn by our responsibilities to both.

Open Access

I am research and scholarship freely available over the Internet. I am partially enacted. Estimates vary. Some say I make between 11% (Björk, Roosr, & Lauri, 2008) and 15% and 20% (Swan & Carr, 2008) of research and scholarly work freely accessible. I am a vision. I have the ability to conceive what might be achieved, what is possible. I am a highly imaginative scheme or an anticipation. I express some foresight. I am explained by the Budapest OA Initiative thus:

By "open access" to this literature, we mean its free availability on the public internet, permitting any users to read, download, copy, distribute, print, search, or link to the full texts of these articles, crawl them for indexing, pass them as data to software, or use them for any other lawful purpose, without financial, legal, or technical barriers other than those inseparable from gaining access to the internet itself. The only constraint ... should be to give authors control over the integrity of their work and the right to be properly acknowledged and cited (Budapest Open Access Initiative, 2002).

The literature they refer to is:

... that which scholars give to the world without expectation of payment. Primarily, this category encompasses their peer-reviewed journal articles, but it also includes any unreviewed preprints that they might wish to put online for comment or to alert colleagues to important research findings (Budapest Open Access Initiative, 2002).

Sometimes I am a vision (Budapest Open Access Initiative, 2002) and sometimes I am a strategic enabling activity, on which research and inquiry will rely (Open Access and Research Conference, 2008)

I am not one. Willinsky (2006) has identified ten flavours of open access. I am multiple and yet I cohere. I inspire journals to become open access and enrol them in my actor-network. I also work with closed access journals inciting them to allow authors to deposit versions of their papers in open access repositories[1]. I motivate authors to publish their work OA in institutional or disciplinary repositories before or after they publish in official journals. By doing so I annoy publishers who do not know how to deal with me. I work hand in hand with these repositories to make these works widely available, thus increasing their readership and citations. This is how I am enacting my vision and growing my OA scholarly publishing actor-network.

A Chorus of Institutional Repositories

We are open access institutional repositories. We are online archives. We are a type of digital library and work with the Internet and web technologies. Our role is to collect, preserve and make freely accessible the research output of the university. That research output may be any kind of paper, or any other product of research. We make them all available to the world. Readers of any kind are welcome to read the work we hold. We rely on information managers to help us look after the content we hold, researchers to put their work into us, software developers to maintain and develop us, and institutions to keep us running. And then we work with the Internet and search engines to provide access to and distribute the papers. Some see our role as primarily to provide OA, but others find other roles for us. Each one of us is different.

JanusWorks - An Institutional Repository

When I began I did not have my own name, instead I was named after the Consortium that gave birth to me. When they were ready to announce me to the world, they held a competition to find a name for me. You can call me JanusWorks. I am built on Fedora, a free and open source robust integrated repository-centred platform that enables the storage, access and management of virtually any kind of digital content. The name Fedora comes from Flexible Extensible Digital Object and Repository Architecture. I am both software platform and information architecture. I like the idea of being free and open source. It is congruent with my role of providing free and OA to the research output of my university. At the time my story begins at Janus University, Fedora was a repository engine, with deep and rich functionality (Payette & Lagoze, 1998). But I did not provide an out-of-the-box experience. To do something useful with me, someone had to write additional software (Treloar, 2005). For many reasons from the practical to the philosophical, my implementers chose to go with a commercial software developer that already had worked at developing the beginnings of a web front end and a Windows based management system for me. There were many features I and my implementers wanted to provide our researchers, but these developments took time. Sometimes I felt a conflict between the open nature of my underlying repository and my OA mission and the proprietary nature of my user interface.

I experienced internal conflict in another way. My implementers started out with a truncated version of OA. At the outset they focused only on research 'not published in the usual way' such as working papers, technical reports and other grey literature.

[We] never went looking for preprints and postprints of already published articles as a way to build the repository…if the published version wasn't freely available on the web, it was still accessible to our community, and if they had published it then it was more than likely in a journal which we took. So we took the line that why would we spend a lot of time and effort in a sense republishing things that have already been published [University Librarian]?

This focus limited my ability to engage researchers with the benefits of OA generally and actively put off those already imbued with the OA vision for their journal and conference papers. Some of those researchers were instead attracted to other methods of achieving OA, such as the disciplinary repositories SSRN, REPEC and arXiv. It held back the spreading of my wings.

My implementers did not want to announce me until I was "shiny".

So in a way it doesn't worry me that in the [IR] project we have spent so much time on technology. It became more of a software development project than I thought it would be. But if you can't get that bit of it right... it's not worth doing. So yep, it's been slower than I thought but I think it should be a better product for it [University Librarian].

The road to "shiny" took longer than expected. I would have been willing earlier to accept more research output, but my human colleagues thought I was a bit messy and difficult. This caused them to postpone my official launch and to appoint my own personal software developer and business analyst. These guys really helped me by finding out what researchers wanted and then inscribing in me affordance for many of those things. My personal developer belongs to an e-list of lots of other repository developers, and together they share information and work to keep us fit, and to keep improving our performance. Recently I have experienced difficulty with both my statistics and search functionality and these have been turned off. My users tell me they miss these features. Researchers place their papers in me of their own free will. I guess those that do value their work being openly accessible to the world, and I work hard to assist them in achieving this goal. However I am reliant on my human colleagues to register me with Google Scholar which they have not yet done. Or at least I think they have not, as papers I hold do not appear there. As at May 2009 I hold 4,430 items. I cannot tell which are full texts and which are metadata only, but 1,581 are PhD theses and 310 Masters by Research theses. Only 550 items were deposited for 2008.

EPrints - An Institutional Repository

I am named after the EPrints free software on which I am built. I like the idea of being free. It is congruent with my role of providing free and OA to the research output of my university. EPrints is a flexible platform for building institutional repositories. EPrints was developed by the School of Electronics and Computer Science, University of Southampton in 2000, and launched in 2001. When I was first installed at Jupiter University my software was still pretty new. I was installed by Library Systems staff onto existing servers in the library. There was no documentation and only a small community of users. The Jupiter University Repository Manager and Library Systems staff worked with what was available to get me up and going. A few tweaks here and there and a customized web front end and I was ready. Of course, since then I have modified and changed as the needs of researchers and the university change.

In my university my becoming was widely announced. The congruence with the university's research mission was made explicit and a policy was instituted to require authors to deposit their work with me. In the OA world this policy is known as a mandate. Every year, academics are required to deposit copies of their published journal articles and conference papers in me. Wherever possible by agreement with the journals and conferences these are available open access. I now (May 2009) have 14,457 items in me and 2,158 people who deposit. 8,828 of those items are open access. 2,252 items were deposited in 2008. Most of my university's authors love my work. When they search their field in Google or Google Scholar they are delighted to see their own works, often near the top of the list of returns. They regularly check my statistics to see how many times their papers are downloaded. They link to their works in me via their email signatures and web pages. Some have even cited my usage statistics in their promotion applications. Some do resent the mandate or have reservations about open access, but mostly my relations with my university and my authors are friendly.

I feel supported and sustained by my relations with the university mission and the policy. More globally Eprints, my software, as opposed to Eprints my self, now has a thriving community who provide feedback to the developers with ideas and requirements. EPrints is continually being modified and improved. As my developers say:

EPrints is both a practical tool and the crystallization of a philosophy. It enables research to be accessible to all, and provides the foundation for all academic institutions to create their own research repositories [http://www.eprints.org/software/].

WHAT DO WE GAIN?

By allowing the non-humans to speak, by presenting the story from numerous actors' viewpoints, we can better describe contradicting developments in OA scholarly publishing and thereby contribute to better understanding of the transformation of scholarly publishing practices and the role that the introduction of an OA IR plays in this transformation.

What does it mean giving non-human actors a voice? They cannot talk or express themselves like humans. So we give them imagined voices based on our experiences of their worlds and their interactions with other actors (including interactions with we researchers). We imagine, for instance, how papers experience the world around them – the authors, journals, peer review and university policies.

When we let the actors speak what do we hear? When actors are given the opportunity to speak for themselves do they appear more alive and lively than they do when spoken of in the third person? Can we learn more about and better present the life of the actor-network which we are researching when we do so? We think so. Their voices resonate. The open access, research papers, peer review, journals and institutional repositories come alive as they speak, firmly and in the first person, as actors. Sometimes they use quotations from interviews (e.g., academics) or documents (e.g., the Budapest Open Access Initiative) to add to the authenticity of their speaking. Importantly each actor presents their position in and their view of the transformation of scholarly publishing.

We have faced challenges in finding the "right" voice to present. There are multiple voices that arise from our engagement and relations with the non-humans actors in this story. Like humans, non-human actors such as atherosclerosis (Mol, 2002) are not singular and they emerge through different relations with us, the authors, and with other actors in the story. The non-human actors in this story are, of course, networks in themselves with their own parts (actors) and histories. We can't study everything at once, our current focus is to increase our understanding of open access in universities by listening to some of the non-human actors in these stories. Thus we have tried to give voice to those different relations and the tensions that arise from our interactions with these actors in our investigations of open access.

This animates the non-humans, gives them identity, and makes coherent their relations with other actors. Thus papers aim to be adopted by journals, they want to be read. They don't want to languish unread and un-cited. Their relationship with peer review is equivocal, as is their relationship with journals. Peer review rejects many papers. Peer review – traditional scholarly publishing's ally – is intended to ensure quality assurance, but it is far from being perfect (its honest voice is so refreshing). Journals only publish some papers. Some journals have such a small readership or subscription base that being published in them sometimes prevents papers from being widely read. Open access expresses itself as a vision that can work with existing actors in scholarly publishing to enable papers to become more accessible to their readers. From the actors' voices we can more clearly see that the peer review would not necessarily be compromised by OA.

Animating new actors such as institutional repositories allows us to better understand how they work with allies such as the Internet and the WWW to collect, preserve and make freely accessible research output such as papers. But their coming into being is not always easy. We learned about two different IR life stories. One by JanusWorks expresses internal conflict: based partially on proprietary software, a limited OA vision expressed by its human colleagues holding back its acceptance within its academic community. The other, EPrints from Jupiter University, speaks to us in a confident voice, supported and sustained by congruence in its use of free software, its explicit relationship with its university's research mission and supported by policies and a strong community.

In our study of IR listening to the voices of the non-human actors helps us to better understand the transformation of scholarly publishing from within, the internal conflicts and contradicting developments. From other actors and from the IR themselves we hear genuine stories how IR are emerging as new actors impacting on this transformation. We can see ePrints, a happy institutional repository, built on a software and inscribed with a mission aligned to the institution's objectives. We see how it works with the authors and papers of its community to help them achieve their ends. We also experience the struggles of JanusWorks as it attempts to become an institutional repository. The stories of non-human actors together with those of human actors help us understand better the ongoing transformation of publishing practices, and the contested alignments and struggles in the enactment of OA vision through conscripting institutional repositories to a program of making research papers open access.

CONCLUSION

Our contribution is twofold. First we illustrate in our narrative the coming alive of actors and their stories. We are more likely to hear human and non-human alike, when they are given the opportunity to speak for themselves. Just as we follow the relations among humans through their voice, so we are better able to follow the relations among non-humans when we hear their own voice, instead of only seeing them separately through human eyes. Secondly, in listening to the actors speak we find messages that can be obscured in other forms of narrative, and this may help universities, librarians, and others in making decisions about how they might implement their repositories. Many of the actors appear in the implementations of repositories and in scholarly publishing and have a presence in universities including both the case universities. We see that they inhabit multiple networks and are closely related to each other. The actions of one influence the actions of another, but they each have their own stories. The stories provide additional and intertwining narratives as counterpoint to the usual narrative of two central actor's becoming (in this case the repositories), adding meaning to the interactions of these actors with other actors. For example, listening to the voices we realised a tension in papers between informing and recognition, and how this can influence their relations with authors, journals and IRs. We hear the voices of peer review – both friend and foe to papers and authors.

We understood the ambiguity that JanusWorks had towards OA reflected a tension in the history of the JanusWorks software as a commercial package built on an open source platform. JanusWorks infers that this ambiguity was reflected in its relations with key human actors such as authors and the university librarian and contributed to its slow growth. On the other hand EPrints felt strong congruence between its name, the nature of its open source platform and open content, its purpose and its ability to work with its university to help achieve the university's mission. Listening to the voices of two repositories, one struggling with ambiguity and uncertainty into existence; the other congruent and stable can provide universities, librarians and other implementers with information to inform their repository development. Congruency, a lowering of ambiguity, the support of policies as well as human actors within the project appears in these cases to contribute to speed and success of implementation.

There is much work yet to be done in understanding how particular interactions of the narratives can be described. There is also the possibility that allowing non-humans to speak might lead to a better understanding of how their scripts evolve with the network (Latour, 1992). Furthermore, it will be interesting to explore the emergence of non-human actors' relations with other actors (human and non-human). Presenting relations from different actors' views may reveal hidden conflicts and contradictions. Allowing contending stories to be heard in the voices of the actors and to intertwine might open the way to represent the true multiplicity of realities (Law, 2004, p. 152).

REFERENCES

Björk, B.-C., Roosr, A., et al. (2008). *Global annual volume of peer reviewed scholarly articles and the share available via different open access options.* Paper presented at the Openness in Digital Publishing: Awareness, Discovery and Access - Proceedings of the 12th International Conference on Electronic Publishing (ELPUB2008), Toronto, Canada.

Boland, R. J. (2000). The Limits of Language in Doing Systems Work. In Baskerville, R., Stage, J., & DeGross, J. I. (Eds.), *Organizational and Social Perspectives on Information Technology* (pp. 47–60). Boston: Kluwer Academic.

Budapest Open Access Initiative. (2002). *Budapest Open Access Initiative*. Retrieved April 7, 2006 from http://www.soros.org/openaccess/

Cecez-Kecmanovic, D., & Nagm, F. (2009). Have you Taken your Guys on the Journey? An ANT Account of Information Systems Project Evaluation. *International Journal of Actor-Network Theory and Technological Innovation, 1*(1), 1–22.

Clarke, R., & Kingsley, D. (2008). ePublishing's Impacts on Journals and Journal Articles. *Journal of Internet Commerce, 7*(1), 120–151. doi:10.1080/15332860802004410

Dale, K. (2005). Building a social materiality: spatial and embodied politics in organizational control. *Organization, 12*(5), 649. doi:10.1177/1350508405055940

Harnad, S. (1999). Free at Last: The Future of Peer-Reviewed Journals. *D-Lib Magazine, 5*(12). Retrieved from http://www.dlib.org/dlib/december99/12harnad.html.

Hosein, I. (2003). A Research Note on Capturing Technology: Toward Moments of Interest. In Whitley, E. A., Wynn, E. H., Myers, M. D., & DeGross, J. I. (Eds.), *Global and Organizational Discourse about Information Technology* (pp. 133–154). Boston: Kluwer Academic Publishers.

Kennan, M. A. (2008). *Reassembling scholarly publishing: open access, institutional repositories and the process of change.* Unpublished doctoral thesis, The University of New South Wales, Sydney, Australia. Retrieved from: http://unsworks.unsw.edu.au/vital/access/manager/Repository/unsworks:3488

Kling, R., & Callahan, E. (2003). Electronic journals, the Internet and scholarly communication. *Annual Review of Information Science & Technology, 37*, 127–178. doi:10.1002/aris.1440370105

Latour, B. (1987). *Science in action*. Cambridge, MA: Harvard University Press.

Latour, B. (1992). Where are the missing masses? The sociology of a few mundane artifacts. In Bijker, W. E., & Law, J. (Eds.), *Shaping Technology/Building Society: Studies in Sociotechnical Change* (pp. 225–258). Cambridge, MA: MIT Press.

Latour, B. (1993). *We have never been modern*. New York: Harvester.

Latour, B., & Woolgar, S. (1986). *Laboratory Life: The Construction of Scientific Facts*. Princeton, NJ: Princeton University Press.

Law, J. (2004). *After Method: Mess in Social Science research*. London: Routledge.

Lynch, C. A., & Lippincott, J. K. (2005). Institutional repository deployment in the United States as of early 2005. *D-Lib Magazine, 11*(9). Retrieved from http://webdoc.sub.gwdg.de/edoc/aw/d-lib/dlib/september05/lynch/09lynch.html. doi:10.1045/september2005-lynch

McDowell, C. S. (2007). Evaluating Institutional Repository Deployment in American Academe Since Early 2005 Repositories by the Numbers, Part 2. *D-Lib Magazine, 13*(9-10). Retrieved from http://dlib.org/dlib/september07/mcdowell/09mcdowell.html.

Mol, A. (2002). *The Body Multiple: Ontology in Medical Practice*. London: Duke University Press.

Open Access and Research Conference. (2008). *The Brisbane Declaration.* Retrieved from http://www.oaklaw.qut.edu.au/files/Brisbane.Declaration.pdf

Orlikowski, W. J. (1992). The duality of technology: Rethinking the concept of technology in organizations. *Organization Science*, 398–427. doi:10.1287/orsc.3.3.398

Orlikowski, W. J., & Scott, S. V. (2008). *The entangling of technology and work in organizations (Tech. Rep.)*. London: London School of Economics and Political Science.

Payette, S., & Lagoze, C. (1998). Flexible and Extensible Digital Object and Repository Architecture (FEDORA). In *Proceedings of the Second European Conference on Research and Advanced Technology for Digital Libraries* (LNCS 1513), Heraklion, Crete, Greece.

Porsander, L. (2005). My Name is Lifebuoy: An Actor-Network Emerging from Action-net. In Czarniawska, B., & Hernes, T. (Eds.), *Actor-Network Theory and Organizing* (pp. 14–30). Copenhagen, Denmark: Copenhagen Business School Press.

Pouloudi, A., & Whitley, E. A. (2000). Representing human and non-human stakeholders: on speaking with authority. In Baskerville, R., Stage, J., & DeGross, J. I. (Eds.), *Organizational and Social Perspectives on Information Technology* (pp. 339–354). Boston: Kluwer Academic.

Suchman, L. (2007). *Human-Machine Reconfigurations: Plans and Situated Actions* (2nd ed.). Cambridge, UK: Cambridge University Press.

Swan, A., & Carr, L. (2008). Institutions, Their Repositories and the Web. *Serials Review, 34*(1), 31–35. doi:10.1016/j.serrev.2007.12.006

Tatnall, A. (2000). *Innovation and change in the information systems curriculum in an Australian University: A socio-technical perspective*. Queensland, Australia: Central Queensland University.

Tatnall, A., & Gilding, A. (1999). *Actor-Network Theory and Information Systems Research.* Paper presented at the 10th Australasian Conference on Information Systems (ACIS), Wellington, New Zealand.

Treloar, A. (2005). *ARROW Targets: Institutional Repositories, Open-Source, and Web Services.* Paper presented at the AusWeb05 the Eleventh Australasian World Wide Web Conference. Retrieved September 13, 2005 from http://ausweb.scu.edu.au/aw05/papers/refereed/treloar/

Van Orsdel, L. C., & Born, K. (2008, April 14). Periodicals Price Survey 2008: Embracing openness. *Library Journal.* Retrieved from http://www.libraryjournal.com/article/CA6547086.html

Vidgen, R., & McMaster, T. (1996). *Black boxes, non-human stakeholders and the translation of IT through mediation.* Paper presented at the IFIP WG8.2 Working Conference on Information Technology and Changes in Organizational Work, Cambridge, UK.

Willinsky, J. (2006). *The Access Principle: The Case for Open Access to Research and Scholarship.* Retrieved from http://mitpress.mit.edu/catalog/item/default.asp?ttype=2&tid=10611

ENDNOTE

[1] Sherpa/Romeo (http://www.sherpa.ac.uk/romeo/) documents which journals allow authors to deposit their papers in OA IR and estimates that at the moment it is around 60% of publishers (http://www.sherpa.ac.uk/romeo.php?stats=yes).

This work was previously published in International Journal of Actor-Network Theory and Technological Innovation, Volume 2, Issue 2, edited by Arthur Tatnall, pp. 1-16, copyright 2010 by IGI Publishing (an imprint of IGI Global).

Chapter 5
A Socio-Technical Account of an Internet-Based Self-Service Technology Implementation:
Why Call-Centres Sometimes 'Prevail' in a Multi-Channel Context?

Rennie Naidoo
University of the Witwatersrand, South Africa

ABSTRACT

Despite the rampant growth in technology-based service delivery options, the implementation of these contemporary forms of service channels continues to be risky and problematic for organisations. Current conceptualisations of IS implementation is rather narrow and highlights only particular aspects of this phenomenon. This paper adopts a socio-technical lens to enhance our understanding of the implementation of an Internet-based self-service technology (ISST) at a major South African healthcare insurance firm. Actor-Network theory's (ANT) key conceptual elements of inscription and translation are used to describe how the design and use of this self-service technology emerged from the co-entanglement between the technological and social. Drawing from a field study, this paper demonstrates the complex interdependencies and interactions among contrasting social, political, economic and technological issues and therefore advances implementation theory for these contemporary service channels in yet another important way.

DOI: 10.4018/978-1-4666-1559-5.ch005

INTRODUCTION

The following statements were made by managers at a healthcare insurance firm, speaking about the challenges in implementing an Internet-based self-service technology (ISST):

Initially it was just to be part of the space. And no one really could draw a more rational reason than that. You have got to be part of this play. The whole world was going to go online ... (CIO Health Systems, interview 36, pp. 1-2)

There was a lot of political wars ... you want to achieve your initial goals so to expose everything is sometimes not the best thing because you are selling something, when you are selling at that moment you are making a claim, and it does not mean that everything that you are selling is the best thing. It's a war in the beginning, it's a business war ... and like in any war the general cannot expose his strategy to the army at any stage, at least at the beginning ... especially in an environment like this if you want to achieve anything ... (Systems architect, interview 021, p. 9)

We tried to follow the industry standards and use what at that stage would have been best of breed technology offerings which we did but not without huge and consistent resistance from other key players ... (Community head, interview 49, p. 3)

You will always have more naysayers and prophets of doom than supporters. Identify the key stakeholders early and engage them. This does not mean become their friends but stay close to them understand their fears, their drivers and their influence and how they can possibly use this to interfere with your plans.. . . . [Community Head, Interview 30, p. 9]

Underpinning the experiences expressed by these practitioners is the view of a power-seeking strategist who, given this new "technology-based self-service" was "plotting" to change the world of servicing healthcare insurance consumers, by enrolling both key human and technology-based allies.

Despite the surge in "technology-based self-service" delivery options, ranging from on-site options such as in-room hotel checkout, and off-site options such as automated airline ticketing by telephone to Internet shopping, implementing these technologies is proving rather difficult for managers (Bitner, Ostrom, & Meuter, 2002). Understanding the strategies of key actors during the implementation journey of these contemporary technologies which radically alters the service encounter is crucial, yet has been a much neglected area. While the literature on implementation is replete with factor-based approaches, which aim to identify a group of variables relevant to ISST implementation outcomes (Naidoo & Leonard, 2007; Lang & Collen, 2005; Pandya & Dholakia, 2005; Zeithaml, Parasuraman, & Malhotra, 2002), some ISST researchers have been calling for the use of multiple theories, concepts, principles and methods to be used in the understanding of ISST problems and issues (Parasuraman & Zinkhan, 2002).

Towards this end, this study uses a socio-technical lens in the form of Actor-Network Theory (ANT) to offer a richer understanding of the complexity of an ISST implementation journey and the ISST service encounter. This study introduces ISST researchers in particular to ANT as a useful theoretical framework for understanding the relationship between technologies and social actors such as designers and users. In the next section, I will review the literature in order to understand what the contemporary debates are in the literature on IS and ISST implementation.

ISST IMPLEMENTATION RESEARCH

The service management literature defines self-service technologies (SSTs) as technological interfaces that enable consumers to produce a service independent of direct service personnel involvement (Meuter, Ostrom, Roundtree, & Bitner, 2000). Robertson and Shaw (2005) further characterises the SST context as threefold: consumer participation in service production and delivery, independent of service personnel; a lack of interpersonal interaction between consumers and service personnel; and consumers being required to interface and interact with technology. In this study, I will focus specifically on off-site options and information based services delivered over the Internet. The Internet in particular has become one of the major forces behind these service innovations. These types of services are becoming popular among software, news, portal, financial services and healthcare firms. Despite the proliferation of Internet-based self-service technology (ISST) in organisations, the implementation of these information systems remains a significant issue (Pandya & Dholakia, 2005). The problems involved are accentuated further in the context of information systems that are deployed to a broader user audience outside of the organisational context. This necessitates a broader conceptualisation of IS implementation for Internet-based self-service technologies.

Given the inherent confusion about what implementation is in the context of IS research and practice, it is not surprising that it is described in the literature in a variety of ways. Generally some IS researchers focusing on the delivery of technical components refer to the conversion and installation process in a systems development lifecycle (Dutta & Roy, 2004). Others focus on the point at which the new system is put to use (Rogers, 1995). A popular definition of IS implementation has been conveyed by Swanson (1988, p. 2) who views the phenomenon as "a decision making activity that converts a design concept into an operating reality so as to provide value to the client". However in the IS context new meanings of IS implementation have been developed over time that transcends Swanson's managerial emphasis. For instance Walsham (1993) suggests that IS implementation encompasses all the human and social aspects of IS implementation in an organisation. However studies that attempt to encapsulate the social and technical are only now gaining prominence.

There are a number of perspectives on IS implementation research. Generally the research stream in IS implementation has been grouped into three dominant streams, factor, process and political research (Swanson, 1988; Kwon & Zmud, 1987; Markus & Pfeffer, 1983; Lucas, 1981). The factor research paradigm has been a dominant paradigm in IS implementation research. Factor studies of implementation have tried to identify variables associated with some measure of implementation success (Lyytinen & Hirscheim, 1987; Swanson, 1988; De Lone & McLean's, 1992). However, this type of research does not capture the realities of self-service technologies where in certain situations it is likely that the impact for the firm may be positive while the user impact may be negative and vice versa. Nevertheless, only a few factors have shown to be important across multiple studies. The influence of factors can be shown to be dependent on the time, history, situation and context in which they are applied. Institutional arrangements, context and technologic and economic constraints reshape the implementation space in which the service innovation is diffused. Though this is acknowledged by some implementation theorists, contending that knowledge of the extent to which factors affect different stages in the implementation process differently is still limited, they still continue to hold on to theories to discover such factors through progressive research. While the factor studies of implementation have attempted to identify the variables associated with some measure of implementation success, process research has focused on the relationship between designer and users and the impact of the system on the organisation (Sabherwal & Robey, 1993). Another example of a process oriented approach is Nolan's (1979) six stage development model which traces the evolution of IT and the organisation in a 'stages of growth' model. The model emphasises the changing role of IT in organisations. On the other hand, user-centric models, actively seek to involve users in the implementation process by improving the interaction between users and designers (Lucas, 1981). Markus and Pfeffer (1983) propose a political view to implementation that is more attuned to organisational or social reality. In this approach, attention is given to the diverse interests of IT stakeholders and how the success of implementation efforts depends on recognising and managing this diversity. She argues that systems implementation does not follow from the separate and independent effects of 'people factors' on the one hand and 'system factors' on the other, but instead is the result of the interactive effects of the two set of factors.

Further understanding of implementation comes from social constructivists who demonstrate the influential role of actors beyond the suppliers or targeted users involved in the innovation (Butler, 2003). According to Sahay and Robey (1996), human actors are assumed to endow technology with social meanings as they engage in processes to propose, design, develop, implement and use the technology. To further overcome some of the mechanistic perspectives that have tended to dominate the IS implementation literature, Myers (1994) proposes critical hermeneutics as another theoretical perspective for understanding IS implementation. In this approach an integrative framework combining interpretive and critical elements is developed. The objective is to make sense of organisations as text analogues, in which the various stakeholders may have confused, incomplete, cloudy, and often contradictory views on implementation issues. It emphasises both the subjective meanings of the individual actor and the social structures that condition and enable such meanings (Butler, 1998). For instance, the structuration perspective emphasises the centrality of the human agency in shaping and appropriating self-service technology (Schultze & Orlikowski, 2004).

In summary then, while many studies have been completed, and a variety of theories of implementation have been suggested, no one theory of implementation has been widely accepted. While some progress has been made, each of the models is rather narrow and highlights only a particular aspect of information systems implementation. Despite ISST being a unique type of IS implementation, the current view of self-service technology implementation in the literature is rather limited, emphasising the relationship between the technology and the end user. Furthermore, perhaps one of the main reasons for the lack of progress is that in most existing theories there is an underlying mechanistic view of the relationship between information technology and organisational change which assumes a separate existence of technology and organisation. Recently, there has been a trend towards a social-technical approach to understand IS implementation (Hanseth & Aanestad, 2004). Implementation research that adopts a socio-technical approach is more important for information systems such as ISSTs, technologies that are entangled in a broader social context. This perspective is discussed in more detail in the next section.

ACTOR-NETWORK THEORY

The major assertion of this paper is that ISST implementation has both technical and social merits at the same time, and that therefore it might be more appropriate to try to overcome the distinction between technical and social for a better understanding of this phenomenon. What sets ANT apart from conventional theories is that neither the inherent properties of the technology, nor some properties of the social context – such as user traits and other actors – drive the success or failure of an implementation. Instead, it is the associations that exist and are created between the technology and its surrounding actors, that is, actors that are both technical and social. ANT also delves into the ways in which networks of relations are arranged, how they emerge and come into being, how they are constructed and maintained, how they compete with other networks and how they are made more durable over time (Tatnall & Gilding, 1999). ANT thus offers a unique approach to theorising innovations such as self-service technologies and their implementation; an approach that resists the essentialist notions inherent in the conventional treatment of self-service technologies.

Understanding the Sociology of Translation

One of the central concepts in ANT is the sociology of translation. For Latour (2005, p. 64), "ANT is the name of a movement, a displacement, a transformation, a translation, and an enrolment. It is an association between entities which are in no way recognisable as being social in the ordinary manner, except in the brief moment when they are reshuffled together". Latour (2005, p. 108) specifically defines translation as a relation that 'induces two mediators into existing'. However, 'translation' is a term used in many different ways. Literally the term 'translation' denotes two meanings, both relevant to ANT. In the first place, it is a change of position and a new interpretation. In other words, translation operates between actors: an actor gives definition to another actor by imputing these actors with interests, projects, desires, strategies, reflexes, afterthoughts. And second, according to Callon (1986), a translation is 'the methods by which an actor enrols others'. These methods involve:

- The definition of roles, their distribution, and the delineation of a scenario
- The strategies in which a future state actor-network renders itself indispensable to others by creating a geography of obligatory passage points
- The displacement imposed upon others as they are forced to follow the itinerary that has been imposed

In the creation of the actor-network or the process of translation, Callon (1986) discerns four 'moments': problematisation, interessement, enrolment and mobilisation.

During the first moment of *problematisation* one actor, the initiator, makes an effort to make other actors subscribe to its own conceptions by demonstrating that it has the right solutions to, or definitions of the problem. Initiators try to demonstrate their quality of being indispensable to the solution of the problem during the initial stage. The problem is redefined or translated in terms of solutions offered by the initiator who then attempts to establish themselves as an 'obligatory passage point' which must be negotiated as part of its solution. To pass through the obligatory passage point, the other actors must accept a set of specific conventions, rules, assumptions and ways of operating laid down by the first actor (Tatnall, 2001). Introna (1997) defines an obligatory passage point as a rhetorical device that presents the solution to the problem in terms of the resources of the agency proposing it.

During the second moment of translation, *interessement*, an attempt is made to impose and stabilise the identities and roles defined in the problematisation on the other actors, thereby locking other actors into the roles proposed for them (Callon, 1986). Gradually existing networks are replaced by the new network.

The third moment is *enrolment*. Enrolment occurs when a stable network of alliances is formed, and the actors yield to their defined roles and definitions. This involves a multilateral political process where the initiators seek to convince other actors. It is for this reason that Callon (1986,

p. 211) states: 'To describe enrolment is thus to describe the group of multilateral negotiations, trials of strength and tricks that accompany the interessements and enable them to succeed.'

The final moment is *mobilisation*. Mobilisation is a set of methods that initiators employ to ensure that allies do not betray the initiators' interests. During mobilisation the proposed solution gains wider acceptance and achieves stability. Stability implies that the technology's content is institutionalised, and is no longer controversial, that is, it becomes taken-for-granted and is 'black-boxed'.

According to Latour (1987), the spread of ideas and their conversion to accepted facts is a rhetorical process. In other words, ideas become more accepted, or taken for granted, as they are translated into inscriptions and incorporated into instruments and technology. For example, the networks constituted by ISSTs are spread in this manner. Challenges are 'muted' as a consequence of the strength which the network achieves as least in part from many of the service providers who deploy these systems. Translation is necessary for stability in these networks, since actors from the outset have a diverse set of interests (Monteiro, 2000). Aligning these interests causes a network to become stable and durable. However, according to Mahring, Holmstrom, Keil, and Montealegre (2004), the translation process does not necessarily pass through all the stages described above. It is plausible, then, that translation processes may fail and halt at any stage, depending on the strength of the network's inscriptions. In contrast to diffusion models, which assume technologies to be immutable, actors in ANT not only reshape technologies, but are themselves changed as the changing artefact spreads through the social network.

Figure 1 shows that actor-networks are configured by the enrolment of various human and non-human allies, via a series of negotiations where one group of actors attempts to impose definitions and roles on other actors. It discerns four 'moments': problematisation; interessement; enrolment; and mobilisation. The model above also demonstrates the notion of weak ties (depicted by broken, thinner and disconnected lines) and strong ties (depicted by darker and connected lines). Whereas actors during problematisation are characterised by fragmented alliances and instability (weak ties), through the process of translation, actors are progressively locked into stronger alliances, whereupon they come together and the network stabilises (strong ties).

Understanding Inscriptions

During the development of a technology and in its placement in an actor-network, inscription also takes place. Inscriptions prescribe a program of action for other actors, which the latter may or may not follow, depending on the strength of the inscription (Latour, 1991). In relation to translation, inscription to a large extent takes place simultaneously and interrelated, that is, it starts as soon as a technology enters the picture and is beginning to be formed by its creators (Latour, 1991). So, inscription implies that a material or technological artefact never begins as a blank slate. In other words, artefacts always embody the designer's beliefs, social and economic relations, previous patterns of use, and assumptions as to what the artefact is about. For example, inscription is used when designers formulate and shape self-service technology in such a way so as to lead and control users. Inscription can also refer to the way technical artefacts embody patterns of use, including user programs of action. The term also encompasses the roles users and the system play (Monteiro, 2000). Since inscription can guide users to join or behave in a way that forces a definition of the form and function of the technology, many actors actively seek to inscribe their vision and interests into the artefact (Faraj, Kwon, & Watts, 2004). Inscriptions may also lead to irreversibility. Irreversibility refers to the degree to which in a certain situation it is impossible to go back to a point where alternative

Figure 1. The four moments of translation (adapted from Callon, 1986, pp. 196-223; also see Naidoo & Leonard, 2009)

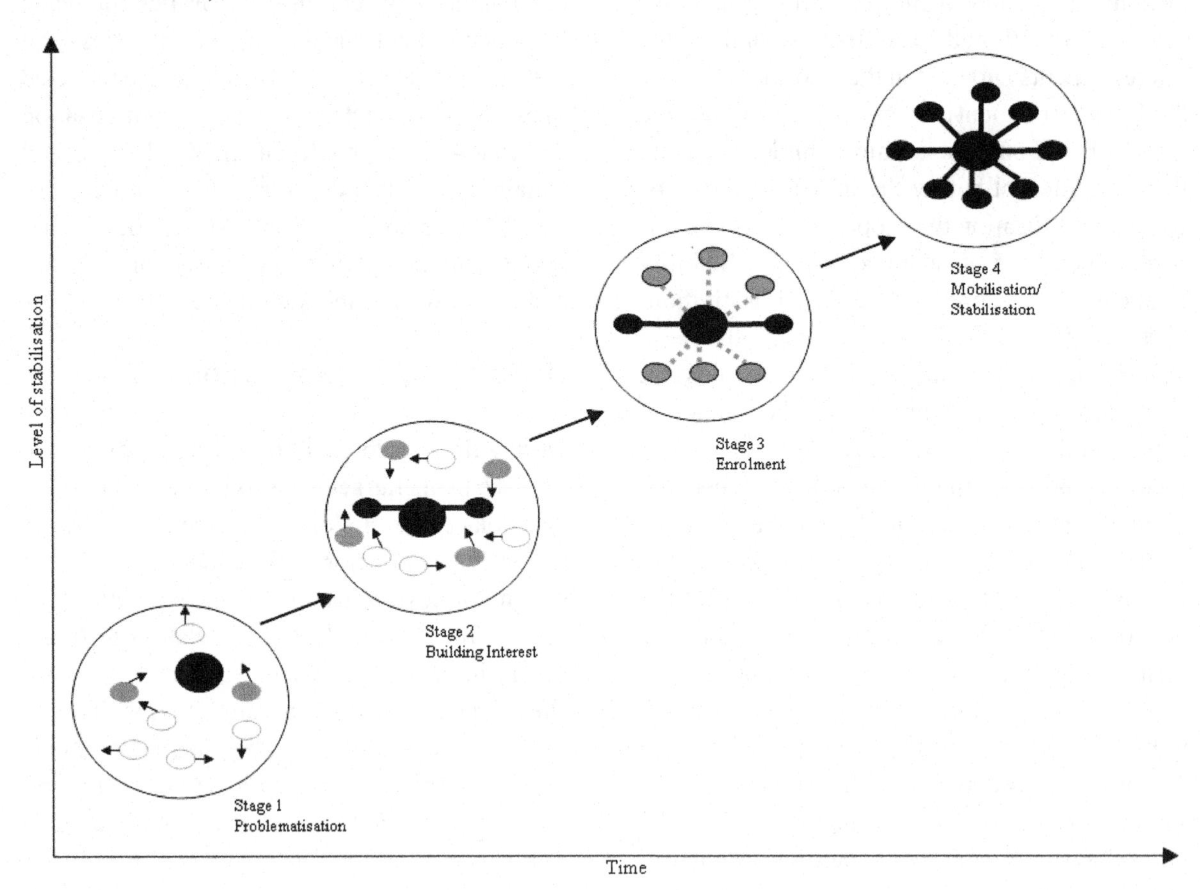

possibilities exist (Callon, 1991). Irreversibility is often the result of the inscription of interests into technological artifacts, whereby those interests become increasingly difficult to change (Hanseth & Monteiro, 1998; Mahring et al., 2004). As ideas are inscribed in technology artefacts and as they diffuse in their relevant contexts, they help achieve socio-technical stability (Latour, 1986). While technology artefacts are, in part, open to interpretation, there are some features that are in practice 'beyond' (re)interpretation and that increase stability in the networks in which technologies are encompassed (Latour, 1991). Walsham (2001) notes that inscriptions developed in software, as frozen discourse, may resist change and display signs of irreversibility.

Hanseth and Monteiro (1997) suggest four notions of inscription and translation that should be emphasised in a study:

- The identification of explicit anticipations or scenarios of use held by the various actors during design
- How these anticipations are translated and inscribed into materials
- Who inscribes them?
- The strength of these inscriptions, that is, the effort it takes to oppose or work around them

ANTs view of implementation as an emergent process initiated and guided by focal actors with specific interests is a particular attraction for the study of ISSTs. Despite facing criticisms of managerialist and Machiavellian tendencies (Moser & Law, 2006), ANTs particular value for ISST research is in the manner in which it traces how actors enact their agendas during the implementation journey through processes of inscription and translation. Following how focal actors mobilise the support of influential actors and decision makers through the processes of inscription and the sub-processes of translation to achieve the ISST vision can assist in teasing out crucial socio-technical relations. The research methodology is discussed next.

RESEARCH METHODOLOGY

The main research strategy selected was an in-depth case study of a single organisation. The case study method was chosen because of its advantages in creating novel and profound insights and its focus on examining the rich social, cultural and political influences on the implementation of SST initiatives. The case study approach is especially useful were contextual conditions of the events being studied are critical and where the researcher has no control over the events as they unfold. According to Yin (1999b) other empirical methods are at a distinct disadvantage in developing our understanding of contemporary developments, specifically with systems such as SSTs that link multiple components in new ways and produce 'mega-systems' of great complexity. The case study approach is used to describe the implementation of an online self-service technology initiative at Africa's largest financial healthcare insurance company, which will be referred to by the anonym 'Healthcare Insurance Company' (HIC). The implementation effort began in the latter part of 1999 when dot.com was at its high point and continued during 2004, the period when I began the fieldwork. The case study was conducted over a two year period beginning in February 2004 and ending in November 2006.

There were several reasons for the selection of this case. The first is that, although the South African economy is perceived to be an emerging market, the South African healthcare insurance industry is widely recognised as being highly developed. In fact HIC is viewed globally as the pioneers in consumer-driven healthcare and was in a fairly advanced phase of implementing their online self-service technology to complement this strategy. Therefore, this case has global relevance. Secondly organisations such as HIC perform an information-intensive activity including processing an insured member's personal details, claim details, service provider details, diseases and conditions information, tariffs and benefits information, and the like. Their systems also integrate with banks, hospitals, clinics, other financial services organisations, employers and so on. Thirdly, organisations such as HIC are made up of traditional and alternative service options such as walk-in centres, branches and call centres which are well institutionalised, providing a richer and more complex environment of study.

Semi structured interviews and secondary source analysis were the main data collection mechanisms. Individual interviews carried out on site were the primary technique used to elicit information from the SST's designers. The duration of these interviews varied from 1 to 2 hours. From June 2004 to July 2005, my main focus was directed at creating a historical reconstruction of the SST implementation from 1999 onwards. During this period I immersed myself in a large number of public and confidential reports given to me by several of the managers and members of the implementation team. The reports included management reports, weekly operations reports, call centre and online customer feedback, strategic plans, press releases and news articles, forms, fliers, prior research reports, presentations, ad hoc studies and so on. The field research for the case study was carried out in three main periods, consisting of 3 months in mid-2005, 3 months in late-2005, and another month in late-2006. In total I conducted a total of 55 formal interviews during this period (Table A1). All 55 interviews were tape recorded and extensive research notes were taken. This practice ensured that everything said was preserved for analysis.

Data Analysis

Because this study was part of a larger research project, the data was systematically coded into as many theoretical themes and categories as possible. As the categories emerged and were refined, I began to evaluate how they related to one another and what the theoretical implications were. I used the conceptual elements of ANT to guide this process. I also used version 5 of ATLAS.ti to code and store these themes and categories at the textual and conceptual level (See Figure 2).

ATLAS.ti was also used for the overall management of the research project and its associated data. This archive consisted of the case study field notes, case study documents, quantitative data and other electronic files generated during the study. These 'files' were catalogued and indexed chronologically as the research process unfolded, and filed for easy access and retrieval. Using ATLAS.ti for easy cross-referencing assisted in maintaining a chain of evidence to support the case study conclusions (Muhr & Friese, 2004; Darke, Shanks, & Broadbent, 1998). These interviews together with the large collection of rich, thick qualitative information from a number of sources played an important role in addressing the complexity of the context studied. This triangulation of data was important in counteracting any biases in the collection and analysis of data (Darke, Shanks, & Broadbent, 1998).

THE HEALTHCARE INSURER CASE STUDY

During the latter part of the 90s, a major multinational South African consumer-driven healthcare insurance firm known for reasons of confidentiality as HIC, offered a fundamental shift in funding healthcare in the local market. Driving HIC's initial growth was the health savings account

Figure 2. Exploring conceptual level structures using network representations

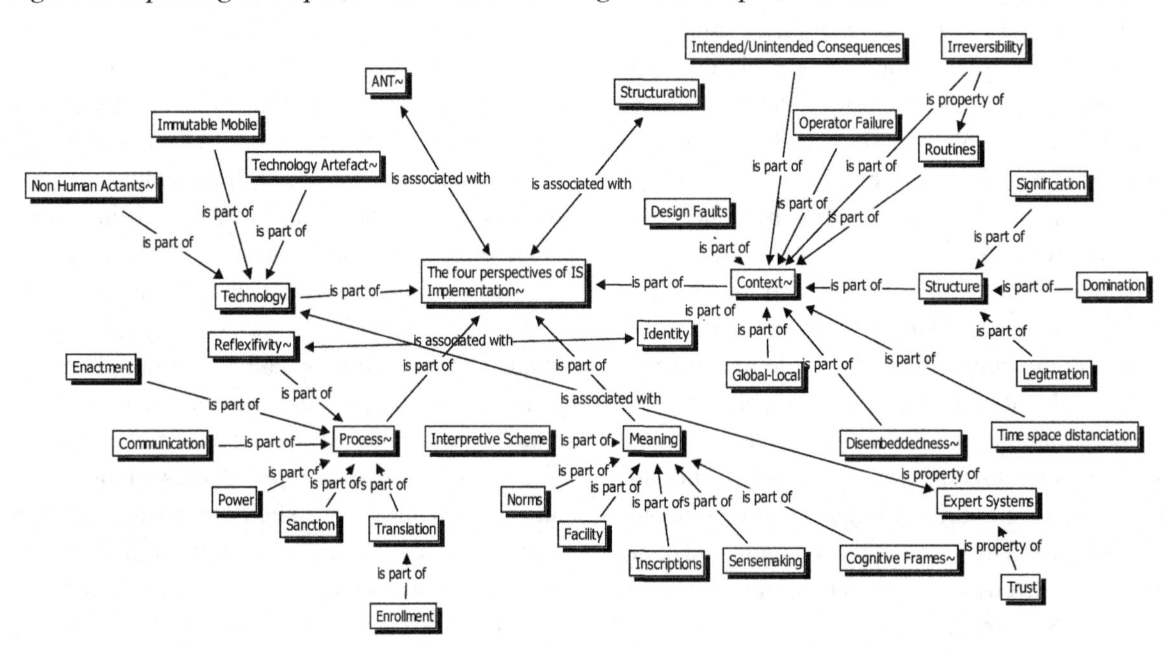

(HSA) component of their product which was at the time a major innovation in healthcare funding in South Africa. This initiative is reviewed in the next section.

The Online Self-Service Project

The development of eHIC began in the latter part of 1999, when excitement about dotcoms was at its zenith. HIC was facing tremendous growth at the time, and the challenge was to overcome the intensifying issues relating to managing massive amounts of paperwork, fending off fraud, and coping with exponential growth in customer demands. At the time it was decided that an online system had the potential to allow health insurance members to keep their personal records up to date, submit their claims, and constantly keep members in the communication loop through direct access to their own medical insurance information.

The business solutions director of the consulting firm was quoted in a special report in InformationWeek, Southern Africa, as saying at the time:

In doing so (using Web technologies), the company is leading an industry trend in closing the gap between itself and its clients, service providers and intermediaries while at the same time reducing the cost of service (InformationWeek, 1998).

Figure 3. eHIC Landing Page (2003 Redesign)

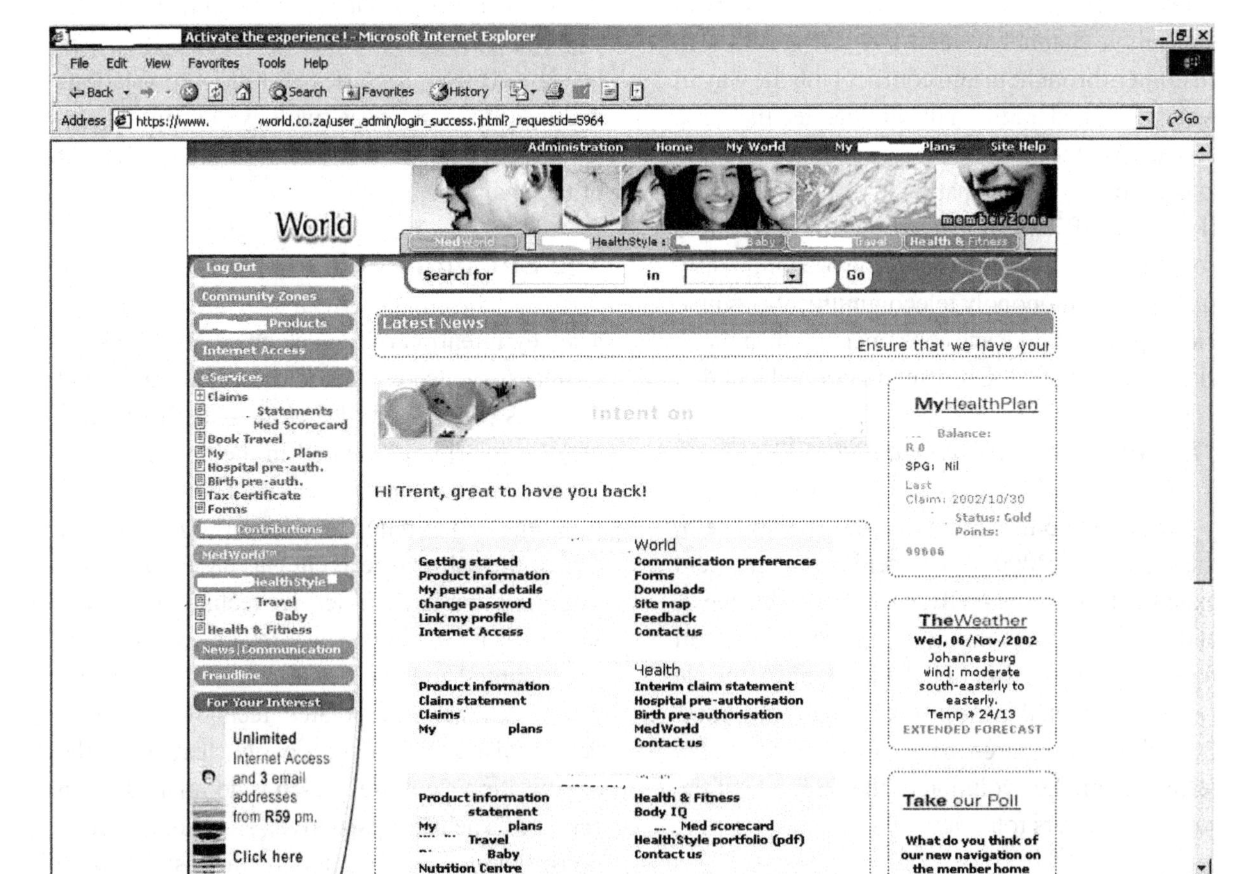

According to the general manager, finance of HIC:

Apart from savings this brings HIC in terms of the efficiency of its administrative process, members enjoy the benefits of being able to interact with the company at any time they choose (InformationWeek, 1998).

However from the outset the newly formed e-business team faced a constant struggle. The systems and business areas were already constrained by a chaotic and an overextended operational environment. This was brought about by servicing the rapidly growing customer base and a plethora of new product development priorities. Furthermore the "integrated, on-line, real-time" concept to which eHIC wanted to operate was foreign to many of the staff at HIC. In addition, the way the online channel wanted to offer services to customers brought in into conflict with the way in which HIC had traditionally architected the same services for the existing service channels. To add to the growing consternation, the online SST was slow and difficult to use. At the time, business connectivity levels offered by the predominantly state-owned monopoly telecommunications provider were very poor and consumer broadband was almost nonexistent. One user mentioned that the:

"The site looks great but is painfully slow to use".

When dotcoms started to falter worldwide in the middle of 2000, HIC's senior management expediently absorbed eHIC back into the business. eHIC was now operating as one of the several functional areas of the IT department. All these issues culminated in the project progressing painfully slower compared to the expectations set. On reflecting on the evolution of the SST, one of the senior managers told me:

"I think, if we look today at where we have come, our initial objective was to convert a channel (call centre) into another channel (online self-service). And lessons are learnt, that you know, this is a social environment, okay. There is no dominant channel. It's apparent to me that the channels are interlinked, merged, and one will use whatever is closest in proximity".

To augment and enrich some of the findings presented in this section, I now employ actor-network theory (ANT).

ANALYSIS

ANT will now be used to help trace the implementation journey of the ISST as the various actors co-evolved. Drawing on empirical data from the case study, I suggest that the ISST can be viewed through a series of shifts or translations and inscriptions. These two key conceptual elements will be used as the scaffolding for the rest of the analysis.

The Substitution Inscription

The key intention of the designers of the HIC e-business was to replace or substitute traditional channels (See Figure 4). More specifically, this major scenario culminated in the desire to substitute the call-centre consultant with the Web front-end. This major inscription to take on the role of the call-centre agent was based on the assumption that the self-service technology would save calls by having answers to key call reasons programmed and made available on the website, using the Web and related technologies. This deterministic approach probably stems from the organisation's culture, which is dominated by an actuarial science perspective. The same inscriptions, founded on formal mathematics, that were

Figure 4. HIC'S servicing architecture (adapted from source: 2003 eHIC strategy presentation)

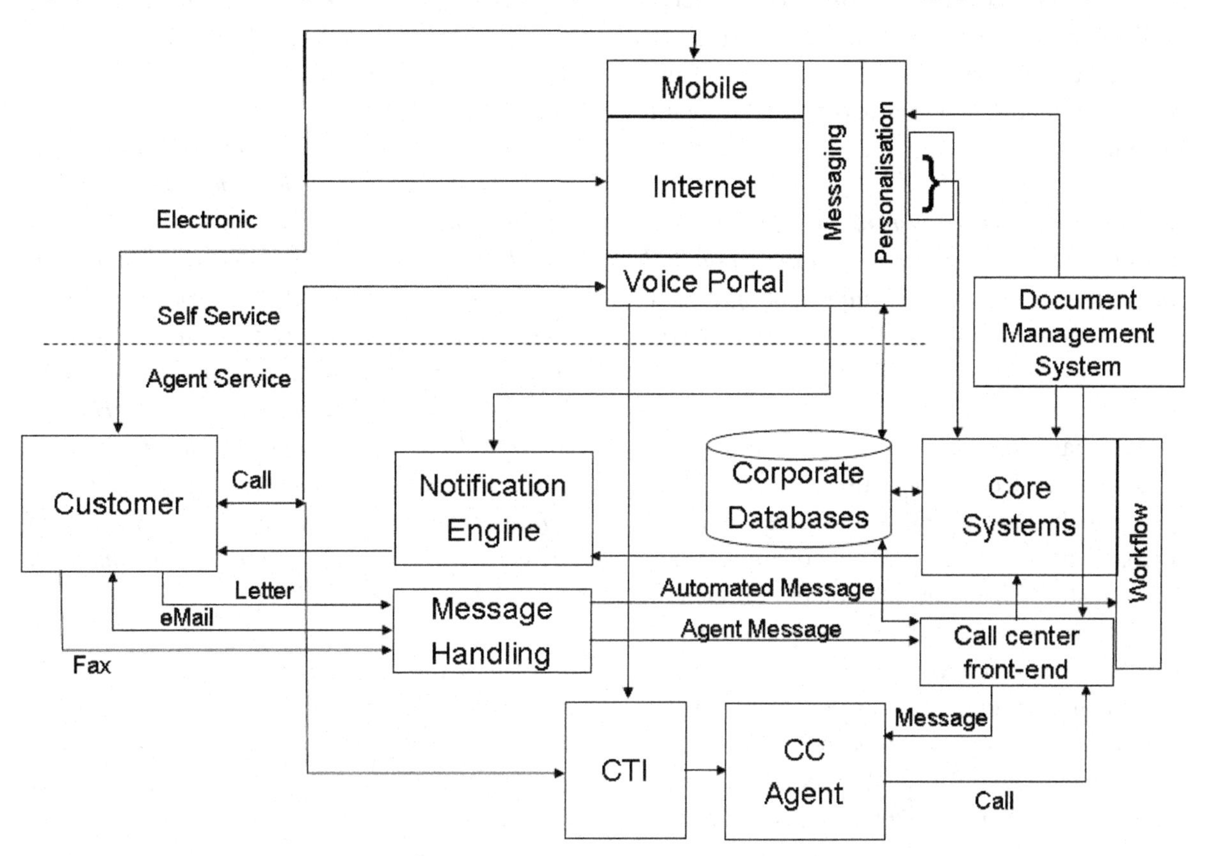

embedded in developing healthcare insurance products such as probability, statistics, finance and economics, were being applied to the ISST's performance.

As opposed to involving users in the requirements analysis process, designers looked at call-log statistics and built online features around popular call reasons, such as submitting and tracking online claims, viewing statements, and checking medical saving account balances. Similar to actuarial models, this call-saving model would soon prove vulnerable because of its assumption-dependent approach. At the time, servicing the rapidly growing customer member base resulted in increasing capital expenditure on call-centre technology. Furthermore, the high fixed-cost base of the call centre, combined with the high labour cost attributed to the growing number of call-centre consultants, all gave strength to this internal inscription of improving service efficiency through automation. This internal inscription was also strengthened by the hype created by the other external steering mechanisms. At the time, the Internet created potential opportunities for new entrants to conventional markets, so called 'pure plays' challenging traditional intermediary niches. This has been termed disintermediation. For instance, the threat of a pure-play helath insurance competitor may seem far-fetched now, but at the time it was viewed seriously by HIC's executive team.

The Internet browser was also positioned as an obligatory passage point (OPP) because it was an 'open', 'electronic' platform that could deliver the paperless environment – vast amounts of paper had plagued healthcare insurers for years.

The provider of the Dynamo suite of e-commerce applications, Applied Technology Group (ATG), offered the following 'objective information and practical guidance' to IT professionals during the dotcom boom:

For all businesses there is an unrelenting pressure to control costs. The pressure of competition and financial investors will not allow managers any relief in their efforts to drive down costs (ATG Technology Guide, 2000, p. 7).

An organising vision – emerging from a heterogeneous collective consisting of the academic world, media, consultant, software vendors, and dotcom start-ups – bestowed a lot of appeal upon this 'substitution claim' and other 'efficiency' inscriptions. Hannemeyr (2003) found that the popular narrative concerning the Internet during the dotcom boom possibly resulted from translations into carefully phrased restatements of fact to support a particular financial or political agenda. Swanson and Ramiller (2004) suggest that this 'bandwagon' phenomenon is especially prevalent where an innovation achieves a high public profile, as with the Internet and e-commerce. Planned action is typically dismissed by the urgency to join the stampeding herd, despite the high costs and apparent risk.

Translating Claims of Substitution

Noticeably the larger community's organising vision was the embarking point for HIC's sensemaking journey with e-commerce. Based on buzzwords such as 'cost advantages' that the media presented about the new channel, the apparent 'rapid rate of adoption' globally, and the 'first mover competitive advantage' this would present at the time, HIC invested significantly in the development of the self-service channel. To show support for the new channel, the leadership of the organisation gave eHIC autonomy to transform the ways in which members interacted with the organisation and were to be serviced. Recalling the mood at the time, one of the senior managers of the initiative stated:

We had direct support from the very top. Andy, Ben and Jim sat on our Exco for the first six to nine months so focused were they on the Internet possibilities. HIC itself was flying having redefined health insurance in South Africa so all in all there was an abundance of goodwill and positive energy. Pretty much anything Tom (referring to the Head of eHIC) and I wanted to do with eHIC we could and we had the support. Our only limiting factor was capacity and time. We did not have enough time and actual people to chase all of the great ideas we had at that time (Community head, interview 049, p. 2)

One of the focal actors – in the form of the newly appointed head of e-commerce – enrolled the executives to establish an exco to support their activities. The exco could assist the newly formed e-commerce organisation to address the criticisms from a number of quarters that were unwilling to participate in this 'new era'. Despite overwhelming support from the CEO and most of the senior members of the executive team, a number of executives expressed a level of apprehension about the merits of eHIC operating as a separate entity. First, there were those who were sceptical about whether eHIC could succeed without closer engagement with HIC's IT and business departments. Linked to this were concerns that incentives would be misaligned in the IT area if the dotcom start-up was conceived separately. In the second place, others in opposition did not believe that HIC's health products could be serviced over the Internet. For these detractors, contact via the call centres had been the hallmark of HIC's success thus far, and was essential in servicing customers.

The *problematisation* in this scenario is overtly concerned with the power relationship between traditional IT, operational call centre managers and the newly conceived e-service. Despite the support and mandate from the exco members, political battles were still being fought at certain levels. After all, there were fears in areas such as corporate systems that the role of the SST was to squash legacy practices.

Nevertheless, the level of optimism was so great at the time that the firm invested significantly in the state-of-the-art technology in the ATG Dynamo suite of applications, which was then the leading and premium Web server technology. Other leading tools such as Documentum for document management and Verity as a search engine formed part of the envisaged solution. The firm chose Java as the development platform instead of .NET as this was deemed to be the best technology for constructing Web applications at the time. Introduced by Sun Microsystems in 1995, Java's 'write once, run anywhere' philosophy made it the ideal language for distributing code across the Internet. Inscribed in Java, among others, were the notion of reuse, shorter time to market, and increased connectivity. Over the implementation period Java's general-purpose programming capability would impose new inscriptions in the overall development environment. The newly formed company sought to recruit for skills in Java, graphic art, and e-commerce generally. Despite its growing popularity and ease of use, Java skills were hard to find, given the exodus of skilled IT workers from the country and the newness of e-commerce at the time. The lack of skills and newness of these technologies would later impinge on the team's ability to deliver on time, with as few 'bugs' as possible, and thus contributed to poor translations of eHIC. One of the senior members of the development team described the immature development environment:

When eHIC was started everyone was in bloody real trouble. People were in real trouble. Everyone was new to all the technologies that were used, new concepts that were introduced, under huge pressure as well as everyone was just hired, everyone was trying to do their best to keep their jobs and it was the job necessity itself that made everyone work so hard, they never did this in their lives before so it was a matter of survival. That kept them together and built strong relationships It was not the leadership ... it was the pressure, the struggle for survival that kept them together (Systems architect, interview 019, p. 2).

Poor translations also involved the internal systems. The predominantly batch mode of processing between internal systems, the use of a non-standard database platform, poor data quality and integration issues all made for weak (ties) inscriptions. The internal Magic-based systems, and a robust client-server application used by the internal operational areas for high-volume data capture were at odds with the Java-based application for developing Web-based applications. The problem of working with the traditional systems department was further articulated by a community head I had interviewed:

HIC was and always has been a mess of technology types, especially in the development environment. A lot of these were not industry standard type of products such as Magic and so had a very particular type of developer and mindset associated with it. With eHIC we very much tried to follow the industry standards and use what at that stage would have been best of breed technology offerings which we did but not without huge and consistent resistance from other key players ... (Community head, interview 49, p. 3).

The Magic-based systems were not readily interoperable with the CORBA standard, which meant that a lot of the business logic was inaccessible to the Java-based applications. Furthermore, a number of the functionally driven Magic systems were built as one monolithic piece of code, and therefore could not be easily adapted for a component-based Web environment. This meant that business rules had to be rewritten, using maintenance-prone Store Procedures to access the data from the already unconventionally designed tables.

Apart from contributing to high maintenance levels, this obviously led to strained relationships. Because the current system environment was designed to support the internal processes, and was not designed for real-time e-commerce, this created a lot of animosity between the eHIC and the systems departments. The e-commerce strategic business unit (SBU) claimed that the current systems were antiquated and not supportive of e-commerce.

I think we were sort of seen as, call it the interloper, ja, that's what we were ... and I think we sort of came in and expected them all to drop everything to give us what we needed. We were dependent on some of these systems. It's like okay you have to deliver this for us. You know so we weren't part of Systems, and also the departments were also treated differently, like eHIC, in the early days we had our own chill room, it might seem silly, we did not go to the systems functions, we had our own functions, so if there was a general systems function we never went. We just did our own thing. And I think that also did not help. And we didn't sit near them, because we were in Eaton House and everything, so ... (Developer, interview 016, pp. 6-7).

There was clearly a feeling of tribalism based on which system one was affiliated to. Magic developers resented the attitude of the ISST's Java developers, particularly as the system they had developed was working fairly well within HIC. They saw eHIC staff as the interlopers, the 'favourite children' of the executive team, and were hostile to the view that eHIC had a 'monopoly on innovation'. The traditional systems departments were also unhappy with the manner in which eHIC representatives 'bullied' them for assistance. This approach was counter to the loosely coupled organisational form in the systems area that was characterised by semi-autonomous reporting relationships and was deemed one of the reasons for their past successes. The introduction of eHIC also exacerbated relations between the business departments and eHIC representatives. As a result of the conflict between the two technologies, and the resultant unsteady support from both systems and business departments, the implementation of the project was completed much later than envisaged. In addition, the frequent system failures created a flood of phone calls to the call centre, which did not help the reputation of the online service internally.

Furthermore, ANT reveals that technical artefacts are not neutral. In this instance, the Magic development environment did not require a skilled systems designer or architect. This led to suboptimal design of the databases. On the other hand, the e-commerce department was a Java-based environment. Java is tied to object-oriented modelling and mapping classes to relational or object-oriented databases. Therefore Java developers tended to have a different set of skills. To add to this, the ISST developers required a single view of the customer and a process view of the organisation. The current stovepipe systems environment and the need to achieve systems integration were at odds with the approach inscribed into the SST. These differences are explained in the following comment:

... There were many data issues which had to be resolved. One of the more complex areas was of profiling. What if a Broker was also a doctor? And a member? And a dependent on another policy? With Wellness? What could he or she see? How would it integrate? This was a significant issue that we had to overcome. It forced a redesigned of our databases from policy driven design to an entity architecture. Extremely challenging but in the end it was well worth it. Another major issue that eHIC introduced was the transparency of our information to our communities. It's easy to hide bad information from your customers over

the phone. But when they log in and view their statements in real time and you have data issues it's very difficult to get around that (Senior business analyst, interview 30, p. 3).

On the other hand, Magic applications were used to sustain robust applications to support the call centre and the myriad functionally based administrative processes. Although Magic supported business growth and rapid changes, it led to suboptimal designs for Java-based concepts such as reuse. Over time, the idea of a database design on an entity model would only gain traction largely because of the ISST's needs. At the outset, the collision of these two (Magic and Java) socio-technical assemblages constrained the way the ISST functioned.

Moving to users, although *interessement* was positioned in the various promotions for convenience, secure and real-time information, from a user perspective the corporate standard to verify user name and password through a call-centre validated process was a major barrier to using the system. Since firms can be held liable for granting consent to users to access a member's information, trust is a concept that applies equally to the firm and the user. In supporting relationships via ISSTs, the firm delegated trust decisions to verify and authenticate the identity claimed by the user to both human and technical systems. The ISST was liable for any breaches of trust or negligence in its use. Therefore a policy for controlling access to the ISST via new roles and profiles had to be established. These were stored in a database. Linked to these new identities were a variety of attributes describing specific relationships, so that the ISST could grant the correct privileges to the user. Some users expressed their frustration that this process was protracted:

The only snag is the registration process. 48 hours is too long to wait for registration confirmation. Everything else, WOW! (Online feedback, June 2001, line 119).

On the other hand, the telephone was ready at hand. Instead of grappling with the cumbersome registration process or the cognitive effort of remembering a password and user name, the member could easily access the firm's phone number and his or her membership number, which was required for authentication. These details were already inscribed on his or her membership card. Given the younger profile of the HIC client base, it is not surprising that most clients who represented a critical mass called the call centre less frequently. In other words, these healthy clients who had low claim incidences had a low need to interact with their health insurer. Despite this, following Pareto's principle, as a collective they represented the majority of calls. To make a significant impact on calls, the SST team would require the arduous task of enlisting these members. However, what would emerge over time is that those members with the greatest servicing need, using multiple channels – in other words high-frequency callers – would also be loyal users of the website. Whereas the intention of the organisation was to develop a channel that was to replace the traditional call-centre channel, different and unexpected patterns of use emerged.

Another reason that negotiating with the SST to become the dominant channel did not work is implicit in the role of the call-centre consultant. It soon became apparent that the call centre agent's role is multidimensional. One of the users expressed her satisfaction with engaging with the call centre in following manner:

... dealing with your Call Centre guys is JUST GREAT ... once you give them the membership number they have the information on their fingertips. Also the folks just seem to be enjoying what they're doing ..a pleasure to deal with ... (Online feedback, June 2001, line 218).

In a typical conversation, the call-centre consultant can play multiple roles, including distilling the information from her system, interpreting it by quickly reviewing historical transactions, and, by combining knowledge of the product and member, offer reasonable solutions to the problem. So the call-centre consultant is also a financial advisor, product expert, and information interpreter - in essence a knowledge worker. In her dialogue with the member she is able to provide an understanding of the problem and opinions based on sound experience. In addition, she has the ability to display empathy, which provides that personal touch which is essential in dialogues that are both sensitive and controversial, such as a query over funds.

Davenport and Prusak (1998, p. 5) define knowledge as follows:

Knowledge is a fluid mix of framed experience, values, contextual information, and expert insight that provides a framework for evaluating and incorporating experiences and information. It originates and is applied in the minds of the knowers. In organisations, it often becomes embedded not only in documents and repositories but in organisational routines, processes, practices and norms.

From this perspective of knowledge, the embedding of the call-centre consultant's work routines was evidently more complex than the programming of Web applications that represented the key call reasons of members. Moreover, informational asymmetries are evident between the customer and the call-centre professional. The service user engages with the call-centre professional from a position of dependency, and the call-centre expert determines what is in the member's best interest, based on his or her professional judgment (Laing et al., 2004). Furthermore, in using the self-service technology, the user is responsible for navigating the pages, finding the information, and expending effort to establish why his or her funds were depleted. In this way, the user interface provides a key contrast when compared with traditional services (Gummerus et al., 2004). However, the user interface is limited to displaying the functionality and content organisation. Thus it supports the look, feel and usability of the ISST, and only passively facilitates the interaction. On the other hand, the call-centre consultant's value is inherent in the ability to dynamically interpret the text. The Web relies on the user for this function and, given the technical complexity of consumer-driven healthcare products in general, this counts as a limitation.

In ANT terms then, the interrelated roles of the call-centre consultant cannot be easily defined and attributed to the Web actor for acceptance. Making the Web front-end function as effective as a call-centre consultant would result in a long and difficult set of negotiations – as future redesign attempts will reveal. Customising a message to address a specific user problem and packaging it into a personalised response is a complex task that human actors tend to dominate. This applies in particular to follow-up queries of a financial nature, such as unpaid or rejected claims, chronic medicine queries, third-party payments, errors with statements, and high-risk transactions, such as hospital authorisation or travel bookings.

Opening the black box of the call-centre consultant then reveals many more actors, many more roles, and many more associations that are not amenable to the Web technology. The telephone was inscribed in the membership card and in the firm's correspondence to members in the form of the claim statements, magazines, fact files and so on. In other words, the telephone number was ready at hand. The rapid increase of cellphones in South Africa further strengthened the ties of the member to the call centre. Even while members were mobile, they had access to the call centre. It is therefore not surprising that the users still contacted the call centre. To add to this, the batch mode of processing meant that the call-centre applications often had information that was timelier than the website. For these reasons, the call-centre channel displayed properties of irreversibility. Successful networks require that allies

Figure 5. Sample membership card

think and act in a way that maintains the network. In contrast, the online service was being negatively hampered by the poor ICT infrastructure provided by the monopoly service provider at the time. Although the firm invested in a virtual ISP arrangement with a leading Internet service provider (ISP) company, this did not appear to alleviate the 'speed' problem. One of the users noted:

Even with a dedicated 64K ISDN line, I have not managed to get to any page I tried to access. Please ensure that there is either more bandwidth for access or the system does not bump you off in too short a time (Online feedback, October 2001, line 533).

The comments from frustrated users suggested that the site had been designed for broadband users. For those home users with a 28.8 k modem, the site would be difficult to access. The typical webpage size was only about 150 k. However, 150 k + the additional 128-bit encryption, made the pages sizeable. Secure Sockets Layer (SSL) would set up an encrypted session between a client and a server using 128-bit session keys once the user logged on. It was assumed that the users would feel more secure in their interaction once the yellow padlock appeared on the bottom of their browser. However, security concerns would exacerbate speed issues. Suggestions included limiting the encryption to areas containing transactional information. However, the custodians of branding and corporate security policy standards – represented by marketing and internal auditing – curtailed these options. The irony is that as computing and networking power increased with the advent of the Internet, there was a pressing need to increase security measures and censor information.

For the most part, even in the context of slow and costly access, the majority of HIC's members simply did not have access to the online service from home. At work, most employers were imposing restrictions on employees against using SSTs in order to alleviate productivity and security concerns. By design then, the online service was accentuating further the social exclusion of marginalised and impoverished members by creating 'information haves' and 'information have-nots'. And even for those members who did have access to the Internet, the openness of the Internet standard was contestable, as members using different browsers continued to undergo varied experiences. As has been shown, the ISST can be described as a heterogeneous network consisting of varied technologies, networks, and standards to support a diversity of application areas over time and space (Hanseth & Monteiro, 1997). At the time, Microsoft and Netscape, the two popular browsers, were in a 'battle' to become the browser standard setter. So while eHIC was attempting to become the dominant service channel, these firms were attempting to grow their install base. Their lack of consensus was creating confusion among HICs consumers as well as software developers. In these early stages many users expressed disappointment that the site was not compatible with their browser versions. For example:

I use a iMac with Internet Explorer 5. Given that IE5 for the Mac and IE5 for Windows support the exact same features with full java support etc. I fail to see why your site disallows my browser. The only reason I can think of is that your programmers never thought it possible that someone with a Mac would want to use the site. I trust that this can be fixed quite quickly (Online feedback, July 2001, line 558).

These examples make it clear that the ICT infrastructure, browser and operating system standards interacted with internal system differences between Magic and Java – and the various beliefs by actors such as management, designers, other departments and users about the role of the Web – to affect the extent to which the SST could become the dominant channel. In contrast to the traditional call-centre channel, stable networks or aligned interests with allies of the SST could not be maintained. Given the properties of irreversibility demonstrated by the traditional channels, there was a realisation among the senior management team that the 'substitution claims' may have been far-fetched. These views are noted in the following comments:

When the dot bomb started happening, you know, the realisation of what happened is that, maybe it really wasn't this tsunami ... (CIO Health Systems, interview 36, pp. 1-2).

From a landscape point of view we may have been a bit blind to the fact that connectivity levels and even on dial-up at that stage were abysmal ... (Community head, interview 49, pp. 1-2).

When the dotcom bomb started, the role of e-commerce in the organisation was subject to further internal evaluation. The inability to deliver the initial projects on time, as well as the inability to convert a majority of the members to the online channel, meant that the intention to substitute the call centre and become the channel of choice was compromised. This led to a shift in strategy as well as a change in the way that the e-commerce organisation was structured to improve internal alignment as well as inter-departmental relationships. While there was still a focus on efficient servicing, major emphasis was being placed on a new paradigm that was emerging, one where the organisation sought to 'dazzle users' with online tools designed to support its new Wellness program.

DISCUSSION AND IMPLICATIONS

From this discussion, using a socio-technical conception of implementation allows us to conclude that the translation of the actors within this ISST's context, failed to achieve its substitution claims and the desired outcome as the preferred channel. The initial network and its loosely formulated OPP – 'to become the channel of choice' – were readily accepted internally by a few of the key senior executives, but remained too weak to mobilise a sufficiently strong network to become the dominant channel. One of the reasons for this outcome was that the advocates of the traditional call-centre channel were aligned with powerful socio-technical networks inside and outside the organisation, so that the substitution vision had to be reformulated. Naturally, a loose formulation of goals such as 'the preferred channel' was not sufficiently convincing for those managers and staff that represented the traditional channels the SST was attempting to substitute. More specifically, during this implementation journey, the interactions with human and non-human actors supporting the traditional channels would be more contentious than collaborative. In this spiralling innovative climate, and increasingly demanding service environment as a result of rapid client membership growth, achieving synergy between departments would prove particularly problematic, largely owing to the various actors having to facilitate multiple and conflicting agendas. As a result, negotiations were often beset by 'clashes' of interest, and these conflicts sometimes became irresolvable.

Successful translations also depend on how faithful key external actors are towards their alliances. Certainly, the local South African ICT infrastructure was not supportive of a self-servicing environment for a majority of the members. Furthermore, standards and security were impeding the Web channel, compared with the traditional channel. In addition, the poor interoperability with internal systems designed to support internal processes, and the lack of technical skills of the newly appointed development team, translated into unsuccessful and unstable translations between internal actors.

While some of the key human actors internally such as the designers of the ISST were convinced of its value, most of the external users were not. Attempts to mobilise, expand and stabilise the majority of users turned out to be complex and frustrating. For the majority of clients, the call centre channel clearly had a better inscription than the web. Allied to the telephone was the membership card, with a membership number and telephone number, which could easily fit into a member's wallet, while a user name and password remained a cognitive challenge. There were simply too many things attached to the use of the call centre. The competing call-centre channel in alliance with the frozen network element of the telephone was now being acknowledged as a black box. While it certainly acquires the features of a black-box for creating and strengthening other network associations, the ISST does not appear to be a convincing inscription for the majority of its users who are placed outside the organisation.

ANT also reveals that many external users used the technology differently from what was inscribed into it. Unlike information systems in the work context, where designers are close to the users and can be prescriptive, and therefore the network into which the intended user behaviour is inscribed is stronger, external users in the context of multiple channels have much more discretion in their use. In other words, despite efforts of designers to customise the channels for segmented audiences, the trend was clearly towards users customising the use of channels to suit their own personal tastes. In this multi-channel context, designers appeared to be at the mercy of what individual users chose to do and how they elected to respond. Ironically, it seems that the essence of being an empowered healthcare customer is not in merely using the Web, but in having the ability to choose from among multiple channels. Weak inscriptions demonstrated by the allies of the ISST and their inability to act in ways that maintained the network led to many members persisting with the use of traditional channels. In this health insurance services context then, Internet-based self-service technologies are deemed most appropriately as a complementary service channel.

CONCLUSION

This paper has argued that researchers and practitioners alike can gain by viewing IS implementation through ANT's socio-technical lens. While conventional theories such as CRM and diffusion suggest that the success of a ISST depends on the ability to retain a critical mass of users, ANT demonstrates how by enrolling other key stakeholder groups with diverse interests to align their interests with the technology, relatively stable technological arrangements can still be created, despite relatively poor use. Notions of continual use as a predictor of IS success are dismissed in an ANT analysis (Bhattacherjee, 2001). Instead, an ISST is deemed successful if networks of aligned interests are created through the enrolment of a sufficient body of allies, and the translation of their interests so that they are willing to participate in particular ways of thinking and acting which maintain the network (Walsham, 1993; Introna & Whitley, 1999). These allies do not necessarily need to be users of the system. After all, there is the politics pursued by health insurance firms and their allies in their encounter with governments, employers, intermediaries, regulators, technology vendors and existing and potential insured members to drive the 'consumer-driven healthcare movement'. The inscribed implication is that the individual should be responsible for his or her own healthcare. After all, the Internet has the ability to "empower the individual", or so the story goes. In this case proponents of the SST had to concede to definition imposed by user behaviour which supported the notion of a 'complementary channel'. Yet, a great deal of rhetoric surrounds ISSTs as being able to empower individuals who are patrons of consumer-driven healthcare products and services. Despite the current irreversibility of call-centres, healthcare insurers may continue to translate the appropriateness of ISSTs as an 'empowerment device' into carefully phrased restatements of fact in order to support their broader political and financial agenda. For now at least existing embedded relationships between the healthcare insured member and the call centre agent appears irreversible or resistant to change.

ACKNOWLEDGMENT

The author would like to thank Kevin C. Desouza for helpful comments on this paper. The author is also grateful to Tim Dröge for making this research possible.

REFERENCES

Bhattacherjee, A. (2001). An empirical analysis of the antecedents of electronic commerce service continuance. *Decision Support Systems*, *32*, 201–214. doi:10.1016/S0167-9236(01)00111-7

Bitner, M. J., Ostrom, A. L., & Meuter, M. L. (2002). Implementing Successful Self-Service Technology. *The Academy of Management Executive*, *16*(4), 96–108.

Butler, T. (1998). Towards a Hermeneutic Method for Interpretive Research in Information Systems. *Journal of Information Technology*, *13*, 285–300. doi:10.1057/jit.1998.7

Butler, T. (2003). An institutional perspective on developing and implementing intranet-and Internet based information systems. *Information Systems Journal*, *13*, 209–231. doi:10.1046/j.1365-2575.2003.00151.x

Callon, M. (1986). Some elements of sociology of translation; domestication of the scallops and the fisherman of St Brieuc Bay. In Law, J. (Ed.), *Power, Action and Belief. A New Sociology of Knowledge*. London: Routledge.

Callon, M. (1991). Techno-economic networks and irreversibility. In Law, J. (Ed.), *A Sociology of Monsters: Essays on Power, Technology and Domination*. London: Routledge.

Darke, P., Shanks, G., & Broadbent, M. (1998). Successfully Completing Case Study Research: Combining Rigor, Relevance and Pragmatism. *Information Systems Journal*, *8*, 273–289. doi:10.1046/j.1365-2575.1998.00040.x

Davenport, T. H., & Prusak, L. (1998). *Working Knowledge*. Boston: Harvard Business School Press.

Delone, W. H., & McLean, E. R. (1992). Information systems success: The quest for the dependant variable. *Information Systems Research, 3*(1), 60–95. doi:10.1287/isre.3.1.60

Dutta, A., & Roy, R. (2004). A Process Oriented Framework for Justifying IT Projects in eBusiness Environments. *International Journal of Electronic Commerce, 9*(1), 49–68.

Faraj, S., Kwon, D., & Watts, S. (2004). Contested artifact: technology sensemaking, actor networks, and the shaping of the Web browser. *Information Technology & People, 17*(2), 186–209. doi:10.1108/09593840410542501

Gummerus, J., Liljander, V., Pura, M., & van Riel, A. (2004). Customer loyalty to content based Web sites: The case of an online health-care service. *Journal of Services Marketing, 18*(2), 175–186. doi:10.1108/08876040410536486

Hannemeyr, G. (2003). The Internet as Hyperbole: A Critical Examination of Adoption Rates. *The Information Society, 19*, 111–121. doi:10.1080/01972240309459

Hanseth, O., & Aanestad, M. (2004). Actor-network theory and information systems: What's so special? *Information Technology & People, 17*(2), 116–123. doi:10.1108/09593840410542466

Hanseth, O., & Monteiro, E. (1997). Inscribing Behaviour in Information Infrastructure Standards. *Accounting, Management & Information Technology, 7*(4), 183–211. doi:10.1016/S0959-8022(97)00008-8

Introna, L. D., & Whitley, E. A. (1999). Limiting the Web: The politics of search engines. *IEEE Computer, 33*(1), 54–62.

Kwon, T. H., & Zmud, R. W. (1987). Unifying the fragmented models of information systems implementation. In Boland, R. J., & Hirscheim, R. A. (Eds.), *Critical Issues in Information Systems Research*. New York: John Wiley & Sons.

Laing, A., Hogg, G., & Winkleman, D. (2004). Health Care and the Information Revolution: reconfiguring the healthcare service encounter. *Health Services Management Research, 17*(3), 188–199. doi:10.1258/0951484041485584

Lang, J. R., & Collen, A. (2005). Evaluating Personal Health Care and Health Promotion Web Sites. *Methods of Information in Medicine, 44*, 328–333.

Latour, B. (1986). The powers of association. In Law, J. (Ed.), *Power, Action and Belief. A New Sociology of Knowledge*. London: Routledge.

Latour, B. (1987). Technology is society made durable. In Law, J. (Ed.), *A sociology of monsters, Essays on power, technology and domination* (pp. 103–131). London: Routledge.

Latour, B. (1991). Technology is society made durable. In Law, J. (Ed.), *A Sociology of Monsters, Essays on Power, Technology, and Domination*. London: Routledge.

Latour, B. (2005). *Reassembling the Social: An Introduction to Actor-Network Theory*. Oxford, UK: Oxford University Press.

Lucas, H. C. (1981). *Implementation: Key to Successful Information Systems*. New York: Columbia University Press.

Lyytinen, K., & Hirscheim, R. (1987). Information system failures: A survey and classification of the empirical literature. *Oxford Survey in Information Technology, 4*, 257–309.

Mahring, M., Holmstrom, J., Keil, M., & Montealegre, R. (2004). Trojan actor-networks and swift translation: Bringing actor-network theory to IT project escalation studies. *Information Technology & People*, *17*(2), 210–238. doi:10.1108/09593840410542510

Markus, M. L., & Pfeffer, J. (1983). Power and the design and implementation of accounting and control systems. *Accounting, Organizations and Society*, *8*(2), 205–218. doi:10.1016/0361-3682(83)90028-4

Meuter, M. L., Ostrom, A. L., Roundtree, R. I., & Bitner, M. J. (2000). Self-Service Technologies: Understanding Customer Satisfaction with Technology-Based Encounters. *Journal of Marketing*, *64*, 50–64. doi:10.1509/jmkg.64.3.50.18024

Monteiro, E. (2000). Actor-Network Theory and Information Infrastructure. In C. U. Ciborra, K. Braa, & A. C ordella (Eds.), *From Control to drift: the dynamics of corporate information infrastructures* (pp. 71-83). Oxford, UK: Oxford University Press.

Moser, I., & Law, J. (2006). Fluid or Flows? Information and qualculation in medical practice. *Information Technology & People*, *19*(1), 55–73. doi:10.1108/09593840610649961

Muhr, T., & Friese, S. (2004). *User's Manual for ATLAS.ti 5.0* (2nd ed.). Berlin: Scientific Software Development.

Myers, M. D. (1994). A disaster for everyone to see: An interpretive analysis of a failed IS project. *Accounting, Management & Information Technology*, *4*(4), 185–201. doi:10.1016/0959-8022(94)90022-1

Naidoo, R., & Leonard, A. (2007). Perceived usefulness, service quality and loyalty incentives: Effects on electronic service continuance. *South African Journal of Business Management*, *38*(3), 39–48.

Naidoo, R., & Leonard, A. (2009). Tracing the many translations of a Web-based IT artefact. In Cunha, M. M., Oliveira, E., Tavares, A., & Ferreira, L. (Eds.), *Handbook of Research on Social Dimensions of Semantic Technologies and Web Services*. Portugal: Polytechnic Institute of Cavado and Ave.

Pandya, A., & Dholakia, N. (2005). B2C Failures: Towards an Innovation Theory Framework. *Journal of Electronic Commerce in Organizations*, *3*(2), 68–81.

Parasuraman, A., & Zinkhan, G. M. (2002). Marketing to and Serving Customers Through the Internet: An Overview and Research Agenda. *Journal of the Academy of Marketing Science*, *30*(4), 286–295. doi:10.1177/009207002236906

Robertson, N., & Shaw, R. (2005). Conceptualizing the Influence of the Self-Service Technology Context on Consumer Voice. *Services Marketing Quarterly*, *27*(2), 33–50. doi:10.1300/J396v27n02_03

Rogers, E. M. (1995). *Diffusion of Innovations* (3rd ed.). New York: Free Press.

Sabherwal, R., & Robey, D. (1993). An empirical taxonomy of implementation processes based on sequence of events in information systems development. *Organization Science*, *4*(4), 548–576. doi:10.1287/orsc.4.4.548

Sahay, S., & Robey, D. (1996). Organizational Context, Social Interpretation, and the Implementation and Consequences of Geographic Information Systems. *Accounting, Management & Information Technology*, *6*(4), 255–282. doi:10.1016/S0959-8022(96)90016-8

Schultze, U., & Orlikowski, W. (2004). A practice perspective on technology-mediated network relations: The use of Internet-based self-serve technologies. *Information Systems Research*, *15*(1), 87–106. doi:10.1287/isre.1030.0016

Swanson, E. B. (1988). *Information System Implementation: Bridging the Gap between Design and Utilisation*. Irwin, Canada: Homewood.

Swanson, E. B., & Ramiller, N. C. (2004). Innovating mindfully with information technology. *Management Information Systems Quarterly*, *28*(4), 553–583.

Tatnall, A. (2001, June). How Visual Basic Entered the Curriculum at an Australian University: An Account Informed by Innovation Translation. *Informing Science*, 510–517.

Tatnall, A., & Gilding, A. (1999). Actor-Network Theory and Information Systems Research. In *Proceedings of the 10th Australasian Conference on Information Systems* (pp. 955-966).

Walsham, G. (1993). *Interpreting Information Systems in Organizations*. New York: John Wiley & Sons.

Walsham, G. (2001). *Making a World of Difference: IT in a Global Context*. New York: John Wiley & Sons.

Yin, R. K. (1999b). Enhancing the Quality of Case Studies in Health Services Research. *Health Services Research*, *34*(1), 1209–1218.

Zeithaml, V. A., Parasuraman, A., & Malhotra, A. (2002). Service Quality Delivery Through Web Sites: A Critical Review of Extant Knowledge. *Journal of the Academy of Marketing Science*, *30*(4), 362–375. doi:10.1177/009207002236911

This work was previously published in International Journal of Actor-Network Theory and Technological Innovation, Volume 2, Issue 2, edited by Arthur Tatnall, pp. 17-38, copyright 2010 by IGI Publishing (an imprint of IGI Global).

Chapter 6
How to Recognize an Immutable Mobile When You Find One:
Translations on Innovation and Design

Fernando Abreu Gonçalves
CEG-IST, Portugal

José Figueiredo
Technical University of Lisbon, Instituto Superior Técnico, Portugal

ABSTRACT

Research involved with Actor-Network Theory (ANT) application in engineering domains often crosses through its fundamentals. In fact, exploring trends that envisage ANT as a paradigm that can prove valid in the engineering design field, researchers sometimes enrol in discussions that drive them to its roots. Obligatory Passage Points (OPP) and Immutable Mobiles (IM) are two of the fundamental concepts that need to be revisited. These concepts are critical to understanding innovation in Actor-Networks, especially for the part of IMs. In the pursuit of that understanding, the authors opt to entangle ANT and engineering design and explore a framework based on Programs of Action where actors are represented as taxonomies of competences. These actors are hybrids but, when human, they are mainly engineers engaged in the scope planning and resource management in engineering design projects or processes. This article exercises and develops a constructive process towards a methodology to approach innovation in engineering design. This research is useful for the first stages of the project design process and, in a broader way, to the full cycle of the engineering design process.

DOI: 10.4018/978-1-4666-1559-5.ch006

INTRODUCTION

We are exploring ways to build practical methodological approaches to engineering design inspired in ANT. In particular we are concerned with the contribution of the concept of IM, (Latour, 1987) and other ANT constructs, namely OPPs and PAs (Latour et al., 1992), to support engineering design and innovation strategies. In this sense we intend to use ANT not only to describe behaviors, but also to support a new approach to engineering design.

To do that in a sound way we needed to build our research on theoretical ANT grounds which took us to review some of the central concepts in this "Theory". The title of this paper is the result of fresh discussions we entailed concerning the centrality of the concept of IM in innovation and/or engineering design.

The aim of the paper can be divided in two main goals. The first one is to explore the meaning of some ANT constructs, namely the meaning of IM, an all present concept sometimes confusing and seldom addressed in a systematic way. Then we apply this research to propose a method to follow engineers "in the making" of design (Callon, 1987). This method is deeply supported and imbedded in the ANT fundamentals and is focused on an application to project scope management in engineering design approaches.

Describing innovation processes is not the same as providing explanations of innovation, (Latour, 1991a, 1996) and what we intend is to gain some understanding of the innovation process as a chain of translations. We undertook a review of the literature, a wide and scrupulously chosen sample, contextualized some engineering design processes, distilled some ANT basics, and tried a proposal for the development of a methodological approach to project scope management. Finally we illustrate the use of the methodological framework in a case study as a *thought description*, a "way of knowing" (Schneider & Ingram, 2007). We finally draw some conclusions.

ENGINEERING DESIGN

Ralph Ford and Chris Coulston (2007) defines the Engineering Design domain as a sequence of steps (with iterations) that can be grouped into a *process phase* (Problem Identification, Requirements Specification, and Concept Generation) and a *technological phase* (Detailed Design, Prototyping and Construction, System Integration, System Test, Delivery & Acceptance, and Maintenance & Upgrade), as we depict in Figure 1.

Project Management can be seen as an engineering process where managing and defining scope acquires special importance. Being sometimes poor listeners and too much confident in the possibilities of technology, we, engineers, need to be aware that it is from the quality of these first phases of project management/and engineering design processes that much is earned to the final quality of the product to be designed and developed.

The *process phase* (design) is critical to the definition of the scope of any engineering design project and the view that the design process is not only a technological endeavor but also a social one has already invaded even the most pure technological domains (Cagan et al., 2001). These authors propose a method that intending to manage the "fuzzy front end of product development" recognizes a socio-technical co-evolution of products and markets.

In this schema the transition from Analysis to Development is through translation, a concept that we can intend as "our" ANT basic operation. Our approach to scope management in engineering design projects is constructed trough looking at the design process as something that has to do with the assemblage of things: designers, users, different supports and artifacts, that is, actors. Engineers must assemble things, durable things, but in order to do it creatively they also need to disassemble things. Engineers should be aware of how translation can be a potent instrument to address social concerns as they build their technical systems.

Figure 1. A comprehensive view of the engineering design process - adapted from (Ford & Chris Coulston, 2007)

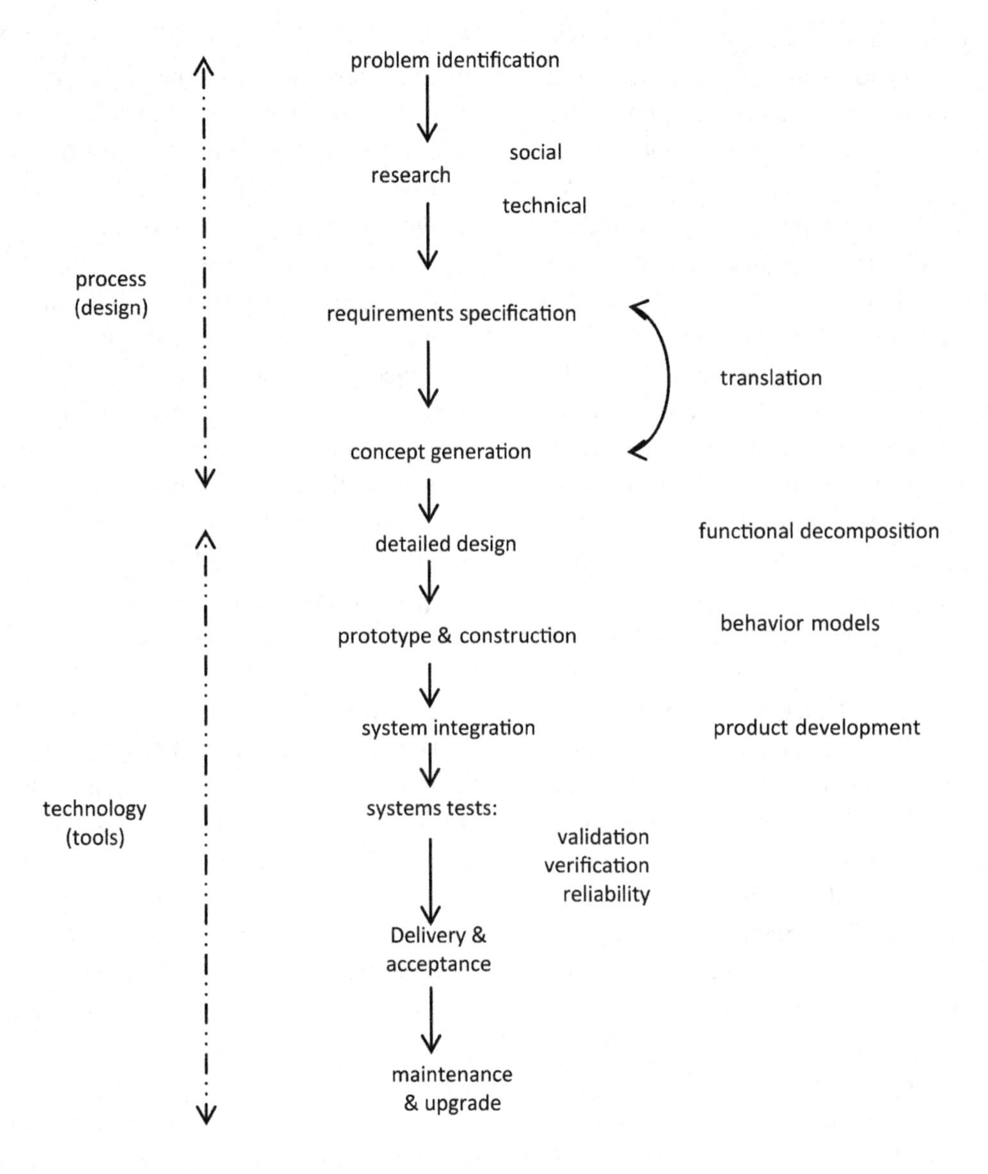

ANT FUNDAMENTALS

Obligatory Points of Passage – OPPs

Following a constructivist approach in our research we have been looking to how we can build upon relevant work already made by others. The view of translation as a "geography of obligatory points of passage" was proposed by Callon (1986a). An OPP is the first component of translation, the *translator*: an entity (a thing) in an *actors-world* that intent to speak on behalf of other actors of that world translating in a way that fits together their interests and behaviors. An alignment of interests on the things involved.

On this subject Law (1986, 1992) considers "network consolidation" the way "networks may come to look like a single point (actor)". The very

Figure 2. Placements and displacements, reductions and amplifications – adapted from (Latour, 1993)

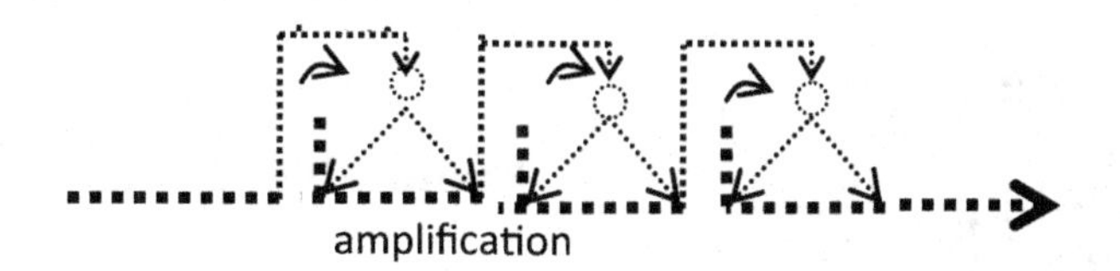

same concept is addressed by Callon (1991) as 'punctualised' organizational actors. Entities, in an earlier ANT perspective, are "actants" (Latour, 1987) that according to the "generalized symmetry principle" (Callon, 1986b) can be all sort of things, humans or artifacts. Nowadays we should address the actor-network mainly as a space of interactions, negotiations and relations. It is in fact a space of action, not entities.

To succeed in its translations the translator attributes roles to other actors and mobilizes them for a *problematisation* that he entails and designs. Then other moments of translation (Callon, 1986b) follow: *interessement, enrolment, and mobilization.*

Inscriptions and Displacements

The translation process needs a support, "aligned interests [are] inscribed into durable material" (Law, 1992). This leads us to the concept of inscription, a concept that has gained a special status in social studies mainly due to the works by Latour and Woolgar (1979).

Inscriptions are embodiments of usage patterns: "Technical objects thus simultaneously embody and measure a set of relations between heterogeneous elements" (Akrich, 1992); and "A large part of the work of innovators is that of inscribing their vision of the world in the technical content of a new object".

Another component of the translation process is the concept of "displacement". Callon (1986a) lists inscriptions as a main type of displacement and says that, to be effective, the network translation implies "displacement" (Callon, 1986a): "otherwise the action at a distance involved in enrolling actors will remain mysterious" (Callon, 1986b; Law, 1986; Latour, 1987).

This concept of displacement is normally associated with Euclidian space but nowadays is more and more related with symbolic spaces. In fact the notion of "displacement" between states is also used to build representations of data in digital systems, Wells (1976). Latour (1990) asserts that the "cascading" of translations that allow actor-networks to go to "simpler and simpler inscriptions that mobilize larger and larger numbers of events in one spot" has been greatly facilitated by their homogeneous treatment as binary units in and by computers". In the IM subsection we will see the relevance of the concept of displacement in relation with the concept of IM.

Reductions and Amplifications, Framing and Summing Up

In Social systems there are infinite opportunities to act by displacements, transformations and codifications, Latour (1988). Using the literal meaning of trans-lation Latour (1990) equates translations to displacements. To deal with the "terrain of *connaisance*" Latour proposes a chain of translations, a reversible chain that transverses things and words. As the translation process unfolds new proposals follow and placements and displacements occur in a process of reductions and amplifications leading to a centre, as we try to represent in Figure 3, adapted from (Latour, 1993).

Figure 3. Mediation uncertainty

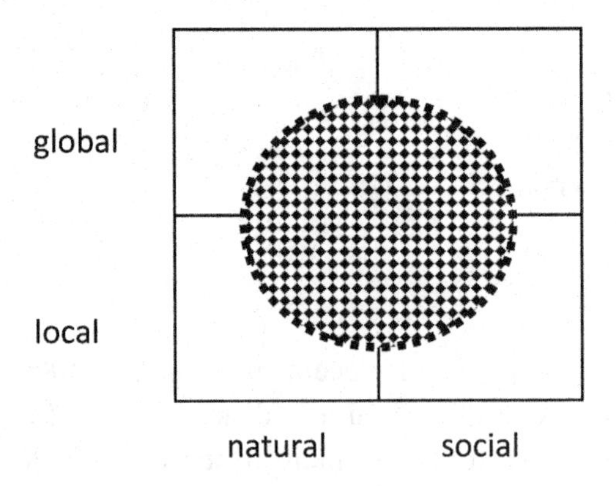

In his keynote speech "On Recalling ANT" Latour (1998) proposes, to avoid mechanistic interpretations of the concepts of actor and network, the use of two operations, "framing" and "summing up", exploring the idea of dealing with different scales and with superimpositions of inscriptions. This view shows that translation, *per se*, does not necessarily add anything useful so we need to look for something to "frame" and "summing-up" and pick some physical thing in the making of a proposal, in a translation process with placements and displacements, reductions and amplifications: "One place gathers in all the others and presents them synoptically to the dissenter so as to modify the outcome of an agonistic encounter" (Latour, 1990).

Competition between Centres of Translation

One centre is never alone so we need to consider several centres of translation, competing and transforming themselves in diverse ways, instead of focusing in only one centre of translation that capitalizes on transformations. This shows that the work of mediation (reductions and amplifications, framing and summing-up) cannot be done without uncertainties. That is what we intend to show with Figure 3 adapted from Latour (1991b).

The idea of social is something between "agency" and "structure", between "macro-social" and "micro-social".

Immutable Mobiles

Latour (1990) describes the concept of IM by means of an enumeration of "the advantages of paper-work" as inscriptions:

- Mobile
- Immutable
- Flat
- Modifiable in scale
- Easily reproducible

And, as a consequence, inscriptions are easily:

- Combined
- Superimposed with inscriptions of different origins
- Integrated into texts

This list ends with an advantage that the author considers as the utmost:

- Being flat, inscriptions allow to be merged with other dimensions, building "re-representations" of objects.

A way to comprehend the work done by IMs is through the concept of "Boundary Object", (Star & Griesemer, 1989). These authors propose the following list of ways of constructing Boundary Objects:

1. Repertoires,
2. Ideal types,
3. Coincident Boundaries
4. Standardized forms.

This fourth way, Standardized forms, is equated to IMs but, as argued by (Figueiredo, 2004), all these types can be thought as being an extension of the concept of IM, opinion we will adopt here.

Law in collaboration with Annemarie Mol (Mol & Law, 1994) and (Law, 2003) contributed with an interpretation of "space and spacialities" in ANT. They address displacements but with different types of spaces: fluids - a kind of "Mutable Mobile" object; regions - "Immutable Immobile" object; network – the place for IMs; and fires - "Mutable Immobiles". Boudourides (2001) has also elaborated in a similar approach.

We agree that there are two ways to circulate inscriptions (Latour, 1993): one is to use it as a norm, as it is, without any innovation, the other is to transform it to sustain and increase the alignment – "to capitalize to the centre". Latour also uses the concept of 'acceleration': 'on passe de mobiles immuables à d'autres encore plus mobiles, encore mieux combinables et toujours plus immuables. Ce qui change – car quelque chose change en effet – c'est l'accélération des déplacements sans transformations' (Latour, 1985).

As we intend to reuse the concept of translation for the study of innovation (Akrich et al., 2002, Part I & II) we opt on mixing two approaches, exploring the richness of Latour's definition of IM, contextualized with Callon's concept of translation: "geography of obligatory points of passage". OPPs are our centers of translation and an IM inscribes something as a go-between in a social space of OPPs, being good enough to find ways to capitalize to a centre. Looking at the positions of OPPs in spaces may give us some information on their strategies and the means to find simpler and simpler ways to allow for a network to grow.

Having revisited and reflected on the fundamentals of ANT we are now ready to explain our Framework in next Section.

Programs of Action and Taxonomies as a Methodological Framework

To focus on the work of learned professionals as it is the case of engineering design professionals and to explore the concept of actor we use, as inscriptions, profiles of competences. We take a generic definition of competences as building blocks of knowledge, encompassing skills, provided that it should be possible to look at competences as something that entails an effective action.

Speaking in a context of literature, Latour (2008) offered a view of IM that we may take to illustrate our use of competences. He looks at IMs as a way to articulate the distinction between "metaphor" and "literal": an IM is an evolutionary script always "between a metaphor and a literal" in the sense that it shares the behavior of an actor enrolling other actors (promoting change) and the behavior of a black-box, a stabilized actor, for example a norm or a standard.

The names of competences may be seen as "metaphors" that turn more and more concrete as the work of translation progress. And considering that a first thing to align is to agree on some division, or classification of the matters, we endow actors with some (provisional) structure of competences – taxonomies - as depicted in the tree represented in Figure 4.

We already have an idea of how translation process develops (OPPs "speak on behalf of other actors"). But describing translations is a complex task especially if you want some resolution (detail). This was the problem that led Callon to introduce the notion of actor-network as a "simplification" (Callon, 1986b).

To describe scripts (translations) in an extreme simplification suitable for our purposes we use tables as representation of socio-technical graphs (Latour et al., 1992) where we follow the negotiation process of translations (acceptances and/or rejections) of competences.

We name these tables Programs of Action (PA) adapting a description by Latour et al. (1992). We have a two-dimensional chart depicting a succession of proposals (paradigms) along a vertical axis (logical OR axis) where different proposals substitute one after another and a succession of syntagms along a horizontal axis (logical AND axis) where associations among actors align, Figure 5.

Proposals and alignments are issued by actors that are 'collections' of professional competences, or artifact's specifications. We explore situations where actants endowed with no a priori profiles of competences become actors, engage in some tasks, and negotiate with other actors in the network in a specific setting. In the course of these negotiations, profiles of competences may alter (translation) and some relevant innovation eventually emerges. At the end, a particular combination of competences will emerge within the PA. This "end" can be reached, for example, by the alignment of all actors involved (they will be all in the same side of the PA) – a black box. Another way of ending may be detected when there is a lack of competences – a trigger for innovation. In this situation the setting changes, (Gonçalves & Figueiredo, 2007).

Where do competences come from? Recognizing that within a professional context (setting) some competences will be generally accepted we will obtain our list of competences from local best practices and experience. This allows us also to address symmetry among actors, being humans or artifacts.

Figure 4. A tree of competence names

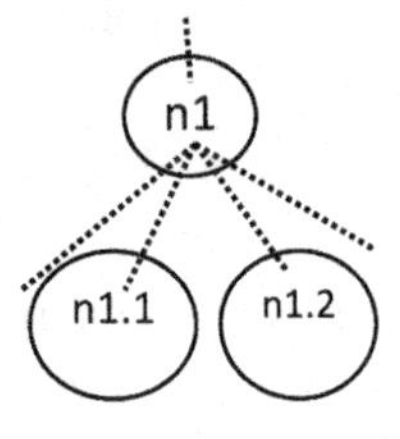

Figure 5. Program of action

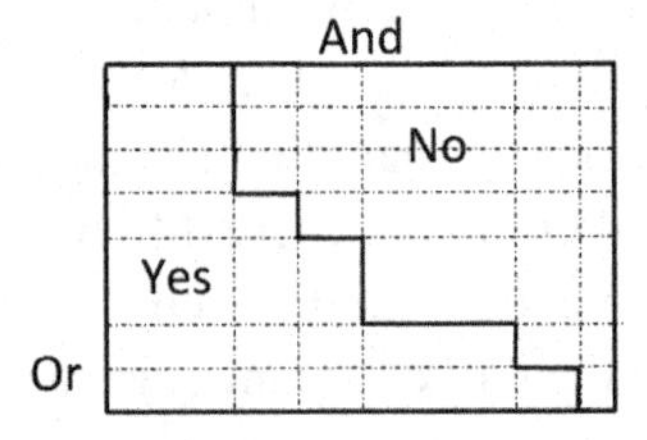

Due Process

A PA is always travelled downwards. This movement is performed diagonally in two components: an AND movement and an OR movement (see Figure 6). The AND movement means some compatibility (adherence) among competences, competences are added. The OR movement means substitution, you alter competences. The OR movement looks more problematic than the AND movement. How to devise new (useful) proposals? How to solve a situation of lacking of competences?

A PA develops within a setting, a situated context for change, where actors may enter and exit. The entry (or exiting) of a new actor can be constructed through a "due process". This term was explored in the context of Artificial Intelligence by Hewitt (1986), a scholar and researcher of this field. Within the ANT context it was used by Latour (1998). Latour addressed three stages to be applied to reject or to accept a new actor in a community (a setting): introducing the actor, asking about its contribution to the community setting, and finally, rejecting or accepting by means of adapting the setting to accommodate the actor (change, evolution, innovation) (Figueiredo, 2004).

Gerson and Star (1986) have shown how a due process can be used to produce boundary objects (IMs). In our framework actors will be followed in several settings so we need a way to deal with the transition between settings. In order to build a machine to travel the network Latour (Latour, 1998; Teil & Latour, 1995) borrowed the concept of 'micro-theory" from Hewitt (1986) as a kind of black-box (or OPP) in the network: 'A *micro-theory* is a relatively small, idealized, mathematical theory that embodies a model of some physical system'.

Network travelling is the producing of 'meaningful statements', 'interpretations in the form of

Figure 6. Design as a "matter of concern" process

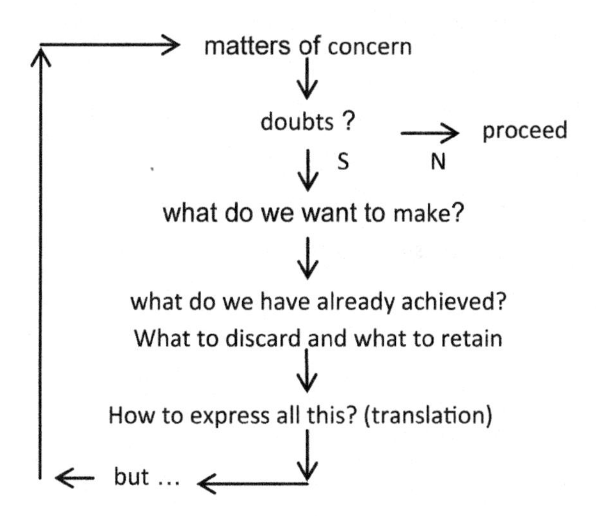

networks possibilities'. This was proposed (Teil & Latour, 1995) on the context of written documents as inscriptions and words as actors. Reflecting the trials of actor-networks the co-occurrences of words in the documents will allow the production of 'meaningful statements about sets of texts in the absence of any micro-theory'.

Translating to the engineering design process our basic blocks are names that denote competences, not words in sentences. And we will take the notion of due process as a comprehensive way to go along the OR axis and to apply the previous rationale to the engineering design process.

Entangling Engineering Design and ANT

In ANT terms a project team is a centre, mobilizing resources to achieve a goal: the product/service to be delivered (artifact). To follow engineering design as a chain of PAs the point of departure inspired by Latour (Latour, 2004, 2007) is to look at a design process from a perspective of 'concerns', not facts. Facts are agreements we settle down when we give up designing anymore. How can we figure a concern here? To see a concern amongst actors is akin to dismantle them, to open the black boxes they have become and reassemble them with other things.

So we picture a situation where someone, something (an actor), states in some way a concern (a problematisation). For instance: someone expressing doubts about a specification of a requirement, or something in the scope that looks odd. We then may achieve a situation where it would be possible to make a decision about a concern on the scope of a project. But decisions have to do with uncertainty. In the process of designing there are uncertainties on what is the thing we want to achieve (prospective object of design) and there are also uncertainties on the way to construct the thing. We then figure a loop of translations that we represent in Figure 6 and is redrawn in Figure 7 as a succession of PAs.

In terms of PAs we identify a focal actor that makes a proposal trying to mobilize other actors to achieve some solution. Some agree and others not, bringing in other details. New proposals may follow until some settlement is reached.

As we have said in order to simplify the discourses we express proposals and consequent answers as taxonomies of features (competences). We expose some competences while hiding others and by the play of the PAs we add/subtract features, enrol other actors, achieve other concerns, until we reach some machination that settle matters.

This way we can look at the engineering design process as a chain of PAs in a space of OPPs.

Scope Management

Scope definition and management are among the most critical processes in project management. Project scope is obtained from project requirements through a series of translations, from project charter, statement of work, environmental factors, organizational process assets, project management methodologies, project communication supports,

Figure 7. Programs of action in engineering design

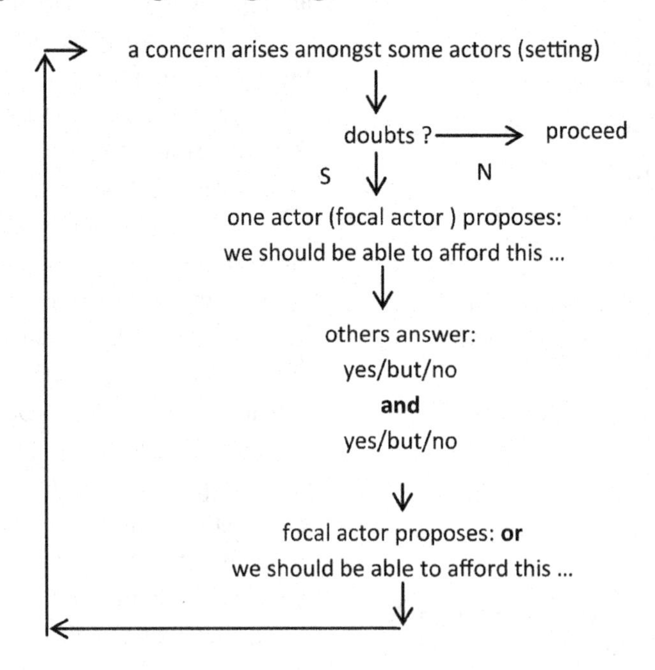

and project information systems (PMBOK Guide, 2004). Project scope management includes the "processes required to ensure that a Project takes care of all the work required, and only the work required, to complete the project successfully" (PMBOK Guide, 2004).

The evolution of project can be seen as a cascade of translations. This way we recognize that as projects evolve irreversibility increases (or it becomes increasingly expensive to change and redefine the scope) although it is always possible, and sometimes mandatory, to review scope and redesign specifications. See Figures 8 and 9.

Applying our framework to scope management in design projects let us try to understand how ANT can help to follow engineers in the making of their work.

We draw a picture to illustrate our framework in Figure 10. The two poles, Names (of Competences) and Literals, structure the space of competences where our IMs will be built. This space will be implemented by means of hierarchies (taxonomies; see also Figure 4).

Popular methods of scope definition as pos-it sessions and brainstorm sessions may be described by means of a cascade of PAs structured this way.

We may apply this view along the full project cycle. That is, the Work Breakdown Structure (WBS) is always provisional. Although it will be more and more costly to do it, there will be, all along the project, scope decisions to be made. In theory it will be possible an infinite succession of redefinitions.

We have here the building of an IM: the "cascade of ever simplified inscriptions that allow harder facts to be produced at greater cost", (Latour, 1990). The challenge is to develop inscriptions allowing suitable artefacts to be produced not paying too much costs. We can propose this assertion because we address projects dealing with innovation, namely engineering design processes.

A particular combination of competences may emerge at the end of a PA but we can also achieve a situation of lack of competences. This situation may represent a trigger to innovation. To illustrate our approach a case where it was possible to do

Figure 8. Project management as a cascade of translations

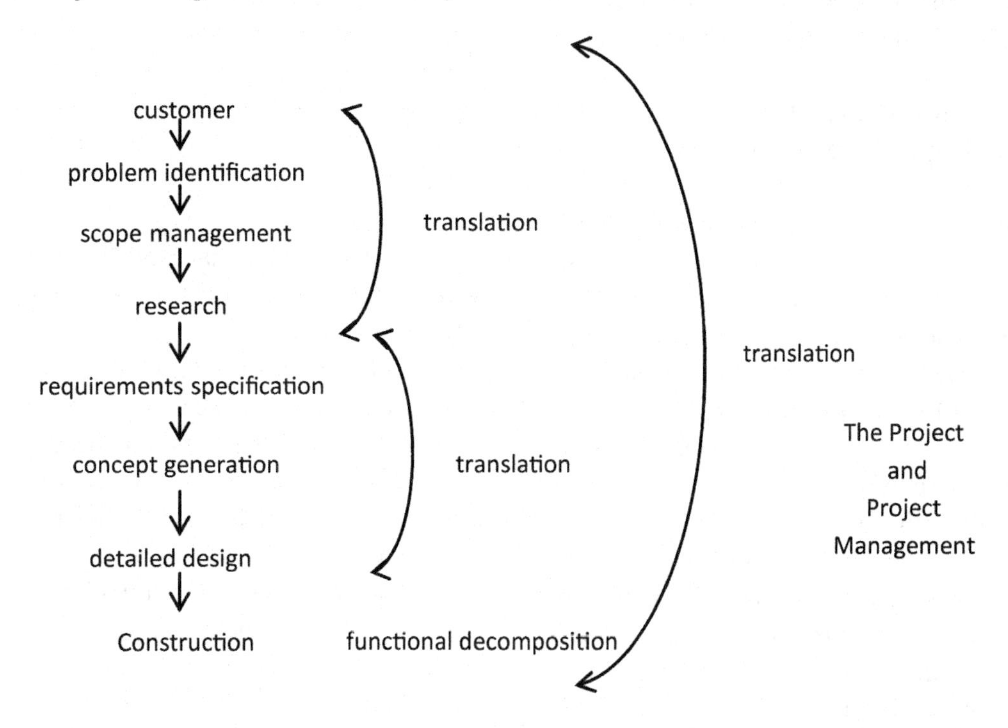

Figure 9. Engineering design as a program of action

Problem	Customer	The Project	Project Management	Construction	
Identification					
Requirements					
Conceptual design					
Detailed design					
Construction					

Figure 10. Names in actor-world

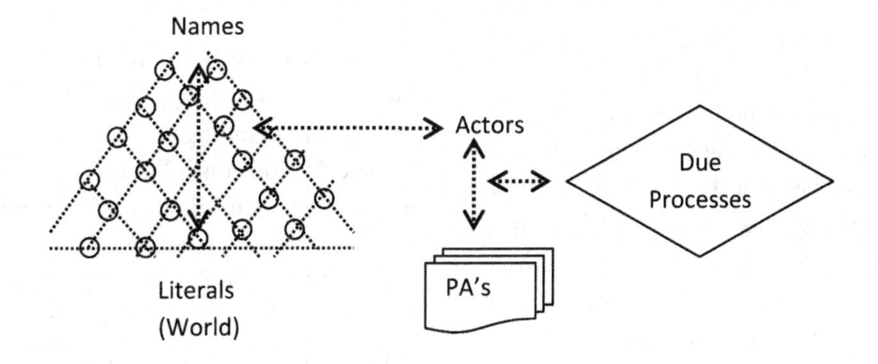

a succession of translations is next described, by means of a cascade of some hypothetical PAs.

A Case to Illustrate Our Methodological Approach

To illustrate scope management in design processes as a process of translations (Latour et al., 1992) (Figueiredo, 2004) we describe a case of innovation in an automation project of a plant in the automotive industry (BAA, 2006). Using this short story we build a case to explore our approach to project scope management. The focal actor (the one that makes proposals that cannot be ignored) will vary along the setting transitions.

A top car manufacturer (out of our setting, but present as a request) requests suppliers to bid for car metal seat frames. This request is our focal actor in the starting setting – *request to bid.* The request is an actor that materializes into a requirements / specification dossier. BL is a company specialized in manufacturing car metal seat frames. BL doesn't assure some technical competences in this request, namely in terms of its operations capacity and time to deliver.

BL intends to answer to the request but relevant transformations are needed. As we can see (using percentages to represent in a very simple way the degree of possible alignments) we assume that BL has 40% of the technical requirements (TR) and 90% of the commercial requirements (CR) needed.

It is mandatory to negotiate with potential partners to assure the missing competences. In fact a potential partner is already available – BAA. In order to bid, BL negotiates with BAA a project to upgrade the production line to be able to manage the requirements within the deadline. BAA is a partner that has collaborated in the past with BL, and is interested in entering the auto industry. Within this background a due process to *enrol* BAA leads to a change of setting and BL becomes the focal actor.

We may sketch a first WBS, Figure 11, and then proceed introducing some schematic PAs.

Table 1. Request to bid

request	BL	missing to BL	BAA
T.R.	40%	60%	?
C.R.	90%	10%	?

Table 1 is a table that intends to simulate a socio-technical graph (a PA) that represents our starting setting.

In Table 2 we inserted the terms 'ok' (aligned), 'x' (not aligned), '+' (needs work), '?' (could be …), and '–' (indifferent), as short descriptions of possible alignments. *Probus* is a specific hardware communication bus that allows the other actor's alignment. It translates as a specific 'ok'.

AC500 is a controller unit that BAA already deploys, but not in the automotive sector. From Table 2 we can observe that in terms of layout and local controlling both BL and BAA are aligned (AC500 is indifferent to this requirements). Tooling section needs integration, a problem that concerns BL and BAA and they can cooperate in this action. BL welding has not enough capacity and needs upgrading.

Table 2. Upgrade the production line

BL	BL in the project	BAA	AC500
layout	ok	ok	-
Local controllers	ok	+ ok	-
welding	+capacity	+ ok	-
tooling	integrate	+ ok	-
Plant-wide control system	x	?	adapt
Communications	-	Probus	-

The AC500 controller must be enrolled in the network. BAA needs to work on this adaptation and a new setting emerges, see Table 3 below, in which BAA becomes the focal actor and a new actor emerges – *SwPlus. SwPlus* is a software firm that develops software CASE tools to deal

Table 3. Adapt AC500

BAA	AC500	SwPlus
Robotics	ok	-
Auto-Industry Standards	+ok	ok

with robot interface standards to the automotive industry. Through *SwPlus*, BAA can *enrol* AC500 in the network of actors.

The concern here for Lander and BAA is to align with a lead firm in the automotive industry. Being on an operational level we have many types of actors. One interesting point to make is about the role of BAA, a global supplier in heavy industries but not in the automotive industry.

Applying symmetry we may view this business in terms of the actor "AC500", considered as an OPP. Its goal will be to control plants, including Auto Industry plants. This way it will mobilize IMs in order to attain its goal: how BAA answers to this? – How it will deploy its resources? This view may be a fruitful exercise to aid in configuring strategies of innovation and development.

Figure 11. Request to bid - upgrading a plant

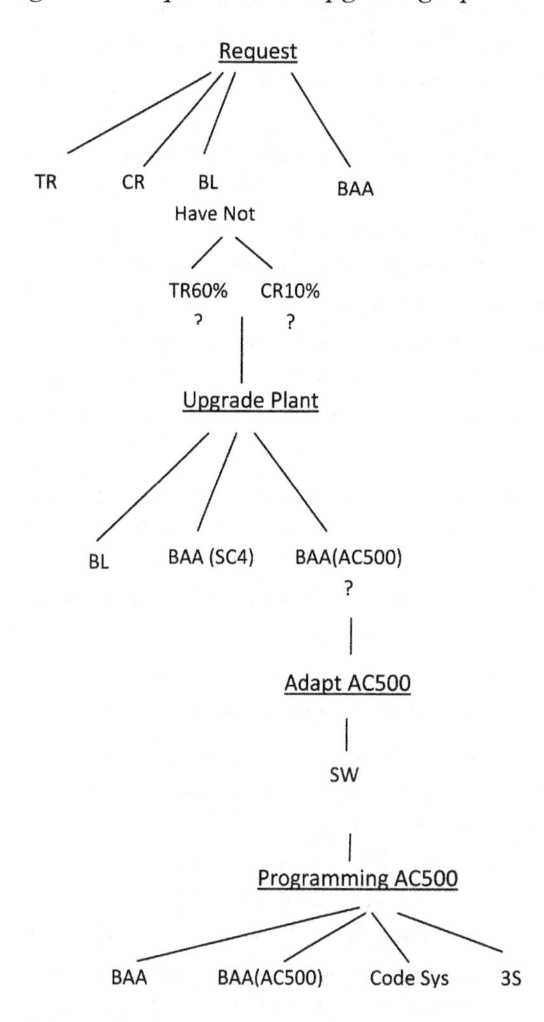

CONCLUSION

ANT provides a way of thinking and a paradigmatic approach that can support the making of a methodology in much diversified domains: strategy management, engineering design, and scope management. That view can be used as an aid in the management of innovation. We tried to explain how this view, with some formalization of the means (editing taxonomies of competences) and the possibility of automating PAs, will make possible to elicit requirements to build a computer tool to assist teams in those domains. We have already advanced some work leading to the design and programming of a prototype that will render our framework operative in practical terms.

So, in our research we explore ideas on how innovation may be constructed. Our title was a challenge: how can we find IMs? In this sense we started looking for IMs using the central concepts of ANT, mainly translation. Translation is a basic operation used by OPPs to move inscriptions and capitalize on their goals. The making of this capitalization, driven by IMs circulations on several types of settings, is a good way to find and recognize IMs. However, in order to capitalize faster enough we need to find suitable IMs, the ones that are able to accelerate to the centre.

In situations where there are no innovations this finding will not be easy. One solution may be to excite the system: introducing a small perturbation in the setting.

Taking a trivial situation that allows a good metaphor: on the road how the driver does know that the wheel shafts are working? – And how does the wheel shafts "know" that the driver is driving? Here we have two IMs (driver and wheel shaft) that are passing through an OPP (the road).

If the car keeps going, it may be that "things are right"; as the car keeps going, there may be that the shaft is in place. But if we want to know better we must envisage some trials. One way is by means of some trials: the driver may speed up a little the speed or force a little on curves. Of course, in this case, electronic instruments will help a lot.

But in the complex mediations of the natural and the social, things are not so neat. The challenge in managing scope in an engineering design project is to develop inscriptions allowing the production of suitable but not so much harder artefacts. That can be achieved by some trial process and we think that our framework helps on this job.

Scope planning and control is an interactive process of building irreversibility along a process of learning (Callon, 1991). Our ANT approach to scope management in design projects accommodates change and the redesign of predefined goals. That is, the goal is itself refined and constructed trough the process of designing and developing.

REFERENCES

Akrich, M. (1992). The description of technical objects. In Bijker, W. E., & Law, J. (Eds.), *Shaping Technology/Building Society: Studies in Sociotechnical Change* (pp. 205–224). Cambridge, MA: MIT Press.

Akrich, M., Callon, M., & Latour, B. (2002). The Key to Success in Innovation Part II: The Art of Choosing Good Spokespersons. *International Journal of Innovation Management*, *6*(2), 207–225. doi:10.1142/S1363919602000562

BAA. (2006). ABB provides turnkey robotic solution in £650k Lander Automotive project. Retrieved from http://www.abb.co.uk/cawp/seitp202/91DE58BEDD547C3CC12571E000533F56.aspx

Boudourides, M. A. (2001, November 1-3). *Networks, Fluids, Chaos*. Paper presented at the International Conference on Spacing and Timing: Rethinking Globalization & Standardization, Palermo, Italy. Retrieved from http://www.math.upatras.gr/~mboudour/

Cagan, J., & Vogel, C. M. (2001). *Creating Breakthrough Products: Innovation from Product Planning to Program Approval*. Upper Saddle River, NJ: FT Press.

Callon, M. (1986a). Some Elements of a Sociology of Translation - Domestication of the Scallops and the Fishermen of St-Brieuc Bay. *Sociological Review. Mongraph*, 196–233.

Callon, M. (1986b). The Sociology of an Actor-Network: The Case of the Electric Vehicle. In Callon, M., Law, J., & Rip, A. (Eds.), *Mapping the Dynamics of Science and Technology: Sociology of Science in the Real World* (pp. 19–34). London: Macmillan.

Callon, M. (1987). Society in the Making: the Study of Technology as a Tool for Sociological Analysis. In Bijker, W. E., Hughes, T. P., & Pinch, T. J. (Eds.), *The Social Construction of Technical Systems: New Directions in the Sociology and History of Technology* (pp. 83–103). Cambridge, MA: MIT Press.

Callon, M. (1991). Techno-economic networks and irreversibility. In Law, J. (Ed.), *A Sociology of Monsters: Essays on Power, Technology and Domination* (pp. 132–161). New York: Routledge.

Figueiredo, J. (2004). *Abordagem sócio-técnica ao desenvolvimento de sistemas de informação inter-institucionais, IST* (Sociotechnical approaches to the design and development of inter-institutional information systems).

Ford, R. M., & Coulston, C. (2007). *Design for Electrical and Computer Engineers: Theory, Concepts, and Practice*. New York: McGraw-Hill.

Gerson, E. M., & Star, S. L. (1986). Analyzing Due Process in the Workplace. *ACM Transactions on Office Information Systems*, *4*, 257–270. doi:10.1145/214427.214431

Gonçalves, A., & Figueiredo, J. (2007). Organizing Competences: Actor-Network Theory in Virtual Settings. *International Journal of Networking and Virtual Organisations*, *6*(1), 23–35.

Guide, P. M. B. O. K. (2004). *A Guide to the Project Management Body of Knowledge* (3rd ed.).

Hewitt, C. (1986). Offices are Open Systems. *ACM Transactions on Office Information Systems*, *4*(3), 271–287. doi:10.1145/214427.214432

Latour, B. (1985). Les "Vues" de L'Esprit. Une Introduction à L'Anthropologie des Sciences et des Techniques. *Culture Technique*, *14*, 5–29.

Latour, B. (1987). *Science in Action: How to Follow Scientists and Engineers through Society*. Cambridge, MA: Harvard University Press.

Latour, B. (1988). *Irréductions, published with The Pasteurisation of France*. Cambridge, MA: Harvard University Press.

Latour, B. (1990). Drawing Things Together. In Lynch, M., & Woolgar, S. (Eds.), *Representation in Scientific Practice* (pp. 19–68). Cambridge, MA: MIT Press.

Latour, B. (1991a). Technology is Society made durable. In Law, J. (Ed.), *A Sociology of Monsters: essays on power, technology and domination*. London: Routledge.

Latour, B. (1991b). *Nous n'avons jamais été modernes: essai d'anthropologie symétrique* (p. 167). Paris: La Découverte & Syros.

Latour, B. (1993). *Petites leçons de sociologie des sciences, III. Les Tribulations de L'Image Scientifique*. Paris: La Découverte.

Latour, B. (1996). *Aramis, or the Love of Technology*. Cambridge, MA: Harvard University Press.

Latour, B. (1998). On Recalling ANT. J. Law & J. Hassard (Eds.), *Actor Network Theory and After*. London: Blackwell.

Latour, B. (2004). Why Has Critique Run out of Steam? From Matters of Fact to Matters of Concern. *Critical Inquiry*, *30*(2), 25–248. Retrieved from http://www.bruno-latour.fr/articles/article/089.html. doi:10.1086/421123

Latour, B. (2007). *Reassembling the Social An Introduction to Actor-Network-Theory*. Oxford, UK: Oxford University Press.

Latour, B. (2008). The Metaphorical/Literal Divide. *Arch Literary Journal*. Retrieved from http://archjournal.wustl.edu/interviews/latour/interview.htm

Latour, B., Mauguin, P., & Teil, G. (1992). A Note on Socio-Technical Graphs. *Social Studies of Science*, *22*(1), 33–57. doi:10.1177/030631279202200l002

Latour, B., & Woolgar, S. (1979). *Laboratory Life: the Social Construction of Scientific Facts*. London: Sage.

Law, J. (1986). On the methods of long distance control: vessels, navigation, and the Portuguese route to India, Power, Action and Belief. In J. Law (Ed.), *A New Sociology of Knowledge*. London: Routledge. Retrieved from http://www.comp.lancs.ac.uk/sociology /papers/law-methods-of-long-distance-control.pdf

Law, J. (1992). Notes on the theory of the actor-network: Ordering, strategy and heterogeneity. *Systems Practice*, *5*(4), 379–393. doi:10.1007/BF01059830

Law, J., & Mol, A. (2003). *Situating Technoscience: an Inquiry into Spatialities*. Lancaster, UK: Lancaster University. Retrieved from http://www.comp.lancs.ac.uk/sociology/papers/Law-Mol-Situating-Technoscience.pdf

Law, L. (1986). On the Methods of Long Distance Control: Vessels, Navigation and the Portuguese Route to India. In Law, J. (Ed.), *Power, Action and Belief: A New Sociology of Knowledge* (pp. 234–263).

Mol, A., & Law, J. (1994). Regions, Networks and Fluids: Anaemia and Social Topology. *Social Studies of Science*, *24*(4), 641–671. doi:10.1177/030631279402400402

Schneider, A., & Ingram, H. (2007, August 29-September 2). *Ways of Knowing: Implications for Public Policy*. Paper presented at the annual meeting of the American Political Science Association, Chicago, IL.

Star, S. L., & Griesemer, J. R. (1989). Institutional Ecology, 'Translations' and Boundary Objects: Amateurs and Professionals in Berkeley's Museum of Vertebrate Zoology. *Social Studies of Science*, *19*, 387–420. doi:10.1177/030631289019003001

Teil, G., & Latour, B. (1995). The Hume machine: can association networks do more than formal rules? *SEHR, 4*(2). Retrieved from http://www.stanford.edu/group/SHR/4-2/text/teil-latour.html

Wells, M. (1976). *Computing Systems Hardware (Cambridge Computer Science Texts - 6)*. Cambridge, UK: Cambridge University Press.

This work was previously published in International Journal of Actor-Network Theory and Technological Innovation, Volume 2, Issue 2, edited by Arthur Tatnall, pp. 39-53, copyright 2010 by IGI Publishing (an imprint of IGI Global).

Chapter 7
Social Network Sites:
The Science of Building and Maintaining Online Communities, a Perspective from Actor-Network Theory

Nisrine Zammar
Université Haute Bretagne, Rennes 2, France

ABSTRACT

This article examines the role of actors in a Social Network Sites and also the triggers and challenges they represent to social networking between today's communities and businesses. A Social Network Sites is the product of the evolution of social liaisons and the emergence of online communities of people who are interested in exploring the concerns and activities of others. A social network is the assembly of direct or indirect contacts; a network is the product of interactions with the actors (individuals, families, enterprises, etc.) enabled by means of the structural design of web 2.0. Social Network Sites bring people together to interact through chat rooms, and share personal information and ideas around any topics via personal homepage publishing tools. This article is intended to be a trigger to deeply and more intensely explore potential roles of actor-network theory in the Social Network Sites context, in today's and tomorrow's world.

INTRODUCTION

This research, as part of my thesis on Information and Communication Science, deals with the role of the actors in a Social Network Sites and also the triggers and challenges they represent to social networking between today's communities and businesses. The methodology is a qualitative study based on observation, as well as in-depth analysis of a group of members and their operation. Moreover, I ran some testing to examine the interactions between these members, their courses of action, and their performance; verifying the convenience of some relative theories.

Social Network Sites is the product of the evolution of social liaisons, and the emergence of online communities of people who are interested in exploring the concerns and activities of oth-

DOI: 10.4018/978-1-4666-1559-5.ch007

ers. This evolution is forever changing societies, organizations, technologies and our imagination. This article looks at the following: can we apply Actor-Network Theory (ANT) in the context of social networking? What are the limits?

The first interest in the quest to find answers to the above-stated questions is to highlight some of the principal characteristics of the Social Network Sites, the evolution of the notion of Network, and hence explore the controversial actor-network theory that insists on the agency of non-humans, where the "*actants*" in a network take the shape that they do by virtue of their relations with one another, suggesting that there is no difference in the ability of technology, humans, animals, or other non-humans to act. As Callon states "we are entertained by showing the false controversies, indignating and dividing colleges" (Dosse, 1995, p.30)

A social network is the assembly of direct or indirect contacts; a network is the product of interactions with the actors (individuals, families, enterprises etc). The networks have revolutionized our relation with space/time. They have allowed a magnificent development of social networks and the expanding of real communities, tearing down barriers.

Social Network Sites (SNS) bring people together to interact with each other through chat rooms, and share personal information and ideas around any topics via personal homepage publishing tools. They are based on the notion that individual computers linked electronically could form the basis of computer mediated social interaction and networking. User profiles could be created (thanks to fonts and graphics), messages sent to users held on a "friends list" and other members could be sought out who had similar interests in their profiles. Research shows that the more extensive the network is, the higher is the potential of diversification. Hence Social Network Sites provide many criteria for category division: family relationships, business fields, markets, lobbies, interest groups etc. Therefore this study is qualitative rather than quantitative, as it does not rely on figures to prove a fact or to highlight a finding in regards to the evolution of communication means.

We define the notion of Social Networks more strictly as: a social network is brought about by a mediator founded on IT communication medium, dedicated to constitute or reconstitute social connections, managing and mobilizing them for personal or professional purposes. In this context, we exclude the secondary services. Therefore we do not assimilate platforms and the internet, because a technical platform does not characterize in any case a social network. According to Haythornthwaite (2008), « social networks enable users to gear and bring to site their own social network, hence, creating new relationships or maintaining « latent relationships », i.e. offline relationships.

Also, a social network can pre-exist on a technical platform that supports it or serves as a base for it, or which the network uses and hence for further development, enabling the characterization of a trend or a certain process of evolution.

HISTORICAL OVERVIEW

Etymologically, a network is a net; a tissue or an interlacement of threads. The word's genealogical illustrations show that this original reference persisted till this very day, but it is "what you can do with the network threads is what has changed with time; corps-cosmos, nature and planet, society and organization" (Musso, 2003). From the beginning to the end of the 17th century the term "Network" was used within the context of the language of medicine. At that time the word "Network" did not refer in any case to communication.

The big advance to the new network concept was its "exiting" out of the human body at the turn of the 18th century: the term network was no longer used exclusively for human flesh; it was used in the context of construction and became a reference to an artifact, and an autonomic technique. The term "Network" becomes artificial rather than natural. By definition, it becomes "to construct"; as a utility it becomes "a machine". The engineer builds it up and constructs it, whereas the doctor observes it.

The notion of "social network" made its first appearance in an article written by the British anthropologist John A. Banes in 1945. Since the start of using the notion of "network" to indicate the assembly of relationships between people or social groups, it became widely common in the field of sciences, as well as in its margins. For example, the number of occurrences of the word "network" in the literature of management multiplied by more then 20, between 1960 and 1990.

The term of "Network" indicates, to a large extent, physical networks (roads, telephone, web ...) more than social networks (relationships between people, the society contacted by other societies, etc.) or modules (neuronal network). The difference is that the physical network exists outside any sort of exchanges, whereas the social network is defined by those exchanges. Yet, physical networks are the product of social activity and social networking, as they are based on enduring relationships. In sociology, a network is a structure formed by exchanging contacts or relationships between people and institutions.

A CONTEMPORIZED IDENTITY

Nowadays, networks carry the image of the modern world- the image of today- after the emerging of IT and swift communication methods, which forever changed societies, politics, sciences, and all sorts of research and studies in general. Hence, a historical overview of the notion of network seems necessary for the purpose of this research and also the expansion of its usages, its evolution and its impact on our life.

The notion of "network" in today's world is omnipresent; and is considered as an omnipotent means in all sectors: in the social sciences it defines the system of relationships (social networks, power lobbies ...), in the sciences it characterizes the analysis, in mathematics it defines the modules of connections, in transportation and energy sectors it revolutionizes the relations between actors on an international scale. Finally, in biology, it characterizes the analyses of the human body.

The 'Internet Network' is a magical product, in which we discover the following traits: it is flexible, can be manipulated, touched and modified every moment of every day, portable, displaceable, and ultimately, it is a valuable product for everyone.

According to Forsé (2005) "a social network is the assembly of relationships between a group of actors. This assembly could be organized (like an enterprise) or unorganized (like a network of friends)." The relationships can be of various influential natures (power, exchanging gifts, etc.), specialized or not, symmetric or not. The actors are very often the individuals themselves, but they can also be households, associations, etc. The main point here is that the object of the study is the relation between elements, in other words, the interaction or the mutual action.

This approach is used to examine the way the organizations interact with each other, which characterizes the numerous informal relationships that bind together the associations, and the connections between the different employees of the different companies. Moreover, the social network seems to play a key role in the success of businesses, and in the turnover of the enterprise.

Network is defined as a source of interactivity between man and machine. This interactivity in the form of importer-exporter, seller-buyer, is the principal distributor of the "technology of the spirit" (Sfez, 1990); but it is also an "intermediary" (Quéau, 1989, 1993), congregating "two opposite couples that are united, overcoming traditional logical differences a situation where the opposing couple is manipulated, and leads to successful interaction of their respective actor-networks. Hence, actor-network theory refers to these creations as *tokens* or *quasi-objects*: somehow ontological" (Sfez, 2003)!

ACTOR-NETWORK THEORY PUT TO THE TEST

It is true that ANT indicates several landmarks and some stepping stones on the road, but it does not provide a clear map, or a compass. ANT - like all comparable methods of study - requires judgment calls from the researcher as to what actors are important within a network, and which are not. But in the absence of 'out-of-network' criteria for judging the relevance of actors, these problems can appear theoretically unmanageable (Cazal, 2007). *"... ANT is less constructive, prefabricated, and ready to be assembled rather than to be built."*

Could we adopt only one perspective of ANT in regards to Social Network Sites? Could such a controversial subject be looked upon from one angle? It is rather more efficient to examine the matter in question from different perspectives, in order to embrace its complexity. In our days, people have contributed to a remarkable interest in what concerns Social Network Sites and their success. We have found in the theory of the Actor-Network a pragmatic concept of the truth: what is efficient is true. For Cazal (2007) the theory of the actor-network is not *"applicable, and not ready for use, while facing the multiples challenges of this emerging process"*.

Actor-Network Theory sees the world as a series of networks, along which 'immutable mobiles' - beings and technology - are transported, unchanged. This theory emphasizes the role of the performers - the actors - who sustain these networks. Any element is only a part of many wider networks, and the functioning of the actors in *performing* and *transforming* their allotted tasks is strongly influenced by their *habitus*. Actor-network theory illuminates the relationships and transformations within networks, across time and space, and rejects artificial divides such as local/global, agency/structure. Although this seems constructivist in concept, this concept is not constructive. Latour, states that Actor-network theory is about *"conflicting with our old thinking habits"* (Latour, 2001). The challenge is in the diffusing and institutionalizing where productivity is limited or dry.

It is not always easy to keep up with Latour when approaching constructivism. He firmly challenges the idea of social constructivism which places an exaggerated importance on society. In this meaning there is no social construction, as a developed notion by sociologists to dissolve everything in the society, and in sociology (Latour, 2004). Nevertheless, Latour admits that we cannot define each entity aside, on the contrary, attention should be drawn to the work of the congregation, to the arranging and the assembling (of alliances in a network), and so the construction process follows the entity: this perspective is relational (according to Caillé, 2001) and "assemblist": this could appear shallow as opposed to the constructivism perspective.

Moreover, Latour (2003) has recently embraced back this term, aiming at saving constructivism (from himself). As he states *"our only defence against fundamentalism is defined as a tendency to deny the constructed and mediated characters of the entities whose public existence have nonetheless to be discussed"*. Latour (2003) pleads *"for a realistic definition of what a construction is"*. Being certain that numerous ways exist to consider constructivism and human and social sciences and in various usages. It helps us to examine the relational perspectives and to analyze how actors in SNSs are represented, and what the SNSs represent for them. ANT does not describe a matter; rather, it provides the means of describing it. Hence, it is a tool for tracing relationships and the movements of multiple entities; it is an invitation to creativity in research.

For Latour and Callon (Flichy, 2007) who refer back to Law (1994), the world should not be thought of in terms of social groups, but in terms of networks. What makes something social is the "connection", the formation of "collectives" and the assembly of mediators that would hold on together and that showcase the social network phenomenon. In that measure we are in the process of directing theories and notions towards designing new phenomenon and practices.

In his work *"we have never been modern!"* Latour (1994) presents a concept of symmetric anthropology "where everything is found of equal importance for analysis ..." The theory assumes that nothing lies outside the network of relations, and as noted above, suggests that there is no difference in the ability of technology, humans, animals, or other non-humans to act (and that there are only enacted alliances.) As soon as an actor engages with an actor-network it too is caught up in the web of relations, and becomes part of the 'entelechy'. From this perspective, the social relations within the Social Network Sites are seen as a product of successive interactions of heterogeneous *"actants"*; that is the members.

For Callon and Latour (in Akrich, Callon, & Latour, 2006) initiators of the "Sociology of Translation", the network is "a meta-organization" gathering humans and non-humans and putting them as intermediaries for each other; seizing situations like an assembly of entities, humans or non-humans, individuals or collectives, defined by their rules, their identities, and their programs. This means re-establishing them under the form of a relative network that we can bring closer to their comprehension. (Serres, 2000).

Nicolas Dodier (1995) notes that "according to Callon and Latour in the domain of sciences and techniques of the innovation, work consists of bringing to existence the socio-technical networks, which means stable associations of humans and non-humans, to consolidate the associations, and if possible to extend their sizes. The success of the enterprise will be judged by its network stability, and at the same time, by the quantity of mobilized beings".

For Callon (1991), the actor usually gathers around himself other entities (intermediaries of all sorts); who are capable of being the Porte-parole of his entities; who redefined the role of identity of his "allies" designing and elaborating a new socio-technological network, a new world, an "actor-network". Serres (2000) states "The network is the product of a big number of translation operations, seeking to associate in an irreversible manner, the heterogenic as well as the dispersed elements. Therefore, the notion of actor-network qualifies this congregation and the birth of a new organization, of a research laboratory, a new artefact ..." After connections are established to form socio-logic articulations; they result into constituting an autonomic network that acts in its turn as an actor. The actor-network, in this perspective, is the product and the result of the process of translation. It does not express any longer an ultimate phase of innovation, but rather an emergence of a new solid reality.

For Callon, an actor (A) defined in the set of roles of the intermediaries of rank N+1, is transformed by these definitions and these attributes to an intermediary of rank N+1. These intermediaries form a series of grouping-entities (or socio-logic articulations) composed of actors or intermediaries, humans or non-humans. These entities are related to the relationships noted r1, r2, r3... and equally defined by A. The final "R (A) is nothing but the course itself that constructs the networks (either by consolidating those already existing, or by emerging new ones), puts the intermediaries in action..." (Callon, 1991) Therefore, an actor-network is a network that constitutes and functions like a totally independent actor. According to Degenne and Forsé (1994) in *"Les réseaux sociaux"*, the couples search in an open network is a trigger for contributions, for more authentic exchanges, and less constraints, with all the "*the strengths and the weaknesses of the interpersonal instituted relations, but at the same time with constituting and perhaps instituting the social essences*".

Central to ANT is the concept of translation which is referred to as **Sociology of Translation**, in which innovators attempt to create a *forum,* a central network in which all the actors agree that the network is worth building and defending. In his widely debated 1986 study of how marine biologists try to restock the St Brieuc Bay in order to produce more scallops, Callon (1986) has defined four moments of translation. These four moments are derived from studying:

1. **Problematisation:** What is the problem that needs to be solved? Who are the relevant actors? Delegates need to be identified that will represent groups of actors. So, a union head represents workers or a Member of Parliament represents his constituency. During problematisation, the primary actor tries to establish itself as an obligatory passage point (OPP) between the other actors and the network, so that it becomes indispensable.
2. **Interessement:** Getting the actors interested and negotiating the terms of their involvement. The primary actor works to convince the other actors that the roles it has defined for them are acceptable.
3. **Enrolment:** Actors accept the roles that have been defined for them during interessement.
4. **Mobilization of allies:** Do the delegate actors in the network adequately represent the masses? If so, enrolment becomes active support.

The notion of the network is found in the core of the sociology of translation. This notion can be defined through 3 dimensions:

- **The descriptive dimension:** the network is characterized and written by other notions like that of the intermediaries and actors.
- **The conceptual notion:** that serves to elaborating specific concepts or notion, in accordance with to sociology of translation like the notion of the "Actors-Network", the "Techno-Economic Networks (TEN)", the notions of the "long networks" and "short networks".
- **The theoretic or philosophic dimension:** that makes of the network a module of reference for the various approaches to sciences and technologies, and innovation.

The Intermediaries

Callon underlines the netlike nature of the intermediaries. Each intermediary writes a network as a group of entities. On the social level, the intermediaries are subject to the same definition as that of actors: "the actors are defined by the intermediaries, whom they put in circulation" (Callon, 1991). Therefore, the society is constructed by technology. The independent does not exist and should be considered within the league of intermediaries that they compose.

Irreversibility vs. Reversibility

But what contributes to the solidity and the healthiness of a network, to the extent that it ends up durable and irreversible means creating a new world around it.

Callon states that the matter of irreversibility is, without any doubt, one of the most important matters in technological sciences, pointing to the irreversibility/reversibility paradox. We note that, for some members of the society, technologies present irreversibility the most. They predetermine the evolutions to come, and orientate the possibilities of change. But, on the other hand, the same technologies "are equally at the heart of transformations and radical incertitude" (Callon, 1991), due to an indefinite system of technology, of prompt innovation, of new worlds that can emerge; of uncertain processes of innovations that will appear.

The Social Network Sites represent this paradox of the system of flaws, they generate incertitude; the kind of irreversibility that creates the reversibility. Because their development is far from being completed, and they are marked by constant socio-technological evolution, that would diversify infinitely the options and the progress.

The Convergence

We see two compositions in the Social Network Sites: *convergence and irreversibility.* According to Callon (1991), the notion of convergence "is to maintain the degree of accordance, engendered by a series of interpretations and by the operation of all intermediaries; and at the same time, maintain the frontiers of techno-economic network" In fact; the degree of convergence allows the categorization of a network under two big categories: convergent or dispersed networks.

- **The convergent network:** the more the network is aligned and coordinated, the more the actors meet and move towards the same target. Effectively, in such a network each actor and each network member have the possibility of mobilizing all the competences and the necessary recourses, which insures them the collection of an individual force. As in the case of groups of humanitarian aids and politics on Facebook, for example.
- **The dispersed network:** in this type of network, the relations of weak density between the actors and the different poles are fragile. And the mobilization of network by an actor is difficult and limited. That is why the construction of such networks is demanding, as Callon underlines in *Réseaux technico-économiques et irréversibilités (1991)* a "long investments, intense efforts of coordination". Therefore, the convergence of a network indicates the degree of stabilization of the multiple translations that enable the construction.

Amongst the exterior indicators to be highlighted is the defining of the degree of convergence of a network. On one hand by the language: the signification of words and shared expressions "A converging network provides assistance through the existence of a linguistic community, common language for researchers, technicians, traders, decision makers, users" (Serres, 2000). On the other hand, by the gathering of the objects of technology, which are coincidental in a space of diffusion in the network.

Finally, because the convergence of a network is defined by the forms of coordination applied to convention, we are placing the highest importance on the structure of the organization and on the conventional protocols that manage the interactions between the actors. These indicators allow the follow-up on the process of construction of the social network, firmly paving the way for a somehow remarkable convergence. We notably think of mobile convergences on Facebook.

The Irreversibility

In order to better illustrate our purpose, we distinguish between the irreversibility of a network and its convergence. For Callon (1991) "the convergence indicates the construction of a record, the irreversibility indicates a record that holds on, retreats, and foresees the interpretations to come." In other words, the irreversibility of a network is anticipated. The only thing that can halt it is a successful convergence. So to make a network irreversible there should be a force of coordination.

Therefore, two conditions are necessary to assure the irreversibility of a translation: the impossibility of withdrawing back from a situation precedent to the translation, and the "predetermination of the translations to come". For Callon (1991), the irreversibility is "a relational attribute that is only actualized in the proof. The sociology and the translation show us that in the process of innovation marked by a big number of operations and interpretations, and huge number of actors, each interpretation competes to become irreversible and to "be imported" by the others.

After the emergence of a Social network and its services, is it impossible to bounce back? There are two qualities of intermediaries that cannot be measured by proof: the durability and the healthiness. Latour (1984) tells us in *Irréductions*, "What is real is found in the proof". For Callon (1991) "the more the interrelations are multi-levelled and intersecting, the more the associated elements are numerous and heterogenic (non-human, human, conventions …). The more the coordination is strong, the more the probability of the resistance to the translation is higher". This idea of heterogeneity, and of the number of elements in a network that makes it resistant, seem to us particularly interesting, especially those of indestructible and irreversible nature.

The Normalization

For Callon (1991), the process of irreversibility is inseparable of that of the normalization, which "manages the standardization of the divers categories of interfaces: actors/intermediaries, intermediaries/intermediaries, intermediaries/actors"

This notion of normalization as a condition or sign of the irréversibilisation seems to be inventive for thinking about the emergence of the social networks and trying to encircle this moment. The irréversibilisation consists of making predictable the behaviour, the chains, the movements, the practices, the relations, etc. For Callon (1991), "an irreversible network is a network that weighed standards of all kinds and thereby slides into metrics and in a codified information system". Thus the more standards and norms of all kinds are defined, and frame (supervise) the actors and their interactions, the more the translation becomes irreversible. We have in mind the different technical protocols that normalize and structure the functions of the actors and their imageries. Also there are implicit social norms that act and interact for the welfare of the social network, being an inseparable aspect of our everyday living.

CONCLUSION

It is true that ANT in the context of Social Network Sites is a recent science; and requires further elaboration and studies. However, this article is intended to be a trigger to deeply and more intensely explore potential roles of Actor-Network Theory, in the Social Network Sites context, in today's and tomorrow's world.

In this sense, ANT invites another method to approach the theory. According to Latour (2004): "As far as it (ANT) is never substantial, it never possesses the explanatory power of the other types of reports". All its interest holds to the credibility that it built itself, by the publications and by the academic recognition … it has for purpose its own extension, solidification and universalization. Latour invites us to get rid of institutionalized way of thinking whose fertility is limited or dried up.

Furthermore, ANT defines itself more frequently by what she is not rather than by what it admits to be. ANT defines itself especially by contrast with the classic approaches and their big dichotomies at which it aims not to overtake or surpass, but by skirting around. Latour invites us not to reduce, rise or to neutralize the uncertainties, but to take the measure, to make them play, what exactly forbids any preliminary positive recommendation.

Finally which wages of *scientificity* does ANT offers in the SNS field? Latour (1995) invites us to an opened construction site: "... build a discipline, develop connections, mobilize the world, create colleagues, and establish collectives, the *scientificity* and the objectivity will follow!" That's what this article has tried to do.

REFERENCES

Akrich, M., Callon, M., & Latour, B. (2006). *Sociologie de la traduction: textes fondateurs*. Paris: Mines Paris, les Presses, Sciences sociales.

Caillé, A. (2001). Une politique de la nature sans politique. *Ecologisme, naturalisme et constructivisme, 17*.

Callon, M. (1986). Eléments pour une sociologie de la traduction. La domestication des coquilles Saint-Jacques et des marins-pêcheurs dans la baie de Saint-Brieuc. *L'Annee Sociologique*, *36*, 169–208.

Callon, M. (1991). Réseaux technico-économiques et irréversibilités. In R. Chavance, B. Godard, & Olivier (Eds.), *Les Figures de l'irréversibilité en économie*. Paris: Editions de l'Ecole des Hautes Etudes en Sciences Sociales.

Cazal, D. (2007). *Traductions De La Traduction et Acteur-Réseau: Sciences, Sciences, Sociales et Sciences en Gestion* ? De Lille: IAE.

Degenne, A., & Forsé, M. (1994). *Les réseaux sociaux*. France: Armand Collin.

Dodier, N. (1995). *Les Hommes et les Machines. La conscience collective dans les sociétés techniques* (pp. 30–31). Paris: Métailié.

Dosse, F. (1995). *L'empire du sens, La Découverte*. Rééd: En poche.

Flichy, P. (2007). *Understanding technological innovation: a socio-technical approach*. Cheltenham, UK: Edward Elgar Publishing.

Forsé, M. (2005). Rôle spécifique et croissance du capital social. *Sociologie et Politique Sociales*, *8*(1), 101–125.

Haythornwaite, C. (2005). *Social networks and Internet connectivity effects.* Information, Communicaion & Society, 8(2), 125-147Latour, B. (1984). *The Pasteurization of France: Irréductions.* Cambridge, MA: Harvard

Latour, B. (1994). *Nous n'avons jamais été modernes. Essai d'anthropologie symétrique*. La Découverte.

Latour, B. (1995). *Le métier de chercheur – Regard d'un anthropologue*. Paris: INRA.

Latour, B. (2001). Réponse aux objections. *Ecologisme, naturalisme et constructivisme, 17*.

Latour, B. (2003). The promises of constructivism. In Ihde, D., & Selinger, E. (Eds.), *Chasing Technoscience: Matrix of Materiality*. Bloomington, IN: Indiana University Press.

Latour, B. (2004). Comment finir une thèse en sociologie? Petit dialogue entre un étudiant et un professeur (quelque peu socratique). *Une théorie sociologique générale est-elle pensable, 24*. Latour, B. (2007). Changer de société, refaire de la sociologie. Paris: La Découverte/Poche.

Law, J. (1994). *Organising Modernity*. Oxford, UK: Blackwell.

Musso, P. (2003). *Réseaux et Société*. Paris: PUF.

Quéau, P. (1989). *Metaxu, Champ Vallon, et Le Virtuel*. France: Champ Vallon.

Serres, A. (2000). *Aux sources d'Internet: exploration du processus d'émergence d'une infrastructure informationnelle*. Description des trajectoires des acteurs et actants, des filières et des réseaux constitutifs de la naissance d'ARPANET. Problèmes critiques et épistémologiques posés par l'histoire des innovations, Rennes.

Serres, M. (1992). *Eclaircissements* (Bourin, F., Ed.).

Sfez, L. (1990). *Critique de la communication* (2nd ed.). Paris: Le seuil.

This work was previously published in International Journal of Actor-Network Theory and Technological Innovation, Volume 2, Issue 2, edited by Arthur Tatnall, pp. 54-62, copyright 2010 by IGI Publishing (an imprint of IGI Global).

Chapter 8
Negotiating Meaning: An ANT Approach to the Building of Innovations

Fernando Abreu Gonçalves
Technical University of Lisbon, Portugal

José Figueiredo
Technical University of Lisbon, Portugal

ABSTRACT

Using an ANT approach based on Programs of Action the authors explore the description of innovation cases to discover internal referents that conveys their meaning. This paper revisits some old and well known histories like the application of ecography to obstetrics and gynaecology and the making and evolution of the computer mouse. Finally, the authors change from these localized cases of innovation to other histories on a more global frame, that is, the cases of two firms, one in the semi conductor industry, and the other in the mould for plastics industry. These descriptions are used as a way to research on the building of an ANT view for engineering innovations and wonder at the ability in which Actor-Network Theory (ANT) adapts and conciliates micro and macro worlds.

INTRODUCTION

Using ANT concepts and travelling along inscriptions and displacements we explore mediation with a semiotic approach into innovation contexts in order to better understand the work of Immutable Mobiles and deploy a method to take advantage of these network actors. We apply this method transversing settings and exploring micro and macro alignments. Our research paradigm is interpretivist, we use the lens of ANT, the method is our own purpose and the tools we use with our method are Programs of Action (PA) with taxonomical trees of competences (referred by their names). These tools are explored in a very simple and low end approach just to help visualization and understanding of what we mean. The innovation addressed is technological innovation and is mainly taken in the shape of engineering design processes.

DOI: 10.4018/978-1-4666-1559-5.ch008

Positioning ourselves in a middle ground we dismantle mediation taking actor-network assertions (reductions, amplifications, framings) to find transversal referents (Latour, 1993a) that allows the emergence of meaning along the construct of artefacts. We reuse the semiotic Latour concepts of *procession* and *network* to address inscriptions used by Immutable Mobiles (IM) and design a method to take advantage of IMs. Then we explain how this method can address situations of technological innovation using the ecography example. We then present our main tools (programs of action and taxonomical trees of names) and we exercise them in the description of the mouse case-study. Our tools are based on the internetworking of names that negotiate their meanings.

The two first short stories addressed are situated in a micro level analysis. Then, taking advantage of the concept of global value chain we explore two more cases as a way to extend our rationale into a macro level analysis. Finally we end up with some conclusions.

CONCEPTUAL POSITIONING

The Mediation Work

The work of mediation (reductions and amplifications, framing and summing-up) (Latour, 1993b) cannot be done without uncertainties. That is what we intend to show with Figure 1, adapted from Latour (1991), where the different influences onto an actor are manifold – an actor is never alone.

It is an ANT ground that there are no pure natural or social facts, which means that we travel in a middle position of a virtual horizontal axis (natural-social), bound by its margins. In terms of the vertical axis (local-global) we also look for another way of viewing how actors align themselves in a network. Of course an actor-network has no local and no global places, has it also has no natural and social bounds. Going from natural to social and from local to global is a simplified way to describe the mediation that is always a messy work in the margins, *Le goût des marges* (Latour, 1991).

To be able to follow the paths of mediation, the referents that enable the understanding of events and actor's work, we reinterpret Latour's formulation as depicted in Figure 2.

In our research we approach the description of some cases of innovation with this ANT based view as a method to understand the management of engineering design processes. That is, what we are trying to do is to figure out a practical way to navigate the work of mediation, a way to register the referents that allows the building of innovations.

Figure 1. Ontological regions and the mediation work, adapted from Latour (1991)

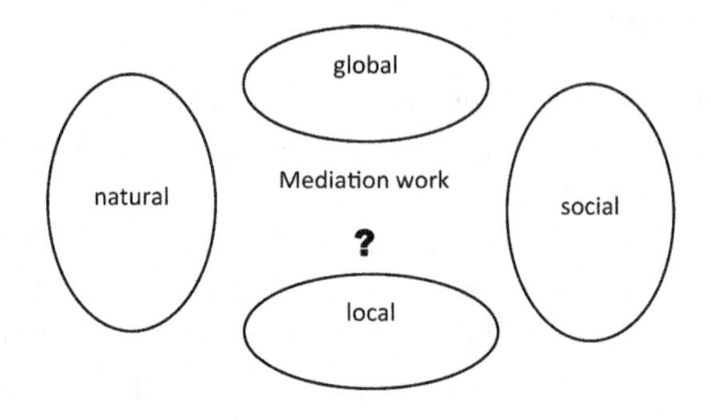

Figure 2. The messy work of the mediation

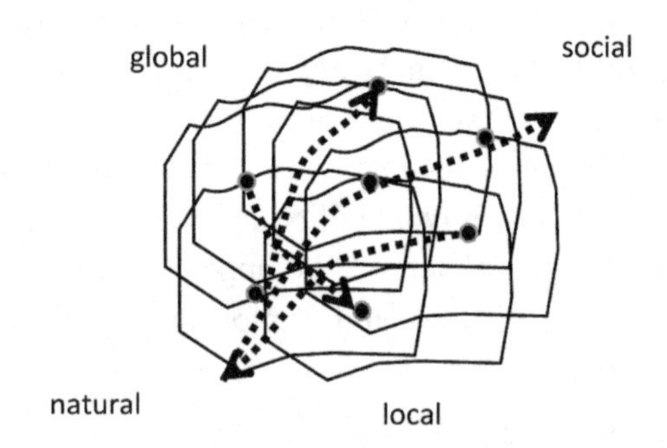

We already proposed this approach as a way to manage scope in engineering design projects (Gonçalves & Figueiredo, 2010). These two papers reflect the constructivist leaning of our research. The use of some practical tools (a methodological approach for field work and a computer-aided tool) whose specifications have being obtained as a result of this research, will hopefully allow us to do practical work on these matters and obtain and report results in a more formalised and concrete way.

A SEMIOTIC APPROACH TO THE WORK OF IMS

A Semiotic Approach to the Work of IMs

Using a semiotic approach to explain the role of IMs in emergence of innovation Latour (1993c) defines two regimes of translation:

- One that is built as *processions* where the *signified* (content) may change its form but the *signifier* (expression) must remain immutable - *Keep expression even if content changes (procession)*
- And one that is built as *networks* where it is possible to maintain the *signified* by changing the *signifier* - *Change expression to maintain content (network)*. This last regime, if successful, allows the capitalization to a center and effaces mediators.

Høstaker (2002) help us understand this semiotic flavour of ANT: *"Hjelmslev distinguishes between two parallel planes of language – that of expression (signifier) and that of content (signified). These planes presuppose each other reciprocally. In addition, within these two planes he distinguishes between form and substance". Meaning* will come from the articulation of forms, *expression* and *content*, see Figure 3.

Forms are crucial to semiotics as are *matter* and *substance* but these references to the natural world are better treated by other disciplines (Høstaker, 2002) namely engineering. Furthering the semiotic approach we may add that the production of signs is continuously elevated to the production of other ones in processes of denotation/connotation and meta-languages (Barthes, 1985). A denotation/connotation occurs when we take a sign (expression and content) as expression of a new sign – *what does this new* (connoted) *content mean*? A meta-language appears when we take a sign (expression and content) as content of a new sign – *how to express this new content*? Designing, making, and using artifacts are all interwoven in translations that we already know

Figure 3. Hjelmslev's model of the Sign (Adapted from Eco, 1976)

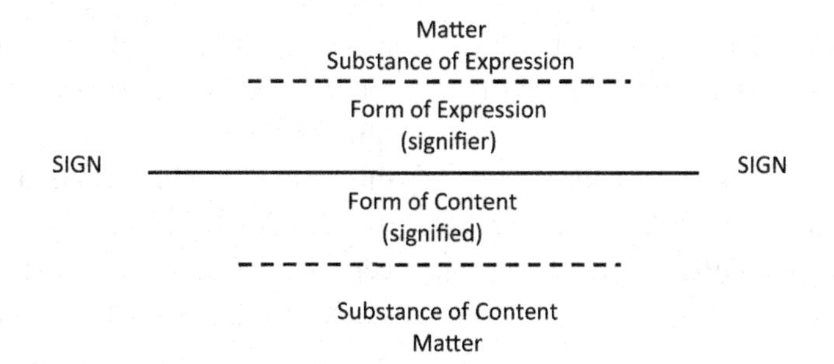

may be looked at as *processions* or as *networks* depending how expressions and contents are worked. This formulation does not explicitly, addresses substance because, as we know, in ANT, substance is not intrinsic to actors but is built relationally.

But we know that we find utilitarian origins for the substance of some expressions: the use is converted into the sign of that use – using cloths is a sign that our body needs protection (Barthes, 1985). In order to take notice that signifier and signified are tied to *matter*, we fold the previous diagram as is shown bellow, and take a view along the SIGN axis, Figure 4.

And if we superimpose into the picture the concepts of *procession* and *network*, the two regimes by Latour, we attain the diagram expressed in Figure 5.

This "closed spatial view" of the two planes of Hjelmslev hints that the two regimes are interconnected and that this interconnection may help us to understand more explicitly the work of Immutable Mobiles in the building of networks: IMs may be found somewhere as an interplay of these two regimes as actants steer to obtain some meaning about their acting.

Schematically, as a first draft to our method, we have the sequence that follows. The method will be tentatively refined along the cases we address.

- In a concrete situation (in Nature or in Society; Locally or Globally) what is the concern? What is the Matter? - choose a Setting.
- Within this setting, what could not be ignored? – identify the Obligatory Points of Passage (OPPs)
- Then, how to meaningfully articulate the two regimes of inscriptions, *processions* and *networks*, for each OPP, in order to design adequate IMs?

In the next section we analyse an application of this reasoning to the use of ecography in the control of foetus development, crossing the settings of Health, Military, and Industry. In doing so we hope to get an understanding of the mediation work that leads to innovations.

ILLUSTRATING THE METHOD BY CROSSING SETTINGS

Ecography: Describing the Birth of an Actor

In the middle of the XX century the application of ultrasounds could be roughly divided into the following three settings (Woo, 2006):

- Military
- Industry
- Health and medicine

Two technological modes were well established (OPPs): Bright (B) mode and Amplitude (A) mode; this one was less sophisticated but precise enough for measuring linear dimensions.

In the late 1950s, Douglass Howry, a radiologist, and John Wild, a surgeon, used the technology of Ecography with different goals. Howry focusing in images explored the more sophisticated technology, (B)-Mode; Wild, looking at diagnostics, used the simpler one, (A)-mode. In these beginnings there are no a priori reasons to choose between Howry and Wild approaches in terms of growth of their networks. A new setting, however, emerged as the Scottish gynaecologist Ian Donald began to explore Ecography in its domain. He was able to build a strong cohesion amongst technology, medics, mothers and foetuses, especially when Dr. Stuart Campbell was able to align the diameter of the foetus's skull, measured by means of the (A)-mode, with the development of the foetus. Foetal cephalometry became the standard method for the study of foetal growth for many years. From the prospect of a health and medicine application we may find the following translations in the building of an internal referent.

Figure 4. Sign as intercept of signifier and signified

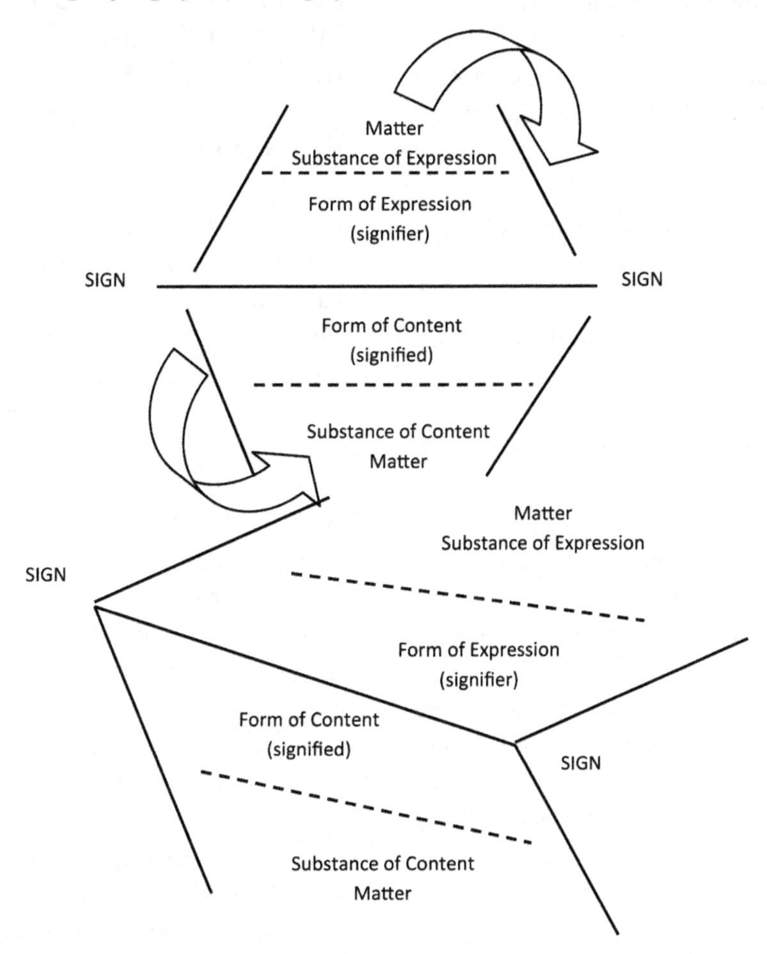

Figure 5. Procession and Network, two regimes of translation

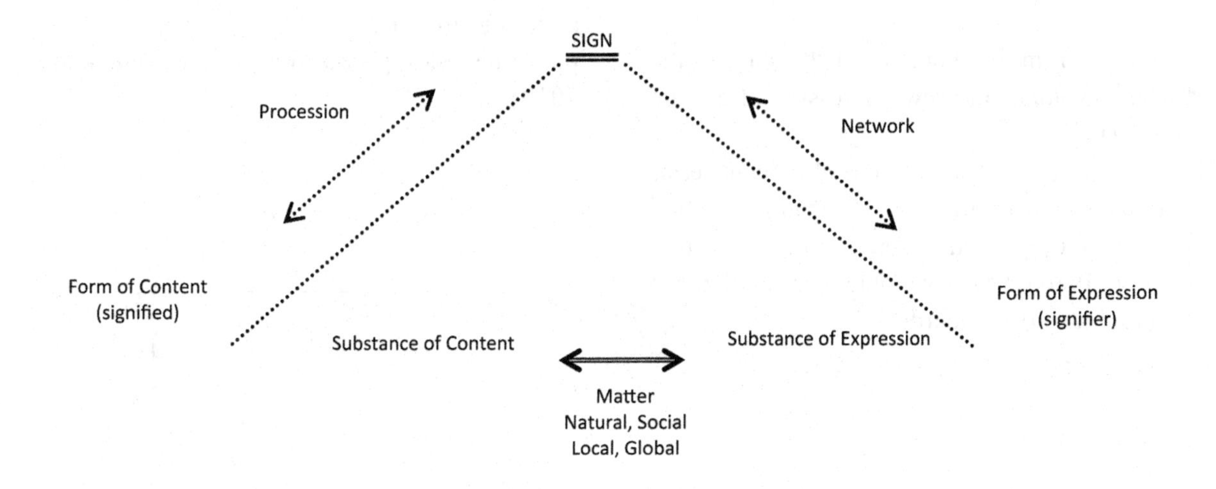

Using the frame described in Figure 1 and Figure 2 we can describe trajectories as follows:

From the social margins to the centre, mixing health and medicine with the military and industrial communities

- *Keep expression even if content changes (procession) –*

Identify differences and similarities between applications

- *Change expression to maintain content (network) –*

Drive technical characteristics from the other to obtain adequate quality in ours

(*ours* is health and medicine and the *others* military and industry)

From the natural margins to the centre, we internalize lessons learned into our own domain

- *Keep expression even if content changes (procession) –*

Figure out a way to use A-linear mode to measure the diameter of the skull (new content)

- *Change expression to maintain content (network) –*

Going from the diameter of the skull to the foetus development (new expression of a same content)

This technology suffered a subsequent series of translations that aligned through industrial and medical settings and a sustainable innovation (Callon, 1986a, 1994) was obtained, stabilized in several industry standards.

PROVIDING TOOLS TO THE METHOD (LOOKING FOR AN INTERNAL REFERENT)

Programs of Action

By means of the interplay of the two regimes of translation, *processions* and *translations*, we have sketched a way to look at "good" places to find IM's. But we need to go deeper to see how meaning is constructed, that is, how the shifting among settings may lead to find suitable internal references.

So we turn into another semiotic flavour of ANT. Latour following Akrich (1992) uses the term "de-scription" to refer to the "retrieval" of scripts that "*define actants, endow them with competences, make them do things, and evaluate the sanction of these things like the narrative program of semioticians*". Programs of Action (PAs), is a "linguistic tool" (Latour, 1992) that allows to follow actors in their translations.

To use this tool we may think of a two-dimension chart depicting a succession of proposals (paradigms) along a vertical axis (logical OR axis) where different proposals substitute one after another. These proposals are, in ANT terms, the inscriptions. Along the horizontal axis (logical AND axis) we have a succession of syntagms, associations among actors. We may follow the meaning of sentences, irrespective of the language, along the frontier Yes/No of the answers to the proposals. See Figure 6 (Gonçalves & Figueiredo, 2010).

Figure 6. Program of action

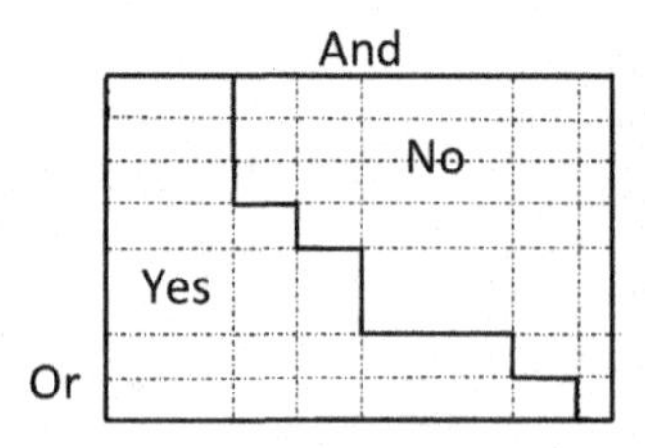

To narrate the things that happen in subsequent settings by means of competences we use "names", descriptions obtained from practices in the settings. Our syntactic structure of sentences will simply be taxonomies of names (taxonomical trees). In practice these taxonomies are temporaries, always prone to new articulations by the play of actants, humans and nonhumans.

The use of names does not mean that we are interested in particular words that represent groups of competences. What we are interested in is the "naming process" as a process of choices of competences, the negotiating of the meaning, Figure 7.

We may simplify the representation of PAs using flat tables where agreements and oppositions between actors (profiles of competences) are registered. Analyzing PAs may allow spotting the meaningful competences in a particular setting; the competences that are necessary to put side by side to obtain a meaningful profile in practice (capability). This knowledge could be used to singularise some competences in several settings and to follow its changes in meaning (Gonçalves & Figueiredo, 2010).

In our PA tables we assume that the first column represents the competence taxonomies that are proposed by an actor, the focal actor. As a label for the table we inscribe the focal proposal (the action in which we concentrate) and action program name. In the next line we display the names of the actors involved in the setting. The focal actor in this setting is the one in the left corner. The columns represent a footprint of actors during the program of action, in the specific perspective we follow them (they have other qualities, we are following these ones).

Inside the cells of the tables we represent the agreements ("ok") and oppositions ("ko", "?") that are at play. They are the result of translations where either due-processes or micro-theories or some simple competence translations have been at work in the particular setting of the network. Here agreements ("ok") and oppositions ("ko", "?") between actors (profiles of competences) are registered. In practical work we can register finer grains of knowledge about the translation processes.

This approach, being very general, does not lead, at a first appreciation, to practical ways of validation. Neither is scientifically grounded in a way to permit the building of frameworks for knowledge management. However, in settings related to practices, is reasonable to postulate that the negotiating of meaning will lead to spectra of convergences in manageable time scales. We may view this approach as a way to permit the building of local theories; a way that may be applied in any setting where a professional practice is dominant.

In the following, we exercise these ideas to make a description of an innovation process - the building of Apple's computer mouse.

Figure 7. Names in Actor-World. (Adapted from Gonçalves & Figueiredo, 2010)

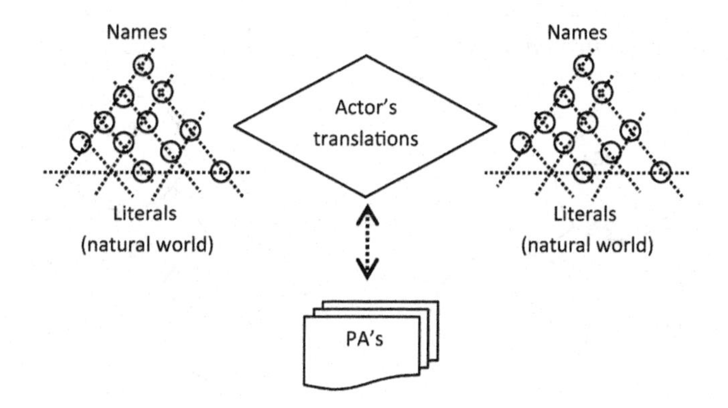

A Micro Setting Case Study - Mouse: Translating Between Two Centres

This story on innovation is about the computer mouse, its design and re-designs through time, (Bardini, 1996; Macintosh Mouse, 2002; American Heritage, 2002). This design process of the mouse can be interpreted as an example of a "no a priory essential features" of actants, actors not yet enrolled in programs. Actors already enrolled change with the settings (Callon, 1986b, 1991; Law, 1992). In fact it is from transitions of settings that relevant features of actors emerge in the actor-network and innovation occurs.

We choose the following settings where "PARC" and "APPLE" met, see Figure 8 and Figure 9. The labels used in the trees are expressions for (provisory) profiles of competences: the name "PARC" represents all competences assembled at Xerox-PARC (and stakeholders) to build the ALTO computer; the name "Steve Jobs" represents the concerns that Steve Jobs had, at the time (1979), in relation to the building of LISA and MAC computers, Figure 8.

We may propose the following PA (see Table 1) to describe the proposal of PARC for a pointing device in a computer monitor.

Describing the translations that took place in Steve Jobs visit to PARC we have Table 2, where we just added a little detail to make our point: the concept of the *mouse* as a pointing device in a computer monitor, its design, and cost.

When Steve Jobs returned to is local world (Apple) he translated the concept of the *mouse* to Dean Hovey – a co-founder of Hovey-Kelley Design firm that have been working for Apple and wanted to scale up its transactions with Apple (Macintosh Mouse, 2002) – "what we need is to build a mouse", Table 3.

This proposal, translated into the specifications of the Mouse conceptual design, worked as an initial IM for the project.

Just to follow a little more within the project we will refer only some focal concerns using, for the sake of simplicity of our descriptions, the names of some principal actors:

- Douglas Dayton: exterior design;
- Jim Sachs and Rickson Sun: the encoding translations (from mechanical to electrical and opting) were critical displacements for meeting the requirements of Cost and Reliability;
- Jim Yurchenko: tolerances allowed for the small parts that were to be built in plastic created problems for the moulding process that were new to the industry.

Another actor was enrolled, an actor with a very interesting network by itself: Micro Molding. This name represents the teams *"of skilled machinists and toolmakers who had first worked for agricultural machinery companies and then electronics manufacturers before getting into computers"* (American Heritage, 2002) (see Table 4).

Figure 8. Translations between two centers

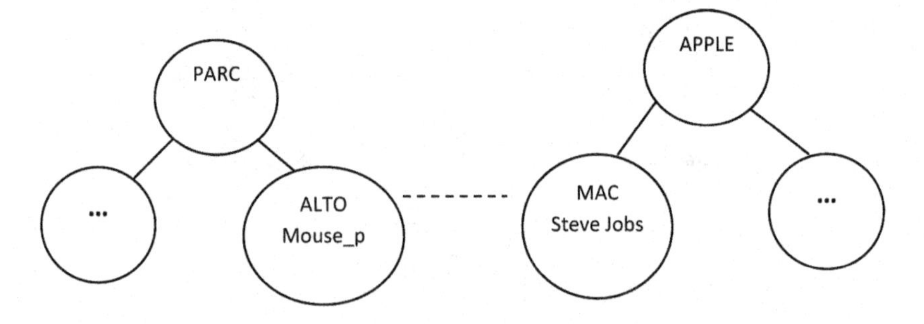

Figure 9. Paradigms from PARC_p

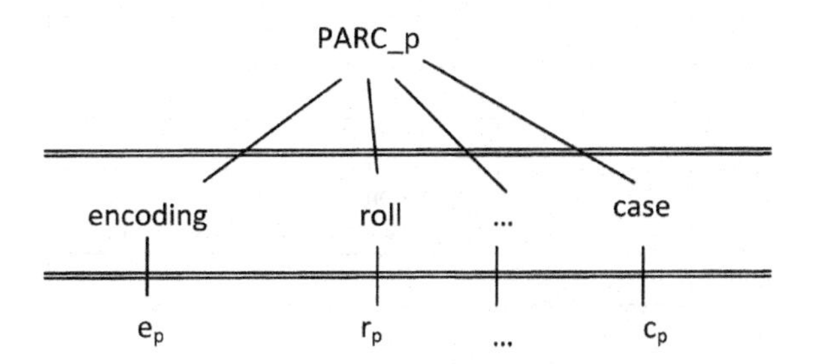

Re-Presentation Using Translation Regimes

Tables 1, 2, 3 and 4 represent the first part of a referent for this innovation. To exercise the analysis of *procession* and *network*, the two regimes of translation, on this chain of PAs, we may observe that what appears in the sintagmatic axis are "signs", that is Expression/Content. The syntagm is a combination of signs (Barthes, 1985), Table 5.

On the other hand paradigms are the domains from where the competences are taken. In another way, Figure 9.

In this formulation, to find the translations-*networks* regimes we follow *keep expression even if content changes*. We must detail some interrogations of the Table 3. For instance, for "roll", Hovey says (Mighty Mouse, 2002): "The ball didn't need to be pushed; it could float". Here we have a transformation of expression, keeping the content the same: to get information where the ball was moving.

Table 1. PARC narrative

PARC_p				
PARC	encoding	roll	buttons	case
...				
design	e_p	r_p	b_p	c_p
....				

Table 2. Steve Jobs displacement to PARC

Mouse_p	
PARC	Steve Jobs
Concept: Mouse, a pointing device	ok
Design (encoding, roll, buttons, case)	?
cost	ko

Table 3. Mouse, Conceptual Design

Mouse, Conceptual Design	
Steve Jobs	Hovey-Kelly
Resolution: 1/100 inch	?
Buttons: 3	?
No special pad to roll on	?
Inexpensive	?
Reliable	?

Table 4. Hovey-Kelly and stakeholders

Mouse, Detailed Design				
Dean Hovey	Douglas Dayton	Jim Sachs and Rickson Sun	Jim Yurchenco	Micro Molding
Exterior design	ok			
Encoding: electrical and optical components		ok		
Mechanics (rib cage)			ok	
Molding			?	ok

Table 5. Signs in PAs: content and expression

PARC_p					
PARC	encoding	roll	buttons	case	content
…					
design	e_p	r_p	b_p	c_p	expression (material mediator of the content)
….					

For the translations-*processions* example (*keep expression to change content*) we may use the case of the buttons going from PARC to Apple the mouse lost a button (Bardini, 1996). We may interpret it as the same expressing (use of buttons for the highlighting and selecting in the monitor space) but with a change in content because the Apple project team intended to avoid complications in the use of the buttons.

We have then showed a formalised way and a meta-language to follow the building of the internal references on innovation cases and also showed how it was possible to detect regimes of translation in chains of PAs. The two stylized regimes, *procession* and *networks*, we think, are both at play in the building of innovations (see Figure 10).

FROM LOCAL TO GLOBAL

A Macro Setting: Global Value Chains

We now turn our attention to management theories that may be useful as "proposals" that we can use at strategic levels. These proposals configure "spaces" where mediations can be made to build strategies. One of those theories is the Global Value Chain Framework (GVC) (Sturgeon, 2001) and (Sturgeon, 2006). We will use it to define our milieu of OPPs and explore our approach in two cases: MIPS/Chipidea (2008) and Iberomoldes (2008).

To illustrate our approach a much simplified classification of GVC, as is in Figure 11, is enough. *Relational* and *modular* governance types are "loosely-coupled" (Brusoni et al., 2001) forms of organisation where there are some complexities in the transactions that preclude decoupled (perfect market) forms. In the *modular* governance type there are economic ways to codify transactions, whereas in *relational* type some intermediary work is needed.

Taking the view of regimes of translation, it is reasonable to assume that transactions along *modular* governance types would align more to a *procession* type. In the *relational* governance type, due to the social work of intermediaries, one cannot reason, a priori, which translation regime would prevail?

To go further in the analysis we will relate on the following two cases, Chipidea and Iberomoldes.

MIPS/Chipidea, a Nice Fit

The Semiconductor Industry (Tuomi, 2009) has responded to the competition on the GVC with a split into Fabs (Foundry) and Fabless (Design) businesses. Fabless companies, tend to re-use their designs whenever possible (EE Times, 2007) which corresponds with a movement towards *modular* governance types of transactions.

Due to the complexity of transactions Intellectual Property (IP) business is oriented towards a *relational* type of governance, but there are strong pressures to improve productivity which implies movements towards a *modular* governance type.

Figure 10. Negotiating meaning

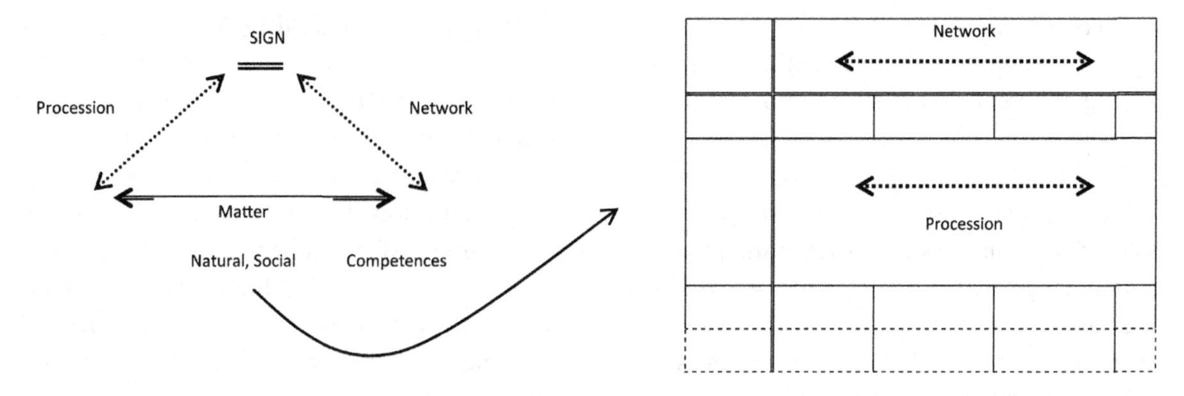

Figure 11. The Global Value Chain

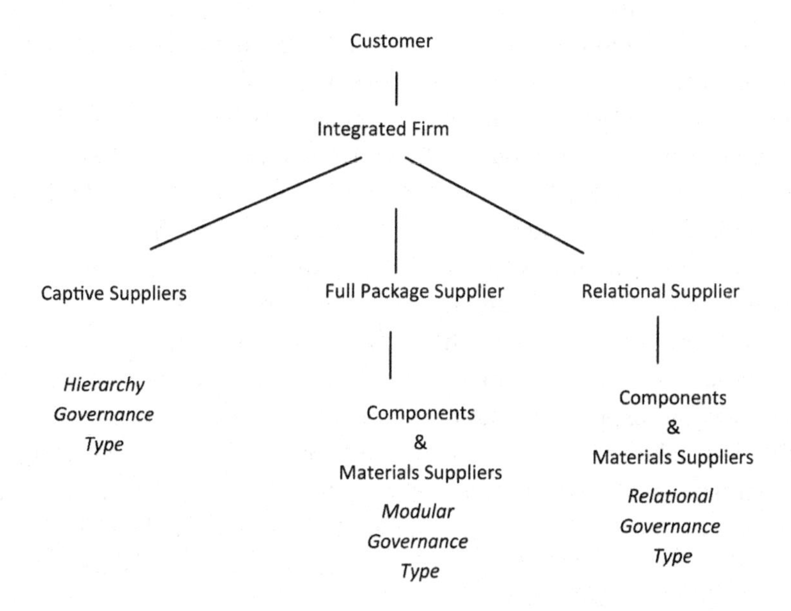

In Figure 12 we present a segmentation of the Intellectual Property (IP) business. MIPS and Chipidea are in this same business but Chipidea is very strong in analog and RF domains whereas MIPS is strong in digital domains.

In March 2007 MIPS acquired Chipidea in a $147 million deal (EE Times, 2007). However the integration was not successful and in August 2009, MIPS sold Chipidea to Synopsys by $ 22 million (Electronic News Weekly, 2009).

Reasoning by means of translations we have two settings to deal with: the management of the IP technology portfolio and the management of the integration of the personnel.

In terms of the technical setting, IP companies will tend to search for solutions that could be capitalized into others; the "ideal" will be to build a virtual system that could be adapted for many situations, although this is a difficult proposition due to the complexities of the business. The so-called systems-on-chip (SoC) are a kind of metaphor for this ideal solution, a new paradigm (Figure 13).

But SoC *"means many things to different people"*, (Sangiovanni-Vincentelli, 2003):

- Japan and Korea: integration of memory and microprocessors

- Elsewhere: anything that uses large numbers of transistors
- For Sangiovanni-Vincentelli: integrating different design styles into a coherent whole

The proposition SoC is not easy to translate in action as its meaning is a question mark. In terms of the management of the resource integration, things are also difficult to deal with. MIPS bet was a *procession* translation - same expression, changing content – integrating Chipidea personnel structure into theirs. That proved not feasible in the conditions of the industry. In face of the bad results, MIPS then favoured a more short term approach: costs and liquidity.

Synopsys, from the technological side is strong in design tools and, having more resources and having invested much less in the buying of Chipidea, is better prepared to pursue the path to a virtual system. As for the integration of personnel it has been keeping the two structures apart: same expression, same content. It could go to, in terms of personnel, trying to find a way to build a *network* solution: changing expression, maintaining content. This will take some time. One forgets frequently that time is, in ANT view, the same as displacement.

Iberomoldes, From Tools Master to Industrial District

Inscriptions may be thought of as displacements through spaces but, to remain alive and strong, fresh displacements are always needed: inscriptions should travel incessantly along networks. Although travelling and communicating is more and more easily done, nonetheless they imply work and some inscriptions do not travel well. The next case (more a short story) shows an industry were local displacements are strongly needed.

The Portuguese plastic mould industry has a very interesting history. It was born from a challenge to create a mould industry without the background of a strong industrial culture, namely precision mechanics. The solution was to translate the traditional Tool Master role into a process of division of labour and this solution has been very successful (the Portuguese plastics mould industry is worldwide class and was the first to widely invest in the CAD technology). Still it is a very sophisticated industry in a region where there are no local markets for their products. It is a *relational* governance type value chain but moving swiftly to a *modular* governance type.

Iberomoldes (2008) is one of the leading firms in this business and on visit to their facilities at Marinha Grande we were somewhere surprised

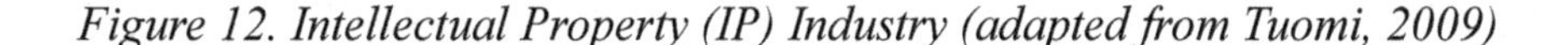

Figure 12. Intellectual Property (IP) Industry (adapted from Tuomi, 2009)

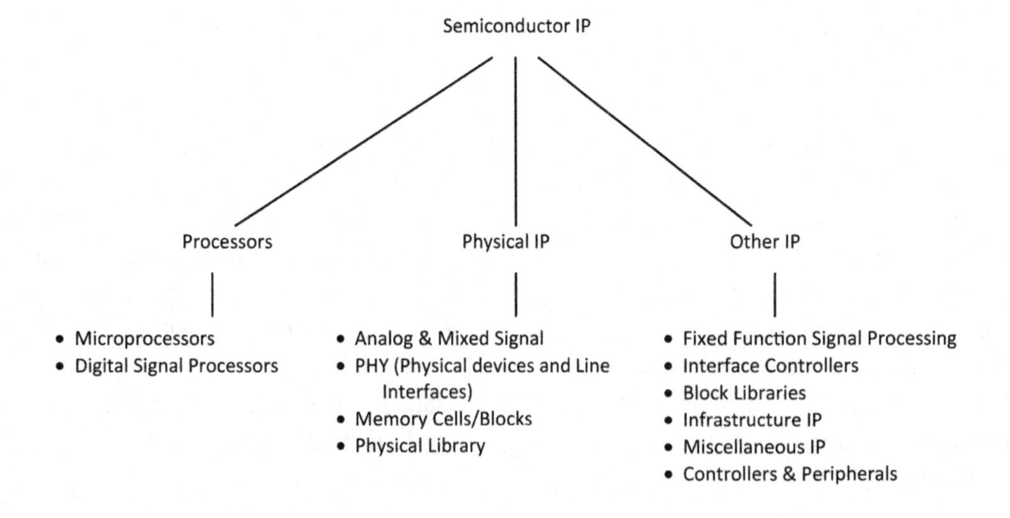

Figure 13. SoC, a new Paradigm?

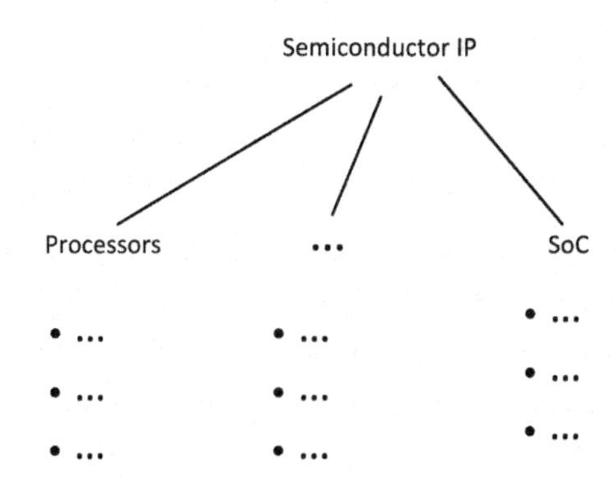

that one strategy that was been to pursue was to join forces, both public and private, in order to enrol another actor, the Full Package Supplier, exploring the good geographic situation of Portugal west coast, to build a transport infrastructure to serve South and Centre Europe.

This move can be described in terms of the regimes of translation: moulds are typically *shifters* within the same referent. Iberomoldes is continuously making new paradigms but for places that are not its local place. That is not enough for Iberomoldes that intends to create new circulations. This proposal, of course, implies the mobilization of different sets of new competences.

CONCLUDING REMARKS

With this paper we intended to clarify how travelling in different and crossing trajectories contributes to the emergence of meaning. We experiment crossing from local to global, from natural to social and vice-versa in crossing spaces. The space where these trajectories are designed is a space of negotiation along the building and dismantling of actor-networks. We addressed mediation and a Latour semiotic approach as ways to give meaning to the work of IMs. *Procession* and *network*, the two regimes of translation, were integrated in the Program of Action framework. This allows following changes in content and expression (construction of meaning) during the execution/construction of the program of action. The method we tentatively express is explored using these programs of action as tools, in the sense we just described. This exploration is experimented in micro and macro settings, travelling from the local to the global.

The referent, one of the main subjects of our paper that we intended to clarify, is to be found along a sequence of programs of action developed in a sustainable alignment.

This paper inscribes in a series of five papers following a research on ANT and Engineering Design. The first paper of this series introduces competences to give meaning to the work of professionals. The Programs of Action were there firstly addressed. The second paper situated the practice of engineering design as a search of IMs. This actual paper details and formalises a method to take advantage of IMs. A fourth will be about the informatics formalization of the method, addressing requirements only. Finally we intend a fifth to be the application of all the knowledge constructed in this research to understand the work of designers (practitioners work).

REFERENCES

Akrich, M. (1992). The description of technical objects. In Bijker, W. E., & Law, J. (Eds.), *Shaping Technology/Building Society: Studies in Sociotechnical Change* (pp. 205–224). Cambridge, MA: MIT Press.

American Heritage. (2002). *The Making of The Mouse*. Retrieved from http://www.americanheritage.com/articles/magazine/it/2002/3/2002_3_48.shtml

Bardini, T. (1996). *Changement et Réseaux Socio-Techniques: De l'inscription à l'affordance, Réseaux (No. 76)*. CENT.

Barthes, R. (1985). *Éléments de sémiologie*. Éditions du Seuil.

Brusoni, S., Prencipe, A., & Pavitt, K. (2001). Knowledge specialization, organizational coupling, and the boundaries of the firm: why do firms know more than they make? *Administrative Science Quarterly*, *46*(4), 597–621. doi:10.2307/3094825

Callon, M. (1986a). On the Methods of Long Distance Control: Vessels, Navigation and the Portuguese Route to India. In Law, J. (Ed.), *Power, Action and Belief: A New Sociology of Knowledge?* (pp. 234–263).

Callon, M. (1986b). The Sociology of an Actor-Network: The Case of the Electric Vehicle. In Callon, M., Law, J., & Rip, A. (Eds.), *Mapping the Dynamics of Science and Technology: Sociology of Science in the Real World* (pp. 19–34). London: Macmillan.

Callon, M. (1991). Techno-economic networks and irreversibility. In Law, J. (Ed.), *A Sociology of Monsters: Essays on Power, Technology and Domination* (pp. 132–161). New York: Routledge.

Callon, M. (1994). *L'innovation technologique et ses mytes*. Gérer & Comprendre.

ChipIdea. (2008). *MIPS-Chipidea merger's goal: 'virtual' SoCs'*. Retrieved from http://www.design-reuse.com/news/16608/mips-chipidea-merger-goal-virtual-socs.html

Eco, U. (1976). *A Theory of Semiotics*. Bloomington: Indiana University Press.

Electronic News Weekly. (2009). *Synopsys pays $22m for MIPS analogue business group*. Retrieved from http://www.electronicsweekly.com/Articles/2009/05/11/46047/synopsys-pays-22m-for-mips-analogue-business-group.htm

Gonçalves, F. A., & Figueiredo, J. (2010). How to recognize an Immutable Mobile when you find one - translations on innovation and design. *International Journal of Actor Network Theory and Technological Innovation (IJANTTI)*.

Høstaker, R. (2002, October 10-13). *Latour – Semiotics and science studies*. Paper presented at the Annual Meeting in the Society for Literature and Science, Pasadena, CA. Retrieved from http://ansatte.hil.no/rohar/artiklar/latourggreimas.htm

Iberomoldes. (2008). *Based on personal communication of the CEO, Mr. Henrique Neto*.

Latour, B. (1991). *Nous n'avons jamais été modernes: essai d'anthropologie symétrique* (p. 167). Paris: Découverte & Syros.

Latour, B. (1992). Where Are the Missing Masses? The Sociology of a Few Mundane Artifacts. In Wiebe, E., Bijker, E., & Law, J. (Eds.), *Shaping Technology/Building Society: Studies in Sociotechnical Change* (pp. 225–258). Cambridge, MA: MIT Press.

Latour, B. (1993a). Les Tribulations de L'Image Scientifique, Le «pédofil» de Boa Vista – montage photo-philosophique. In *Petites leçons de sociologie des sciences* (pp. 213–219). Paris: Éditions La Découverte.

Latour, B. (1993b). Les Tribulations de L'Image Scientifique, Le Travail de l'image ou l'intelligence savante redistribuée. In *Petites leçons de sociologie des sciences* (pp. 165–168). Paris: Éditions La Découverte.

Latour, B. (1993c). Les Tribulations de L'Image Scientifique, Les anges ne font pas de bons instruments scientifiques. In *Petites leçons de sociologie des sciences* (pp. 234–252). Paris: Éditions La Découverte.

Law, J. (1992). Notes on the theory of the actor-network. *Ordering, strategy and heterogeneity. Systems Practice*, *5*(4), 379–393. doi:10.1007/BF01059830

Macintosh Mouse. (2002). Retrieved from http://library.stanford.edu/mac/mouse.html

Mouse, M. (2002). Retrieved from http://www.stanfordalumni.org/news/magazine/2002/marapr/features/mouse.html

Sangiovanni-Vincentelli, A. (2003). *The Tides of EDA, IEEE CS, CASS*. Retrieved from http://embedded.eecs.berkeley.edu/research/hsc/class/papers/d6sang.lo.pdf

Sturgeon, T. J. (2001). *How Do We Define Value Chains and Production Networks*? Retrieved from www.inti.gov.ar/cadenasdevalor/Sturgeon.pdf

Sturgeon, T. J. (2006). *Conceptualizing Integrative Trade: The Global Value Chains Framework*. Retrieved from www.dfait-maeci.gc.ca/eet/research/TPR_2006/Chapter_3_Sturgeon-en.pdf

Times, E. E. (2007). *MIPS-Chipidea merger's goal: 'virtual' SoCs*. Retrieved from http://www.eetimes.com/showArticle.jhtml?articleID=201803503

TimesAsia, E. E. (2007). *MIPS boosts analog IP line with Chipidea acquisition*. Retrieved from http://www.eetasia.com/ART_8800477579_480100_NT_8dd61497.HTM

Tuomi, I. (2009). *The Future of Semiconductor Intellectual Property Architectural Blocks in Europe*. Retrieved from http://ipts.jrc.ec.europa.eu/publications/pub.cfm?id=2799

Woo, J. (2006). *A Short History of the Development Of Ultrasound In Obstetrics And Gynaecology*. Retrieved from http://www.ob-ultrasound.net/history1.html

This work was previously published in International Journal of Actor-Network Theory and Technological Innovation, Volume 2, Issue 3, edited by Arthur Tatnall, pp. 1-16, copyright 2010 by IGI Publishing (an imprint of IGI Global).

Chapter 9
Theoretical Analysis of Strategic Implementation of Enterprise Architecture

Tiko Iyamu
Tshwane University of Technology, South Africa

ABSTRACT

In the past and present, organizations experience difficulty in managing information, technology, changing from system to system, implementing new technology, maintaining compatibility with existing technologies, and changing from one business process to another. It is thought that these challenges could be prohibitive to the organization, and in this regard, many organizations deploy Enterprise Architecture (EA) in an attempt to manage the situations. The deployment of EA does not go without its challenges from development to implementation. This study focuses on the implementation of EA by using two case studies. The case studies are theoretically analysed from the perspective of Actor-Network Theory (ANT) to gain better understanding of the socio-technical influence in the implementation of EA in the organisations. This was done by following the negotiation process that took place among the actors, both humans and non humans.

INTRODUCTION

From the perspective of computing, Enterprise Architecture (EA) is a paradigm, which promises to address and reduce the challenges currently encountered by both business and technology (Kappelman, 2002). The development and implementation of EA has impact on the entire organisation that deploys it. This could be attributed to its intention to enable the organisation in addressing and achieving the balance between Business efficiency and IT innovation. Despite some constraints, EA has the potential to solve problems of imbalance during transition and implementation (Zachman, 1996). EA allows the organisation to directly, or through its individual business units, to innovate safely in their pursuit of competitive advantage. At the same time, it assures the needs of the organization for an integrated IT strategy, permitting the closest possible synergy across the extended enterprise (Spewak, 1992).

DOI: 10.4018/978-1-4666-1559-5.ch009

There is no unique approach for developing EA (Zachman, 1996; Cook, 1996). Irrespective of the development approach adopted, the output is intended to address business and technology needs. This involves meaning, interaction and translation associated to EA during implementation. This is the main justification of the study.

There are many domains of EA. The study explored the approach which prescribes four main domains, namely, Enterprise Business Architecture (EBA), Enterprise Information Architecture (EIA), Enterprise Application Architecture (EAA), and Enterprise Technical Architecture (ETA) (Ross et al., 2006; Tapscott & Caston, 1993). These domains are interdependent in implementation, primarily because of the relationship in their focuses and deliverables. The problematisation, development and implementation of EA hugely depend on people, technology and process. The interdependency and interrelated nature of the activities makes implementation heterogeneous and encompasses networks.

The deployment of EA within the context of a specific business enables an organisation to create a joint Business and IT planning and execution process (Cook, 1996). Spewak (1992) emphasised planning as a concrete foundation for development and implementation. Rationale for the deployment of EA in many organisations include integration of business and IT planning, which could result in quicker time to market; an increase in customer intimacy; and greater operational efficiency enterprise-wide (Zachman, 1996).

Many organisations have developed (blueprint of) EA. The executives and stakeholders approval for the deployment of EA is arguably based on the promising nature as presented by the promoters. Many of the developed EA encounter problem during implementation. Others are never implemented. According to Ross et al. (2006, p. 65), "most of these architecture exercises end up abandoned on a shelf". Some of the problems encountered during implementation have social context orientation. Implementation requires the power to enforce. According to Mintzberg (1983), power has the capability to effect (or affect) organisational outcomes. Power is a productive force that organises, formats and solidifies actors into various sorts of agents that perform actions. As such, the relationship in the union between the business and IT units is seen as critical factor, particularly in the areas of roles, responsibilities and ownership related to EA implementation in many organisations. The study seeks to understand better strategic approach for the implementation of EA in the organisation. The case study approach was adopted and Actor-Network Theory (ANT) was applied for the analysis of the data.

The paper is organized into five main sections. The first section presents the literature review, exploring available literature on enterprise architecture (EA) and information technology (IT) strategy. The second section covers the research methodology and approach that was adopted in the study. In the third and fourth sections, the paper presents and discusses the analysis and empirical findings, respectively, of the study. Finally, the paper concludes with highlights of the contributions of the empirical findings of the study.

LITERATURE REVIEW

For a company to be successful, it must adapt quickly and spend less time reminiscing about the norms of the organisation's pursuits (Porter, 2008). The EA approach is a framework for developing business driven objectives through architecture. Through an evolutionary, iterative process, the current and future state definitions of the architecture are continuously developed, evaluated, and updated in order to assure EA alignment with changing business requirements and emerging technology (Zachman, 1996). It is suggested that EA has "audiences" across the organisation, fundamentally because it serves as a basis for analysis and decision-making in the business and in the life cycle of systems.

EA is not just a design; in fact it leads to the development and deployment of consistent, multiple software- and technology-based changes in the business, and amalgamation of the both the IT and the business. According to Iyamu (2009), EA is a technical mechanism which defines the role of the business, information, technical and application architectures that best enable the needs of the organisation. This definition is provided to guide the study. Architecture invigorates the need to design and redesign as well as continuously improve the functioning of enterprises. Schekkerman (2004) argued that EA is a complete expression of the enterprise; a master plan which acts as a collaboration force between aspects of businesses and it enables technological infrastructure. EA is intended to reduce the cost of deployment, maintenance and management of technology and processes in the enablement of business goals and objectives. It could be used to achieve significant organisational advantage over competitors in a competitive marketplace. It does this through process effectiveness and efficiencies arising from the eliminations of non-value adding and redundant tasks, streamlined information flow, systems placement, and business restructuring (Ross et al., 2006). EA is intended to provide methodology for modelling what business functions are performed, who (or what) performs them, where and when the functions are performed, how the functions are performed, and most importantly, why the business needs to perform these functions (Gibson, 1998).

The scope of EA is seen as a union of the enterprise, the business engineering and development that is applied to it, and the technical domains that support it in the organisation. This scope is defined through pragmatism, thereby enacting the importance of EA in the organisation. However, the meaning, interactions and interpretation brought into the implementation of EA is significance to the outcome. Armour (2007) emphasises the potential challenges in the implementation as critical to the deployment of EA in the organisation. Like every other subject, implementation of EA has never been easy. Implementation of EA involve social context, which include process and people. From the perspective of ANT, the concept of translation is particularly important in implementation, where human actors are expected to adapt, translate and innovate in carry out their task (Tatnall, 2009).

Due to the significance role of EA, as a bridge between business and IT (Zachman, 1996; Ross et al., 2006), it is of paramount importance to measure it. Organisations have different requirements and method for the measurement of EA in their various organisations. DeLone and McLean (1992, 2003) developed a model consisting of six categories of IS success: Systems quality; Information quality; Use; User satisfaction; Individual impact; and Organizational impact. This model has been extensively used in the computing environment, including empirical studies.

In order to understand the social context in the strategic implementation of EA, the study employed the concept of Actor Network Theory in the analysis of the data. This is primarily because of its social orientation. Social is not simply human, other materials are involved (Law, 1992). Bielenia-Grajewska (2009, p. 41) emphasised that, "*we should remember that a person is not only determined by some factors, but it is also a factor himself or herself, determining the shape of the environment*". One of the key features of the Actor-Network Theory is that it doesn't place emphasis human above non human entities (Tatnall & Davey, 2005). That is, when people interact with other people, the interaction is mediated through objects of various kinds, and such interactions are in turn mediated through additional networks of objects and people. Iyamu and Dewald (2009) argue that networks grow changes and possibly stabilises during the deployment of technology. These various networks both participate in and shape the social, and therefore, if the material in these networks were to disappear, then the social order(s) would too (Law, 1992). Hence, the view in ANT is that a particular order is an effect generated by heterogeneous means. An actor is seen as produced from or as an effect of these heterogeneous relations between people and objects, and an actor is also, always, a network (Law, 1992).

RESEARCH METHODOLOGY AND APPROACH

ANT focuses on how people and objects are brought together in stable, heterogeneous networks of aligned interests through processes of translations and negotiations (Law, 1992). Latour (1996) emphasises that heterogeneous networks overcome issues related to identity, and avoid arbitrary dichotomies and structures. According to Latour (1996), the heterogeneity is reflected in different organisational principles that are in simultaneous action. The combination makes it possible to engage in a balance between identified and or known different interests and values.

According to Latour (1996), each element in the network is simply defined by the heterogeneous list of its associates. Entities are hence defined through their existence and their specific associations with other entities and they are not substitutable. The elements within a network, whether human or non-human, acquire power through the number, extensiveness and stability of the connections routed through them.

ANT has frequently been revised and extended, and there is, therefore, no unified body of knowledge. There are, however, some relatively stable key elements of the theory (Walsham, 1997). In Table 1, Walsham (2001) identified the following key concepts of Actor-Network Theory:

The key concepts of Actor-Network Theory as tabulated in Table 1 are defined and briefly discussed as follows.

Actor or Actant: Actors are defined as all entities that are able to connect texts, humans, money, etc., to build more or less effectively a world that is filled with other entities having their own history, identity and relations (Callon, 1991).

Actor-Network: When actors and their interactions are taken together they form a network. An actor-network that is known and predictable in a certain situation and context can be assimilated into a black box. Such a punctualisation is a temporary simplification of a network that acts as a single unit so that the network behind can be effaced into one actor (Law, 1992).

Table 1. Key Concepts of ANT (Walsham, 1997)

Concept	Description
Actor (or Actant)	Any material, i.e., human beings or non-human actors
Actor-network	Related actors in a heterogeneous network of aligned interests
Translation	How actors generate ordering effects by negotiating or manoeuvring others' interest to one's own with the aim to mobilise support
Inscription	Embodied translations into a medium or material
Enrolment	Mobilise support by creating a body of allies through translations
Irreversibility	The degree to which it is subsequently impossible to go back to a point where alternative possibilities exist
Black box	A temporary simplification of a network that acts as a single unit so that the network effaces into one actor
Immutable mobile	A materialised translation that can be interpreted in essentially the same way in a variety of contexts

Translation: Translation implies transformation, which refers to how actors engage with other actors to generate ordering effects (Law, 1992). Actors negotiate or manoeuvre others' interest to their own with the aim of enrolling actors into the network. When such translations get embodied into a medium or material, they are referred to as inscriptions (Akrich, 1992). Such inscriptions prescribe a program of action for other actors, although they can vary in strength and flexibility (Hanseth & Monteiro, 1996).

Inscription: Inscription is the act of proposing a pattern of use as the solution followed by the attempt to enforce it onto others. Inscriptions may lead to irreversibility, which refers to both the degree to which in a certain situation it is impossible to go back to a point where alternative possibilities exist, and the extent to which it shapes and determines future translations (Hanseth & Monteiro, 1996).

Enrolment: ANT proposes that enrolling allies creates aligned interests and the translation of their interests must be such that participation will lead to the network's maintenance. A form of translation is required to align individuals' perception with their ambitions and interests.

Irreversibility: Irreversibility is a measure of how difficult it is to undo decisions and the extent to which these determine subsequent ones. Callon (1991) argue that the degree of irreversibility depends on the extent to which it is subsequently impossible to change, including the extent it shapes and determines subsequent translations.

Black Box: Within ANT, when enough cohesion is obtained in order that an organised whole is formed from an assembly of disorderly and unreliable allies, when "many elements are made to act as one" (Latour, 1996) then a 'black box' can be said to have been created. A black box has properties of irreversibility, for it cannot be easily disassociated, dismantled, renegotiated or re-appropriated. Networks that are anchored in places to black boxes will therefore tend to be more stable and resilient that those that are not.

Immutable Mobile: A materialised translation, hence mobile, that can be interpreted in essentially the same way in a variety of contexts (i.e., relatively stable in space and time) is referred to as an immutable mobile. Such immutable mobile entities often possess strong properties of irreversibility, e.g., information technology architecture standards in the computing environment.

Interpretive approach was employed in the study. This is primarily because interpretive approach within information systems research is particularly aimed at producing an understanding of the social reality, the context and process whereby information systems influences and are influenced by the context (Walsham, 1993). According to Klein and Myers (1999), interpretive research explicitly demonstrates the reasons for the understanding of a text. It does not aim to explain and predict but to understand and to make sense of others' actions (Myers & Avison, 2002; Lee, 1994).

The set of principles proposed for conducting and evaluating interpretive research studies by Klein and Myers (1999) were useful in the data collection of the study. The study took cognisance of these principles (the Principle of the Hermeneutic Circle, Contextualisation, Interaction between the Researchers and the Subjects, Abstraction and Generalisation, Dialogical Reasoning, Multiple Interpretations and Suspicion) which are all related and interdependent, with the hermeneutic orientation as a golden thread connecting them all. Hence the principles were not applied mechanically. These principles have been applied in many works such as Monteiro and Hanseth (1996). The importance and relevance of each principle is partly derived from the manner in which the others are applied to the collection and interpretation of the field material (data). As a result, the set of principles were not used mechanically in the study.

The study adopted dual case study methodology to investigate how EA can be successfully implemented in organisations. Two case studies were used to gain an insightful, qualitative interpretation of how the implementation process has been carried out in the organisations that deploys it.

To begin, a preliminary investigation was conducted to establish which organisation deploys EA. Criteria were formulated to identify successfulness of EA in the organisations. Of the few organisations who met these criteria, two were selected for the study, a financial institution and a Government department. The organisations have different cultural backgrounds and settings, and each provides some evidence of success based on the criteria, which were based on DeLone and McLean (1992, 2003). The financial institution has more than 10,000 employees which include 450 personnel in the IT division. The Government department has about 6,000 employees of which 250 are in the IT computing unit.

The criteria were used in designing the detail of the questionnaire, and the structured interviews in the two cases. The study adopted interpretive, dual case study and qualitative approaches. The decision was informed primarily because of the social implications of the implementation.

The research applies the case study method, primarily because it allows in-depth exploration of the complex issues involved in the study. Two case studies were conducted. Data sources included interviews and documentation. The number of interviewees varied as a result of the size of the organisations. A set of balanced respondent demographics was a key factor in achieving a true reflection of the situations. Targeted respondents were from both the Business and the IT units. The respondents were at various levels of the structure within the organisations. The respondents from the business unit included Business Analysts, Project Managers, Team Leaders, Development Managers and Head of Departments. Similar to the Business, the respondents from the IT unit were Application, Technical, Business and Information Architects, Technicians, Business Analysts, IT Managers, IT Project Managers and IT Executives.

The research employs a qualitative methodology to study how EA is implemented in the organisation that deploys it. Qualitative research is more suitable for this type of study as it allows clarification from respondents to questions when asking respondents to explain who, what, how, when, where and why. This enabled the researcher, through close interaction with interviewees, to develop a deeper understanding of the situation. Qualitative research is argued and described as a very useful method for complex situations and theories (Boucaut, 2001). In studying events in their natural setting, the case study makes use of multiple methods of data collection such as interviews, documentary reviews, archival records, direct and participant observations (Yin, 1994). Walsham (1993) believes that the most appropriate method for conducting empirical research in the interpretive tradition is the in-depth case study.

The data collected were relevant to EA with focus on the implementation approach. Data collected came from semi-structured interviews, as well as from relevant documentation from both business and IT units. The interviews were recorded and transcribed. Therefore, the case study approach is especially useful in situations where contextual conditions and events being studied are critical and where the researcher has no control over the events as they unfold. The case study, as a research strategy, should encompass specific techniques for the collection and analysis of data, directed by clearly stated theoretical assumptions.

Through the use of the interpretive method, findings were made from the data collected. These findings are presented in the next section.

FINDINGS

Many organisations face complex and unwielding challenges in assessing and articulating the components required in the implementation of EA in their organisations. The aim of this paper has been to contribute towards understanding of how EA is implemented in the organisations that deploy it. This section presents a combined result of the two case studies. As shown in Figure 1, five components were revealed to be most critical in the successful implementation of EA. These components are regarded as the key strategic components by the organisations. The components include Guiding Principles, Policy, Strategic Relationship and Ownership, Performance Measurement, and Conformance.

GUIDING PRINCIPLES

In the context of this study, Principles is defined as guiding statements of positions that communicate fundamentals, vision and mission that must be exhibited by the organisation during implementation of EA. The purpose of principles was to enable the organisation to take an incremental and iterative approach to transitioning to formal modelling, while allowing it to execute allocated and influence decision making immediately and consistently in the implementation of EA.

To successfully implement and maintain the EA in the organisations, principles were needed. EA contains principles, which reflected the collective and common will of the entire organisation as positioned by the business strategy. These

Figure 1. EA implementation components

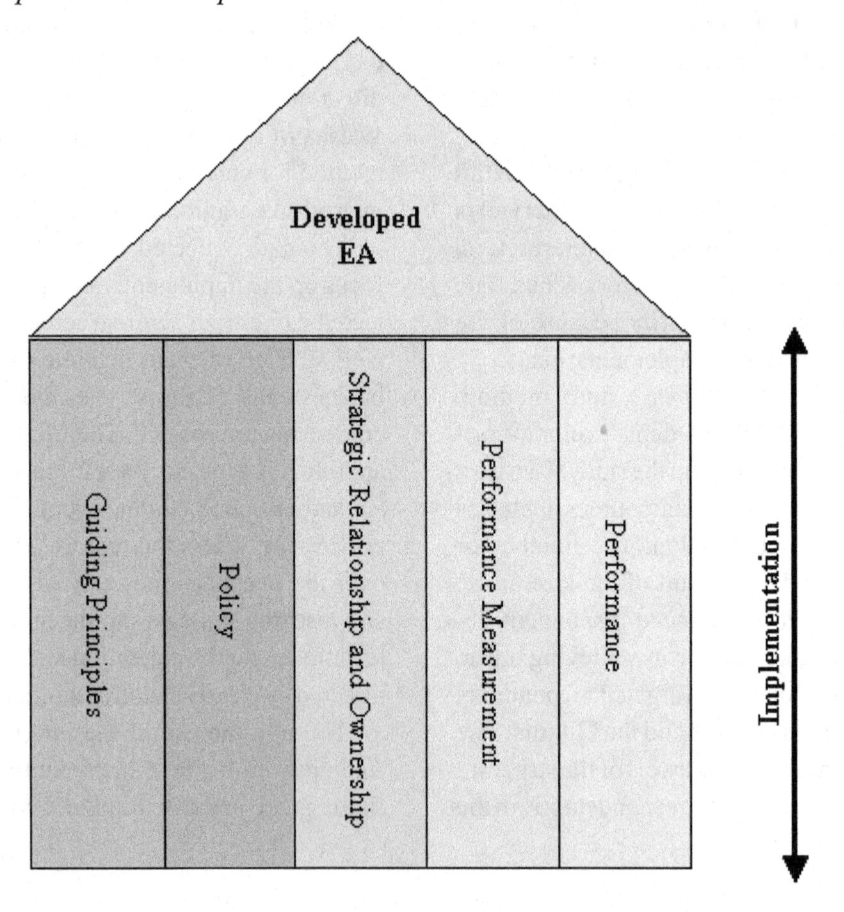

principles were basic philosophies that guided the process of implementation of EA. The principles guided the enrolment including execution of tasks of individual and team employees. Principles play a part in all the components of the domains. In the organisations, principles were primarily and consistently applied on diverse EA related matters in the various units of the organisation to achieve its results. It was used as evaluation criteria in the absence of detailed models that direct decision making more discretely and comprehensively. Based on this empirical evidence, the degree to which an organisation can establish principles across EBA, EIA, ETA, and EAA is dependent on its ability to identify and apply best practices in each area.

The implementation principles were related to each of the domains of EA and were derived from the principles which guided and ensured the delivery of business objectives as defined in the conceptual architecture (as illustrated in Figure 2). These principles leads to rationale and procedures and were used to give guidance to the designers, developers and implementers of the EA in the organisations. The rationale for the principles were documented along with procedures and guidelines associated with them. Table 2 is an example of a template which was used for the recording as well as documentation of the implementation principles. This template was populated and used to support strategic analyses over time in the organisations. Every technology deployed in the organisations was expected to be populated into the template.

There exists at least a principle for each element of EA implementation in the organisations. The principles were based on the business strategy. Each principle guiding the implementation had both business and IT (Technical) rationale, benefit to the organisations. The procedural elements needed for the implementation of EA were defined. The guidelines required to implement the principle in the implementation of EA in the organisation were defined. The guidelines include time frame, roles and responsibilities.

During implementation of EA in the organisations, principles had a significant impact mainly because they were stable. The principles provided guidelines and rationales for the constant examination, reengineering and re-evaluation of technology plans. The principles were generally derived from an intensive discussion with senior IT and business management, then validated in discussions with the highest IT Committee. These principles were viewed as a starting point for subsequent decisions that impacted the EA.

Application of principles, the above approach (Table 2) has contributed to a successful implementation of EA in the organisations, particularly from the perspective of the following:

i. Effective removal of hardware obsolescence. Removal of vendor dependency, which was costly during application re-engineering. The approach allowed for more flexible use of developmental program for staff and minimises training costs and requirements.
ii. Enable information systems to be periodically reviewed to ensure that they continued to meet the business needs and to avoid technological obsolescence.
iii. Ensured that the rapidly changing external businesses and technical environments adhered to significant changes within the organisations.

Table 2. Implementation principles

Principle	Rationale	Procedure	Guideline
Elements of vision and mission were represented and identified with a name.	For each of the principle, potential benefit was identified.	Modus of operandi and methods to consistently achieve the goals and objectives.	Boundaries, scope rules and regulations within which principles were carried out.

Figure 2. Enterprise Architecture domains

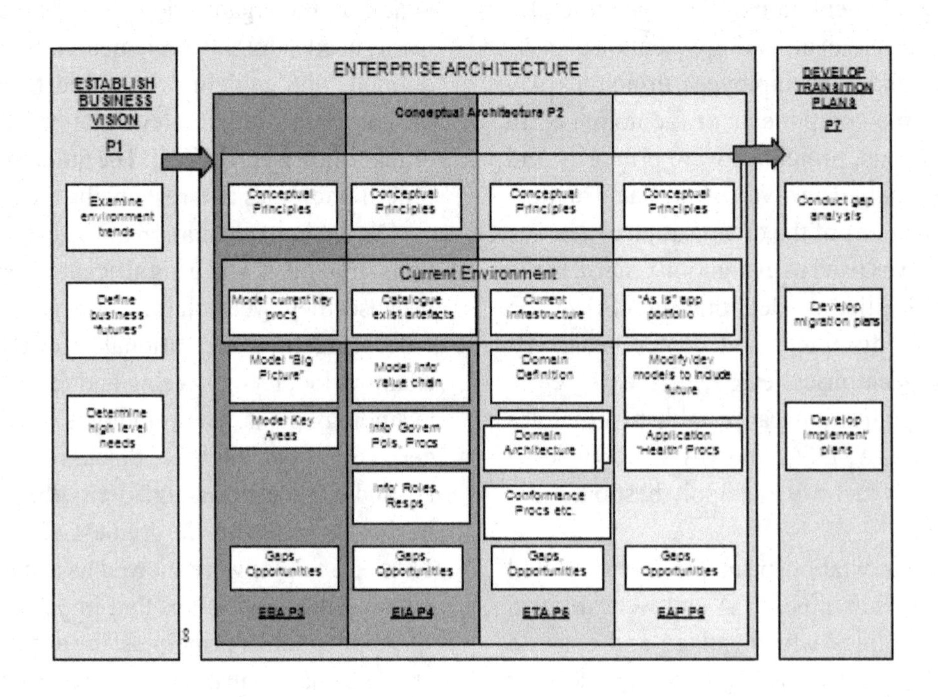

These changes required an ongoing evaluation process to protect the investments in information systems by keeping them current with the changing needs of the organisations.

IMPLEMENTATION POLICY

The implementation policy was made obligatory passage point (OPP) by the CIOs of the organisations and the various business units who subscribed to EA. This was mandated by the organisations and was meant to enforce rules and regulations during EA implementation.

The implementation policy lays down the requirements of the EA process and the constraints under which it must proceed and be implemented. Typically, some of the key policy statements included the following:

i. The EA must be driven by business strategies and take into account the full context of the enterprise (and its environment) in which the Enterprise Architecture will be applied.
ii. The EA implementation must continuously evolve through an iterative process.
iii. The implementation of EA must enable rapid change in the enterprise's business processes and the applications that enable them.
iv. The implementation of EA will guide the engineering of the enterprise's processes, information systems and technology infrastructure.
v. The EA must be understood and supported by senior management and lines of business and must therefore be marketed accordingly.
vi. All management that is involved in the engineering of the enterprise's processes, information systems and technology infrastructure will be held accountable for ensuring conformance with the EA requirements.
vii. All projects are to be assessed in terms of architectural fit, at certain stages of the project life cycle, as part of the Project Quality Assurance (QA) process.

The policy statements were sanctioned by the executive and they were enforced through performance contracts of individual executive members. This was drilled down to employees in the lower ranks. The performance contract was used to determine the employees' annual bonus and financial incentives, including promotions.

STRATEGIC RELATIONSHIP AND OWNERSHIP

Fundamentally, this component was critical in the implementation of EA. It clarifies ownership, accountability and responsibility of key elements that needed to be implemented. Table 3 shows example matrix cross-references the implementation elements as they apply to the individual architecture areas. "O" = Owner, "A" = Applicable.

PERFORMANCE MEASUREMENT

Performance measurement emerged as a key aspect of the implementation of EA in the organisations. Establishment of the right performance measure has been key to the success of EA in the cases studied. Executive members of both organisations had the belief that an enterprise must be able to tell whether progress is being made on its goals and objectives, and whether stakeholder expectations are being met.

Performance measures were built, as part of allocated tasks in individuals and teams performance contract in the organisation. The performance contract was an obligation, which was mandated by the rules and regulations of the organisation.

There were a large number of constraints, some natural, which were inevitably required attention in order to achieve the implementation of EA in the organisations. Some of examples include the following:

i. The inherited technological environment that existed at the initiation of the process;
ii. New technologies constantly emerging that must be accommodated;
iii. Immediate concerns such as providing information technology support for a new headquarters building, and
iv. The fact that any information systems architecture is always in transition and ever changing and evolving.

EA assists in the development of performance measurement criteria that could be linked to the business and IT strategies, objectives, and goals. It allows us to organise documentation in support of performance measurement and determines not only the content of reports, but also the path of the data from source to final report recipient. The combination of all the reports of all the performance measures became the basis for a data warehouse and an EA report that was truly tailored to the enterprise's vision and way of working. These reinforced initiatives, reward behaviour, support change and enhance strategies.

CONFORMANCE

EA conformance procedures should be implemented to ensure adherence to the EA process, thereby enabling the business to realise its strategic goals whilst maximising business value – this was after all the primary benefit derived from the EA.

The architecture conformance procedure was applicable to all parties involved in the engineering of the organisation's processes, information systems and technology infrastructure i.e. all those who were affected by the EA Policy.

It applies to all Business and IT related projects as well as change requests, regardless of whether they were initiated by the Business or IT. In some instances, the reviews will also be event-driven,

Table 3. Matrix of best practices and principles

Elements of Implementation	EBA	EIA	ETA	EAA
Common Vision	O	A	A	A
Corporate Planning process	O	A	A	A
Visible Strategy	O	A	A	A
Enterprise Models	O	O	O	O
Open standards		A	O	A
Technology standards		A	O	A
Portability and scalability			A	O
Technology innovation	A		O	A
Data Management		O	A	A
Information Sharing	A	O	A	A
Information Protection	A	O	A	A
Architectural governance	A	A	O	A
EA planning and implementation	A	A	A	A
"*Build*" or "*Buy*" applications			A	O
Message-based interfaces		A	O	A
Network interface			O	A
Logical/Physical server boundaries			O	A
Virtual Data Centre			O	A
Infrastructure patterns			O	A

e.g. time-based reviews to ensure that existing processes, information systems and technology infrastructure, were still in line with the EA.

Architecture conformance assessment reviews were conducted as part of the quality assurance (QA) process at the various stages of the Systems Life Cycle, as well as the Project Life Cycle as principled by EA in the organisations. At each stage of these life cycles, sets of questions from each of the four architectural perspectives (EBA, EIA, ETA and EAA) enabled the QA reviewers to determine whether or not the EA strategy has been complied with. Only those projects and change requests that were likely to have an architectural impact were required to go through the detailed architectural conformance assessment reviews.

In summary, due to performance contracts which each of the employees agreed to, there was a degree of irreversibility of allocated tasks thereby making the process of EA implementation institutionalised. This creates a black box in carrying out individual tasks in the implementation of EA in the organisations. Activities of the implementation which were anchored in places to black boxes seem stable and resilient.

ANALYSIS OF THE DATA

The above findings were analysed using an ANT perspective. This was to gain an understanding at the actor level of the factors which influences the strategic implementation of EA in the organisation. This includes understanding of the spheres of influence of actors and the influence of power in the implementation of EA. The analysis was done through 'processes of the ANT concepts' (Walsham, 1997) as earlier discussed.

Preliminary investigation was conducted on thirteen organisations to determine which organisation has successfully implemented EA. The organisations operates in different cultural settings, have different business disciplines, but few were in competition. A summary profile of the organisations which participated in the preliminary investigation is tabulated in Table 4.

On each of the organisations, interviewing of the employees came to conclusion when the interviewer reached a point of saturation. This is the point when no new information was forthcoming.

The preliminary investigation revealed that for most organisations, EA is primarily based on common expectation which was the minimal threshold of shared knowledge, theory, and experience which must be achieved from both Business and IT perspectives. This leads to cohesiveness and adaptiveness in the efforts to achieve a common goal. The preliminary investigation revealed that for an EA to be considered successful it must meet certain criteria. The criteria used in this context were extracted from objectives as set by its sponsor and stakeholders in the organisations and the reviewed literature. These criteria are tabulated in Table 5.

Columns 2 and 3 in Table 5 below were measured relatively to the ration of individual respondents in each of the organisations. The measurement was based on grading of 1 (lowest) to 5 (highest). For example, if number respondents exceeded average, it was considered a response.

What was even more critical and important was the implementation of the developed EA. It has proven to be very challenging as many organisations have been unsuccessful in the discipline. Of the thirteen organisations that participated in the preliminary investigation, only five have been successful in the implementation of EA. Others have rather concentrated on Application or Technical architecture. The elements of Delone and McLean (1992, 2003) model of IS success was validated as being important to the delivery of the implementation EA in the organizations. The elements of the model align with the explicit requirements of the organization as explored during the study and tabulated in Table 5.

The process model presented is reached from the analysis of the data from the study. It reflects the consistent approach which was employed by organisation to build, maintain, and apply EA. The model emphasises a holistic approach to architecture development by recognising the perspectives and components that make for a complete view. It should be applied uniquely to each organisation's needs, which depends upon its business strategies, architectural maturity, priorities, organisational culture, and the general computing environment.

People, technologies and processes were the actors involved in the strategic implementation of EA in the organisations. Each of these actors belonged to one or more networks. The networks were based on the activities and the interest of the actors. The networks of people heterogeneously covered area of expertise, roles and responsibilities, which simultaneously overlapped during EA implementation in the organisations. Architect worked with other employees in different teams such as software development and network administration units. According to one of the interviewees, *in the things that I do as a technical architect, many people from other units are stakeholders in my tasks. They include people from the business, software developers and other architects. The same people are involved in other works including that of my colleagues.* There were also groups of friends. This formed networks of common interest.

The driving factors and requirements for the deployment of EA in the organisations were capital expense; ongoing operating costs; return on investment; usability; and manageability. Principles, policies and standards EA were developed based on these factors and requirements.

Network in information technology is different from Actor Network Theory definition of networks. A network incorporates both technical and

Table 4. Participants in the preliminary investigation

No.	Size of Organisation	Size of IT	No. of interviewees	Industry Type
1	=> 20 000	750 or more	16	Financial
6	10000 – 19 999	500 - 749	Average of 21	Financial (2); Energy (3); Telecommunication (1)
3	5000 – 9999	250 – 499	Average of 17	Government (2); Telecommunication (1)
2	1000 – 4999	50 – 249	Average of 6	Telecommunication (1); IT (1)
1	100 – 999	10 – 49	3	Information Technology and Communication

Table 5. Metrics for selection of organisation for the study

Metrics	No. of organisations who responded	No. of organisations who agreed
Business and IT strategy alignment.	13	13
Percentage of cost reduction in the IT projects as result of EA process.	9	4
Bridge the communication gap between Business and IT and increase mutual understanding	8	3
Achieve an increased uniformity and consistency in IT practices	10	5
Achieve greater effectiveness of contract administration process and reduce the number of contract disputes	11	4
Reduce time to resolve disputes and controversies in the selection of technologies.	12	5
More than fifty percent of IT projects has undergone through EA processes to date.	12	4
More than fifty percent of Business and IT employees' actively participating in EA processes.	13	5
More than fifty percent of IT projects adherence to EA standards.	13	4
More than fifty percent of Business units who sees value in participation of EA process.	13	4

non-technical actors with linkages consisting of stabilised translations and interactions between actors Latour (1997). According to Wickramasinghe, et al (2009:21), "*This is a network of materially heterogeneous actors that is achieved by a great deal of work that both shape those various social and non-social elements*". This is different from technology infrastructure network as deployed in the computing environment. The networks of technologies include technologies of the same compatibility, deployed on the same platform or collaborate with other technology deployed on different platform to form an entity. An example is applications deployed on a server to carry out business processes. For example, there were applications deployed on separate server infrastructures but collaborate to carry business process. This was to be enabled by the principles, policies and standards in order to ensure it achieve the *operandi* of the organisation. A senior explained that *all technology deployment must meet the architectural guidelines, which include principles, policies and standards.*

Different processes were applied in the implementation of EA in the organisations. The processes were related and depended on each other to exponential degree. Similar to people and technologies, processes were critical in the implementation of EA in the organisations. The processes outlined the rules and regulations within which implementation of the various tasks of EA were carried out. The processes included roles and responsibilities, principles, policies and standards (such as measurement and conformance).

Individuals and various teams interpreted and translated the technologies and processes differently. The translation of meaning were based and influenced by the different networks the individuals and teams belong to. In most cases, the managers were dominating, as such were able to persuade the employees to accept his or her translation of processes and technologies. This was based on trust some of the employees had on their managers. Others had no choice as the rules and regulations of the organisation weren't flexible for negotiation.

As illustrated in Figure 2, there was routine in the implementation of EA. The routine involved seven stages in the development and implementation of EA. The development stages were business vision and conceptual framework. This included documenting the current and future of the Enterprise Business Architecture (EBA), Enterprise Information Architecture (EIA), Enterprise Technical Architecture (ETA) and Enterprise Application Architecture (EAA) domains of EA. The implementation stages were the transition plan, gap analysis and execution of plans. The study focuses on the implementation only. This routine was considered the norm. No employees could act different from the processes outlined in Figure 2. Otherwise, it was considered act of insubordination. One of the employees expressed as follows: *it is very important for us not to change it, otherwise, we would continue to explore without result . . . we are all used to this process and it is part of orientation for new employees.*

Figure 2 shows a geographical illustration of the EA model. EA is a process which intends to address all aspects of bridging from strategy to implementation and deal with the gaps that consistently challenge the achievement of significant enterprise change (Kling, 1995). This process was expected to enable prioritisation of analysis and implementation effort. This was based on value delivered and therefore allows organisation to proceed at its own pace while progressing in the change at the same time.

The building blocks as shown in Figure 1 were within the principles, policies and standards as set by the organisation and translated by employees, particularly managers. The building blocks were allocated to individuals and teams, periodically. Executions of the tasks were incentivised through annual financial bonuses and promotions. Most employees subscribed to managers' interpretation mainly because of the incentives associated to the executions of the allocated tasks. An attempt to reverse or interpret the processes or technologies other than the managers' embroiled conflict, which was sometimes considered insubordination.

Principles, policies and standards, which included measurement and conformance, were critical components in the implementation of EA. The components were applied in all the domains of EA in accordance to the requirements and specifications. Allocations of tasks were also carried out and evaluated within the principles, policies and standards of EA in the organisation. The principles, policies and standards were primarily to avoid individual interpretation and translations of meanings during implementation of EA. Some employees expressed in affirmation: *we are glad that we have the governance bodies who define for us the principles, policies and standards and our managers goes to workshop to understand the meaning including the boundaries.*

CONCLUSION

The EA process must address all aspects of bridging from strategy to implementation and deal with the gaps that consistently challenge the achievement of significant enterprise change. These problems impact significantly on business performance and will continue to do so if not addressed. This process must enable prioritisation of analysis and implementation effort based on value delivered and must allow an organisation to proceed at its own pace while progresses change at the same time.

The findings of the study, the adoption of EA support and emphasises on the value of collaborative work in the process of change, work that institutionalises the interaction between different levels and participants in the enterprise vision and the strategies that deliver it.

The result of the study emphasises an approach to EA development by recognising the perspectives and components that make for a complete view. The success of EA in any organisation greatly depends on how the change elements are managed.

The study contributes to the understanding of the criticality of social relationship between people, technology and process in the implementation of EA in the organisation. It highlights the importance of the influence of non technical factors in the implementation of EA. this help the IT managers in terms of area of focus during deployment of EA.

Another contribution of the study is to both IS research and professionals in the area of EA. It helps to understand better the importance of heterogeneity of activities and networks of various interests in the implementation of EA.

REFERENCES

Akrich, M. (1992). The description of technical objects. In Bijker, W. E., & Law, J. (Eds.), *Shaping technology, building society* (pp. 205–224). Cambridge, MA: MIT Press.

Armour, F., Kaisler, S., & Bitner, J. (2007). Enterprise Architecture: Challenges and Implementations. In *Proceedings of the 40th Hawaii International Conference on System Sciences* (pp. 217-217).

Bielenia-Grajewska, M. (2009). Actor-Network Theory in Intercultural Communication – Translation through the Prism of Innovation, Technology, Networks and Semiotics. *International Journal of Actor-Network Theory and Technological Innovation*, *1*(4), 39–49.

Boucaut, R. (2001). Understanding workplace bullying: A Practical Application of Giddens' Structurational Theory. *International Education Journal*, *2*(4), 65–73.

Callon, M. (1991). Techno-economic networks and irreversibility. In Law, J. (Ed.), *A sociology of monsters. Essays on power, technology and domination* (pp. 132–164). London: Routledge.

Cook, M. A. (1996). *Building enterprise information architectures: reengineering information systems*. Upper Saddle River, NJ: Prentice-Hall.

DeLone, W., & McLean, E. (1992). Information Systems Success: The Quest for the Dependent Variable. *Information Systems Research*, *3*(1). doi:10.1287/isre.3.1.60

DeLone, W., & McLean, E. (2003). The DeLone and McLean Model of Information Systems Success: A Ten-year Update. *Journal of Management Information Systems*, *19*(4).

Gibson, S. (1998). Evangelizing about Enterprise Architecture. *PC Week*, *15*(38), 78.

Hanseth, O., & Monteiro, E. (1996). Developing Information Infrastructure: The tension between standardization and flexibility. *Science, Technology & Human Values*, *21*(4), 407–426. doi:10.1177/016224399602100402

Iyamu, T. (2009). The Factors affecting Institutionalisation of Enterprise Architecture in the Organisation. In *Proceedings of the 11th IEEE Conference on Commerce and Enterprise Computing* (pp. 221-225). Washington, DC: IEEE Computer Society.

Iyamu, T., & Dewald, R. (2010). The use of Structuration and Actor Network Theory for analysis: A case study of a financial institution in South Africa. *International Journal of Actor-Network Theory and Technological Innovation*, *2*(1), 1–26.

Kappelman, L. A. (2002). We've Only Just Begun to Use IT Wisely. *Management Information Systems Quarterly*, *887*, 116.

Klein, H., & Myers, M. (1999). A set of principles for conducting and evaluating interpretive field studies in Information Systems. *Management Information Systems Quarterly*, *23*(1), 67–93. doi:10.2307/249410

Latour, B. (1996). Social Theory and the Study of Computerised Work Sites. In Orlikowski, W. J., Walsham, G., Jones, M. R., & DeGross, J. I. (Eds.), *Information Technology and Changes in Organizational Work* (pp. 295–307). London: Chapman & Hall.

Law, J. (1992). Notes on the theory of the actor-network: ordering, strategy, and heterogeneity. *Systems Practice*, *5*(4), 79–393. doi:10.1007/BF01059830

Mintzberg, H. (1983). *Power In and Around Organizations*. London: Prentice-Hall.

Monteiro, E., & Hanseth, O. (1996). Social Shaping of Information Infrastructure: On Being Specific about the Technology. In Orlikowski, W. J., Walsham, G., Jones, M. R., & DeGross, J. I. (Eds.), *Information Technology and Changes in Organizational Work* (pp. 325–343). London: Chapman and Hall.

Myers, M. D., & Avison, D. (2002). An Introduction to Qualitative Research in Information Systems. In Myers, M. D., & Avison, D. (Eds.), *Qualitative Research in Information Systems: A Reader* (pp. 3–12). London: Sage publications.

Porter, M. E. (2008). The five competitive forces that shape strategy. *Harvard Business Review*, *86*(1), 78–93.

Ross, J. W., Weill, P., & Robertson, D. (2006). *Enterprise Architecture as a Strategy: Creating Foundation for Business Execution*. Boston: Harvard Business School Press.

Schekkerman, J. (2004). *How to survive in the jungle of Enterprise Architecture Frameworks*. Victoria, Australia: Trafford.

Spewak, S. H. (1992). *Enterprise Architecture Planning: Developing a Blueprint for Data, Applications and Technology*. New York: John Wiley & Sons Inc.

Tapscott, D., & Caston, A. (1993). *Paradigm shift: The new promise of information technology*. New York: McGraw-Hill.

Tatnall, A. (2009). Information Systems, Technology Adoption and Innovation Translation. *International Journal of Actor-Network Theory and Technological Innovation*, *1*(1), 59–74.

Walsham, G. (1993). *Interpreting information systems in organizations*. Chichester, UK: John Wiley & Sons.

Walsham, G. (1997). Actor Network Theory and IS Research: Current Status and Future Prospects. In Lee, A. S., Liebenau, J., & DeGross, J. I. (Eds.), *Information Systems and Qualitative Research*. London: Chapman & Hall.

Walsham, G. (2001). *Making a World of difference: IT in a Global context*. Chichester, UK: John Wiley & Sons.

Wickramasinghe, N., Bali, K. R., & Goldberg, S. (2009). The S'ANT Approach to Facilitate a Superior Chronic Disease Self-Management Model. *International Journal of Actor-Network Theory and Technological Innovation*, *1*(4), 15–26.

Yin, R. K. (1994). *Case Study Research, Design and Methods* (2nd ed.). Newbury Park, CA: Sage Publications.

Zachman, J. A. (1996). Enterprise Architecture: The View Beyond 2000. In *Proceedings of 7th International Users Group Conference for Warehouse Repository Architecture Development*.

This work was previously published in International Journal of Actor-Network Theory and Technological Innovation, Volume 2, Issue 3, edited by Arthur Tatnall, pp. 17-32, copyright 2010 by IGI Publishing (an imprint of IGI Global).

Chapter 10
RAD and Other Innovative Approaches to Facilitate Superior Project Management

Rajeev K Bali
Coventry University, UK

Nilmini Wickramasinghe
RMIT University, Australia

ABSTRACT

Rapid Application Development (RAD) is promising to bring many benefits and state-of-the-art uses to the discipline of software engineering. The plethora of low cost RAD tools, together with the claims made by advocates of this methodology, has lead to an explosion in the use of this technique across the field. Unfortunately, however, there has been comparatively little regard in context to the project management issues of adopting RAD methodologies on which this paper will focus.

INTRODUCTION

RAD is a linear sequential software development process model that emphasises extremely short development cycles (Pressman, 1997) and was conceived as a means of reducing time-to-market. RAD was trumpeted as the way to reduce software development time which, according to Reilley (1995) would cost less than traditional methods and which would deliver higher quality products that better met business requirements.

The promise of low-cost and high-quality would require the support of radically new tools and precepts in order to meet these aspirations. Again, Reilley (1995) has stated that these tools and techniques would include Developers creating requirement diagrams using automated tools (rather than by hand), Group interviews (in which customers and developers discuss application design together - replaced one-to-one interviews) and the introduction of Time-Boxing to set time limits on tasks.

DOI: 10.4018/978-1-4666-1559-5.ch010

Martin (1991) discusses how software practitioners have dramatically reduced development times of IS dramatically whilst maintaining, or in some cases *improving*, quality. The key to this success has not only been the implementation tool used. Correct application of the technique to the correct projects (or parts thereof) together with an appreciation of the less visible, although equally important, management style displayed is of vital importance.

EXAMINING FITNESS FOR RAD

It is vital to understand which projects will benefit from the introduction of RAD techniques, and why. The indiscriminate application of the RAD methodology will not achieve the projected improvements in productivity. RAD will not work especially well in large and complex projects or in environments where bureaucracy is an endemic characteristic.

However, Connell and Shafer (1989) take the view that most IS applications can benefit from rapid prototyping and that it is the tools and techniques behind the methodology which will limit the effectiveness of RAD in the development process. The Authors do concur with Martin (1991) by saying that RAD will not be effective where there is little or no user involvement.

REQUIREMENTS SPECIFICATION

The requirements specification process comprises a high level of user involvement which should reduce the risk of misunderstanding the specification. Additionally, interactivity at this level acknowledges the efficacy of the group process whilst reducing the risk of an unusable specification.

The user of a system or product may not necessarily be a specialist in the field of software engineering; as a result, familiarity (or unfamiliarity) of technical concepts may lead to a "comprehension gap". One consequence of this may be a final specification which does not accurately reflect the true nature of the users' requirements. RAD attempts to alleviate this danger by the inclusion of the user in the development team and process. No attempt should be made to unduly progress a specification to the next iteration or stage as each iteration should attempt to produce some form of usable system.

Cost Analysis

Traditional process decomposition techniques or function point analysis can be used to estimate the likely duration of a RAD project in the same way as they can for a traditional project. Due regard should be paid to:

- The production of time estimates from these breakdowns
- The RAD tools' ability to reduce the number of lines of code required to implement each function point or process block
- The likely benefits of future productivity.

Resources should be optimised (for effective use of manpower) and so planning the duration of tasks and the division of tasks into smaller "subtasks" is a major element of the project planning process. RAD projects use relatively small teams (compared with traditional IS projects) who working on subtasks concurrently Reilley (1995), delivering components on an incremental basis. Planning the delivery of these installments would create pivotal milestones for the project upon which project progress can be measured or monitored.

Organisational Culture

In order to see significant benefits from the RAD process, it is necessary to motivate the development team and maintain this motivational momentum throughout the duration of the project. Martin (1991) advocates that the development team should be made to feel valued and important, perhaps extending to the provision of an isolated, customised, environment that they have helped design and implement.

Involvement in the RAD process should be viewed as a "win-win" situation. Software developers should be made to feel inspired and motivated (as they are achieving high quality results efficiently) and, equally, because they are producing good results efficiently, they become inspired and motivated.

It is imperative that the development team be well trained in the use of RAD tools and at least one member of the team should have prior experience of building applications using the tools. Barriers between the development team and the customers using and testing the system should be removed and both sides should be encouraged to communicate as much as possible.

According to Brooks (1975), system requirements are likely to change from what was originally anticipated. The appeal of the RAD process is that it gives the users an opportunity to use prototype systems relatively early in the project lifecycle. Users should be made aware that the systems they are testing early in project lifecycle are only prototype models which are designed to give a "feel" for how the final system may be implemented. If users are not made to feel an integral part of the process, such trials will be counter-productive, perhaps leading to apathy and user listlessness for the final system.

Risk Management

Butler (1994) takes the view that, like all process models, the RAD approach has some drawbacks. These include the requirement of sufficient human resources to create the correct number of RAD teams and the requirement of developers and customers who are committed to the necessary rapid-fire activities to complete a system in a reduced time frame. If commitment is lacking from either party, RAD projects might well fail.

These two points serve to highlight the type of difficulties which may occur in a RAD project. To be of any real value, the cultural aspect should be considered as an integral part of the initial team formation stage.

In any development methodology which uses small, highly focused teams, there is a danger that, often at the most inconvenient time, the team may suffer the loss of a key team member. However, the flexible and dynamic nature of most small teams can often compensate for this (as other team member assume additional tasks if required).

If there are any changes in the structure or mission of the customer, the project may suffer a loss of commitment from the RAD team. The high dependency on the customer-developer relationship means that any user-planned tasks may result in complications later in the programme.

If there is insufficient commitment to the project by the development team, the failure of the project may be inevitable, as time and financial overshoots may cause the project to be seen as a non-viable venture for the customer. In the worst case scenario, if the product is a vital part of the customer's business strategy, complications may result in severe and far-reaching repercussions for the customer.

Additionally, there is a risk of code failure in RAD projects. Carmel (1995), during his discussion on methodologies, recognises that disregarding a formal design phase may lead to little or no software re-use, resulting in a system which is brittle and hard to maintain.

To counter this, the Project Manager may select a candidate piece of software as the first prototype, further iterations of which would be refinements of code that has been re-used or extended – this maintains the advantage of using proven code. Many 4GL's rely on libraries of proven code in order to link together components of the application being written. This high degree of code-robustness means that the code may well become graphically similar to the Application's informal solution.

It should be recognised that some unprofessional developers working in a RAD environment may regard the technique as an excuse to "hack" code together in the name of prototyping. Carmel (1995) agrees with this and states that today's technology (such as RAD) allows developers to act as Artists rather than Programmers.

THE DEVELOPMENT PROCESS

RAD uses a development technique that more closely follows the process of natural invention (Goldense, 1994). My own experience of software engineering demonstrates an inclination to prototype an idea, try it out, refine it, re-try it, and refine it yet further. This process is inevitably open-ended. This relatively unorthodox development process is quick to get the main 90% of a project on its feet, but there is a risk that the final 10% will never be complete.

The RAD technique of "Time-Boxing" limits the duration and iterations of the development process, thereby stopping at the 90% example point, which permits sufficient refinement for the user. When combined with concurrency, this procedure can greatly shorten the delivery period.

RAD also permits users to take on additional tasks - such as unit testing - after the initial run-through (Reilley, 1995). This allows developers to return to their main task of coding. Inevitably this practice may be restrictive as the project plan is locked into these dates, making contingency planning very difficult. The most likely result is that if these milestones are firmly established, the development maturity of the milestone will be defined on a worst case basis.

PROJECT CONTROL AND MONITORING

When writing about difficulties controlling prototyping projects, managing problems can affect any type of project, not just those using prototyping methodologies (Maude & Willis, 1991). For inexperienced developers, the flexibility offered by prototyping therefore needs careful control. As RAD uses a highly flexible approach, this view would apply to the management of this technique.

The evolutionary nature of RAD poses the extra problem of accurately defining the status or maturity of the project where the developers' inclination is to produce just one more refinement iteration. Time-Boxing can limit the duration of a project phase but may in itself present the project manager with the decision of Timing versus Maturity.

Other factors involved in progress monitoring become evident when the user is part of the project team. The user's organisation may not recognise the authority of the project within its organisational structure, particularly if the main project development is taking place off-site. Planned dependencies within the project plan may be in direct conflict with other projects run by the user and this quandary emphasises the importance of full commitment from the customer.

A change in requirements remains a potential threat to all projects. RAD projects are no exception to this but it can be argued that the intrinsic incremental delivery process allows greater flexibility in the later phases of the project. Unlike non-RAD projects, moderate changes in direction are permitted. Change Control may be more manageable within a RAD project but this should be viewed with caution, as thorough re-planning should be undertaken to fully assess the ramifications of any change.

The danger of feature-creep (Carmel, 1995) means that RAD projects must be well scoped. The danger of complacency at this point assumes that the use of the RAD methodology will be beneficial as it makes a provision for altering the project scope later. Project metrics should be defined when the project is first planned, identifying those milestones that give feedback points to the control process. It must be noted that if the project scope changes part way through a plan, the project should re-planned to redefine the metrics and the significant milestones.

KNOWLEDGE-BASED IMPLICATIONS

The last but possible most important aspect is that of trying to incorporate the tenets of the knowledge-based economy. In managing projects this not only means that they must be rapidly designed and incorporate the essential germane knowledge present, but it must also mean that as time progress the solution must be continuously adapting and thereby building on the existing extant knowledge base yet always being relevant and enhanced in the future state (Wickramasinghe & von Lubitz, 2007; Wickramasingeh & Goldberg, 2007). This is depicted in Figure 1.

What is essential is that for both the diagnostic and prescriptive stages the tools, techniques and technologies of the knowledge economy are effectively and appropriately applied. This means that essential business intelligence and analytic techniques coupled with data mining tools and knowledge management tactics are applied (i.e., the intelligence continuum is applied). Figure 2 highlights how the intelligence continuum is utilised in this fashion as well as emphasising how this approach is continuous for the life of the system.

DISCUSSION

In addition to the adoption of RAD, we contend that to be even more effective and result in heightened success it is necessary to adopt an appropriate lens of analysis. We contend that ANT (Actor Network Theory) provides such a lens.

ANT was developed by British sociologist, John Law and two French social sciences and technology scholars Bruno Latour and Michel Callon (Callon, 1986; Latour, 1987; Latour, 2005; Law & Hassard, 1999; Law, 1992; Law, 1987;

Figure 1. Adaptive mapping

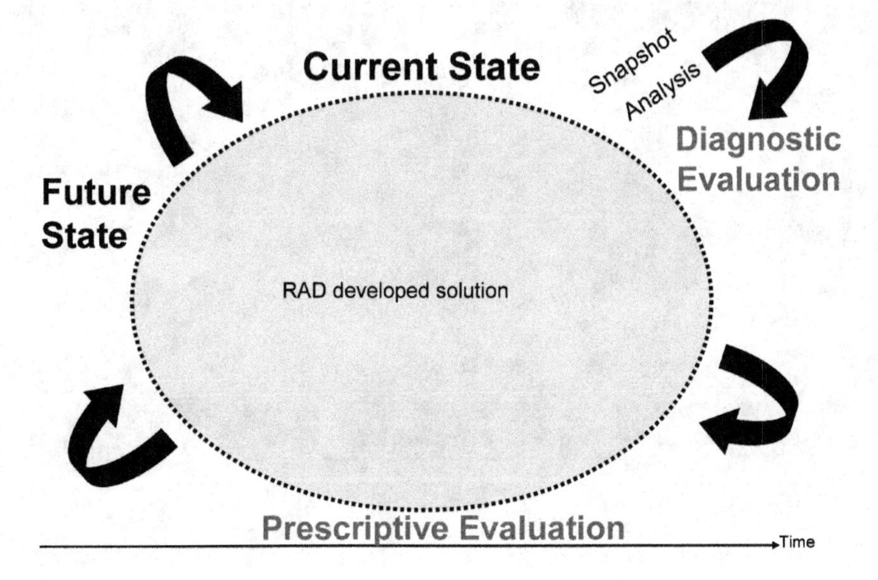

Callon, 1986). It is an interdisciplinary approach that tries to facilitate an understanding of the role of technology in specific settings, including how technology might facilitate, mediate or even negatively impact organizational activities and tasks performed. Hence, ANT is a material-semiotic approach for describing the ordering of scientific, technological, social, and organizational processes or events.

Although named "theory", ANT is neither a theory in a social theory sense nor is it trying to explain the behaviour of social actors. ANT is more of a framework based upon an array of concepts. It is based upon the principle of generalized symmetry, which rules that human and non-human objects/subjects are treated with the same vocabulary. Both the human and non-human counterparts are integrated into the same conceptual framework.

CONCLUSION

Project Management techniques should be adapted to fit the new RAD methodology, reducing the associated overheads at all times. Of principal importance is the need to reduce bureaucracy. More effort must be spent motivating people and getting users and developers communicating effectively. Progress measurement methods also need revision and both the project manager and the project plan need to be flexible and adaptable to the changing requirements.

This paper has argued that RAD is based on the understanding that the fundamental advantage offered is *freedom* and the ability to experiment and to constantly explore. This freedom may well be stifled by a more structured management approach to the project. The paper has postulated that, whilst there may be a trade-off between flexibility and control in the management of projects, this trade-off need not be so rigid when managing prototyping projects.

Figure 2. Knowledge-based systems development model

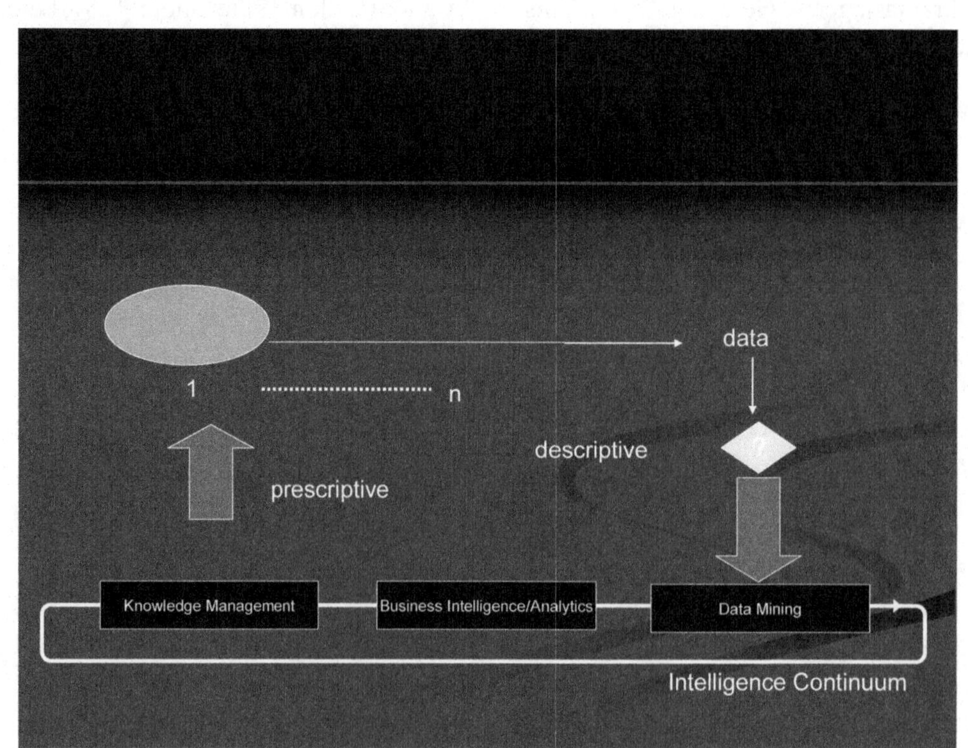

In addition in this paper we have tried to bring together tools, techniques and tactics from a knowledge-based perspective so that continuous improvements will always ensue. To do this we believe it is essential to embrace a rich analytic lens and we have thus suggested the role for incorporating ANT. In closing we call for more research into this important area that will further demonstrate the benefits of our proffered strategies.

REFERENCES

Brooks, F. (1975). *The Mythical Man-Month*. Reading, MA: Addison-Wesley.

Butler, J. (1994). Rapid Application Development in Action–Managing System Development. *Applied Computer Research*, *14*(5), 6–8.

Callon, M. (1986). Some Elements of a Sociology of Translation: Domestication of the Scallops and the Fishermen of St Brieuc Bay. In Law, J. (Ed.), *Power, Action and Belief: A New Sociology of Knowledge*. London: Routledge & Kegan Paul.

Connell, J. L., & Shafer, L. B. (1989). *Structured Rapid Prototyping*. Yourdon Press.

Goldense, B. L. (1994). Rapid Product Development Metrics. *World Class Design to Manufacture*, *1*(1), 21–28. doi:10.1108/09642369210049924

Latour, B. (1987). *Science in Action: How to Follow Scientists and Engineers Through Society*. Milton Keynes: Open University Press.

Latour, B. (2005). *Reassembling the Social: An Introduction to Actor-Network-Theory*. Oxford, UK: Oxford University Press.

Law, J. (1987). Technology and Heterogeneous Engineering: The Case of Portuguese Expansion. In Bijker, W. E., Hughes, T. P., & Pinch, T. J. (Eds.), *The Social Construction of Technological Systems: New Directions in the Sociology and History of Technology*. Cambridge, MA: MIT Press.

Law, J. (1992). *Notes on the Theory of the Actor Network: Ordering, Strategy, and Heterogeneity*. Retrieved from http://www.lancs.ac.uk/fss/sociology/papers/law-notes-on-ant.pdf

Law, J., & Hassard, E. (Eds.). (1999). *Actor Network Theory and After*. Oxford, UK: Blackwell.

Martin, J. (1991). *Rapid Application Development*. New York: Macmillan Publishing Company.

Maude, T., & Willis, G. (1991). *Rapid Prototyping, The Management of Software Risk*. Pitman.

Pressman, R. S. (1997). *Software Engineering a practitioners approach* (4th ed.). New York: McGraw Hill.

Reilley, J. P., & Carmel, E. (1995). Does RAD Live Up to the Hype? *IEEE Software*, 24–26. doi:10.1109/52.406752

Smith, M. F. (1991). *Software Prototyping, Adoption, Practice and Management*. New York: McGraw-Hill.

Wickramasinghe, N., & Goldberg. (2007). Adaptive Mapping to Realisation Methodology (AMR) to facilitate Mobile Initiatives in Healthcare. *International Journal of Mobile Communications*, *5*(3), 300–318. doi:10.1504/IJMC.2007.012396

Wickramasinghe, N., & von Lubitz, D. (2007). *Knowledge-Based Enterprise: Theories and Fundamentals*. Hershey, PA: IGI Global.

This work was previously published in International Journal of Actor-Network Theory and Technological Innovation, Volume 2, Issue 3, edited by Arthur Tatnall, pp. 33-39, copyright 2010 by IGI Publishing (an imprint of IGI Global).

Chapter 11
Desituating Context in Ubiquitous Computing:
Exploring Strategies for the Use of Remote Diagnostic Systems for Maintenance Work

Katrin Jonsson
Umeå University, Sweden

Jonny Holmström
Umeå University, Sweden

Kalle Lyytinen
Case Western Reserve University, USA

Agneta Nilsson
Umeå University and Gothenburg University, Sweden

ABSTRACT

Context awareness forms a core concern in ubiquitous computing and goes hand in hand with today's extensive use of sensor technologies. This paper focuses on the use of sensors as part of remote diagnostic systems (RDS) in industrial organizations. The study shows that the process of desituating context, that is, capturing context and transferring it to another context, is critical for the successful use of the technology. The processes of capturing and transferring context are explored in industrial maintenance work through interviews with suppliers and users of RDS. To successfully manage the desituation of context, industrial organizations must find strategies of creating and managing a center of calculation, a center where the captured contexts meet and merge. To enable the long-distance control of the equipment, all data must be compiled into one manageable view without losing the specifics of the local contexts. The data collection must be designed with this in mind. Moreover, to bridge the gap between the digital and the physical world created by the new way of organizing the maintenance work, a new kind of maintenance network must be formed, one in which local technicians' practices are reconfigured and instituted.

DOI: 10.4018/978-1-4666-1559-5.ch011

INTRODUCTION

Context awareness forms a core concern in ubiquitous computing and goes hand in hand with today's extensive use of sensor technologies in industrial organizations. As noted by Dey et al. (2001), sensors enable close attention to detail in their context and allow for automatic data collection. However, capturing context is not enough in ubiquitous computing environments. In this paper, we will see that desituating context – capturing context and transferring it to another context – is essential for ubiquitous computing use. This paper focuses on remote diagnostics systems, an application family within ubiquitous computing (Lyytinen & Yoo, 2002b). To date, the use of RDS has primarily focused on enabling effective and timely equipment maintenance (e.g., Jonsson et al., 2008). Sensors and network access are installed into equipments – mostly equipments and engines in industrial settings – to collect and access data remotely related to their performance. Critical performance indicators of industrial equipment can be monitored to ensure continuous and satisfactory performance and to guarantee timely and cost-effective maintenance. With RDS, centralized service centers can monitor and diagnose a large number of equipments remotely. Maintenance groups at these service centers engage in problem diagnostics and solving as well as value-adding services such as learning from failures and formulating forecasting models for equipment performance (Kuschel & Ljungberg, 2004; Tolmie et al., 2004).

RDS is often viewed as a harbinger of a new kind of practice that offers new possibilities for organizing maintenance. Improved uptime and lowered cost motivate the organizational use of RDS immersed in new settings and equipments. The impact of this technology may be observed in new work routines that separate technicians and the monitored equipment over time and space. In contrast to traditional maintenance, where local skilled workers use their senses and local data as the main source of information during maintenance, remote diagnostics depend on the content and quality of data plus the process of collecting and transferring it to the remote service centers. Local maintenance work has also been shown to be organized around communities characterized by collaboration and information sharing (Brown & Duguid, 1991). RDS reach beyond these local practices by transforming equipment's physical condition into a digital representation, which is then transferred from the local setting to a remote site for analysis. To this end, context is desituated: captured and transferred to another context.

The term "context" can seem obvious but at the same time obscure. Commonly, people find it hard to elucidate what it is, and in attempts to explain its meaning, synonyms as background, situation, milieu, and environment are often used. Dahlbom and Mathiassen (1993) argue that our understanding of context varies between individuals' own choice of underlying thinking and perspectives. Hence, context could be understood as a perceptual condition that to some extent is flexible and negotiable rather than a factual environment.

In context-aware computing, typical context information is: location, identities of nearby people and objects, and changes to all these things over time (Dey, 2001; Schilit, 1995). Dey (2001, p. 5) elaborates the definition of context as "any information that can be used to characterize the situation of an entity. An entity in such a view is a person, place, or object that is considered relevant to the interaction between a user and an application, including the user and applications themselves."

Contextualism in organizational change means that events should be explained within the context of their occurrence (Pepper, 1948). It views organizational life as complex with interconnected events and continuously changing patterns. In this tradition, context is dichotomized into the outer and inner contexts of organizations (Pettigrew et al., 2001). The outer context includes the economic, social, political, and sector environment.

The inner context is defined as features of the structural, cultural, and political environments through which ideas and actions for change proceed. The widely adopted socio-technical approach to information systems (IS) research on organizational change has been criticized for its limited view of context, its narrow perception of the duration and scope of innovation, and its sociologically naive view on technology innovation and social change (Avgerou, 2002). She emphasizes that the dynamics has to be studied as a situated emergent phenomenon, in which actor-network concepts provide a valuable analytical approach. The translation processes need to be understood by analysis of the relevant institutional contexts and their interactions.

In this study we deal with context-aware computing as well as contextualism in organizational change. RDS generate some of the new challenges associated with the interpretation of the computing context. Grudin (2001, p. 284) says that sensors "...can pick up some but not all context that is acquired through senses. Some context is lost, some is added, and captured context is presented in new ways... Missing or altered context disrupts our processing of information in ways that we may not recognize." RDS give insight into the complexity of working with contextual information, and the focus on equipment and their condition expands context beyond the current focus on individuals and their location and identity (Abowd & Mynatt, 2000). While desituating context is an essential ability for many ubiquitous computing application (Andersson & Lindgren, 2005; Lampe et al., 2004; Olsson & Henfridsson, 2005), current research has not explored this ability from an organizational perspective in any detail. This paper will contribute to this gap in research by exploring how the process of desituating context is managed in organizations using RDS. ANT is applied as an analytical lens for the contextualist inquiry into the use of an advanced RDS in six organizations.

To understand technology in a social context, it is important to focus on the relationship between technological artifacts and technology-in-practice (Hanseth et al., 2004). By conceptualizing the world as heterogeneous socio-technical networks, ANT can help analyzing and understanding the intertwined relationship between human agency, technology, and contexts to further our knowledge about desituation of context. ANT has gained increased interest in IS research (Holmström & Robey, 2005; Jones, 2000; Mähring et al., 2004; Walsham, 1997; Wickramasinghe et al., 2007). Applied to studies of IT, ANT guides the investigation of networks of people, organizations, software, and hardware (Latour, 1996; Walsham, 1997). For example, Moser and Law (2006) use ANT and argue that information in healthcare is fluid, referring to it being open, uncertain, in process and unstable. Mort May and Williams (2003) show how remote diagnosis in healthcare was made possible by the quality of the inscriptions of patients created by the nurse intermediaries. Walsham and Sahay (1999) analyze the development and use geographical information systems (GIS) in district-level administration in India. Their analysis shows that none of the districts studied created stable heterogeneous networks with aligned interests related to GIS. Consequently, the Western GIS was not adapted to the local Indian settings and Walsham and Sahay's (1999) study is a good example of ANT's principle that social and technical stability resides in the mutual dependency between technological properties and social context.

In the next section, we will review previous research on ubiquitous computing and draw on the ANT notions of action at a distance and centers of calculation. We then present the research method and the organizations forming part of the case study. The empirical results of the exploration of how the process of desituating context is managed in the case companies are also presented. Based upon the empirical results in relation to the literature, we identify two issues for which organizations dealing with the desituation of context need to find strategies. Finally, we conclude the paper with a summary of the findings.

LITERATURE REVIEW

Ubiquitous Computing

The computer has moved from dedicated operating rooms, via the desktop into our homes, and has now reached the status of innate or invisible objects in our everyday environments. Ubiquitous computing devices that weave computing into the environment are characterized by simultaneous potential for mobility, increased levels of embeddedness (Avital & Germonprez, 2003; Lyytinen & Yoo, 2002a) and context awareness (Dey et al., 2001). Due to mobility and embeddedness, they harvests large amounts of contextual data from environments, users, and equipments and use them in intelligent ways both locally and remotely. By being mobile, ubiquitous computing separates data from technology instrumental in collecting it (Avital & Germonprez, 2003) and allows data transfer over time and space. These computing environments can support knowledge work (Davis, 2003) and enable new ways of working (Garfield, 2005), learning (Chae, 2003), collaboration (Grudin, 2003) and business processes (Giles & Purao, 2003; Medovich, 2003). From a business perspective, data about customers as well as access to the customer's context can give business opportunities to develop new offers, as the present ubiquitous technology gives companies data and knowledge that was not previously available (Gershman & Fano, 2005).

Capturing context and informing an application of the context is a key challenge in the field of ubiquitous computing (Dey et al., 2001; Grudin, 2001). As Grudin (2001) points out, context that is captured is by default removed from its original context. This process of capturing context and transferring it to another context is what we label as desituating context. Recent research on context-aware ubiquitous computing applications is mainly focusing on identity and location (Abowd & Mynatt, 2000; Dey et al., 2001; Grudin, 2003) as well as focusing on context as something physically connected to people (Olsson & Henfridsson, 2005). Henfridsson and Lindgren (2005), identify multi-contextuality of use as particularly challenging in the design of ubiquitous services. As ubiquitous computing follows its user while moving through different spatial contexts and shifting temporally between different co-existing computing contexts, "context switching" capabilities become critical to support the user. Context is here defined in relation to persons and the situations they encounter. In contrast, Dey et al. (2001) show that context can be understood in a broader fashion both in terms of focus and content than what is assumed by current ubiquitous applications. In contrast to many other context-aware ubiquitous computing technologies, RDS not only address the context issues of identity (i.e., the ability to identify and separate equipments from each other) and location (i.e., where a equipment is located), but also pay attention to status (i.e., a snapshot of the performance of a equipment/process) and time (i.e., data on how such performance varies over a certain period). RDS thus goes beyond context in relation to people by also focusing on equipments (things).

Figure 1 presents an overview of organizing maintenance work based on the RDS's ability to collect data in remote contexts. New interactions and tensions emerge due to a new type of relationship between the technology embedded in a equipment and remote technicians' access to generated information. This way of working need to be contrasted with previous maintenance models, which to a great extent are based on the physical presence of technicians. Through the use of RDS, context is thus desituated: captured in a certain context and transferred to a remote setting. At the remote service center, technicians are located working with analysis of data as a base for planning maintenance. This way of organizing maintenance work, separating information from its context, enables the remote technicians to act from a distance. In the following section, we will explore this possibility of understanding what it means to act from a distance and what issues become critical in such a process.

Action at a Distance and Centers of Calculation

ANT seeks to explain social order through the construction and transformation of socio-technical networks, i.e., connections between human agents, technologies and objects (Callon, 1986; Latour, 1987). The argument behind the inclusion of both humans and non-humans, and the ordering of these, is that the social is not simply human; it is intrinsically related to other materials too (Law, 1992). ANT has frequently been revised and extended, and there is, therefore, no unified body of knowledge. In Table 1, we summarize some of the key concepts in ANT (adapted from Walsham, 1997).

'Action at a distance' is a concept proposed by Latour (1987) to describe how actors influence and control a remote context. What enables this process is the possibility of accumulating and transferring information about a remote object. During the information transfer, a translation process takes place. 'Translation' (Callon, 1986) implies transformation, which refers to how actors engage with other actors to generate ordering effects (Law, 1992). Translation goes beyond the traditional definition of action as it deals with mutual definition and inscription. When such translations get embodied into a medium or material, they are referred to as 'inscriptions' (Akrich, 1992). Such inscriptions prescribe a program of action for other actors.

Figure 1. Maintenance organization with the use of RDS

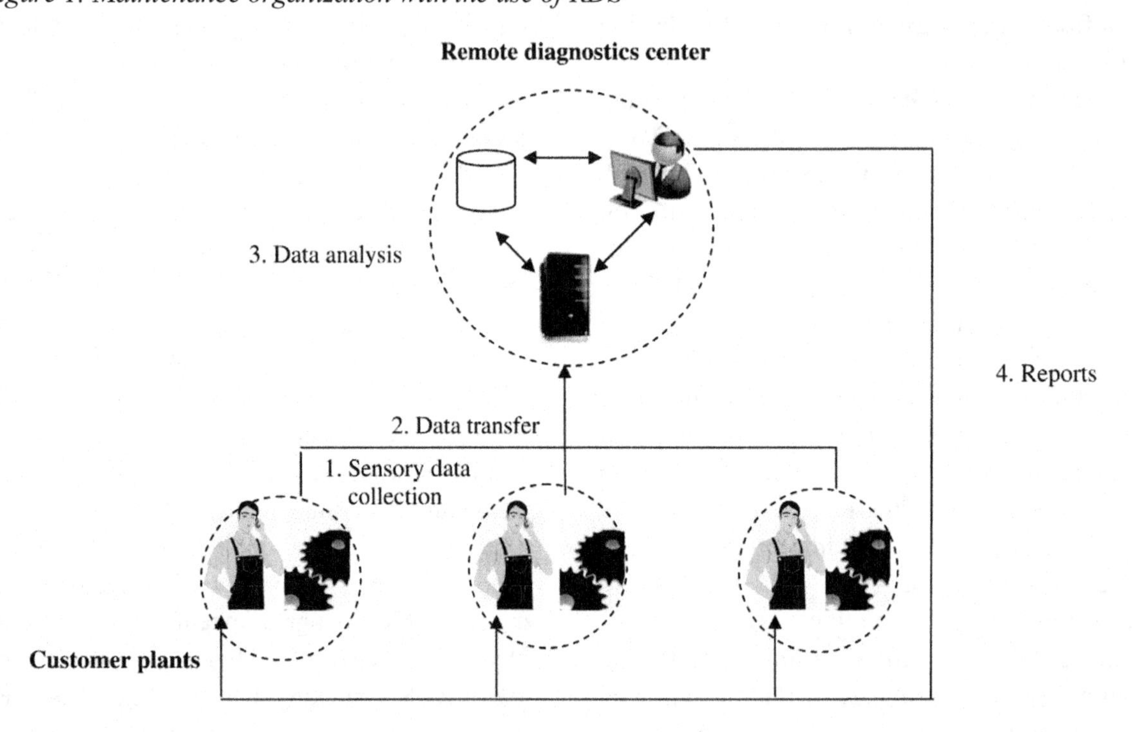

Table 1. Key concepts in actor network theory

Concept	Description
Actor (or actant)	Any material, that is, human or nonhuman actors
Actor-network	Related actors in a heterogeneous network of aligned interests
Action at a distance	How actors influence and control a remote context
Translation	How actors generate ordering effects by negotiating or maneuvering others' interest to one's own with the aim to mobilize support
Inscription	Embodied translations into a medium or material
Immutable mobile	A materialized translation that can be interpreted in essentially the same way in a variety of contexts
Center of calculation	A location for accumulation, synthesis and analysis of observations
Modes of ordering	Recurring patterns as part of the ordering of human and non-human relations

A critical issue becomes how to render the contextual information mobile, presentable, readable and combinable with other pieces of information, a state referred to as immutable mobile (Latour, 1987). Such immutable mobiles (Law, 1987; Mol & Law, 1994) can move in time and space while being interpreted in essentially the same way in a variety of contexts. Examples of such objects are writings, maps, graphs, figures, and formulas. Even though objects remain unchanged during their moves, locality and particularity are lost in the transfer from local to remote settings, while compatibility, standardization, and universality are gained (Latour, 2000). Translations can thereby make objects appear different to an individual at a remote site than it may appear to an individual close to the physical object.

'Center of calculation' (Latour, 1987) is a location for accumulation, synthesis and analysis of observations, i.e. collection of immutable mobiles. Examples of such centers of calculations are scientific laboratories or census offices. In these centers, information is accumulated about things, processes, people or places to facilitate prediction and control (Bloomfield, 1991).

According to Latour (1987) the information-accumulation process changes the relationship between remote and local actors. As the information goes from being locally situated to being universally applicable, the local actors lose their unique access to information, and the remote actors' position grows stronger. Consequently, the local actors are moved into the periphery if actions are not taken to make sure they are properly instituted in the network of remote actors and center of calculation (Bloomfield, 1991). The new information flows allow for new ways of organizing. The concept 'modes of ordering' (Law, 1994) is used to explain the multiple, often implicit, strategies and practices that hold an organization together. Organizing is about complex relations between the different modes of ordering (Law, 1994).

RDS are made up by a collection of technologies including sensors, which are diffused into equipments throughout a plant or a factory. The amount of contextual information collected by the sensors is quickly growing. However, merely collecting a large amount of data is not enough; we need to interpret and act upon the data in a holistic manner. The information containing the captured context needs to be effectively transferred into centers of calculations, where all the local data are merged; creating an overall sense of the context that is interpreted. Supporting this desituation of context seems to be of crucial concern for ubiquitous computing, and in the next section, we will explore this empirically in the use of RDS.

RESEARCH METHOD

Research Approach

As this study seeks to explore the desituation of context in maintenance work, organizations with experience of RDS were selected as objects of study. The research data were collected in six different organizations. The companies are MacGregor Cranes (MGC), Monitoring Control Centre (MCC), PowerDrive, Alpha, Beta and Gamma (fictitious names on the last four), all located in Sweden. The selection of the sites had theoretical rather than statistical reasons (Yin, 1989), as the primary aim is to understand more than it is to generalize. The results might thus not be generalizable, but this does not exclude the possibility that they can contribute to the collective body of knowledge of a discipline (Kautz & McMaster, 1994). The selection of the sites was based on their willingness to cooperate, the availability of multiple sources and the possibility of purposeful sampling (Peppard, 2001; Yin, 1989).

Table 2 presents an overview of the case organizations and their relation to the RDS. Further details of the organizations are presented. The study employed a qualitative data collection technique using semi-structured interviews. In all, the study includes 31 interviews, conducted by two researchers of which one is the first author of this paper. Four interviews were conducted at MGC, four at PowerDrive, seven at MCC, five at Alpha, six at Beta and five at Gamma. The interviews lasted between 45 minutes and 3 hours, with an average of about 60 minutes. Each interview was audio taped, which allowed the researchers to focus upon the respondent and formulate follow-up questions. The interviews were transcribed to enhance the analysis. All interviews were conducted on-site at the respondents' workplace, which allowed the researchers to gain some insight into the work context. When choosing participants, we wished to include individuals with different relationships to the technology. No restrictions in participation were imposed from management, and a contact person at each company helped us choosing respondents for the interviews. At all organizations respondents were chosen to cover both individuals in a managerial position and people working with equipments equipped with the RDS.

The data collection covered questions related to sensory data collection, data transfer and respondents' view of this process, issues of value, and the benefits and challenges of using this technology. Depending on the respondent's experiences, follow-up questions were formulated during the interview.

The results of this study were developed in a three-stage analysis. During stage one, the transcription from each interview was read through.

Table 2. The organizations in the study

Organization	***Activity***
MGC	Manufacturer of shipboard cranes, RDS provider
PowerDrive	Manufacturers of motors, RDS provider
MCC	RDS provider
Alpha Customer to PowerDrive and MCC	Mining industry company, RDS user
Beta Customer to PowerDrive	Processing industry company, RDS user
Gamma	OEM to processing industry, RDS provider

While reading, notes were taken to summarize the material. Stage two involved a cross-analysis of the interviews to find similarities and differences. Each interview gave an explanation of the case from a certain perspective; for example, a technician's view could be compared with a manager's view of the technology. This crosschecking of different perspectives ensures validity, as the case interpretation is built up from multiple sources. The empirical investigation is based on the two processes of capturing and transferring context, which together constitute the desituation of context. The third stage of the analysis included a cross-case analysis, searching for similarities and differences between the cases regarding the processes of capturing and transferring context. ANT was used as a lens to make sense of the empirical findings as a theoretical abstraction by challenging or generalizing concepts (Walsham, 1997).

The Case Organizations

MGC is a manufacturer of cranes and has recently developed a first prototype of a RDS. Sensors are installed into the crane to collect data about its condition. These data are sent to a server at MGC every time the crane is turned off, where they are analyzed to find out when maintenance is needed. As the cranes travel around the world, they are also equipped with a Global Positioning System that shows where the cranes are at the moment. This position is sent to MGC every six hours and is valuable when scheduling the maintenance.

PowerDrive is a manufacturer of motors that also has developed a RDS for enhancing preventive maintenance. Their system is also based on sensors embedded into the equipment that collect data about its condition. Data are collected every 30 seconds and are temporally stored in the system before they are transferred to a server at PowerDrive for analyses, once every day. If something is detected, an alarm is automatically sent out to technicians via SMS or e-mail with information about the problem. A report that summarizes the equipment's condition and detected problems is also compiled every month and sent to the customer.

MCC is a provider of preventive maintenance services based on RDS. Unlike MGC and PowerDrive, they are not manufacturers and do not develop RDS on their own, but participate in such projects with other companies. MCC take responsibility for implementing the RDS into the customers' equipments, and they also take responsibility for analyzing the collected data and informing the customers when maintenance is needed.

Gamma is a supplier of installations for the processing industry. These installations include equipment produced by PowerDrive. Gamma has developed a RDS for its installations, but it does not measure any specific parameters of the motor. The customer can choose to use both a RDS from Gamma and from PowerDrive, as these two systems complement each other. Like the other manufacturers, Gamma also has a group of technicians specialized in analyzing data collected in remote systems. The last two organizations, Alpha and Beta, have RDS installed at their plants.

All companies have experience of either developing or using RDS, which gives a rich view of remote diagnostics and issues associated with such applications from both a local customer perspective and a remote supplier perspective.

DESITUATING CONTEXT

In this section, the desituation of context is explored empirically based on the results from the case study. In the desituation of context, two different processes take place. First, context is captured and second, transferred to another setting. In RDS, context is captured via sensors, and the data contain information about a equipment's condition, identity, time and, if the equipment is mobile, its position. These data are then transferred to a remote centers with technicians specialized in analyzing this type of data. To understand the desituation of context and how it can be managed, this section will explore these two processes - capturing context and transferring it - in the industrial setting.

Capturing Context

The equipment's physical condition is transformed into a representation (an immutable mobile), by the sensors, which record information without a technician physically visiting the equipment. The data collection is viewed primarily as creating a stable and regular flow of data, whereas manual collection could result in corrupt data due to irregularities in time and variation in the use of measurement instruments. A developer of RDS at Gamma explains:

Manual measuring is not acceptable. People are not good at repeatable accuracy. You don't use [the instrument] in the same way each time, you don't hold it in the same way and you are not able to place the measuring circuit in the same position each time. What people are good at are analyses.

According to this developer, the stability of the data is enhanced with automatic data collection. The developer argues that the collection is more reliable with sensors, as the measuring technique always remains the same, which enhances the quality of the data. Moreover, the sensors expand human sensing, as they can monitor things that humans cannot and in places where humans cannot go. For example, a sensor can pick up sounds that the human ear cannot recognize. In the processing industry, there are many safety regulations, and with fewer people present on the floor, the risk of accidents decreases. When the equipments are running, it is sometimes impossible for humans to get access to them and measure parameters. Sensors thus create possibilities for a stable and safe data collection. The digital sensor technology also transforms the equipment's condition into a mobile state, where it can be transferred via network connections to remote sites.

An uncertainty observed among the organizations in this study regarding the data collection is the potential for faulty sensors. Abnormal data can be caused either by problems with the sensor or by real problems in the equipment. If faulty sensors cause them and this is not detected, this will lead to misinterpretations of the equipment's condition. The organizations try to avoid these problems through regular calibrations of the sensors. The technicians can sometimes detect problems with the sensors by their experience of what values are normal and what are not. If the measured values are substantially deviant, technicians begin to suspect problems with the technological equipment.

When equipment is to be monitored, a number of parameters have to be chosen. During the development process at MGC, the technicians had a long list of parameters they wished to gain access to. During the process, this list was reduced both due to technical reasons (no sensors were available that could collect the parameter) and due to costs (some sensors were too expensive relative to the overall value of the system). Picking out the relevant parameters is crucial for condition-based maintenance, as overlooked parameters may be the ones causing an unplanned break. The providers in this study show a tendency to wish for a constant increase in the number of parameters being collected. Even the customers experience the growing data collection; the director of maintenance at Alpha says:

We do measure parameters that we don't get any benefit of. But if you haven't measured them, the data are lost.

By collecting more and more data, the companies want to build an all-embracing model of the equipments to perform better analysis and to detect abnormal conditions and trends. Collecting more data can also be a strategy to minimize the uncertainty of incorrect sensors. If many parameters are captured, values can be cross-checked when uncertainties arise. However, even though increased data collection can minimize uncertainties and give more information about the equipments, all organizations stress the risk of information overload. The amount of data is growing fast, often faster than these organizations are able to analyze them.

Transferring Context

After the sensors have captured the data, this information is transferred to remote centers for analysis. When the equipment is mobile, wireless connections are used for the transfer. In this study, the remote centers are located within the suppliers' organizations. At these centers, specially trained technicians work with analyzing the collected data and compare them with previous measurements. Through this analysis, the technician can detect abnormal variations and, hopefully, prevent breakdowns. To companies offering services based on the collection and analysis of data, the technology allows for a seamless service solution, as the technology is always present and enables context to be transferred to remote sites. To the suppliers, this presence creates opportunities for new types of services. MCC, for example, has their technicians in the northern part of Sweden but envisions becoming a global service provider of remote diagnostics solutions without opening new offices at new locations. MGC also highlights the time and space independence in promoting their RDS. In their brochures, they say:

Wherever you are— we are there...we provide seamless service solutions...we monitor the condition and performance of your cargo handling equipment, wherever the ship is in the world.

MGC's presence at customer sites is, of course, via the RDS by which it monitors the shipboard crane at a distance. PowerDrive also offers a RDS, where data are collected from equipments all around the world and then transferred to the company's main office, where analysis takes place.

Transfer of data from many dispersed objects into one place enhances the possibility of comparing data, and the technicians performing the analyses gain experience from many different equipments and settings. The remote centers act as centers of calculation, collecting large amounts of data about objects in the periphery. To the manufacturer, this possibility creates new business opportunities in the after-sale market while at the same time giving it important feedback about its equipments. With the remote diagnostics of equipments, the manufacturer gets a better picture of how its equipments work in actual settings and whether or not common problems exist within equipment runs. PowerDrive, for example, has been using its system to test equipments before they are launched, which has been valuable in equipment development, as it gives an overall picture about the performance of certain equipment categories.

The companies in this study highlight that even though the equipments are constantly monitored with RDS, only data about a specified number of parameters can be collected. Thus, the picture a remote technician gets is not "complete." As the director at MCC expresses it,

When you physically walk around in the plant, you get a lot of other signals; you see, hear, and feel.

The diagnoses that can be performed with the system are limited to the number of parameters that are monitored. A physical walk-around by an experienced technician who can see, hear, and feel when something is abnormal can detect things that the technology and the remote technician cannot. A hydraulics technician at Beta also notes:

You have to learn to know the equipments individually. You don't do that remotely.

This highlights a limitation with the RDS compared to an experienced technician walking around in the plant. Although the system can detect conditions by detailed analysis that the local technician cannot, many of the respondents point out the importance of keeping in mind that the limitation of the collected data. The hydraulic technician at Beta expresses both a risk and a limitation of the technology:

With more monitoring, you can work more and more online and less people will be out among the equipments. You won't get the same feeling for the equipments. The only things you see are, for example, temperature, pressure, and flow. You don't know how it sounds.

The RDS and the remote technicians are limited to the data collected by the sensors. At Beta, they gave an example of problems with a motor due to poor oil quality – a parameter that the RDS did not monitor. Another example is given by an technician at Alpha, who described how the company installed a RDS at one of the oil pumps that monitored the oil level. The system was supposed to be a complement to the operators' traditional regular walk rounds in the plant. When the oil level sank, an technician located in another building called the operator and instructed him to fill it with more oil. After a while, the operator got accustomed to the phone calls and stopped walking around in the plant. One day the equipment almost broke down due to other problems that the system did not detect, but the operator would have seen it had he walked by the equipment. To him, the phone calls from the remote center had become a work practice that would indicate all possible problems with the equipment. As a result, he viewed the walk rounds as unnecessary.

The example highlights the constraint of transferring context to another setting; the depiction of the reality is limited, and not all problems can be detected. However, the example also gives insight into another potential constraint to the possibility of transferring context. The RDS can create a remote closeness where the remote technicians can get "close" to the equipment, and at the same time, create a local distance at the plant, which is what happened at Alpha. The operator stopped physically walking by the equipment, as he relied on the RDS and the new procedure of getting an alarm when something had to be done. The example highlights the potential loss when the local operator or technician is not instituted in the new work practices, which creates a local physical distance between him and the equipment.

With the use of RDS follows the critical issue of managing both the benefits and the limitations of capturing and transferring context. Not only must the remote centers be well functioning, the local technicians must also be incorporated into the maintenance work; otherwise, they may be pushed into the periphery. The director at MCC expresses it as such:

When the company buys services from the remote group, the local group seems to view the remote group as responsible for everything, at the same time as the remote group views the local group as responsible for basic monitoring and walk rounds. This happens when the borders are not clear; the responsibility has to be clearly expressed.

The "remote closeness" came as a result of the use of RDS and the possibility of transferring context. The "local physical distance" came as a result of the local groups assessing walk-arounds as unnecessary and shifting responsibility. The local groups seem to interpret the RDS as a replacement of the old work routines, although they are aware of the technology's limitations.

DISCUSSION

With RDS, contextual data is desituated – that is, captured and transferred to another setting. Managing the desituation of context is thus of crucial concern in ubiquitous computing environments. In this paper we aspired to identify strategies for how to deal with the desituation of context in ubiquitous technology use through a case study of six different organizations either developing or using RDS. In what follows we identify two main strategies for accomplishing this: creating a center of calculation and bridging the gap between the physical world and the digital world.

Creating a Center of Calculation

With RDS, maintenance work faces new ways of organizing and working, and different modes of ordering extended through people in order to include technologies and organizational arrangements. Acting based upon the interpretation of automatically collected data is a challenging task in an environment used to basing actions on physical presence and manual skills. Grudin (2001) argues that learning to work in a world of context-aware applications is one of the greatest challenges that we face today. Through the use of RDS, data about equipments can be automatically captured and transferred to remote settings, which is a process whose management becomes crucial. A strategy for dealing with the desituation of context has to take into consideration how to organize and deal with the data flow that emerges. In the case of RDS, the technicians at the remote centers serve as key actors in the process of handling the data flow and analysis.

With the remote technology, data are automatically captured with sensors, transferred via a digital network, and combined in the centers of calculation where they provide the technicians with data about the equipments' performance and condition. When data are transferred from the local setting to these centers of calculation, the context is desituated. The transformation of the equipment's condition into digital numbers makes it possible to compare different equipments with their ideal condition and with each other, independent of their physical location. At the centers, a crucial activity is to create an overall picture of the equipment's status that can be analyzed without losing the specifics of the local contexts. The overall picture will make it easier to analyze the equipment's condition and perform timely maintenance. To successfully manage the desituation of context– we need these centers of calculation as a place in which the captured local contexts meet.

To enable the creation of centers of calculation, data must be transferable and still remain the same i.e. an immutable mobile. The digital network makes data perfectly mobile by making it possible to transfer them thousands of kilometers in milliseconds. It is also possible to combine binary data; data can be received from different sources, combined and compared with other data sources. The data collected by the RDS have in this study shown a degree of immutability in their character, as they can be captured and transferred to the centers of calculation. Concerning the stability of the data, uncertainty can arise due to the potential of incorrect sensors. It is thus the capturing of context that is perceived as being more uncertain than the transportation process. The three characters of the immutable mobile - mobility, stability, and combinability - seem to be characteristics important for RDS and essential to the creation of centers of calculation.

Bridging the Gap between the Physical World and the Digital World

To the technicians at the remote centers, the equipments are represented digitally via the captured parameters. As this study has shown, such inscription, a digital representation, gives the technicians a remote closeness to the equipments, as they can constantly monitor its condition and performance, independent of the physical distance. RDS does thereby decrease the gap between the world of information and the physical world, as the local contexts are desituated to the remote centers. However, in this study, this process showed to be a struggle between information gain and information loss, which retains the gap between the two worlds. The created remote closeness was accompanied with local physical distance where the local technician quit the walk-rounds and relied on the RDS. This require the organization to use different modes of ordering (Law, 1994) extended through people to include technologies and organizational arrangements to make the local technician instituted in the new work practices. A sense of locality is lost when specified data are collected and transferred via the digital network to a remote place, which creates a limited view of the monitored context. Context that is not captured is totally invisible to the remote technician. The second strategy to pursue when context are desituated is thus to find ways of bridging the gap between the physical world and the world of information.

To compensate for this gap, organizations engage in increased data collection, even though they cannot fully be used in the analyses. However, digitally represented contexts will always be different, as the captured context is by default moved from its context. The process of desituating context will always imply a process of abstraction, as the sensors will never capture a full context. All abstractions are limited, but they have another value; they can be represented and made mobile across time and space. The process of abstraction and a limited picture will thus be permanent in desituating context, and it is the process of abstraction that enables data containing contextual information to become an immutable mobile and transferred to the remote centers.

New data will always be available through sophisticated sensor technology in RDS. Therefore, it is a challenge to resist engaging in collecting more and more data. Constantly adding new sensors to capture additional context leads to an escalation of the amount of data that needs to be compiled, but the picture will still be limited. Capturing context digitally is also associated with certain costs. While some data are expensive to capture, other data are easier to collect. With RDS, these costs must be balanced with the benefits in terms of possibly preventing the breakdown of equipment. Increased data collection also raises questions about privacy, accuracy and interpretation (Grudin, 2001) which stresses the importance of balancing the data collection process and not letting it escalate beyond control.

According to Fleisch (2002) sensor technologies make the digital and the physical world approach each other and slowly merge together. However, even though the digital world includes more and more data, the remote picture available to the technicians is limited. A physical visit to the equipments gives maintenance workers information through all of the senses. This is lost when the equipment is diagnosed remotely via a specified number of parameters, as the sensors only detect what they are designed to. One should, however, bear in mind that sensors can observe things that the maintenance workers cannot and in places where they cannot go. Nevertheless, a sense of locality is lost when specified data are collected and transferred away via the digital network to a remote place. In this study, both the local maintenance groups and the remote groups were aware of both their own and the other group's benefits and limitations. The remote groups knew they were not able to diagnose the equipment at full capacity, and the local groups knew that they were not able to predict the condition of the equipments with the same precision as the RDS. Although both parties were aware of the limitations in their own work, some of the providers emphasize the risk of putting the local technicians in periphery when the RDS is installed. Neglected maintenance from the local group could result in an overall unsuccessful maintenance strategy, as these two groups complement rather than replace each other.

Decisions based on analyses of the digital world must thus be combined with insights from the physical world; otherwise, critical information can be lost. The separation of technicians and equipments demands a compensating network of practice, which in this case is the practice of the local technicians. It is thus important to find ways of combining these two groups of actors, modes of ordering these organizational arrangements (Law, 1994). Together these two groups and the technology constitute a collective of humans and non-humans (Latour, 2000), a hybrid collectif (Callon & Law, 1995). This maintenance network is growing, as each member as well as the network as a whole learn and improve their performance in relation to remote diagnostics. Managing the implementation of RDS and the gap between the remote and the local contexts can then be seen as the cultivation of such a collective. The local practices on the field must be reconfigured and instituted in the collective for RDS to become safe and workable. RDS thus makes it necessary for the local practices to change and adapt and for the remote centers to ensure that they are instituted in the collective. Only then can the benefits of the RDS be reached.

CONCLUSION

In this paper we have seen how the desituation of context is of crucial concern in ubiquitous computing environments. With the aim of identifying strategies of dealing with the desituation of context, we have explored how the process of desituating context is managed in organizations using RDS.

RDS goes beyond the current context-aware ubiquitous applications focusing on identity and location of users through its use of identity, location, status and time to diagnose the condition of equipment. The results reveal that capturing and transferring context - desituating context - is an important issue to address in ubiquitous computing. To manage this process, organizations need to find strategies of creating and managing the center of calculations, which serves an important role in the process of remote diagnostics. Moreover, they need a strategy of bridging the gap between the digital and the physical world created by this new way of organizing the maintenance process.

The creation and management of centers of calculation involve setting up a global site where captured contexts meet and merge into a remote setting. To enable long-distance control, all data must be compiled into one manageable view without losing the specifics of the local contexts. Data collection must thereby be designed with this in mind. To bridge the gap between the digital and the physical world, a new kind of maintenance network must be formed, one in which local technicians' practices are reconfigured and instituted.

The findings of this study challenge the existing assumptions of ubiquitous computing. While context awareness in relation to people will draw our attention to issues such as context switching as users move between different locations, context awareness in relation to things allow for a ubiquitous information environment with local contexts meeting in a global setting. Managing ubiquitous information environments thus also involves managing the desituation of context. By appreciating this, and by appreciating the challenges that arises when contexts are desituated in relation to RDS use, adopters of the technology stand a good chance of realizing the benefits of ubiquitous information environments.

REFERENCES

Abowd, G., & Mynatt, E. (2000). Charting past, present, and future research in ubiquitous computing. *ACM Transactions on Computer-Human Interaction*, 7(1), 29–58. doi:10.1145/344949.344988

Akrich, M. (1992). The de-scription of technical objects. In Bijker, W., & Law, J. (Eds.), *Shaping technology/building society: Studies in socio-technical change*. Cambridge, MA: MIT Press.

Andersson, M., & Lindgren, R. (2005). The mobile-stationary divide in ubiquitous computing environemnts: Lessons from the transport industry. *Information Systems Management*, *22*(4), 65–79. doi:10.1201/1078.10580530/45520.22.4.20050901/90031.7

Avgerou, C. (2002). *Information Systems and Global Diversity*. Oxford, UK: Oxford University Press.

Avital, M., & Germonprez, M. (2003, October 23-26). *Ubiquitous computing: Surfing the trend in a balanced act.* Paper presented at the Workshop on ubiquitous computing, Cleveland, OH.

Bloomfield, B. P. (1991). The role of information systems in the UK national health service: Action at a distance and the fetish of calculation. *Social Studies of Science*, *21*(4), 701–734. doi:10.1177/030631291021004004

Brown, J. S., & Duguid, P. (1991). Organizational learning and communities-of-practice: Toward a unified view of working, learning, and innovation. *Organization Science*, *2*(1), 40–57. doi:10.1287/orsc.2.1.40

Callon, M. (1986). Some elements of a sociology of translation: Domestication of the scallops and fishermen of St Brieuc Bay. In Law, J. (Ed.), *Power, action and belief: A sociology of knowledge?* London: Routledge.

Callon, M., & Law, J. (1995). Agency and the hybrid collectif. *The South Atlantic Quarterly*, *94*(2).

Chae, B. (2003, October 24-26). *Ubiquitous computing for mundane knowledge management: Hopes, challenges and questions.* Paper presented at the Workshop on Ubiquitous computing environment, Cleveland, OH.

Dahlbom, B., & Mathiassen, L. (1993). *Computers in Context: The Philosophy and Practice of Systems Design*. Cambridge, MA: Blackwell Publishers Inc.

Davis, G. B. (2003, October 24-26). *Affordances of ubiquitous computing and productivity in knowledge work.* Paper presented at the Workshop on ubiquitous computing, Cleveland, OH.

Dey, A. K. (2001). Understanding and Using Context. *Personal and Ubiquitous Computing*, *5*(1), 4–7. doi:10.1007/s007790170019

Dey, A. K., Abowd, G., & Salber, D. (2001). A conceptual framework and a toolkit for supporting the rapid prototyping of context-aware applications. *Human-Computer Interaction*, *16*, 97–166. doi:10.1207/S15327051HCI16234_02

Fleisch, E. (2002). Von der Vernetzung von Unternehmen zur Vernetzung von Dingen. In M. T. Schögel & T. Belz (Eds.), *Roadm@p to E-business* (pp. 124-136). St Gallen: Thexis.

Garfield, M. J. (2005). Acceptance of ubiquitous computing. *Information Systems Management*, *22*(4), 24–31. doi:10.1201/1078.10580530/45520.22.4.20050901/90027.3

Gershman, A., & Fano, A. (2005). Examples of commercial applications of ubiquitous computing. *Communications of the ACM*, *48*(3), 71. doi:10.1145/1047671.1047711

Giles, C. L., & Purao, S. (2003, October 23-26). *The role of search in ubiquitous computing.* Paper presented at the Workshop on ubiquitous computing, Cleveland, OH.

Grudin, J. (2001). Desituating action: Digital representation of context. *Human-Computer Interaction*, *16*, 269–286. doi:10.1207/S15327051HCI16234_10

Grudin, J. (2003, October 23-26). *Implications of technology use throughout organizations.* Paper presented at the Workshop on ubiquitous computing, Cleveland, OH.

Hanseth, O., Aanestad, M., & Berg, M. (2004). Guest editors' introduction–Actor-network theory and information systems. What's so special? *Information Technology & People, 17*(2), 116–123. doi:10.1108/09593840410542466

Henfridsson, O., & Lindgren, R. (2005). Multi-contextuality in ubiquitous computing: Investigating the car case through action research. *Information and Organization, 15*, 95–124. doi:10.1016/j.infoandorg.2005.02.009

Holmström, J., & Robey, D. (2005). Understanding IT's organizational consequences: An actor network approach. In Czarniawska, B., & Hernes, T. (Eds.), *Actor-Network Theory and Organizing* (pp. 165–187). Stockholm, Sweden: Liber.

Jones, M. (2000). The moving finger: The use of theory. In Baskerville, R., Stage, J., & DeGross, J. (Eds.), *Organizational and social perspectives on information technology* (pp. 1975–1999). Boston: Kluwer Academic Publishers.

Jonsson, K., Westergren, U. H., & Holmström, J. (2008). Technologies for value creation: an exploration of remote diagnostics systems in the manufacturing industry. *Information Systems Journal, 18*(3), 227–245. doi:10.1111/j.1365-2575.2007.00267.x

Kautz, K., & McMaster, T. (1994). Introducing structured methods: An undelivered promise? - A case study. *Scandinavian Journal of Information Systems, 6*(2), 59–78.

Kuschel, J., & Ljungberg, F. (2004, September 6-10). *Decentralized Remote Diagnostics: A Study of Diagnostics in the Marine Industry.* Paper presented at the 18th British HCI Group Annual Conference, Leeds, UK.

Lampe, M., Strassner, M., & Fleisch, E. (2004, March 14-17). A ubiquitous computing environment for aircraft maintenance. In *Proceedings of the Proceedings of the 2004 ACM Symposium on Applied computing*, Nicosia, Cyprus.

Latour, B. (1987). *Science in action*. Cambridge, MA: Harvard University Press.

Latour, B. (1996). Social theory and the study of computerized work sites. In Orlikowski, W. J., Walsham, G., Jones, M., & DeGross, J. (Eds.), *Information technology and changes in organizational work.* London: Chapman & Hall.

Latour, B. (2000). *Pandora's hope: Essays on the reality of science studies*. Cambridge, MA: Harvard University Press.

Law, J. (1987). On the methods of long-distance control: Vessels, navigation and the Portuguese route to India. In Law, J. (Ed.), *Power, action and belief: A new sociology of knowledge* (pp. 234–263). London: Routledge & Kegan Paul.

Law, J. (1992). Notes on the theory of the actor-network: ordering, strategy, and heterogeneity. *Systemic Practice and Action Research, 5*(4), 379–393.

Law, J. (1994). *Organizing Modernity*. Oxford, UK: Blackwell Publishing.

Lyytinen, K., & Yoo, Y. (2002a). Issues and challenges in ubiquitous computing. *Communications of the ACM, 45*(12), 63–65.

Lyytinen, K., & Yoo, Y. (2002b). Research commentary: The next wave of nomadic computing. *Information Systems Research, 13*(4), 377–388. doi:10.1287/isre.13.4.377.75

Mähring, M., Holmström, J., Keil, M., & Montealegre, R. (2004). Trojan actor-networks and swift translation: Bringing actor-network theory to IT project escalation studies. *Information Technology & People, 17*(2), 210–238. doi:10.1108/09593840410542510

Medovich, M. (2003, October 23-26). *Pervasive computing and pervasive economies in the 21st century.* Paper presented at the Workshop on ubiquitous computing, Cleveland, OH.

Mol, A., & Law, J. (1994). Regions, networks and fluids: Anaemia and social topology. *Social Studies of Science, 24*(4), 641–671. doi:10.1177/030631279402400402

Mort, M., May, C. R., & Williams, T. (2003). Remote Doctors and Absent Patients: Acting at a Distance in Telemedicine? *Science, Technology & Human Values, 28*(2), 274–295. doi:10.1177/0162243902250907

Moser, I., & Law, J. (2006). Fluids or Flows? Information and Qualculation in Medical Practice. *Information Technology & People, 19*(1), 55–73. doi:10.1108/09593840610649961

Olsson, C.-M., & Henfridsson, O. (2005). Designing context-aware interaction: An action research study. In Sorensen, C., Yoo, Y., Lyytinen, K., & DeGross, J. I. (Eds.), *Designing ubiquitous information environments: Socio-technical issues and challenges*. New York: Springer. doi:10.1007/0-387-28918-6_18

Peppard, J. (2001). Bridging the gap between the IS organization and the rest of the business: plotting a route. *Information Systems Journal, 11*(3), 249–270. doi:10.1046/j.1365-2575.2001.00105.x

Pepper, S. C. (1948). *World Hypotheses: A Study in Evidence*. Berkley, CA: University California Press.

Pettigrew, A. M., Woodman, R. W., & Cameron, K. S. (2001). Studying organizational change and development: Challenges for future research. *Academy of Management Journal, 44*(4), 697–713. doi:10.2307/3069411

Schilit, B. N. (1995). *System architecture for context-aware mobile computing*. New York: Columbia University.

Tolmie, P., Grasso, A., O'Neill, J., & Castellani, S. (2004, September 7-10). *Supporting remote problem-solving with ubiquitous computing: Research policies and objectives.* Paper presented at the Ubicomp Conference, Giving help at a distance workshop, Nottingham, UK.

Walsham, G. (1997). Actor-network theory and IS research: Current status amd future prospects. In Lee, A. S., Liebenau, J., & DeGross, J. (Eds.), *Information systems and qualitative research* (pp. 466–480). New York: Chapman & Hall.

Walsham, G., & Sahay, S. (1999). GIS for district-level administration in India: Problems and opportunities. *Management Information Systems Quarterly, 23*, 39–66. doi:10.2307/249409

Wickramasinghe, N., Tumu, S., Bali, R. K., & Tatnall, A. (2007). Using actor-network theory (ANT) as an analytical tool in order to effect superior PACS implementation. *International Journal of Networking and Virtual Organisations, 4*(3), 257–279. doi:10.1504/IJNVO.2007.015164

Yin, R. K. (1989). *Case study research: Design and methods*. Newbury Park, CA: Sage.

This work was previously published in International Journal of Actor-Network Theory and Technological Innovation, Volume 2, Issue 3, edited by Arthur Tatnall, pp. 40-55, copyright 2010 by IGI Publishing (an imprint of IGI Global).

Chapter 12
Negotiating the Socio-Material in and about Information Systems:
An Approach to Native Methods

Fletcher T. H. Cole
University of New South Wales, Australia

ABSTRACT

Recent moves to more explicitly account for the relationship between the social and the material in the Information Systems discipline, under the banner of socio-materiality, also imply the need for a closer examination of practice. Using John Law's (2004) exposition of "method assemblage" as foregrounding and backgrounding a re-reading of Jonathan Grudin's (1990) account of the various delineations of the computer interface is attempted. It is offered as a preliminary orientation to some of the native "ethno-methods", (discursive and embodied practices) which might be deployed to negotiate sociality and materiality in IS and other technical arenas.

INTRODUCTION

This paper is motivated by the observation that references to the idea of socio-materiality are scant in the Information Systems (IS) academic literature, especially when compared with cognate fields. Recent moves to more explicitly account for the social and the material, their relationship and significance in different situations, in IS and other technical arenas, also imply the need for a closer examination of practice. Orlikowski (2007, p. 1444), for instance, proposes that "*all* practices are always and everywhere socio-material, and that this sociomateriality is constitutive, shaping the contours and possibilities of everyday organizing". Or we might recognise the opposite, that practice in its particulars is constitutive of the social and the material (and much else). Just how to characterise "practice" is not uncontested and, as with any term, will relate to a host of theoretical and practical considerations (Bourdieu, 1972).

DOI: 10.4018/978-1-4666-1559-5.ch012

As a way of explicating these proposals I use John Law's (2004) discussion of "method assemblage", and offer a re-reading of Jonathan Grudin's (1990) account of the extension of the computer interface as it "reaches out". I do this to provide an *orientation* to some of the native "ethno-methods" (discursive and embodied practices) used to negotiate notions of sociality and materiality, and which seem relevant to a discussion about IS. I wish to retain the modes of expression used by practitioners themselves. The intention is to avoid the situation where the observer, drawing on an unfamiliar (to practitioners) social theory framework, always "gets the last word", perhaps even imputing "self-deception to the natives who do not acknowledge or recognise the [alternative] analytical explanation" (Lynch, 1993, p. 32).

The line of thought in this paper owes a great deal to the many discussions and demonstrations I have overheard among those who bravely attempt to work according to *Ethnomethodology's Program* (Garfinkel, 2002). The outcome is a practical suggestion as to where to look for contrasting modes of IS practice; and there may be parallels also in other technical fields.

CRAFTING PRESENCE AND ABSENCE

In his exploration of "mess in social science research", John Law, in post-ANT mode, resorts to an idea of "method assemblage", defining it as the bundling or crafting of "ramifying relations" that shape, mediate and separate representations and objects into the visible "in-here", and the seen and unseen "out-there". Foreground implies Background. Some things are highlighted; some things receive little or no attention, or are deliberately forgotten. The characterisation is reminiscent of and has antecedents in the phenomenology of Edmund Husserl (1938, 1970), and in much earlier debates (Shapin, 1996). In the "praxiological coupling of material relations with mathematical forms" Galileo's perfect curves have a forgotten genealogy, "indifferent to human historicity and purpose" (Lynch, 1993, p. 119). The actual work involved is made invisible, and tricky to reproduce.

Law then draws on post-structuralist vocabulary to characterise method assemblage further as "the enactment of *presence*, *manifest absence*, and *absence as Otherness*" (Law, 2004, p. 84):

Method assemblage becomes the crafting or bundling of relations or hinterland into three parts: (a) whatever is in-here or present; (b) whatever is absent but also manifest in its absence; (c) whatever is absent but is Other because, while it is necessary to presence, it is not or cannot be made manifest.

Both the Other and the Manifest Absent are necessary to Presence, but sometimes that which is evident disappears in Otherness "because what is being brought to presence and manifest absence cannot be sustained unless it is Othered" (p. 85) – much of the social and cultural context, perhaps.

Another way of putting it is that any assemblage is the result of considerable collective effort, some acknowledged (brought to Presence), most of it not, most of the time. The precise nature of this effort is a matter of some interest. The process of assemblage is also about "crafting and enacting of boundaries" between categories and "normative methods [that] try to define and police boundary relations in ways that are tight and hold steady" (p. 85). This suggests that the *methods* through which categories are negotiated are important to be aware of.

What Law is after is social science Method but, from his examples alone, his discussion has a wider reach. To anyone aware of ethnomethodology, with its preoccupation with identifying the "immense variety of discursive and embodied practices" that constitute human affairs (Lynch, 1993, p. 297), this is familiar stuff. It directs us not only to query what those "normative methods" might be, it also requires us to investigate a host of other practices, whatever happen to be deployed at the time.

There is also perhaps some correspondence with Garfinkel's early observation (1967) about our reliance on much which is assumed to be there, but which needs no direct reference – the "seen but unnoticed". Disclosure of this Othered "unnoticed", in relation to what is noticed as the Present, has been one of ethnomethodology's durable research goals.

Law further elaborates the process of Othering, in his reading of Shapin & Schaffer's classic history of science study of Robert Boyle and Thomas Hobbes (1985). In order "to produce statements about the world which would carry conviction" (Law, 2004, p. 119), Boyle was faced with two problems, one epistemological (how to report) and the other social (how to convince). The solution was to be found in set of "interrelated and mutually embedded 'technologies'", which nevertheless needed to be disentangled, by being made subject to the methodical trifecta of drawing out Presence, manifestly moving into Absence, and unobtrusively Othering. These technologies included:

1. **Material:** an elaborate and temperamental air-pump in an equally elaborate laboratory.
2. **Social:** the laboratory was a social space in which appropriate people could witness the experiments, and assess their worth. An appropriate person needed to be an independent agent, not beholden to anyone; in practice, a gentleman of independent means. The artisans who built, ran and repaired the pump were not likely to qualify.
3. **Literary:** in practice few people could visit the laboratory to witness the experiments in London; some kind of indirect or virtual witnessing was therefore necessary, which involved "the production in the reader's mind of such an image of an experimental scene as obviates the necessity for either its direct witness or its replication" (Law, 2004, p. 119, quoting Shapin, 1984).
4. **Trust:** accomplished through a representation of reality (an image of the pump), a verbose though modest, matter-of-fact style (to enhance verisimilitude), and some discussion of the experiments that failed.

Law comments (120) that "if it is to witness reliably then the scientific assemblage needs to detach itself from the personal" (the witness "speaks for nature, and then modestly disappears") and to detach … from social interests and social context … from geographical location … from the specific material forms (this particular air-pump). … "In this enactment of knowing, most of the social, the geographical and the technical are rendered invisible. But it is only achieved because of a hidden set of carefully organised relations with the social, the geographical and the technical" (p. 121).

The method assemblage owes its success to "distinguishing between a public discursive reality and a private heterogeneity", between a purified Scientific Presence, and a residual and differentiated order on which it depends. Nature is "always entangled with culture and society" (p. 121). Here we are reminded about Latour's observation that "modernity" is characterised by its insistence on purity for itself, but further "by pure forms, pure distinctions on the one hand, and a proliferation of heterogeneities, impurities and hybrids on the other" (p. 82, referring to Latour, 1993).

From this account, a simple filtering out of the "material" from the "social" would seem to be too primitive a way of characterising the work that went into the "method assemblage" of Boyle's experimental science. So too perhaps are simple oppositions of social and material too primitive in information systems research, and similar fields. The scant attention paid in IS to matters of socio-materiality may be part of the way purifications have been established and continue to be maintained, with the entanglements with "heterogeneities, impurities and hybrids" being systematically obscured. This might entice some researchers into attempting to identify the precise ways in which material and social aspects are made Present or Absent in various research programs. The intermittent calls to tease out a widening range of neglected entanglements, sometimes beyond the designated social and material, may come as a welcome surprise (Orlikowski, 2007; Basden, 2008), but they do represent an unfolding challenge to disciplinary boundaries, preoccupations and modes of discourse.

OTHER APPROACHES

Challenges to prevailing assemblages are the stuff of history. So, outside IS, historical studies of technology, science and business that feature information systems to varying degrees provide rich case material. Probably the most accomplished at keeping both the Social and the Material (and the Technical) to the Fore are those historians (e.g., Mackenzie, Galison, Yates, Maloney) whose historiography allows them (and us) to identify significant entanglements.

Another resource is provided by the smaller field of workplace studies (Heath & Luff, Garcia, Rawls), which regularly includes reference to information systems; inevitably, given the nature of work today. It too is more inclusive of the entanglements that constitute the Present, and generally pays more attention to the actual practices and methods through which this takes place. Ethnomethodological concerns guide a great deal of this work. As Heath and Luff comment:

Contemporary sociological research concerned with technology seems in various ways to separate systems, both technical and human, from social action, so that we are unable to recover just how tools and artefacts and the 'rest of the furniture' of the modern organisation is constituted in and through the activities of the participants themselves.

Closely related to workplace studies is the field of computer-supported collaborative work (CSCW). Lucy Suchman explains that "the emergence of increasingly distributed, networked computing during the late 1970s and early 1980s raised questions that clearly went beyond the limits of the human-machine interface narrowly construed to involve collective forms of computer use" (Suchman, 2007, p. 276). A re-configuration of the method assemblage (which was HCI) was on the cards, involving a "turn to the social among computer scientists and information systems designers" (some of them anyway) fortuitously converging with and "accompanied by an intensification of interest among social researchers in the material grounds of sociality" (p. 276). Suchman recalls: "Among those of us immersed in ethnomethodology and newly engaged with the enterprise of computer systems design, absence of attention to the social and material organization of relevant forms of practice … was an obvious site for generative intervention." Steady streams of studies in this vein have proceeded ever since (Suchman, Randall et al., 2007). Suchman concludes that "the central argument of those studies is that the nature and relevance of environment, objects, and actions are reflexively constituted through the ongoing activities of their habitation, engagement and recognition" (p. 277). The "just how" of the activities of participants, the native methods, became more of a focus.

However, as a summarising gloss this fits poorly with the native language of IS or software engineering, or of the studies themselves, which tend to stick very close to operational detail or the specifics of method (e.g., when conducting a conversation). The summary is the voice of a visitor. Somewhat paradoxically, making the familiar visible to all, both natives and outsiders, is yet another challenge. To native practitioners it is only in the familiar details of their methods of assemblage that the resulting accounts can make any workable sense. But, referring back to Law's discussion, what is made Present through Purification, is not all that is familiar. There is much of the Other to which the native, in the interests of Purity, never refers directly, but which is familiar, and necessarily so. Bringing the Absent and the Other to our attention, in terms which we, both as natives and visitors appreciate, demands some ingenuity.

By dint of necessity this ingenuity is exercised in inter-disciplinary settings and when practitioners of different traditions are required to collaborate (i.e., when method assemblages collide). One example is provided by Peter Galison (1997), where he explicates the specific sites or zones which developed to accommodate the interests of diverse discipline and practice communities: viz. image and logic traditions in experimental particle physics, with their long histories of interaction with a range of engineering, managerial and data processing practices, and with their more recent exploitation of computing and simulation techniques.

Intelligibility in the experimental enterprise was achieved and maintained within an on-going process of *negotiation and exchange* among these various discipline and practice communities. Galison points out the various locations, or "trading zones" (borrowing from culture-contact anthropology), in which such exchanges took place; some zones as small as a blackboard (as when young Julian Schwinger, quantum physicist, developed equivalent circuits for microwave engineers in the dead of night at MIT during WWII), or some zones materially manifest, and massively so, as in the successful operation of the large Mark I detector.

Ethnomethodologists, in order to draw attention to the Absent and the Other, seek out "perspicuous settings" (Garfinkel, 2002). For Lynch (2007) such a "site is a researchable organization of activity in which participants raise, address, and locally explicate problems, topics, and conceptual distinctions that have a central place in academic philosophy, social theory, and methodology" (p. 107). Such topics as "socio-materiality" perhaps. Garfinkel (2002, 2007) finds everyday queues endlessly fascinating (but many other settings also) in alerting us to the "seen but unnoticed"; Lynch in his studies has ranged from bioscience laboratories to expert witnesses in law courts.

An ethnomethodological distinctive is "to relocate topics of socio-theoretical argument and debate within specific organizations of activity" in contrast to the visitor who resorts to "models that employ specialized conceptual and mathematical resources – resources that are drawn from literatures independent of the domains of conduct investigated" (Lynch, 2007, p. 108) and which tend to make the site unrecognisable to natives. As a perspicuous site Galison's trading zone not only needs to accommodate natives from several regions but also a few strangers as well.

Identifying perspicuous sites may not be too difficult, for it involves locating familiar settings with the potential to disclose the "specific organizations of activity" that constitute the Present, the Absent and the relevant Other, in which for our purposes we also want to locate the social and the material. A perspicuous site provides an orientation to the task of identifying native methods, and it affords the reporting of these in terms that both natives and foreigners might understand. One possibility for our purposes is the "Interface" between people and their computers; on the face of it a classic and obvious site or cluster of sites, for simultaneously investigating what counts as social and material, and how it counts. The relevance to IS comes if we regard the various assemblages of the Interface (the part) as also pertaining to the System (the whole).

RE-USING GRUDIN'S SCHEMA

A prescient account of the same turn to the Social that Suchman identified was provided by Jonathan Grudin (1990) in the days when CSCW was separating (re-assembling) itself off from the HCI community (Bannon, 1997). The historiography he deployed was of a "trajectory of interface research and development", involving the "shifting" in the "focus" or extent of "the interface" between people and their computers, through five stages (Figure 1). Grudin provided a history, but his account can also be used to outline a little more clearly the respective assemblages at each stage, potentially locating a series of perspicuous sites. Thus, alternatively, we could take this account as an *orientation* to the Interface, in its various definitions, and a *proposal* for the study of "specific organizations of activity" (the native ethnomethods) constituting the assemblage at each site.

In Stage 1, "the interface was located at the hardware itself … most users were engineers working directly with the hardware" (p. 262). It is the domain of electronic engineering. In terms of our discussion, and following its lead in many respects, we could speculate that the socio-material assemblage formed at this stage is one in which the Material is Present, but some aspects are Other; the Social is Other. This sets the stage for pursuing the question about the methods used in constituting the interface. Even under this view, establishing material standards involves intense social activity, as it did in Boyle's experience. For instance, Mackenzie (1996) reports on the controversy about the design of addresses for floating-point numbers. This is not presented as part of the official standard, but its acceptance has depended on resolving that controversy, utterly.

In Stage 2, attention shifted to "the programming task … as users were freed from the need to be familiar with the hardware". The domain is computer science and software engineering. Here, the Material of the previous stage becomes manifestly Absent; the othered Material is now brought to the Fore. The Social remains other. The previous users have now become exclusively

Figure 1. The five foci of interface development

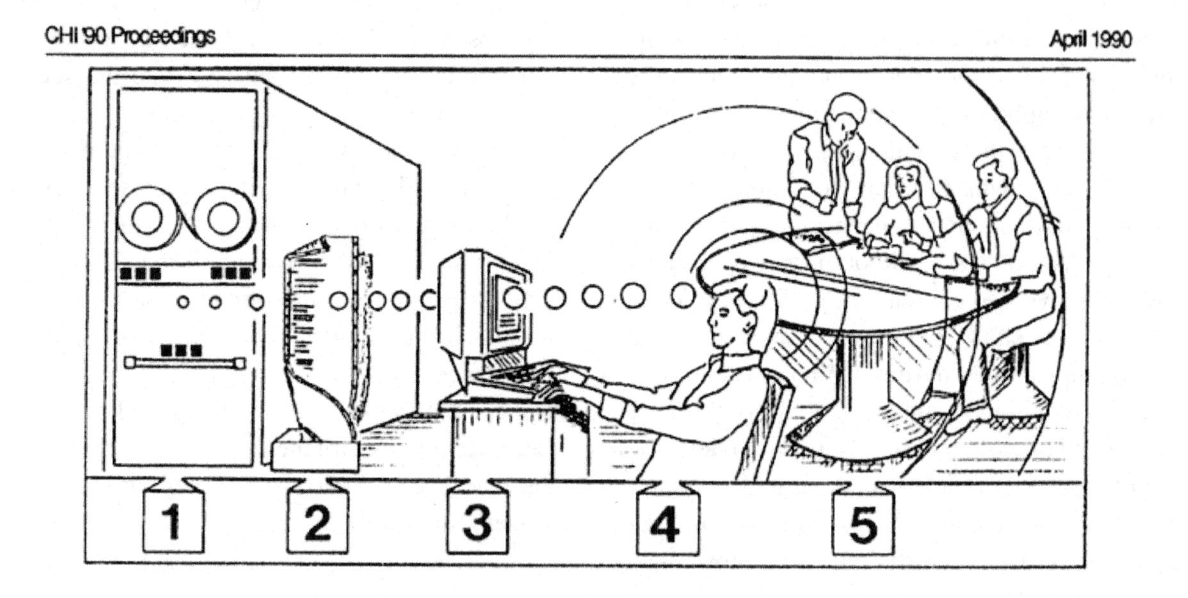

producers. The challenge of keeping track of hardware components and their characteristics has been overcome, made Absent, by means of facility with catalogues of components, sensible labelling of switches and layout, although a manager of hardware company might not quite "say this to my people" (p. 262). More pressing are the needs of programmer-users who have to get increasingly capable machines to do increasingly complicated routines, and do so without getting lost. The symbolic systems materialised in programming languages of varying distances, at different "levels", from the hardware, are the means through which the Interface is manifest. Various graphical devices are developed (VDU, WIMP) that unobtrusively facilitate the manipulation of symbols. The sociality of the world of the programmer is characterised by the mix of languages that are written and spoken. Only some are noticed; all are seen.

In Stage 3, "with the widespread appearance of interactive systems and non-programming 'end-users', the user interface shifted to the display and keyboard, with early attention to perceptual and motor issues". The domain is human factors HCI. The Social is starting to become Present, but specified in Material terms; the Material is retreating to the Absent; much of the Social remains Other. The community of "users" share common needs, but it is further differentiated into specialist IS professionals and everyone else. The boundary, the "end" of the interface (and the information system) is marked by the individual non-specialist, solely reliant on their own personal resources and those provided by the system, much like Robinson Crusoe. Beyond this is uncharted territory.

In Stage 4, "deeper cognitive issues underlying the learning and use of systems" extend the interface "past the eyes and fingers, into the mind". The domain is of cognitive and psychological HCI. The Social becomes more Present; the Material is absent; much of the Social remains Other. The basic configuration of the user community and the boundary of the system remains, but the interface is seen in less mechanical terms, to account for "higher" human cognitive functioning and, for some, a notable relationship to a "wild" social world (Hutchins, 1995), even if these terms only afford a "weaker scientific base" (Grudin, p. 264). Evidence is gathered through studies of human planning, problem-solving and other "complex tasks", producing keystroke logs and interaction dialogues (with the machine, and with users "thinking aloud"), which might be amenable to psycholinguistic and cognitive psychological analysis. The personal history of the user is becoming more relevant, inviting exploration of the (mostly othered) social context in which cognition functions. Design goals might seek

Interfaces that develop a sense of the user by modeling users' goals or plans, by retaining past user actions to develop in the computer a sense of dialogue with the user, and by adapting or tailoring the interface to an individual over time (p. 264).

In Stage 5, the advent of "groupware" sees the focus "extend out into the social and work environment" (262). It is the domain of CSCW. In this assemblage, the Social is Present; the Material is Absent; any Other is liable to be made Present. The potential in Stage 4 for taking greater account of the social is exploited. Robinson Crusoe has been taken off his island, and repatriated to his country of origin and his fellow citizens. The focus in the interface shifts from the machinery of the system, the material artefact, to its place in the wider world. The design rationale is that

Since most work occurs in a social context, computers will support it more successfully if they implicitly or explicitly incorporate social and organizational knowledge (p. 264).

Because the extent of the interface has shifted, so has the "end" for end-users, who much of the time may not actually directly use, or be aware of using, the system at all (such as, most customers,

CEOs, grandparents who get their grandchildren to write their e-mails). The community of users, and their encounters with the interface, differentiates to reflect the variety of social settings to which they belong. This includes those closely associated with the interface as defined in previous stages, the workgroups of CSCW, as well as those much more socially diverse and distant.

As a consequence, the methodological problems of research multiply, as Grudin somewhat ruefully comments:

... studying groups is difficult – group processes are often variable and context-sensitive, and usually unfold over time and in different locations; organizational change that results from introducing technology may take even longer to observe; and generalizing from observation is difficult (p. 264).

However, not all social knowledge, whatever is presumed to be its limits, is likely to be relevant in this dramatically broadening view. Which leaves us with the ongoing questions for any particular setting – What of the material and social remains Present? What is now Absent? What continues to be Other? *Just how* does all this take place? *And how can we possibly find out?*

TOWARDS A STUDY POLICY

Grudin's five stages in the evolution of the IS Interface could also be an account of the emergence of information systems research, as in its materialistic history IS has increasingly declared its intent to regard more of the human and the social as relevant to the system. The precise nature of this regard for the "system" parallels that of the "interface" in its wide variety of theoretical and methodological commitments.

To Grudin the progression from stage to stage is a "natural" migration of the Material:

When we have solved the most pressing problems at one level – or can handle them adequately – human and computer resources are available to work on the next level. In a sense, the computer is colonizing its environment – or, less threateningly, computers are progressively learning more about the world around them. This learning has generally been implicit, reflected in improved system and application design (p. 263).

An alternative to this singular view of the Material is that of Suchman's, that

The singularity of "the interface" explodes into a multiplicity of more and less closely aligned, dynamically configured moments of encounter within socio-material configurations, objectified as persons and machines (Suchman, 2007, p. 268).

This seems to fit better with our discussion of the ways in which the Social and the Material are liable to assume several guises, and be crafted through diverse means, whether commonplace or exotic, depending on where attention is focussed. The diversity represents alternative practical resolutions of the problem of maintaining the coherence and integrity of complex and differentiated socio-material phenomena. They indicate a variety of intelligible courses of action in grappling with material cultures which incorporate information systems. For both the interface and the system as a whole (the view of IS), the "moments of encounter" suggest where and when to look.

The relationship between the Social and the Material varies in significance according to the prominence which is given to its multiple aspects in specific situations. For a deeper understanding of this varying relationship we need to examine how these priorities are accomplished in the course of practice. Identifying fruitful locations for examining practice is important, and the suggestion here is that the computer interface is one of these.

As a practical conclusion, the method assemblage at each of Grudin's stages could be taken as directing us to a perspicuous site where we can identify just how foregrounding and backgrounding are achieved, just how in this process a particular socio-material configuration manifests itself. In short, his account provides us with a study policy to work with, but one which demands intellectual diversity in our research programmes. As an account of the ethno-methods by which the socio-material is negotiated it only goes so far, but it does provide some idea of what else we might expect when we do eventually attempt to find out.

ACKNOWLEDGMENT

An earlier version of this paper was presented at the University of New South Wales – Bentley University Working Conference on Sociality, Materiality and Sociomateriality of Information Systems and Organizations, 12-13 March 2010, Sydney, Australia.

REFERENCES

Bannon, L. J. (1997). Dwelling in the "Great Divide": The case of HCI and CSCW. In Bowker, G. C., & Star, S. L. (Eds.), *Social Science, Technical Systems, and Cooperative Work* (pp. 355–377). Mahwaw, NJ: Lawrence Erlbaum Associates.

Basden, A. (2008). *Philosophical Frameworks for Understanding Information Systems*. Hershey, PA: IGI Global.

Bourdieu, P. (1972). *Outline of a Theory of Practice*. Cambridge, UK: Cambridge University Press.

Galison, P. (1997). *Image and Logic: A Material Culture of Microphysics*. Chicago: University of Chicago Press.

Garcia, A. C. (2006). Workplace studies and technological change. *Annual Review of Information Science & Technology, 40*, 393–437. doi:10.1002/aris.1440400117

Garfinkel, H. (1967). *Studies in Ethnomethodology*. Englewood Cliffs: Prentice-Hall.

Garfinkel, H. (2002). *Ethnomethodology's Program: Working out Durkheim's Aphorism. Lanham: Rowman & Littlefield* (Rawls, A. W., Ed.).

Garfinkel, H. (2007). Lebenswelt origins of the sciences: Working out Durkheim's aphorism. *Human Studies, 30*(1), 9–56. doi:10.1007/s10746-007-9046-9

Grudin, J. (1990). The computer reaches out: The historical continuity of interface design. In *Proceedings of the SIGCHI Conference on Human Factors in Computing Systems: Empowering People (CHI'90)* (pp. 261-268). New York: ACM.

Heath, C., & Luff, P. (2000). *Technology in Action*. Cambridge, UK: Cambridge University Press. doi:10.1017/CBO9780511489839

Husserl, E. (1938, 1970). *The Crisis of European Sciences and Transcendental Phenomenology.* Evanston: Northwestern University Press.

Hutchins, E. (1995). *Cognition in the Wild*. Cambridge, MA: MIT Press.

Latour, B. (1993). *We Have Never Been Modern*. Cambridge, MA: Harvard University Press.

Law, J. (2004). *After Method: Mess in Social Science Research*. London: Routledge.

Lynch, M. (1993). *Scientific Practice & Ordinary Action: Ethnomethodology and Social Studies of Science*. Cambridge, UK: Cambridge University Press.

Lynch, M. (2007). Law courts as perspicuous sites for ethnomethodological investigations. In Hester, S., & Francis, D. (Eds.), *Orders of Ordinary Action: Respecifying Sociological Knowledge* (pp. 107–120). Aldershot, UK: Ashgate.

MacKenzie, D. A. (1996). Negotiating arithmetic, constructing proof. In *Knowing Machines: Essays on Technical Change* (pp. 165–183). Cambridge, MA: MIT Press.

MacKenzie, D. A. (2001). *Mechanizing Proof: Computing, Risk, and Trust*. Cambridge, MA: MIT Press.

Mahoney, M. S. (2005). The histories of computing(s). *Interdisciplinary Science Reviews*, *30*(2), 119–135. doi:10.1179/030801805X25927

Orlikowski, W. J. (2007). Sociomaterial practices: Exploring technology at work. *Organization Studies*, *28*(9), 1435–1448. doi:10.1177/0170840607081138

Randall, D., Harper, R., & Rouncefield, M. (2007). *Fieldwork for Design: Theory and Practice*. London: Springer.

Rawls, A. W. (2008). Harold Garfinkel, ethnomethodology and workplace studies. *Organization Studies*, *29*(5), 701–732. doi:10.1177/0170840608088768

Shapin, S. (1984). Pump and circumstance: Robert Boyle's literary technology. *Social Studies of Science*, *14*, 481–520. doi:10.1177/030631284014004001

Shapin, S. (1996). *The Scientific Revolution*. Chicago: University of Chicago Press.

Shapin, S., & Schaffer, S. (1985). *Leviathan and the Air-Pump: Hobbes, Boyle, and the Experimental Life*. Princeton, NJ: Princeton University Press.

Suchman, L. (2007). *Human-Machine Re-configurations: Plans and Situated Actions* (2nd ed.). Cambridge, UK: Cambridge University Press.

Yates, J. (2005). *Structuring the Information Age: Life Insurance and Technology in the Twentieth Century*. Baltimore: Johns Hopkins University Press.

This work was previously published in International Journal of Actor-Network Theory and Technological Innovation, Volume 2, Issue 4, edited by Arthur Tatnall, pp. 1-9, copyright 2010 by IGI Publishing (an imprint of IGI Global).

Chapter 13
On Actors, Networks, Hybrids, Black Boxes and Contesting Programming Languages

Arthur Tatnall
Victoria University, Australia

ABSTRACT

In the mid 1990s the programming language Visual Basic (VB) fought hard to enter the undergraduate information systems curriculum at RMIT University, against resistance from two incumbent programming languages. It could not, of course, work alone in this and enlisted the assistance of a human ally known as Fred. The incumbent programming languages, Pick Basic and the Alice machine language simulator, also had their human allies to assist them in resisting the assault of the newcomer. In many ways, it is useful to think of all these programming languages as black boxes made up of hybrid entities containing both human and non-human parts, along with a conglomeration of networks, interactions, and associations. The non-human cannot act alone, but without them, the human parts have nothing to contest.

INTRODUCTION

This paper provides an actor-network account of how Visual Basic (VB) entered the information systems (IS) curriculum at RMIT University in Melbourne in the 1990s. The first question I must address, however, is: Why is something that took place in one university in the 1990s still relevant? Although the events recounted here took place over 15 years ago, I will argue that similar processes, interactions and associations to those here described are likely to be found in any curriculum innovation and indeed in most situations of change. I will argue, through this example that actor-network theory is able to shed light on the processes involved in change.

DOI: 10.4018/978-1-4666-1559-5.ch013

Analysis of the events described in this article does, however, assume that the academics and educational institutions involved here had some choice in determining the details of their curriculum. While in some countries much of the IS curriculum is pre-determined by 'bodies of knowledge' and accreditation processes set up by professional associations or otherwise prescribed, this is not the case in Australia where individual universities control their own curricula.

Until the late 1980s and early 1990s Australia had a dual system of tertiary education comprising both Universities and Colleges of Advanced Education. The original idea in setting up this dual system was that the previously established universities would continue to handle the academic work and perform research while the Colleges would handle more vocationally and practically related tertiary teaching. In the late 1980s the Federal Government took a decision to support only one type of tertiary educational institution, and initiated a process of mergers of Colleges and Universities to create a smaller number of 'new' or 'merged' Universities. By the mid 1990s this process was complete and Australia had a smaller number of larger, and in many cases multi-campus, tertiary institutions, all of which were known as universities.

This story begins at a time when two Colleges of Advanced Education (CAE) in Melbourne: Phillip Institute of Technology (PIT) and RMIT[1] were about to merge to form RMIT University (Tatnall & Davey, 2001; Tatnall, 2007). It will be considered in four parts:

1. Existing programming languages in the IS curriculum at RMIT before the merger
2. Fred's discovery of Visual Basic at PIT and his first attempts at its use in the IS curriculum
3. Entry of Visual Basic into the IS curriculum at RMIT University
4. How VB continued to maintain its place in the curriculum despite challenges.

RMIT

The institution now known as RMIT University opened its doors to students in June 1887 as the Working Men's College. Unlike its London namesake which was devoted to "literary subjects, Christian principles and the humanities" (RMIT, 1997b), the Working Men's College in Melbourne was more concerned with general and technical education, and in 1899 it began to offer full-time diploma courses in Engineering and Applied Science (Murray-Smith & Dare, 1987). During the 1950s, the college developed new courses in Food Technology, Transport Studies, Accountancy, Real Estate and Advertising. In 1960 it adopted the name Royal Melbourne Institute of Technology (RMIT). In 1965 RMIT became a member of the Victorian Institute of Colleges, and the non-tertiary parts of RMIT were reconstituted as RMIT Technical College (RMIT, 1997b), later to become RMIT TAFE (Technical and Further Education) and VET (Vocational Education and Training). After the merger with Phillip Institute in 1992, RMIT was granted formal university status and adopted its current name: RMIT University.

RMIT had always prided itself as being a "technological educator" (RMIT, 1997a), and had worked closely with industry over the years to justify this title indicating, at the time of events described in this paper, that:

"We emphasise education for employment, and our research solves real-world problems. Our courses and research projects are technologically oriented, client focused, creative, innovative and - above all - practical." (RMIT, 1998)

RMIT has always maintained close ties with industry and commerce and made every effort to keep its courses relevant to the needs of industry. This vocational orientation has been maintained, and the university's teaching and learning strategy at the time of this story (RMIT, 1995) emphasised that students' educational experiences would be a preparation for working life. In 1997 the university's Web pages proclaimed:

"We pride ourselves on providing our students with 'education for employment'. We provide vocationally relevant courses which ensure our graduates are highly employable in their chosen field. And for mature-age students we offer courses that concentrate on upgrading their existing skills. We've been doing it for 110 years!" (RMIT, 1997a)

In line with this vocational focus, many of RMIT's courses included opportunities for periods of professional practice, and all undergraduate business degree programs incorporated a cooperative education year. The university claims to work actively with industry to reinforce the applied emphasis of its education and training programs.

"This is achieved through the participation of skilled industry representatives in the design and evaluation of RMIT programs, the appointment of teaching staff with industry experience, and the extensive employment of guest and visiting lecturers." (RMIT, 1997a)

RMIT's long tradition, and the regard with which it is held in filling an important place in higher education in Melbourne, have been powerful inducements in convincing its staff, students, Course Advisory Committees, and courses to accept and adopt the particular definition (or *problematisation* (Callon, 1986)) of higher education it has proposed. Higher education at RMIT meant an *applied professional education* that took serious regard of the current needs of industry and commerce. This was, of course, differentiated from industry *training* that was undertaken in RMIT TAFE and VET programs. As far as possible, RMIT curricula aimed to use materials and examples that reflected the situation in industry. In Information Systems this meant, where possible, teaching with 'industry standard' hardware and software, and 'real' programming languages used in the computer industry by professional programmers.

WHAT IS REAL?

Being considered to be 'real' was seen as important for any new topic or entity introduced into the Information Systems curriculum at RMIT. This was the case whether the addition was a new programming language, a new IS approach, a new systems development methodology, a new operating system, a new piece of technology or any other addition. In asking the question: 'Is it real?' what was really being asked was: would this new approach, application or technology be used in 'the real world' of industry, commerce or business? Being 'real' was seen as important in catering for industry's needs, and to RMIT this was paramount. It was important because it gave legitimacy to the inclusion of this addition to the Information Systems curriculum.

This article looks at the introduction of a new programming language, Visual Basic into the IS curriculum and the idea of a programming language being 'real' is a key element as it was commonly used as a device for securing or blocking alliances at RMIT. How a programming language comes to have this status conferred upon it is the subject of this paper. One of the questions often asked of a programming language at RMIT was whether or not it is a 'real programming language', normally meaning 'is it a language that is used extensively in the computer industry?' Of the programming languages used in the RMIT Information Systems curriculum in the mid-1990s and discussed later in this article, Cobol, Pick/BASIC and Visual Basic were all considered 'real' by the Information Systems academic staff and Courses Advisory Committee, but Pascal and Alice (an assembly language simulation) never quite managed to achieve this status.

'What is REAL?' asked the Velveteen Rabbit one day, when they were lying side by side near the nursery fender, before Nana came to tidy the room. 'Does it mean having things that buzz inside you and a stick-out handle?' (Williams, 1922, p. 14)

The question of whether or not something is 'real' has often also been put of computers and other technological entities (Tatnall, 2005; Tatnall, 2007). The Apple II computer was briefly popular with business in the late 1970s and early 1980s because it allowed users to run VisiCalc – the first spreadsheet program (Sculley & Byrne, 1989). Sculley, CEO of Apple during this period, notes that VisiCalc was responsible for "putting the Apple II on many business desks" (Sculley & Byrne, 1989; p. 207) but that when the IBM PC came along with Lotus 1-2-3 in 1983, business dropped the Apple and VisiCalc in favour of the IBM combination. The Apple II was thus never entirely 'real' for very long, except perhaps in education. (It is interesting that something can be seen as real for a period and then loses this status!) It was the spreadsheet program that business wanted, and the Apple II was just a means of delivering this software. The IBM PC, on the other hand, quickly moved from the status of an expensive toy used only to play games and run Lotus 1-2-3, to being considered a real and useful machine (Sculley & Byrne, 1989). Following the IBM PC's successful acceptance by business, other microcomputers of the MS-DOS variety were soon also considered real. When the Apple Macintosh was released in 1984 it was a long time before it was used enough by business to eventually be considered real, although even then only in some areas (Tatnall, 2005).

'Is it a real ... ?' tends to be a question asked by human actors of non-human actors in an attempt to decide how seriously to take them; to decide whether they are worth further investigation and could possibly be of some use. People asked this question, although probably not in these words, of the first mobile phones, of electronic organisers, Blackberries, digital cameras, smart phones and of other technological innovations they were unsure whether they could find a use for (Franklin, 1990). It is interesting to note that in respect of a given (non-human) actor the question 'Is it real?' is fairly uncontroversial and most people will agree on the answer. Although they would probably use a quite different vocabulary to express it, almost everyone would agree that mobile phones, digital cameras and PCs are now 'real', but that videophones, SmartCards and nano-technology are at present not real.

It is probably true to say that initially most new technologies are not considered to be real, and only become real after some time. People need a period in which to evaluate the innovation to see whether or not it might be of use to them and so become something they might think of as real. This raises the question of how something becomes real.

'Real isn't how you are made,' said the Skin Horse. 'It's a thing that happens to you. When a child loves you for a long, long time, not just to play with, but REALLY loves you, then you become Real.' (Williams, 1922, p. 14)

Victor Frankenstein (Shelley, 1818) never permitted his creation to become real. His revulsion at what he had done, and his refusal to accept the creature or even to give it a name, meant that the creature's quest to become real and so to be accepted was doomed to failure. But if Frankenstein's monster never succeeded in becoming real in the world of Shelley's novel, in many ways it has become real, even if only as a concept, in our world. We have found a use for the analogy of Frankenstein's monster to describe any 'unnatural creation' of modern technology. The concept of creating something that seems to go against the natural order of things (Anderson, 1999) is one that is closely linked in our minds with the monster of the novel, and Frankenstein's monster has become real in that sense. In using the concept of a monster like this, we have made it 'real' in much the same way that the term Luddite became real as a concept used to refer to those people who opposed the increased use of technology. Of course the Luddites (Grint & Woolgar, 1997) did actually exist whereas Frankenstein's monster is only a work of fiction, but in each case it is the *concept* that is real, and it is real because we have found a good use for it.

The recent series of the BBC TV program Dr Who has also raised considerable issues of what is real, especially when time travel and parallel universes are allowed. Can something be real in someone's mind that is not real in the world at large? Can something be real in one situation and not real in another? The answer to these questions must probably be 'yes'.

Whether or not a programming language is considered to be 'real' within the Information Systems community is generally related to its use in industry and in commerce. Cobol and Fortran were considered real because they had long been used, and indeed relied upon, in commerce and science respectively. Pascal, with its academic origins and quite small user-base in business has never been thought of as real (Juliff, 1992). Basic, which was invented over thirty years ago as a simple teaching language, has had great difficulty shaking off its unstructured, 'quick-and-dirty' image, and its image as a language for beginners in programming. Although never seriously used as a mainframe programming language, the growth in respectability of the microcomputer in the 1980s contributed to making Basic, and later Visual Basic, the 'real programming languages' they were seen as being in the 1990s. Not all computer professionals *like* Visual Basic, but few would challenge its reality. In actor-network terms, what matters is the length of the network, its allies, and the intermediaries it is able to marshal on its behalf. By the time this story takes place VB's network had grown quite long; it had attracted many allies and was able to make use of many intermediaries.

PROGRAMMING LANGUAGES IN THE IS CURRICULUM AT RMIT BEFORE THE MERGER

In the late 1980s RMIT and Phillip Institute were two independent CAEs, and we begin this story by looking at the situation at RMIT at this time. This part of the story begins with eight actors: RMIT, Pick/BASIC, Alice, Cobol, the Department of Business Information Systems, the IS curriculum (the non-humans) and two humans: Stephen and James. It is important to remember, however, that in ANT terms each of these actors also constitutes a network which can be considered as a black box (Callon, 1986) but pulled apart for detailed internal examination if and when required. If we were to do so for RMIT itself, however, we would find a large number of entities, many of whom cannot be considered as relevant actors in this story, so we will consider just those relevant to the action taking place here. In this article, when I refer to RMIT, I am really referring to just those aspects of RMIT that relate to the Department of Business Information Systems and its curricula.

Pick/BASIC

Today few people have heard of Pick, which is a specialised database-oriented operating system that makes use of a programming language called Pick/BASIC (Johnson, 2009). In the late 1980s and early 1990s Pick was in its ascendancy and Stephen, a Senior Lecturer in the Department of Business Information Systems, was in the process of assembling a network that would assist Pick's entry into the Information Systems curriculum at RMIT. Pick worked by incorporating a form of database access directly into the mini-computer's operating system (Stephen, 1997). Originally the Pick system could be programmed only in assembler, but by the mid 1970s a procedural programming language called Pick/BASIC had been developed (Tatnall, 2007). Pick and Pick/BASIC soon gathered an enthusiastic following of programmers and users who saw a place for this database-oriented operating system as a suitable alternative to Unix to run the business applications they needed. Pick had successfully enrolled them to its use.

Pick could not have entered the Information Systems curriculum at RMIT unaided and needed to expand its network by the addition of a local ally who was in a position to assist, and who could be convinced to do so. That local ally was Stephen who had come across Pick when doing a private consulting job for an organisation that used this system. Stephen (1997) decided to have a go at using Pick/BASIC with his students and describes how his students quickly adapted to Pick and were able to gain "a very rapid understanding of the business problems" he wanted them to consider. Using Pick also provided a potential niche market for RMIT students to gain future work in this field as no other higher education institution in Melbourne then offered teaching in Pick/BASIC programming. Pick also met RMIT's criteria for a 'real programming language' as it filled an important place in local business usage. Pick/BASIC thus entered the RMIT curriculum in an introductory programming subject taught by Stephen.

In the 1980s, one of the drawbacks in using the Pick operating system was that an organisation had to choose to use *either* Pick *or* Unix, and Unix was rapidly gaining in market popularity (Stephen, 1997). For any organisation, choosing Pick instead of Unix would have been seen as a "courageous decision" (Lynn & Jay, 1984). To counter this advantage, in the late 1980s a version of Pick known as Universe was developed to run under Unix. This new development meant that an organisation using Unix could now run Universe and so also make use of Pick (Stephen, 1997). It would not have to problematise its programming as taking place *either* through Pick or Unix. This translation of Pick into a product that did not have to challenge Unix in an all-out, win or lose battle succeeded in strengthening Pick's hold on its market segment and succeeded in strengthening Pick's network of allies and supporters. Now that an organisation which was using Pick did not have to choose either to stay with Pick, and so miss out on what the computer press increasingly praised as the advantages of Unix, or to desert Pick and move to Unix, most Pick users adopted Universe to retain the advantages of both. Pick's network had avoided the desertion of its user allies and so had survived the Unix challenge; for the moment. It had survived, however, by neutralising Unix' attack, and without weakening or challenging Unix' supremacy; the result could be considered to be a draw.

The network that could be thought of as Pick/BASIC consists of more than just the Pick/BASIC programming language and is a kind of hybrid (Latour, 1993) of RMIT and some aspects of Pick and Pick/BASIC that fitted with RMIT's definition of what a business programming language should be. By appealing to the benefits of a market niche in Pick programming for RMIT students, Stephen and his allies also performed a process of interessement (Callon, 1986) that locked the Course Advisory Committee and the Department of Business Information Systems into continued support for Pick by raising effective barriers against any challengers, or other competing networks such as Pascal.

Assembly Language Programming: the Alice Simulator

In the late 1980s James began development of a new one-semester introductory subject in computer architecture and operating systems for the Information Systems degree at RMIT. James began this course development not because of a suggestion from the Course Advisory Committee, but because he himself saw a need for his students to understand more about how a computer works internally. While developing this subject James decided to build a software simulator to make the teaching of assembly language more concrete (James, 1997). The idea was that when using this 'virtual machine' the students would be better able to understand what goes on inside a computer. James maintained that they would do so more easily, and in a shorter time than if performing real assembly language programming which he judged to be more the province of Computer Science. In the development process James designed several simulators ending up with one called Alice.

These simulators were all designed to be used predominantly as teaching machines and James had successfully problematised (Callon, 1986) a need for students to understand how a computer worked by using his simulators. This definition, or problematisation, was the key to Alice's existence: if Information Systems students needed to have a deep understanding of the internal operations of a computer; of registers, accumulators, assembly language, program counters and I/O buses, then Alice deserved a place in the curriculum. True, Alice was not 'real' in the sense that Pick was, but the concepts it was *teaching* were seen as real and necessary, and so it was accepted, although perhaps somewhat grudgingly. Alice then entered the RMIT curriculum in the computer architecture and operating systems subject taught by James (Tatnall, 2007).

Cobol had been taught, on and off, for some years at RMIT and it had some strong supporters on the institute's Course Advisory Committee. There could be no doubt that it was a 'real' programming language: it probably had the best claim of any language to this title at the time as it had been used to a very large extent in business over a very long period of time (Juliff, 1992). Nevertheless, Cobol's problematisation of business programming in the Information Systems curriculum at RMIT was weak as it was not liked by most of the teaching staff who thought it to be 'old hat' and past its time.

FRED'S DISCOVERY AND USE OF VISUAL BASIC IN THE IS CURRICULUM AT PIT

At Phillip Institute in the early 1990s before its merger with RMIT, Fred, a newly arrived Information Systems academic, was teaching Cobol on the Digital Equipment VAX mini-computer and Pascal in MS-DOS on PCs (Tatnall, 2007). What he quickly discovered, however, was that in writing a program in either of these languages, everything you wanted to add to a form in order to display this to the user had to be instigated by a separate line of program code, and this was found by the students to be quite hard going.

Unconnected with his teaching, Fred had discovered Visual Basic for MS-DOS when undertaking an outside programming job (In a way rather similar to that in which Stephen had discovered Pick). He instantly liked the way that VB allowed the programmer to get to a good looking prototype solution very quickly, and with much less bother than other approaches. Fred liked the fact that VB allowed the programmer to put a useful program together in a short time and that the program had a good professional look to it and became convinced that he should introduce VB to his students at PIT. He did this by exploring and experimenting with VB in several existing subjects. One of the subjects Fred had just started teaching at PIT at the time was an introductory IS subject that required use of a screen prototyping tool in one topic. This topic had always been hard to teach because PIT did not have a suitable prototyping tool that could be easily used in the MS-DOS student labs, meaning that this topic could not really be handled practically (Tatnall & Davey, 2001). After his recent experience with VB, Fred wondered whether some aspects of the MS-DOS version of VB could do the job. Fred was not interested in the programming features of VB in this, just those involved in its screen design. Fred could only use VB in this way by *translating* (Callon, 1986) it from a 'programming language and visual programming environment' into a 'screen prototyping tool'. He could do this by selecting some features of VB, including its visual interface, while ignoring the others (Tatnall & Davey, 2001).

In another subject on operating systems programming Fred decided to try out teaching with the Windows version of VB on a PC in place of Unix on the mini-computer. He achieved this by leaving out all of VB's visual aspects and concentrating on just those aspects of VB that related to operating systems extensions for Windows. Experiences with these two programming subjects were enough to *enrol* (Callon, 1986) Fred in using Visual Basic for a variety of teaching applications and started him on the road to *mobilising* (Callon, 1986) others in using Visual Basic. Fred (1997, 1998) now saw a significant place for Visual Basic in the Information Systems curriculum at PIT, and later at RMIT, and so adopted the position of *heterogeneous engineer* (Law, 1987) in an attempt to convince and so mobilise other actors to this same belief.

ENTRY OF VISUAL BASIC INTO THE IS CURRICULUM AT RMIT UNIVERSITY

After the merger between PIT and RMIT, in order for the new enlarged RMIT University to subsume its component institutions and have the appearance of a *single* university it was necessary to quickly merge the curricula for each degree at each of the former CAEs. Discussions and negotiations about the new course continued over almost a two-year period before formal accreditation of the final version. During this period however, a significant event occurred when Visual Basic made its appearance in a new elective subject on graphic user interface (GUI) and event-driven programming thanks to Fred's efforts.

After deliberation by the Course Review Panel, the structure of the new combined degree agreed upon included four core programming subjects. Choice of the programming languages to be used was not built into the accreditation process and was to become an implementation decision to be taken not long before each subject was offered for the first time to students (Tatnall, 2007). The VB network, led by Fred, made every effort to find a significant place in these core programming subjects but the network that Stephen had engineered around Pick was by now so long and powerful that any attempt to remove it was almost unthinkable. Dismantling this network would have proved very costly (Grint & Woolgar, 1997) as it would have required the weakening of a lot of associations, and convincing a large number of Pick's allies to change their allegiances. It was thus decided that the first two programming subjects were to be taught using Pick/BASIC.

The Course Review Panel's idea for the third programming unit was that it would start the shift into some of the newer programming issues such as graphical user interface, client-server concepts and possibly multiple platforms. With a little help from Fred, Visual Basic was the language chosen for this subject with another translation of VB to become 'Visual Basic the language for rapid application development with databases'. As the final programming subject was not scheduled to run for several years, a decision on the language it should use was postponed.

Despite severe criticism from a number of lecturers during the course review, Pick/BASIC had survived the merger and this had a potentially significant effect on the future of Visual Basic, as had Pick not survived as the main programming language in the course, the way would have been opened for Visual Basic to become a challenger in this role. Pick, with Stephen's support, had proceeded into a position of sufficient strength at RMIT to withstand almost any challenge at this stage. It could take the line: '*Slander my attributes and capabilities if you like, but I've got powerful friends, and I can provide a niche market for your graduates that you can't afford to lose. You need me in your curriculum*' (Tatnall, 2007)![12] It was a winning line.

Despite most lecturers thinking it to be a good product, the Alice virtual machine did not find a place in the new degree. The difficulty was that the problem Alice had been designed to solve – teaching important concepts about the internal workings of a computer – had by now become largely irrelevant to Information Systems students, and Alice was not able to adapt. Alice could not possibly adapt and still continue to exist in anything like its present form: "*How could I accept a change to another role and so deny the very reason for my existence?*" Alice could not accept that having a deep understanding of a computer's internal workings was unimportant to these students, when this was exactly what it was built to teach. (If Alice has been designed with Computer Science students in mind the situation would have been different as their problematisation of computing did still involve the computer's internal workings.) Alice could not adapt and still be true to itself (Tatnall, 2007) and thus lost its place in the RMIT curriculum.

HOW VB MAINTAINED ITS PLACE IN THE IS CURRICULUM AGAINST NEW CHALLENGERS

Debate on programming languages at RMIT did not stop after the new IS course was accredited. Paul (1997) reported that programming languages were often a matter for consideration and heated debate at the degree Course Team meetings, and described one recent meeting where the possibility had been raised of a new elective using ABAP/4, SAP's programming language, in the light of possible industry accreditation for students taking this subject. Increasingly, however, the debate was turning towards the value of introducing object-oriented (OO) programming somewhere into the degree. The entry of a new actor, or a translation in the role taken by an actor already present, often destabilises and poses a threat to existing networks (Grint & Woolgar, 1997). At this point, we see a new actor: Object-Oriented Technology and its associated network, poised for an attempt to enter the curriculum. The OO actor-network had been growing steadily for several years and its increasing influence and importance was well known to many academics in the Department of Business Information Systems (Tatnall, 2007).

Debate now centred on choice of a programming language for the final core programming subject. If this subject was to be based on the use of an object-oriented language, two questions now emerged: which language to use for this subject, and whether Visual Basic was still appropriate in the preceding subject that would then need to introduce object concepts. One possibility was to use Visual Basic for both subjects. Although early versions of VB had been 'object-based' and had made considerable use of object concepts, they had not previously been 'object-oriented' in the technical sense, but this had begun to change in 1995 with the release of VB-4 and continued with the release of VB-5 earlier in 1997.

If it had been unprepared to face this threat the Visual Basic network would probably have been substantially weakened by OO and perhaps even displaced from at least one Information Systems subject. Fortunately for VB however, the OO threat had been building up for several years and by the time it eventually came to a fore Microsoft had ensured that VB was well prepared. Visual Basic had always made use of objects in designing screens, and its whole programming approach was *object-based.* Early versions however, could make no claim to being *object-oriented*, a classification that required conformance to a set of specific rules. Microsoft had seen the impending OO threat and successive versions of VB had been moving nearer and nearer to having fully object-oriented status. Visual Basic had responded to the gathering OO menace by itself becoming object-oriented (Tatnall, 2007).

After much debate, in the end, the language chosen for this final programming subject was Java, but it was decided to stick with Visual Basic for the previous subject and to teach this subject stressing the OO aspects of VB as an introduction to object concepts. VB had not done its 'sales job' well enough to be able to muster sufficient support to be seriously considered for both subjects. The network developing around VB's object-oriented features had not yet gained enough allies and had not created enough *immutable mobiles* (Latour, 1987) to give it a good chance of adoption in this role. Although this meant a change of role for VB in this subject that would require further negotiations, it had survived, for the moment. At RMIT it is seen to be important that students get jobs immediately upon graduation, and so a programming language in the curriculum must be seen to have 'commercial credibility'; it must have a substantial number of commercial allies; it must be 'real'. Java was certainly seen as real and, the moment at least, Visual Basic did still fit this criterion and so survived in the curriculum.

CONCLUSION

Visual Basic had, by 2000, become quite real in the Information Systems curriculum at RMIT University but it had not been seen as real when Fred first experimented with it at Phillip Institute. During the time between these events the ground had changed. At first it had few allies and had not yet managed to attach any intermediaries to further its network, but by the mid 1990s this had changed. How does something gain a 'real place' in the curriculum? I would argue that VB became real in the RMIT Information Systems curriculum when it started to become popular with the computer industry. This led to a consensus among the academic staff that VB occupied a useful place in the curriculum and fitted in well with RMIT's educational mission of preparing its students to cater for industry needs. It became real when it had enrolled enough of the academic staff in its support, and mobilised them to speak on its behalf.

Visual Basic took its first small step to becoming real in the curriculum when Fred formally implemented it as a serious screen prototyping tool at PIT by incorporating its use as part of student assessment. This assessment was able to act as an intermediary (Callon, 1991) that added to the durability of VB 's network. VB took another step, acquired more intermediaries, and gained more allies when Fred also incorporated it into the *operating systems programming* subject and a giant leap when it was given its own subject in *'Graphical User Interface and Event-Driven Programming'*. VB was now almost at the point of mobilising business programming at RMIT. The final step to Visual Basic becoming totally real and occupying a significant place in the curriculum, however, was its adoption as the programming language used in a core computing subject. This last adoption put VB in a similar position to Pick/BASIC as an indispensable part of the Information Systems curriculum. By 2000, Visual Basic had acquired a network that would be very difficult to disassemble, making VB very hard to challenge for some time into the future (Tatnall, 2007). What happened to VB's place in the RMIT curriculum after this time is, however, not part of this story.

REFERENCES

Anderson, A. (1999, March 20). Beware the F Word, Unless You Know What it Means. *New Scientist, 3*.

Callon, M. (1986). *Some Elements of a Sociology of Translation: Domestication of the Scallops and the Fishermen of St Brieuc Bay. Power, Action & Belief. A New Sociology of Knowledge? Law, J* (pp. 196–229). London: Routledge & Kegan Paul.

Callon, M. (1991). *Techno-Economic Networks and Irreversibility. A Sociology of Monsters. Essays on Power, Technology and Domination. Law, J* (pp. 132–164). London: Routledge.

Franklin, U. (1990). *The Real World of Technology*. Montreal, Quebec: CNC.

Fred. (1997). *Interview on Programming Curricula at RMIT*. Melbourne, Australia: RMIT.

Fred. (1998). *Interview on Programming Curricula at RMIT*. Melbourne, Australia: RMIT.

Grint, K., & Woolgar, S. (1997). *The Machine at Work - Technology, Work and Organisation*. Cambridge, UK: Polity Press.

James. (1997). *Interview on Programming Curricula at RMIT*. Melbourne, Australia: RMIT.

Johnson, W. (2009). *Pick, Universe, Unidata Resources*. Retrieved from http://knol.google.com/k/pick-universe-unidata-resources#

Juliff, P. (1992). *Interview on Business Computing Curriculum*. Melbourne, Australia: RMIT.

Latour, B. (1987). *Science in Action: How to Follow Engineers and Scientists Through Society. Milton Keynes*. UK: Open University Press.

Latour, B. (1993). *We Have Never Been Modern*. UK: Hemel Hempstead.

Law, J. (1987). Technology and Heterogeneous Engineering: The Case of Portuguese Expansion. In Bijker, W. E., Hughes, T. P., & Pinch, T. J. (Eds.), *the Social Construction of Technological Systems: New Directions in the Sociology and History of Technology* (pp. 111–134). Cambridge, MA: MIT Press.

Lynn, J., & Jay, A. (1984). *The Complete Yes Minister - The Diaries of a Cabinet Minister*. London: British Broadcasting Corporation.

Murray-Smith, S., & Dare, A. J. (1987). *The Tech: a centenary history of the Royal Melbourne Institute of Technology*. Melbourne, Australia: Hyland House.

Paul. (1997). *Interview on Programming and Curriculum at RMIT*. Melbourne, Australia: RMIT.

RMIT. (1995). *Teaching and Learning at RMIT: philosophy and principles*. Melbourne, Australia: RMIT.

RMIT. (1997a, December 1). About RMIT University. *RMIT hotTYPE*.

RMIT. (1997b). Key Dates in RMIT University's History. *RMIT hotTYPE, 1*(1). Retrieved February 1997, from http://www.rmit.edu.au/About/hotTYPEv1n1/keydates.htm

RMIT. (1998, December). About RMIT University. *About RMIT*. Retrieved from http://www.rmit.edu.au/About/

Sculley, J., & Byrne, J. A. (1989). *Odyssey: Pepsi to Apple*. London: Fontana.

Shelley, M. (1818). *Frankenstein, or the Modern Prometheus*. London: Penguin Classics.

Stephen. (1997). *Interview on Business Computing Curriculum at RMIT*. Melbourne, Australia: RMIT.

Tatnall, A. (2005). Real-Life Learning, What is Meant by 'Real.' In Weert, T. v., & Tatnall, A. (Eds.), *Information and Communication Technologies and Real-Life Learning - New Education for the Knowledge Society* (pp. 143–150). New York: Springer. doi:10.1007/0-387-25997-X_16

Tatnall, A. (2007). *Innovation Translation in a University Curriculum*. Melbourne, Australia: Heidelberg Press.

Tatnall, A., & Davey, B. (2001). How Visual Basic Entered the Curriculum at an Australian University: An Account Informed by Innovation Translation. In *Challenges to Informing Clients: A Transdisciplinary Approach (Informing Science 2001)*, Krakow, Poland, Informing Science.

Williams, M. (1922). *The Velveteen Rabbit, or How Toys Become Real*. London: Heinemann.

ENDNOTES

1. Although formally known since the 1960s as the Royal Melbourne Institute of Technology, since the 1980s and 1990s RMIT has used just the acronym for its name
2. Although this sort of language coming from a non-human object may sound strange, it is one way that ANT allows the same treatment for the contributions of both human and non-human actors.

This work was previously published in International Journal of Actor-Network Theory and Technological Innovation, Volume 2, Issue 4, edited by Arthur Tatnall, pp. 10-20, copyright 2010 by IGI Publishing (an imprint of IGI Global).

Chapter 14
From Intermediary to Mediator and Vice Versa:
On Agency and Intentionality of a Mundane Sociotechnical System

Antonio Diaz Andrade
Auckland University of Technology, New Zealand

ABSTRACT

Assuming symmetry between human and nonhuman actors is a tenet of actor-network theory (ANT), i.e., an actor, anyone or anything that modifies a state of affairs. This symmetric perspective entails granting agency attributes to both human and nonhuman actors, an approach that has been often criticised. By means of a combination of research observation and participation, the use of electronic mail systems, especially the automatically generated "Out of Office" message, is examined in this article to emphasise the distinction between agency and intentionality. The fundamental assumption is that work practices are nothing less than technology mediated activities and the use of electronic mail and its multiple tools is an inherently sociotechnical practice. The notions of intermediaries and mediators are introduced not only to corroborate that the division between the social and the technical is artificial but also to reveal the difference between nonhuman agency and human intentionality.

INTRODUCTION

Social interactions take place in the social space. The social space does not necessarily mean activities taking place in contiguity; coordinated social activities can be performed at a distance too. The availability of ubiquitous connectivity redefines the space where social interactions take place (Castells, Fernández Ardèvol, Qiu, & Sey, 2007). In nowadays organisations most of the communications are conducted through electronic mail system. It is hard to imagine an organisation, regardless of its size (e.g., small, medium or large), its purpose (e.g., for profit, non for profit or government department) or its sector (e.g., mining, hospitality or banking, just to mention a few) running their operations without

DOI: 10.4018/978-1-4666-1559-5.ch014

an electronic mail system at the present time. This is not only true for the communication across different organisations but also between employees sitting at contiguous offices and even for workers sitting close to each other in an open floor space. The messages transmitted are utterances, which the recipients are expected to act upon. Being electronic mail a system that essentially modifies a state of affairs, this study – through the theoretical lens of actor-network theory (ANT) – will stress the distinction between agency attributes and intentionality.

This article is structured as follows. In the next section, I present the foundations of ANT and the constitution of sociotechnical systems, with emphasis on the notions of intermediaries and mediators. Then, electronic mail is conceptualised as a sociotechnical system. Following this, the agency attributes and human intentionality of electronic mail systems are analysed through the lens of ANT, stressing the passage between intermediary and mediator. Finally, I conclude by discussing the implications of the analysis and suggest future research avenues.

SOCIOTECHNICAL SYSTEMS

Heidegger's (1977) forceful statement "the essence of technology is by no means anything technological" (p. 4) emphasises the intricate nature between the social and the technical. Science and technology and their interaction with the social context constitute a "seamless web" and their study should take a systemic approach (Hughes, 1986).

Callon (1986) and Latour (1986) put forward ANT as a framework theorising on the symmetry existing between human and nonhuman actors. ANT stresses the need of including both the social and the technical when studying sociotechnical – sociotechnical, without the hyphen – systems: "To insist on symmetry is to assert that *everything* deserves explanation and, more particularly, that *everything* that you seek to explain or describe should be approached in the same way" (Law, 1994, pp. 9-10, emphasis in the original). ANT perceives the border between people, technology and their context as a negotiation process (Hanseth, Aanestad, & Berg, 2004), which can be revealed by unpacking the "black box" constituted by the sociotechnical system (Latour, 1999b). ANT can assist researchers in circulating the tension between agency and structure (Latour, 1999a) and has demonstrated its value in researching the social and technical assembly (cf., Akrich, 1992; Latour, 1992; Law & Callon, 1992).

As Latour (1999b) convincingly argues, "we are sociotechnical animals, and each human interaction is sociotechnical. We are never limited to social ties. We are never faced only with objects" (p. 214). Although the assumption of symmetry has been criticised because power structures might hide behind objects designed by humans (Whittle & Spicer, 2008), ANT does recognise agency attributes of nonhumans, but not intentionality at all. Attributing causal agency – i.e., intentionality – to objects is merely technical determinism (Latour, 2005). Humans are empowered with intentionality, while nonhumans are not; Durkheim affirms that the latter lack "motivating power" and do not "release social energy" (cited by Latour, 2005, p. 73). The purpose of studying the interaction between human and nonhuman actors in a symmetric fashion is to avoid imposing "a priori some spurious asymmetry among human intentional action and a material world of causal relations" (Latour, 2005, p. 76).

ANT challenges the generalised assumption that humans and technology tend to constitute a stable and predictable system (Latour, 1987). To be sure, humans and technology do constitute a sociotechnical arrangement; however, this arrangement is neither stable nor predictable. In ANT, the word social designates an association, an association of both humans and nonhumans; if either one of them is missing the association is no longer possible (Latour, 2005). The sanctioning of scientific facts requires several stages, on which technical only aspects are not enough; it necessitates the combination of different interests to form an amalgamated entity. Indeed, for a discovery or an innovation to become socially accepted, the process starts with the collection of samples in the field and continues with the appropriate methods of analysis that make it significant. Then, it is the set of connections within the discipline that creates allegiance to the novel object, which is subsequently socialised. Ultimately, the novel object can be upheld only if there are "links and knots" that maintain these heterogeneous elements together (Latour, 1999b).

Building upon ANT tenets, sociomateriality has recently emerged as a fresh and promising perspective to studying both technology and social organisation together as an indivisible compound. Conceptualising the organisation as a sociotechnical system contributes to optimise the joint use of both technical and social resources in a well-balanced way (Daft, 2007). Sociomateriality moves beyond the social contructivist view that conceptualises the social and the technical as mutually dependent ensembles, whereby one shapes the other; sociomateriality perceives the social and the technical as an entangled unit (Orlikowski & Scott, 2008). A basic assumption of sociomateriality is that the social and the technical have agency properties because the system they both constitute is continuously reconfiguring the world (Barad, 2003).

Intermediaries and Mediators

Social life cannot be explained without reference to technology (Latour, 1992). Hence, gaining understanding of social practices requires studying the continuous interactions between humans and technology. Among the rich conceptual lexicon that ANT provides, Latour (2005) offers two terms that should prove useful in the subsequent argument on agency and intentionality: intermediaries and mediators. The former do not produce transformations in the sociotechnical system; they just maintain the assembly of humans and nonhumans. For instance, the sociotechnical system comprised by a truck driver, a truck and a road constitutes an intermediary if every element is working well. As soon as, say, the truck breaks down, the components of the association are exposed and they become a mediator. Mediators "transform, translate, distort and modify the meaning or the elements they are supposed to carry" (ibid., p. 39). The passage from invisible intermediaries to visible mediators, and vice versa, makes apparent the artificial division between the social and the technical.

Although the weight of technology may be quite overwhelming in a car factory assembly line, technology is also present in less technically-oriented organisations like a legal office. While material objects are far more rigid in terms of opportunities of the user to modify them, the flexible characteristics of information systems possess make them unique in terms of both the negotiation processes and transformations they generate. Indeed, information systems users are continuously accommodating social practices in relation to the logic inscribed in the former and simultaneously adjusting the technology to their particular needs (Orlikowski, 2000).

To be sure, the opportunities to generate accounts of momentarily visibility of the human-nonhuman dyad are practically unlimited (Latour, 2005). The human-nonhuman interaction can also be observed beyond the infrequent encounters with current innovations, the gap existing between technical instruments and their would-be users, the occurrence of breakdowns, the historical accounts of inventions and discoveries and the imaginary portrayals of counterfactual history. Everything can be studied using ANT; even mundane artefacts such as the now ubiquitous electronic mail system.

ELECTRONIC MAIL SYSTEM AS A SOCIOTECHNICAL SYSTEM

Electronic mail system, or e-mail for short, evolved from file directory. At the beginning, it was just a message added in another user's directory, so the recipient could see it when they logged in. *MAILBOX*, originated at Massachusetts Institute of Technology in 1965, was a pioneer message system. It simply allowed sending messages among various users of the same mainframe computer.

A proper e-mail system indicating to whom the messages should go was invented in 1972 when computers became interconnected to each other over networks. It was then when the @ symbol was introduced and the convention of nominating the addressee by *name-of-the-user@name-of-the-computer* was adopted. Later on, the first e-mail commercial packages began to appear – e.g., *Eudora* in 1988 and *Pegasus* in 1990 – followed by a wide range of e-mail systems available now – e.g., *Hotmail* in 1996, *Yahoo!* and *Outlook* in 1997, *Entourage* in 2000, among others. Certainly, e-mail communications is one of the most popular uses of the Internet. As August 2008, the number of e-mail users was estimated in 1.3 billion worldwide (Tschabitscher, 2010).

One of the key features of e-mail systems is that they are highly interactive. An e-mail message prompts actions upon its recipients by making possible a direct two-way communication between two or more users, besides the ability to keep others informed of the communication exchange among the parties either overtly – by using the carbon copy (Cc) function – or covertly – by using the blind carbon copy (Bcc) function. Moreover, not only that these communications in the form of written texts can be responded but also can be saved, forwarded, copied and/or deleted.

E-mail has become part of the ample "communication repertoire" (Haddon, 2005) we enjoy these days. We can easily jump from face-to-face interaction to communication through telephone calls (using either fixed-line or mobile phones) to communication through the World Wide Web. Indeed, we are living an era where convergent technologies facilitate communication and allow remote interaction – cf. "technological affordances" (Wellman, Quan-Haase, Boase, Chen, Hampton, Isla de Díaz, & Miyata, 2003).

The Use of E-mail Systems in Organisations

Generally speaking, information systems are socially situated, immersed in an economic, political and cultural environment with a particular set of procedures interacting with a whole array of practices (Orlikowski & Iacono, 2001). E-mail, as a specific information systems application, is intrinsically interactive and undeniably flexible. Technology-mediated communication, like the one by e-mail, is nothing else but a sociotechnical process. It allows the user to customise, create, override or just ignore the developer's intentionality embedded on certain functionalities as well as the organisational procedures that delineate the way it should be used. Therefore, e-mail systems can function either as an intermediary, if they allow the communication exchange as has been conceived, or as a mediator, if they produce a disruption in the communication flow.

A high degree of familiarity with social practices and, at the same time, keeping oneself distant from them help the researcher in gaining an inside understanding of social practices that take place within the intertwined unit formed by both users and e-mail system. Attention must be paid to the uniqueness of the social actors and their context in an attempt to unpack the social and technical characteristics that constitute the practice of using e-mail systems. Both participation and observation is conducive to knowledge creation to understand how information technology is constituted and reconstituted by social actors. By combining research observation and participation, the researcher can gain a deep understanding of the continuous negotiation process (ten Have, 2007).

This knowing creation exercise entails treating the obvious and usual activities – like using an e-mail system – as a phenomenon, where social behaviour in concrete situations is thoroughly described (Knorr-Cetina, 1988).

Understanding how social practices are configured requires studying them not as a sporadic event but as part of the organisational life without presupposing the pre-existence of either humans or technology (Orlikowski, 2007). By adopting an ANT perspective, the researcher can see the usually hidden-from-view aspects of the entangled practices involving humans and technology and to understand organisational life as a "relational ontology" that grants agency attributes to the combined configuration of individuals and objects (Orlikowski, 2010). This relational ontology, which conceptualises both the technical and the social as an entangled unit, poses a major challenge from an epistemological point of view. A relational ontology does not distinguish the observer and the observed as separate components. It perceives them as an indissoluble unit with "intra-acting" components and conceptualises phenomena as "ontologically primitive relations – relations without pre-existing relata" (Barad, 2003, p. 815).

DISCLOSING THE AGENCY ATTRIBUTES AND HUMAN INTENTIONALITY OF E-MAIL SYSTEM

More often than not, behind an e-mail message there is a human sender. It is not hard recognising the human agency behind an e-mail communication that has been written and sent by a person with the intention to put across a message. E-mail messages can convey commands, instructions, enquiries, information, compliments or a combination of any of these. Without doubt they provoke an action on the recipient, whether to make a decision, to execute a task, to provide an answer, to keep up on what is going on or increasing one's sense of worth. What is important to note here is that no matter what the purpose of the message is, the computer-mediated communication does modify a state of affairs – i.e., it becomes an actor (Latour, 2005). A careful observation reveals than an e-mail system is in fact a constitutive relationship of humans and nonhumans with hybrid agency (Introna, 2007).

To illustrate the difference between agency attributes of nonhuman actors and intentionality of human actors and further elaborate on the concepts of intermediaries and mediators, I will use the atypical yet widespread episode of the automatically generated "Out of Office" rule of e-mail systems as a case in point. The e-mail service has been designed by engineers and is configured by its users in a certain way to facilitate communication in organisational life. The "Out of Office" automatic function allows the user to communicate his/her temporary unavailability, usually in days or weeks, to those who are trying to reach him/her by e-mail. The user just needs to specify the period when he/she is not going to be available and any time a message gets into his/her mailbox, an automatically generated reply goes back to sender of the original message. Most of the e-mail applications include such function with different degrees of customisation by defining the parameters where the rule does not apply. If the user sets up the "Out of Office" automatic reply, he/she is intentionally articulating his/her inaccessibility through and in the e-mail system – paradoxically, using the tools the system designed to facilitate communication itself affords.

Unsurprisingly, the opposite is also possible. The user can override the "Out of Office" function altogether. It could be because he/she will continue reading and replying the incoming e-mail messages or simply because does not want to let others know about his/her temporary unavailability status. It is also possible for the user not to set up the "Out of Office" auto-responder because he/she wants to avoid disturbing his/her contacts. Since the "Out of Office" reply is by and large not selective, it goes out to the individual who is trying to contact the addressee and also, indiscriminately, to the list group members the addressee may have subscribed to who become knowledgeable of the status of the replier, without even being interested on it. Incidentally, a recent poll has just confirmed that the automatically generated "Out of Office" reply is ranked among the top 20 most irritating technological inventions (Telegraph.co.uk, 2010).

The interesting point here is that whether the user sets up the "Out of Office" function or not, the action or the omission reflects a human intention. Although it can be argued that technology – through its several layers – and morality are profoundly mingled (Latour, 2002), nonhuman actors do not possess intention. In the case of e-mail technology, individual and managerial assumptions define the way it is going to be used in a particular organisation (Zuboff, 1982). In the contemporary networked organisation, characterised by fluidity and flexibility, a particular technology can be adapted depending on the individual and/or organisational interests (Castells, 2000). For instance, some organisations have explicit policies in place encouraging their staff to set up the "Out of Office" auto-responder whenever they are to be absent from their workplace – e.g., on vacation, on a business trip, at a seminar, etc. The purpose is not only to know the actual status of the employees (i.e., availability or unavailability) but also to have an accurate headcount in case the premises have to be evacuated after a disaster – e.g., earthquake, fire, etc. On the other hand, some organisations recommend not using the "Out of Office" assistant in order to avoid confirming the validity of employees' e-mail addresses to spammers and thereby increasing the spam mail received by the organisation – it is estimated that 45% of e-mail traffic is made up of junk messages.

Regardless of organisational policies or human intentions, nonhuman actors possess agency. Even the automatically generated "Out of Office" message prompts actions on the recipient. An extreme case demonstrating the high degree of interactivity occurred in the historical city of Swansea, Wales in 2008. Being a bilingual country, road signs in Wales must be in both English and Welsh. So when the local authority e-mailed its in-house translation service requesting a translation into Welsh of the sign "No entry for heavy goods vehicles. Residential site only", the Swansea Council literally became lost in translation. When the automatic reply, "I am not in the office at the moment. Send any work to be translated", came back, the council officials hastily put up the sign in both languages with the original version in English and its wrong Welsh translation.

The aforementioned case is an extraordinary example of the agency attributes of technology. It did modify the state of affairs, although the resulting road sign did not reflect the intention of the participating human actors – neither the translator's nor the city council officials'. Only human actors have intentions; nonhuman actors do not. Furthermore, this example reveals the passage from an indiscernible intermediary to a conspicuous mediator.

Some personal experiences also serve to illustrate the difference between agency and intentionality as well as the intermediary/mediator duality. It happened to me that I had been in frequent correspondence with colleagues, who were in fact absent from work – sometimes even enjoying holiday overseas. Even though the first reply I received when I tried to contact them was an automatically generated "Out of Office" message, immediately afterwards I received a proper message in response to my first communication. Moreover, given the nature of the topic we were discussing, sometimes the correspondence by e-mail spanned over several days or weeks while my correspondents were in fact out of office. It became clear that the intention of my contacts was not to stop the communication flow, although they had originally set up the automatic reply. This scenario also portrays the intermediary – i.e., the nonhuman agency announcing my colleagues' hiatus – becoming the mediator – i.e., the human intention rendering the nonhuman agency ineffective. Of course, there were occasions when I received "Out of Office" messages and had no option but waiting until the return of the person I was trying to contact. Under these circumstances, the nonhuman agency mirrors the human intention with no transformation in the sociotechnical system – i.e., intermediary.

My experience when I set up the "Out of Office" reply was similar. Depending on the urgency of the subject matter, the relevance of topic according to my own interests and the person who was trying to reach me, I made the decision whether to answer or not the incoming e-mail message. If I judged the message as one that required a rapid response, if the content of the message was of special importance to me, or if the sender was close to me, I immediately proceeded to prepare an answer, overriding the pre-set rule. The human intention prevailed over the nonhuman agency reversing the sociotechnical system by modifying the meaning it was supposed to carry – i.e., mediator. Otherwise, I just left the message to be answered until I was back to office. In this case, the sociotechnical system just continued operating as envisaged.

The practice of using e-mail technology to tell others that we are not available but acting in a way that either confirms or cancels out what we say reveals the contradiction between the utterance and the performance. The occurrences explained in the paragraphs above reflect the selective criterion the user can apply to answer e-mail communications when he/she is not at work. Nevertheless this selective behaviour, it seems that e-mail technology, which was designed to make possible communication over networks, give individuals the power to control the flow of communication breaking the notion of "perpetual connection" (Gergen, 2002) on ad-hoc considerations. It becomes apparent that e-mail technology in general and the "Out of Office" rule in particular can be used to produce a state of affairs – "I am away and will get back to you on my return to office" – that does not represent reality – "I am here reading your message". If the recipient is reading the incoming e-mails, the "Out of Office" message is merely announcing a fictitious situation, giving the opportunity to be well informed of what is going on while no creating no expectations of an immediate reply. The "Out of Office" reply is more than an expression informing about one's status; it produces an action on both the sender and the receiver.

CONCLUSION

A combination of research observation and participation, whereby the knowing process and the knowledge produced are informed by both observation and practice has made possible the analysis of the e-mail, a sociotechnical system that is commonplace nowadays. Using the conceptual vocabulary provided by ANT, the agency attributes of nonhuman actors have been outlined and contrasted against the intentionality that human actors possess.

The antecedent discussion has contributed to emphasise the difference between agency attributes and intentionality by tracking the negotiation process that goes on in the daily interaction between individuals and technology at work. Taking the automatically generated "Out of Office" message as a case in point, this study demonstrates that it is an indexical expression that artificially creates a specific state of affairs. It produces a surrealist situation where the person who gives the utterance can modify the created reality depending on specific circumstances. Furthermore, the notions of intermediaries and mediators have shed light on the variability of the systems; they have contributed to show how the agency attributes embedded in the "Out of Office" expression can be eventually subordinated to human intentionality. In this sense, organisational norms, power related issues and individual choices in the presence of a specific technology shape the assembly constituted by both human and nonhuman actors making the sociotechnical entanglement unpredictable.

Work practices are supported, modified and created by technology to the same extent that technology is supported, modified and created by work practices. Before the introduction of e-mail technology – and even mobile telephones – into organisational life, employees' situation in relation to their workplace was restricted to binary options: being either present or absent. If they were absent, co-workers had absolutely certainty that they could not rely on the missing colleague for any activity or communication. With the introduction of new technological tools in the workplace, there is always the possibility to reach the absent colleague, who is constantly at arm's length (cf., Fortunati, 2005). Perhaps, in the time of pervasive and ubiquitous information and communication technologies there is no longer a place for an "Out of Office" rule in the networked organisation.

Future research could explore further the role played by power on nonhuman agency attributes and human intentionality. It is possible to speculate that the physically absent actors can reveal their status when deciding whether to reply or not incoming e-mails. While an employee in a subordinated position might feel anxious for not answering an e-mail request from his/her manager while not in the office (situation that can be aggravated for the tracking system that allows the sender to check whether or not the e-mail has been opened), a person in a senior position may use the same technology to read e-mail messages and decide not to respond them to demonstrate who is in a powerful position in relation to the sender. Alternatively, the subordinate might take advantage of the technology to demonstrate his/her devotion to the organisation and answer e-mails during his/her time off.

REFERENCES

Akrich, M. (1992). The De-Scription of Technical Objects. In Bijker, W. E., & Law, J. (Eds.), *Shaping Technology/Building Society: Studies in Sociotechnical Change*. Cambridge, MA: The MIT Press.

Barad, K. (2003). Posthumanist Performativity: Toward an Understanding of How Matter Comes to Matter. *Signs: Journal of Women in Culture and Society*, *28*(3), 801–831. doi:10.1086/345321

BBC. (2008). *E-mail Error Ends Up on Road Sign*. Retrieved February 24, 2010, from http://news.bbc.co.uk/2/hi/uk_news/wales/7702913.stm

Callon, M. (1986). Some Elements of a Sociology of Translation: Domestication of the Scallops and the Fisherman. In Law, J. (Ed.), *Power, Action and Belief*. London, UK: Routledge & Kegan Paul.

Castells, M. (2000). *The Information Age: Economy, Society and Culture - The Rise of the Network Society* (2nd ed., *Vol. 1*). Malden, MA: Blackwell Publishing.

Castells, M., Fernández Ardèvol, M., Qiu, J. L., & Sey, A. (2007). *Mobile Communication and Society: A Global Perspective*. London: The MIT Press.

Daft, R. L. (2007). *Organization Theory and Design* (9th ed.). Mason, OH: Thomson South-Western.

Fortunati, L. (2005). Mobile Telephone and the Presentation of Self. In Ling, R., & Pedersen, P. E. (Eds.), *Mobile Communications: Re-negotiation of the Social Sphere* (pp. 203–218). London: Springer.

Gergen, K. J. (2002). The Challenge of Absent Presence. In Katz, J. E., & Aakhus, M. A. (Eds.), *Perpetual Contact: Mobile Communication, Private Talk, Public Performance* (pp. 227–241). Cambridge, UK: Cambridge University Press. doi:10.1017/CBO9780511489471.018

Haddon, L. (2005). Research Questions for the Evolving Communications Landscape. In Ling, R., & Pedersen, P. E. (Eds.), *Mobile Communications: Re-negotiation of the Social Space* (pp. 7–23). London: Springer Verlag.

Hanseth, O., Aanestad, M., & Berg, M. (2004). Guest Editors' Introduction: Actor-Network Theory and Information Systems. What's so Special? *Information Technology & People*, *17*(2), 116–123. doi:10.1108/09593840410542466

Heidegger, M. (1977). *The Question Concerning Technology, and Other Essays* (Lovitt, W., Trans.). New York: Harper Torchbooks.

Hughes, T. P. (1986). The Seamless Web: Technology, Science, Etcetera, Etcetera. *Social Studies of Science*, *16*(2), 281–292. doi:10.1177/0306312786016002004

Introna, L. D. (2007). Maintaining the Reversibility of Foldings: Making the Ethics (Politics) of Information Technology Visible. *Ethics and Information Technology*, *9*(1), 11–25. doi:10.1007/s10676-006-9133-z

Knorr-Cetina, K. D. (1988). The Micro-social Order: Towards a Reconception. In Fielding, N. G. (Ed.), *Action and Structure: Research Methods and Social Theory* (pp. 21–53). London: Sage Publications.

Latour, B. (1986). The Power of Association. In Law, J. (Ed.), *Power, Action and Belief*. London: Routledge & Kegan Paul.

Latour, B. (1987). *Science in Action*. Boston: Harvard University Press.

Latour, B. (1992). Where Are the Missing Masses? The Sociology of a Few Mundane Artifacts. In Bijker, W. E., & Law, J. (Eds.), *Shaping Technology/Building Society: Studies in Sociotechnical Change* (pp. 225–258). Cambridge, MA: MIT Press.

Latour, B. (1999a). On Recalling ANT. In Law, J., & Hassard, J. (Eds.), *Actor Network Theory and After* (pp. 15–25). Oxford, UK: Blackwell Publishers.

Latour, B. (1999b). *Pandora's Hope: Essays on the Reality of Science Studies*. Cambridge, MA: Harvard University Press.

Latour, B. (2002). Morality and Technology: The End of the Means. *Theory, Culture & Society*, *19*(5/6), 247–260. doi:10.1177/026327602761899246

Latour, B. (2005). *Reassembling the Social: An Introduction to Actor-Network-Theory*. Oxford, UK: Oxford University Press.

Law, J. (1994). *Organizing Modernity*. Oxford, UK: Blackwell.

Law, J., & Callon, M. (1992). The Life and Death of an Aircraft: A Network Analysis of Technical Change. In Bijker, W. E., & Law, J. (Eds.), *Shaping Technology/Building Society: Studies in Sociotechnical Change*. Cambridge, MA: The MIT Press.

Orlikowski, W. J. (2000). Using Technology and Constituting Structures: A Practice Lens for Studying Technology in Organizations. *Organization Science*, *11*(4), 404–428. doi:10.1287/orsc.11.4.404.14600

Orlikowski, W. J. (2007). Sociomaterial Practices: Exploring Technology at Work. *Organization Studies*, *28*(9), 1435–1448. doi:10.1177/0170840607081138

Orlikowski, W. J. (2010). The Sociomateriality of Organisational Life: Considering Technology in Management Research. *Cambridge Journal of Economics*, *34*(1), 125–141. doi:10.1093/cje/bep058

Orlikowski, W. J., & Iacono, C. S. (2001). Desperately Seeking the "IT" in IT Research - A Call to Theorizing the IT Artifact. *Information Systems Research, 12*(2), 121–134. doi:10.1287/isre.12.2.121.9700

Orlikowski, W. J., & Scott, S. V. (2008). Sociomateriality: Challenging the Separation of Technology, Work and Organization. *The Academy of Management Annals*, *2*(1), 433–474. doi:10.1080/19416520802211644

Telegraph.co.uk. (2010). *Car Alarms Are "Most Irritating Piece of Technology Ever Invented", Poll Finds*. Retrieved January 12, 2010, from http://www.telegraph.co.uk/technology/news/6950876/Car-alarms-are-most-irritating-piece-of-technology-ever-invented-poll-finds.html

ten Have, P. (2007). Ethnomethodology. In C. Seale, G. Gobo, J. F. Gubrium, & D. Silverman (Eds.), *Qualitative Research Practice* (Concise paperback ed., pp. 139-152). London: Sage Publications.

Toffler, A. (1971). *Future Shock*. London: Pan.

Tschabitscher, H. (2010). *How Many Email Users Are There?* Retrieved February 16, 2010, from http://email.about.com/od/emailtrivia/f/how_many_email.htm

Wellman, B., Quan-Haase, A., Boase, J., Chen, W., Hampton, K., & Isla de Díaz, I. (2003). The Social Affordances of the Internet for Networked Individualism. *Journal of Computer-Mediated Communication*, *8*(3).

Whittle, A., & Spicer, A. (2008). Is Actor Network Theory Critique? *Organization Studies*, *29*(4), 611–629. doi:10.1177/0170840607082223

Woolgar, S. (2005). Mobile Back to Front: Uncertainty and Danger in Theory-Technology Relation. In Ling, R., & Pedersen, P. E. (Eds.), *Mobile Communications: Renegotiation of the Social Sphere*. London: Springer Verlag.

Zuboff, S. (1982). New Worlds of Computer-mediated Work. *Harvard Business Review*, *60*(5), 142–152.

This work was previously published in International Journal of Actor-Network Theory and Technological Innovation, Volume 2, Issue 4, edited by Arthur Tatnall, pp. 21-29, copyright 2010 by IGI Publishing (an imprint of IGI Global).

Chapter 15
Using Actor-Network Theory to Facilitate a Superior Understanding of Knowledge Creation and Knowledge Transfer

Nilmini Wickramasinghe
RMIT University, Australia

Arthur Tatnall
Victoria University, Australia

Rajeev K. Bali
Coventry University, UK

ABSTRACT

Given today's dynamic business environment it becomes essential for organisations to maximise their intellectual assets in order to ensure that they are able to support flexible operations and sustain their competitive advantage. Central to this is the ability to extract germane knowledge to enable rapid and effective decision making. At present, knowledge creation techniques tend to focus on either human or technology aspects of organisational development and less often on process-centric aspects of knowledge generation. However, to truly understand knowledge creation and transfer, thereby enabling an organisation to be better positioned to leverage the full potential of its intellectual capital, it is important to view knowledge creation and all socio-technical organisational operations that result in knowledge generation through a richer lens. Actor-network Theory is proffered in this article as such a lens.

DOI: 10.4018/978-1-4666-1559-5.ch015

INTRODUCTION

Knowledge is now considered to be central to organisational performance, and integral to the realisation of a sustainable competitive advantage (Bali et al., 2009; Wickramasinghe & von Lubitz, 2007; Davenport & Grover, 2001; Drucker, 1993). The rapidly evolving field of knowledge management (KM) provides various tools and techniques necessary for the enhancement of the efficiency of core business processes, the support of continuous innovation and the facilitating of rapid decision making in dynamic and complex environments; all being essential ingredients of a sustainable competitive advantage.

A central issue within KM concerns the way knowledge is created and transferred. Since this naturally has a very important bearing on all subsequent steps of the KM process it should come as no surprise that a significant amount of attention has been devoted to the manner in which knowledge is generated (Bali et al., 2009; Davenport & Grover, 2001; Drucker, 1993; Malhotra, 2000; Wickramasinghe, 2003; 2006; Markus, 2001; Alavi & Leidner, 2001). Within the KM literature many different conceptual frameworks exist for explaining knowledge creation. To date however, these frameworks tend to view knowledge creation from one of two perspectives; either a people-oriented perspective (Bali et al., 2009; Wickramasinghe, 2003, 2006; Polyani, 1958, 1966; Nonaka & Nishiguch, 1994; Nonaka, 1994; Newell et al., 2002; Schultz & Leidner, 2002), or a technology-based perspective (Bali et al., 2009; Adriaans & Zaninge, 1996; Cabena et al., 1998; Bendoly, 2003; Fayyad et al., 1996; Holsapple & Joshi, 2002; Choi & Lee, 2003; Chung & Gray, 1996; Becerra-Fernandez & Sabherwal, 2001). More recently, we can see the appearance of a third process-centric perspective (Bali et al., 2009; von Lubitz & Wickramasinghe, 2006; Wickramasinghe & von Lubitz, 2007). Recognising the limitation of taking a narrow perspective to knowledge creation many have advocated the need for a new holistic approach (von Lubitz & Wickramasinghe, 2006; Wickramasinghe, 2006; Bali et al., 2009) in order to provide a more flexible instrument for interaction with the increased dynamics of the business environment. We contend that in order to enable such a perspective a rich framework is required in which a wide lens can be used to identify knowledge created through various socio-technical organisational operations. In this article we propose that Actor-network Theory (ANT) provides such a suitable lens since it enables the analysis of all the socio-technical operations of an organisation in one inter-connected network which combines actants; including both technology and people and their interactions.

KNOWLEDGE CREATION

Succinctly, knowledge management (KM) involves four key steps of creating/generating knowledge, storing knowledge, using/re-using and dissemination of knowledge throughout the organisation (Bali et al., 2009; Davenport & Grover, 2001; Drucker, 1993; Malhotra, 2000; Wickramasinghe, 2003; Markus, 2001; Alavi & Leidner, 2001; Holsapple & Joshi, 2002; Becerra-Fernandez & Sabherwal, 2001). Given that knowledge creation is the first step, it is important that the quality of inputs is high and that the knowledge generated is germane since this impacts the consequent steps and thereby will also determine the quality of the output (Wickramasinghe, 2006; Bali et al., 2009).

To date the domain of knowledge creation has been dominated by two main streams of thought. We classify one of these as people-centric as it has its roots in behavioural theories, and the other as technology-centric as it is strongly rooted in its computer science ancestry. Furthermore, knowledge itself has also been viewed from various philosophical perspectives; Burrell and Morgan's (Schultze & Leidner, 2001) well-established framework of objective and subjective characterisations or a more recent approach elaborated on by Schultze and Leidner (2001) using Deetz's four discourses of organisational inquiry namely; consensus/dissensus and emergent/a priori have all emerged to represent these various perspectives. The underlying philosophical perspectives being Lokean /Leibnizian or Hegelian/ Kantian (Wickramasinghe, 2006; Wickramasinghe & von Lubitz, 2007) and if one looks at Churchman's work on inquiring organisations then it is necessary to also include the Singerian perspective (Wickramasinghe, 2006; Wickramasinghe & von Lubitz, 2007). We briefly summarise the key points from these respective streams in the following sections.

People-Centric Approaches

Nonaka's knowledge spiral (Nonaka & Nishiguchi; 2001; Nonaka, 1994) is arguably the most widely known and used framework for knowledge creation. Grounded in the ideas of Polyani's tacit and explicit knowledge (Polyani; 1958, 1966) it views knowledge primarily as an object existing in two forms of explicit or factual knowledge (i.e., 'know-what') and tacit or experiential knowledge (i.e., 'know – how') (Schultz & Leidner; 2002; Wickramasinghe, 2006). Central to this model is the dynamic nature of knowledge (Becerra-Fernandez & Sabherwal, 2001; Wickramasinghe & von Lubitz, 2007) and the continuous conversion of one type of knowledge to another to form new knowledge, i.e., "the knowledge spiral" (Nonaka & Nishiguchi, 2001; Nonak, 1994). In doing so, Nonaka also recognises knowledge as a subject and in his socialisation step in particular, sense making activities (Nonaka & Nishiguchi, 2001; Nonak, 1994) are necessary in creating new knowledge.

Nonaka identifies four principal conversion forms (Nonaka & Nishiguchi, 2001; Nonaka, 1994):

- **Socialisation (tacit to tacit knowledge):** usually occurs through apprenticeship type relations where the teacher or master passes on the skill to the apprentice
- **Combination (explicit to explicit knowledge):** formal learning of facts
- **Externalisation (tacit to explicit knowledge):** articulation of nuances
- **Internalisation (explicit to tacit knowledge):** associating newly acquired facts to enrich one's pre-existing expertise and skills.

Like Nonaka, Spender's model recognises the existence of both explicit and implicit knowledge but he emphasises an individual and social sense (Wickramasinghe, 2006; Newell et al., 2002). This serves to underscore the sense making perspective (Nonaka & Nishiguchi, 2001; Nonaka, 1994). Spender's definition of implicit knowledge corresponds well with Nonaka's tacit knowledge (ibid).

In contrast, Blackler's approach (Wickramasinghe, 2006; Newell et al., 2002) emphasises the fact that knowledge is not a binary construct but can exist in several forms (encoded, embedded, embodied, encultured and/or embrained) that span the continuum of tacit (embrained) to explicit (encoded) knowledge. The embedded, embodied and encultured types of knowledge exhibit varying degrees of tacit (implicit)/explicit combination and serve, essentially, as the transitional links between the two extremes.

Technology-Centric Approach

The dominant technical perspective to knowledge creation has its roots in computer science and views new knowledge as being discovered from data and hence is known as knowledge discovery in databases (KDD) or simply data mining (Bali et al., 2009; Adriaans & Zaninge, 1996; Cabena et al., 1998; Bendoly, 2003; Fayyad et al., 1996; Holsapple & Joshi, 2002; Choi & Lee, 2003; Chung & Gray, 1996; Becerra-Fernandez & Sabherwal, 2001). KDD focuses on how data are transformed into knowledge by identifying valid, novel, potentially useful, and ultimately understandable patterns within data sets that would remain opaque without purposeful extraction and analysis (Bali et al., 2009; Adriaans & Zaninge, 1996; Cabena et al., 1998; Bendoly, 2003; Fayyad et al., 1996; Holsapple & Joshi, 2002; Choi & Lee, 2003; Chung & Gray, 1996; Becerra-Fernandez & Sabherwal, 2001). Consequently, KDD-based creation of knowledge is based on providing common (superior) structure to often widely dispersed data sets. Other technology-centric approaches to knowledge creation include the newer sub-fields of business intelligence and business analytics (Wickramasinghe, 2006). In any of these approaches knowledge is primarily considered to be an object.

Process-Centric Approach

This is a newer approach to knowledge creation which tries to emphasise the dynamic nature of knowledge creation. One model that does this is the intelligence continuum (Wickramasinghe & Schaffer; 2006; Wickramasinghe et al., 2009) while another is derived from the work of Boyd (Boyd, 1976; Wickramasinghe & von Lubitz; 2007). Contrary to either people- or technology-centric models, the process-centric concept is based on de-structuring pre-existing domains, selection of their relevant components, then recombining these components into an entirely new domain relevant to the activities within the changed environment.

The pivotal notion of all models of knowledge creation is the demand that the generated product – usable knowledge – remains the paramount concern to any organisation, be it a small business or a nation-state.

Knowledge, then like so many other concepts in organisational theory, is a complex construct. In trying to understand knowledge creation it is necessary to not only understand its binary nature i.e.; its objective and subjective components (Alavi & Leidner, 2001) but what enables effective knowledge creation. While we have the frameworks of Burell and Morgan as well as Deetz to help us to understand the complex philosophical underpinnings of knowledge the KM literature lacks a strong and robust lens of analysis to view organisational operations and thereby understand knowledge creation more fully. Given the prevalence and importance of ICT (information communication technology) in organisations' today it is vital that such an analytic lens takes a socio-technical perspective. Bearing this in mind, we suggest that Actor-network Theory (ANT) provides a rich and suitable framework since it enables the viewing of all organisational operations as one inter-connected network of people and technology actants.

ACTOR-NETWORK THEORY (ANT)

Much research in information systems is based on an essentialist paradigm that asserts that a technological innovation embodies some essential capacity, 'information' or 'essence' that is largely responsible both for the way is works and the way we relate to it. Grint and Woolgar (1997), contend that essentialist accounts which distinguish between human and non-human elements are forced to treat the 'technology' as something with a set of fixed, intrinsic properties, and the human elements as a context within which the technology is used.

Actor-Network Theory (ANT) considers both social and technical determinism to be flawed and proposes instead a socio-technical account (Callon & Latour, 1981; Latour, 1986; Law & Callon, 1988) in which neither the social nor technical positions are privileged. In this socio-technical order nothing is purely social and nothing is purely technical (Law, 1991). What seems, on the surface, to be social is partly technical, and what may appear to be only technical is partly social. ANT deals with the social-technical divide by denying that purely technical or purely social relations are possible. To address the need to treat both human and non-human actors fairly and in the same way, actor-network theory is based upon three principles: agnosticism, generalised symmetry and free association (Callon, 1986). The first of these tenets, agnosticism, means that analytical impartiality is demanded towards all the actors involved in the project under consideration, whether they be human or non-human. Generalised symmetry offers to explain the conflicting viewpoints of different actors in the same terms by use of an abstract and neutral vocabulary that works the same way for human and non-human actors. Neither the social nor the technical elements in these 'heterogeneous networks' (Law, 1987) should then be given any special explanatory status. Finally, the principle of free association requires the elimination and abandonment of all *a priori* distinctions between the technological or natural, and the social (Callon, 1986; Singleton & Michael, 1993).

"ANT was developed to analyse situations in which it is difficult to separate humans and non-humans, and in which the actors have variable forms and competencies." (Callon, 1999, p. 183)

In summary, under the principles of agnosticism, generalised symmetry and free association, actor-network theory attempts impartiality towards all actors in consideration, whether human or non-human, and makes no distinction in approach between the social, the natural and the technological. As Callon puts it:

"The rule which we must respect is not to change registers when we move from the technical to the social aspects of the problem studied." (Callon 1986, p. 200)

Actor-Network Theory and Knowledge Management

It is useful to consider Knowledge Management in terms of the socio-technical as both human and non-human elements are involved and it is difficult to separate these. We argue that they need to be seem in terms of 'heterogeneous networks' (Law, 1987) involving both human and non-human aspects and that to attempt to identify which aspects are human and which are non-human is not productive. This does indeed appear to be an area where actor-network theory fits very well.

CONCEPTS OF ACTOR-NETWORK THEORY

The Key concepts of ANT that are relevant to the present context of KM research include the following.

1 Actor/Actant

Typically actors are the participants in the network and include both the human and non-human objects and/or subjects. However, in order to avoid the strong bias towards human interpretation of Actor, the neologism **actant** is commonly used to refer to both human and non-human actors. Examples include humans, electronic instruments, technical artefacts, or graphical representations.

Be it the people-centric, techno-centric or process centric approach to knowledge creation all involve actors and by taking the ANT interpretation of actor as both human and/or non human arms the researcher with a more powerful lens to observe and identify knowledge that is created in many more areas and through multiple interactions. This is especially the case when considering KM and ICT together.

2 Heterogeneous Network

An Actor-network or Heterogeneous Network is a network of aligned interests formed by the actors. This is a network of materially heterogeneous actors that is achieved by a great deal of work that both shapes those various social and non-social elements, and 'disciplines' them so that they work together, instead of 'making off on their own' (Latour, 2005) For example, 16th century Portuguese navigation successfully combined improved sailing vessels, the magnetic compass, knowledge of trade winds, and a new method for the astronomical determination of latitude. The result was a 'durable network' that was capable of resisting hostile forces, including currents, winds, and Muslim navigators (Law, 1990; Law & Hassard, 1999).

ANT claims that in principle all actors, whether they be human or non-human, have equal importance and that the difference between such actors, their characteristics, and their apparent relative importance are all generated within a web of relations. The power of an actor is something which emerges out of the effect of network of relations.

In such a network the creation of knowledge is occurring continuously. What is of particular importance is the movement of this knowledge throughout the network, i.e., the transfer and use of knowledge. An understanding in this regard for KM would enable analysis to be made pertaining to importance and germaneness of the created knowledge, its use, usefulness and useability.

3 Tokens/Quasi Objects

Tokens or Quasi Objects are essentially the success outcomes or functioning of the Actors which are passed onto the other actors within the network. As the token is increasingly transmitted or passed through the network, it becomes increasingly punctualised and also increasingly reified. When the token is decreasingly transmitted, or when an actor fails to transmit the token (e.g., the oil pump breaks), punctualisation and reification are decreased as well.

In looking at KM initiatives one of the key success outcomes is superior decision making while errors will multiply and propagate quickly hence it is a critical success factor that the integrity of the network is maintained at all times. Identifying appropriate tokens and quasi objects in a particular context will enable the analysis of the flows of knowledge that enable successful decision making to be observed.

4 Punctualisation

Punctualisation is similar to the concept of abstraction in Object Oriented Programming. A combination of actors can together be viewed as one single actor. These sub-actors are hidden from the normal view. This concept is referred to as Punctualisation. An incorrect or failure of passage of a token to an actor will result in the breakdown of a network. When the network breaks down, it results in breakdown of punctualisation and the viewers will now be able to view the sub-actors of the actor. This concept is often referred to as depunctualisation.

For example, an automobile is often referred to as one unit. Only when it breaks down, is it seen as a combination of several machine parts, or in a knowledge management context the uploading task of one key actor is often in reality a consequence of the interaction and co-ordination of several sub-tasks. This only becomes visible when a breakdown at this point occurs and special attention is given to analyse why and how the problem resulted and hence all sub tasks must be examined carefully.

5 Obligatory Passage Point

The obligatory passage point (OPP) broadly refers to a situation that has to occur in order for all the actors to satisfy the interests that have been attributed to them by the focal actor. The focal actor defines the OPP through which the other actors must pass and by which the focal actor becomes indispensable (Callon, 1986).

In understanding knowledge creation, obligatory passage points might include meetings that must take place, reports that must be submitted or audits and other activities that must occur. Any or all these scenarios have the potential to impact the knowledge creation network.

6 Irreversibility

Callon (1986) states that the degree of irreversibility depends on (i) the extent to which it is subsequently impossible to go back to a point where that translation was only one amongst others and (ii) the extent to which it shapes and determines subsequent translations.

Given the very complex nature of unstructured decision making in dynamic scenarios irreversibility is generally not likely to occur. However it is vital that chains of events are continuously analysed in order that future events can be addressed as effectively and efficiently as possible.

STAGES OF ANT RELEVANT TO A STUDY OF KM

In addition to the key concepts of ANT, three critical stages are also important to consider.

1 Inscription

Latour (2005) describes inscription as a process of creating technical artefacts that would ensure the protection of an actor's interests. Inscriptions – including texts, but also images of many sorts, databases, and the like – are central to knowledge work. Some say that texts (including journal articles, conference papers and presentations, grant proposals, and patents) are among the major, if not *the major*, products of scientific work. Inscriptions make action at a distance possible by stabilising work in such a way that it can travel across space and time and be combined with other work.

Texts are also central to the process of gaining credibility. They carry work to other people and institutions. They attempt to present work in such a way that its meaning and significance are irrefutable. Texts are where authors establish equivalences among problems, which Callon et al. (1986) identifies as a major strategy of enrolling others. An important part of the standard journal article or grant application, for example, is to say, in essence, "If you are interested in X (major issue) you must be interested in Y".

2 Translation

Translation is the central concept of Actor-network theory. The stage of translation can also be called the stage of negotiation. After an Actor-Network is actually created, there would obviously be several actors. For the purpose of clarity and simplicity, a powerful and/or primary actor will translate other's interests into his own, by negotiating with them. This is the stage when all the actors come to an agreement to determine if the network is worthwhile to be built and defended. Michel Callon (1986) defined four important sub-stages of Translation. They are:

2.1 Problematisation

Problematisation is the first stage of translation. This is the stage, where the problem that needs to be solved is identified. The actors and their interests are also identified and framed. To each group of actors with similar interests, a primary actor is chosen as the head of the group. This primary actor establishes itself as the obligatory passage point (OPP) between the other actors and the network, rendering it indispensable.

2.2 Interessesment

This second stage of Translation involves the primary actor identified in the first stage to convince other actors and to negotiate their terms of involvement. The primary actor works to convince others that the roles defined by it are acceptable and feasible and thus works towards getting the actors interested in the network.

2.3 Enrolment

The third stage of translation is the stage of acceptance by the actors of roles defined by the primary actor in the prior stages. The actors, after being convinced by the primary actor, accept their role and interests in this stage.

2.4 Mobilisation of Allies

The primary actors identified in the above stages are supposed to represent the actors of each respective group. During this stage, a re-examination is made to identify if the primary actors identified in the prior stages accurately represent the masses. If the answer is Yes, then the enrolment becomes active support.

3 Framing

This is the final stage of ANT, which gives a sort of stabilisation to the network. As the key issues and debates get resolved within the network, technologies can become stabilised over time.

AN ANT APPROACH TO RESEARCHING KNOWLEDGE CREATION AND TRANSFER

The approach used in ANT to identify and trace networks is to "follow the actors" (Latour 1996:10) and investigate all the relevant leads each new actor suggests. This means that it is primarily the actors themselves, and not the researcher, that determine the direction taken by the investigation. The first step is thus to identify these actors (or actants), remembering that an actor is someone or something that can make its presence individually felt and can make a difference to the situation under investigation. When looking at knowledge creation and transfer the actors are many and varied and this includes various decision makers and knowledge workers as well as the technologies and tools they use to support their tasks and the organisations with which they interact. In a particular scenario it is important to identify all relevant actors before proceeding further.

The next step is to 'interview' the actors. With human actors this is, of course, quite straightforward, but with non-humans it is necessary to find someone (or something) to speak on their behalf. For a non-human item, i.e., a tool or technology this might be its designer or user, or it might just be the instruction manual. The aim of this step is to see how these actors relate to each other and the associations they create – to identify how they interact, how they negotiate, and how they form alliances and networks with each other. These 'heterogeneous networks' consists of the aligned interests held by each of the actors.

In ANT change results from decisions made by actors and involves the exercise of power. Latour (1986) argues that the mere 'possession' of power by an actor does not automatically confer the ability to cause change unless other actors can be *persuaded* to perform the appropriate actions for this to occur. The notion that power is an attribute that can be *possessed* by an actor is an essentialist one, and Latour contends that rather than this it is the number of other people who enter into the situation that indicate the amount of power that has been exercised.

The key to the success of a new approach or the use of a new technology is the creation of a powerful enough consortium of actors to carry it through, and when a medical or education innovation, for example, fails to be taken up this can be considered to reflect on the inability of those involved to construct the necessary network of alliances amongst the other actors. Getting this innovation accepted calls for strategies aimed at the enrolment of others.

At times during any ANT-based research it will be convenient to consider some groups of actors as operating from inside a black-box. We do this to remove the need to investigate the detail of these actors further at this time and so consider them only as a single actor. At some later time, however, it may be necessary to lift the lid of the black box and investigate the enclosed network in detail.

The main advantage of the ANT approach when considering or researching knowledge creation and knowledge transfer is that it provides the researcher with a powerful lens to enable the identification and ability to explore the real complexity involved in a systematic and robust fashion. Other approaches to technological innovation, Innovation Diffusion and the Technology Acceptance Model (TAM) for example, put much stress on the properties of the technology or organisation themselves, at the expense of looking at how these interact. Unfortunately in doing this they often tends to oversimplify very complex situations and so miss out on a real understanding. The ANT approach of investigating networks and associations provides a useful means to identify and explain these complexities.

Case Vignette: 1: Healthcare Knowledge Exchange

This example revolves around a collaborative partnership to develop a secure information network between two regions in Europe. One of the regions is in the UK, the other (Country X) remains confidential at this stage due to ongoing funding applications and existing confidentiality agreements. Pseudonyms shall be used where appropriate to preserve anonymity.

The first stage of the project involves capturing the principles of the partnership by way of a pilot project, the aims of which are to analyse and understand the value of outsourcing (digital) medical images. Key issues in the delivery of services in Country X are: a widely dispersed population, healthcare provision in remote environments and an overall shortage of medical image professionals. Within the UK, the routine analysis of digital medical images is becoming a growing issue with increased recruitment in other core medical disciplines not being matched in medical imaging.

The pilot project's objective is to establish the added value in outsourcing digital medical images over a secure and potentially portable Public Key Infrastructure (PKI) based system for remote diagnosis across international borders. Added value relates to both improvement in quality of patient care and clinical outcomes, and financial/operational benefits to individual healthcare organisations.

Within the UK, analysis and delivery of more cost-effective healthcare services by individual National Health Service (NHS) Trusts (hospitals) is encouraged by the introduction of a tariff-based system through 'Payment by Results' by the Department of Health. The UK Government medical imaging outsourcing targets encourage international collaboration, but there are barriers which must be overcome to enable successful partnership, namely: (i) to establish clinical trust between countries and organisations, (ii) to establish common data security policies and (iii) to ensure full integration with existing healthcare ICT systems.

The following research areas will therefore be considered as part of the pilot project: (i) clinical trust and security issues in the health care domain (in the UK and Country X), (ii) the importance of integration with existing systems, (iii) the effect and added value of technology intervention, (iv) the impact of outsourcing in health care (including barriers to delivery) and (v) the relevance of process simulation.

Delivery of the project will be managed through five distinct stages: Stage 1 (to develop project and research plans (including trial methodology), identify individual leads within partner organisations and potential sources of regional, national, and EU funding); Stage 2 (to establish organisational trust, define PKI functional requirements (framework of reference), and build a PKI network between Country X and the UK NHS Trust under a common security policy; Stage 3 (to implement and integrate the PKI system into the existing medical imaging applications in Country X and the UK NHS Trust, to train end users in the application through the use of videoconferencing and eLearning techniques); Stage 4 (to execute full trial, collate and report results) and Stage 5 (to extend technology to other clinical areas).

The link of this scenario to an ANT framework can be depicted by the following schematic. This would seem at first glance to be relatively simplistic and easy to understand, but the scenario becomes increasingly complex when additional actors and/or countries are added (for example, once the proposed pilot exchange is validated and expanded). Hence, understanding of the simple scenario and its correct implementation is vital before any expansion, proposed or otherwise, can take place (Figure 1).

Case Vignette: 2: Knowledge Management in Malaysian Universities

University governance can be divided into three parts: leadership and the responsibility of managing the institution, teaching and research faculty and administration to implement and handle support services. This second vignette reports two studies that are investigating aspects of whether adopting a knowledge management culture facilitates or restrains effective practices in higher educational administration in Malaysia. The aim of each the studies is to investigate whether Malaysian university administrative staff and managers view knowledge management as a useful innovation, and to investigate and understand how organisational culture is affecting KM practices in universities. One of the studies is concentrating

Figure 1. International linkage

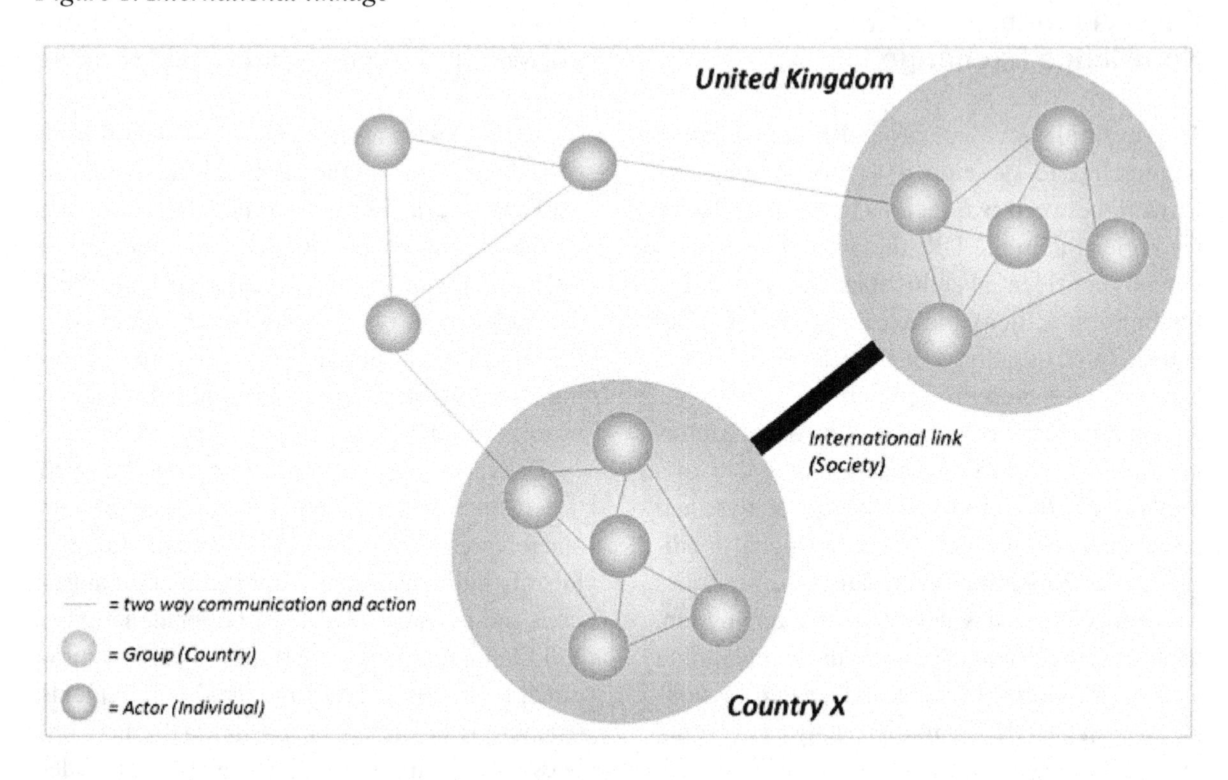

on adoption and use of KM in the administration of research universities while the other is looking at KM adoption and use in all public universities.

While innovation can be understood as the introduction of something new and useful (Tatnall, 2009), such as new methods, practice or products, knowledge management involves another concept that refers to a management function to create or locate knowledge, manage the flow of knowledge and ensure that knowledge is used effectively and efficiently for the long-term benefit of the organisation (Darroch & McNaughton, 2002). An organisation's competitive advantage does not depend only on its existing knowledge, but also depends on its ability to apply this existing knowledge to effectively create new knowledge (Dasgupta & Gupta, 2009). In many ways organisational culture relates to human decisions and actions and is a vital factor for organisations to create value to leverage their knowledge assets and an important source of an organisation's competitive advantage. Organisational culture has also become a powerful determinant of innovative potential in order to sustain an innovative culture (Ahmed, 1998; Wan Ismail & Abd Majid, 2007). These studies are investigating how organisational culture in the administration of Malaysia's universities affects the adoption and use of knowledge management which is seen to be able to provide competitive advantage and to improve effectiveness and efficiencies.

As the potential adoption of knowledge management tools, techniques, processes and methods involves both people and technology, an ANT approach is appropriate. These studies need to identify all the actors, both human and technological, and to investigate the formation of networks connecting these actors (Tatnall & Tatnall 2007). They need to look for tokens, quasi objects, punctualisations, obligatory passage points, reversibility/irreversibility, and to question how this innovation is being adopted. To be successful, those working for the adoption of KM in these universities need to form alliances and to persuade both other people, and also the ICT tools and infrastructure, to work with them. These studies will make use of ANT to consider these issues, and make use of conceptual frameworks linking people, processes, strategy and technology as shown in Figure 2.

Figure 2. Knowledge management practices in university administration

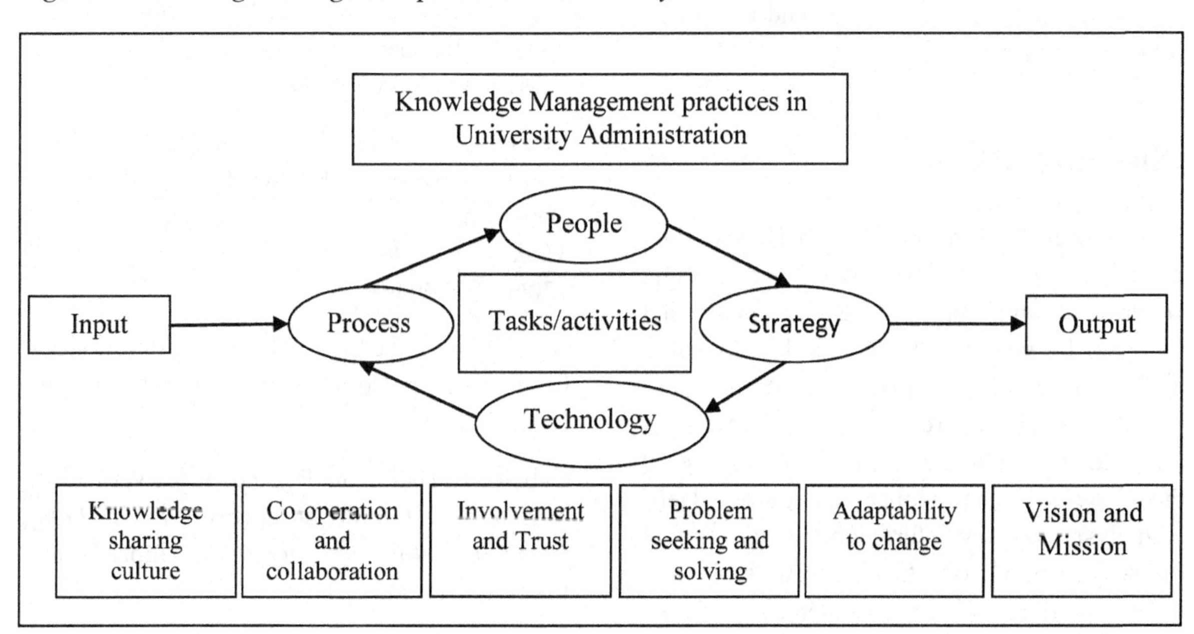

DISCUSSION

The preceding case vignettes serve to illustrate several key points. First, especially in complex contexts (as tends to be typical of most modern business activities) where multiple activities occur concurrently it is essential to have a robust and rich lens of analysis that can capture all these diverse operations at once. In addition, it can be seen that the multiple roles of knowledge workers is inextricably linked with and to the tools, techniques, processes and methods they utilise in carrying out their myriad of duties. Moreover, these involve people and technology as well as simultaneously draw upon the people, technology and process centric perspectives of KM. Hence, ANT, as we have outlined, not only provides a significantly rich lens to correctly capture all these operations but also enables a systematic evaluation of all tasks and activities to enable a thorough analysis to ensue which in turn leads to a full understanding and the identification of critical barriers and facilitators essential to ensure on-going success and sustained competitive advantage. Conversely, without the use of ANT we contend that it is not possible to fully understand the key dynamics of such complex operations and thus decision making and consequent outcomes would always be sub-optimal at best.

CONCLUSION

More than ever before organisational knowledge, its creation, transfer, use, re-use and storage, are critically important for organisations so that they can be viable and successful in dynamic and complex global operations. While there has been much research done into the types of knowledge we contend that it is not only useful but of significance to adopt a more powerful lens of analysis as we try to further our understanding of knowledge, the tools tactics, technologies and techniques of knowledge management; and how organisations can extract germane knowledge from various networks and systems to enable them to achieve a sustainable competitive advantage. In this article then we have proffered the use of ANT as just such a rich lens and provided two case vignettes to illustrate our ideas. We close by calling for more research in this important area.

REFERENCES

Adriaans, P., & Zantinge, D. (1996). *Data Mining*. Reading, MA: Addison-Wesley.

Ahmed, P. K. (1998). Culture and climate for innovation. *European Journal of Innovation Management*, *1*(1), 30–43. doi:10.1108/14601069810199131

Alavi, M., & Leidner, D. (2001). Review: Knowledge Management And Knowledge Management Systems: Conceptual Foundations And Research Issues. *Management Information Systems Quarterly*, *25*(1), 107–136. doi:10.2307/3250961

Bali, R. K., Wickramasinghe, N., & Lehaney, B. (2009). *Knowledge Management Primer*. New York: Routledge.

Becerra-Fernandez, I., & Sabherwal, R. (2001). Organizational Knowledge Management: A contingency Perspective. *Journal of Management Information Systems*, *18*(1), 23–55.

Bendoly, E. (2003). Theory and Support for Process Frameworks of Knowledge Discovery and Data Mining from ERP Systems. *Information & Management*, *40*, 639–647. doi:10.1016/S0378-7206(02)00093-9

Boyd, J. R. (Col USAF). (1976). Destruction and Creation. In R Coram (Ed.), *Boyd*. New York: Little, Brown & Co.

Cabena, P., Hadjinian, P., Stadler, R., Verhees, J., & Zanasi, A. (1998). *Discovering Data Mining from Concept to Implementation*. Upper Saddle River, NJ: Prentice Hall.

Callon, M. (1986). Some Elements of a Sociology of Translation: Domestication of the Scallops and the Fishermen of St Brieuc Bay. Power, Action & Belief. A New Sociology of Knowledge? *Law, J. London*, 196-229.

Callon, M. (1999). Actor-Network Theory - The Market Test. Actor-network Theory and After. *Law, J. and Hassard, J*, 181-195.

Callon, M., & Latour, B. (1981). Unscrewing the Big Leviathan: how actors macro-structure reality and how sociologists help them to do so. In Knorr-Cetina, K., & Cicourel, A. V. (Eds.), *Advances in social theory and methodology. Toward an integration of micro and macro-sociologies* (pp. 277–303). London: Routledge & Kegan Paul.

Darroch, J., & McNaughton, R. B. (2002). Examining the link between knowledge management practices and types of innovation. *Journal of Intellectual Capital*, *3*(3), 210–222. doi:10.1108/14691930210435570

Dasgupta, M., & Gupta, R. K. (2009). Innovation in Organizations: A Review of the Role of Organizational Learning and Knowledge Management. *Global Business Review*, *10*(2), 203–224. doi:10.1177/097215090901000205

Grint, K., & Woolgar, S. (1997). *The Machine at Work - Technology, Work and Organisation*. Cambridge, MA: Polity Press.

(2000). Knowledge management and new organizational form. InMalhotra, Y. (Ed.), *Knowledge Management and Virtual Organizations*. Hershey, PA: IGI Global.

Latour, B. (1986). The Powers of Association. *The Sociological Review*, *32*.

Latour, B. (1996). *Aramis or the Love of Technology*. Cambridge, MA: Harvard University Press.

Law, J. (1987, 1990). Technology and Heterogeneous Engineering: The Case of Portuguese Expansion. In W. E. Bijker, T. P. Hughes, & T. J. Pinch (Eds.), *The Social Construction of Technological Systems: New Directions in the Sociology and History of Technology* (pp. 111-134). Cambridge, MA: MIT Press.

Law, J. (1991). Introduction: monsters, machines and sociotechnical relations. In Law, J. (Ed.), *A Sociology of Monsters: Essays on Power, Technology and Domination*. London: Routledge.

Law, J., & Callon, M. (1988). Engineering and Sociology in a Military Aircraft Project: A Network Analysis of Technological Change. *Social Problems*, *35*(3), 284–297. doi:10.1525/sp.1988.35.3.03a00060

Markus, L. (2001). Toward a Theory of Knowledge Reuse: Types of Knowledge Reuse Situations and Factors in Reuse Success. *Journal of Management Information Systems*, *18*(1), 57–93.

Newell, S., Robertson, M., Scarbrough, H., & Swan, J. (2002). *Managing Knowledge Work*. New York: Palgrave.

Nonaka, I. (1994). A dynamic theory of organizational knowledge creation. *Organization Science*, *5*, 14–37. doi:10.1287/orsc.5.1.14

Nonaka, I., & Nishiguchi, T. (2001). *Knowledge Emergence*. Oxford, UK: Oxford University Press.

Polyani, M. (1958). *Personal knowledge: towards a post-critical philosophy*. Chicago: Chicago University Press.

Polyani, M. (1966). *The Tacit Dimension*. London: Routledge & Kegan Paul.

Schultze, U., & Leidner, D. (2002). Studying Knowledge Management In Information Systems Research: Discourses and Theoretical Assumptions. *Management Information Systems Quarterly*, *26*(3), 212–242. doi:10.2307/4132331

Singleton, V., & Michael, M. (1993). Actor-Networks and Ambivalence: General Practitioners in the UK Cervical Screening Programme. *Social Studies of Science*, *23*(2), 227–264. doi:10.1177/030631293023002001

Tatnall, A. (2009). Information Systems, Technology Adoption and Innovation Translation. *International Journal of Actor-Network Theory and Technological Innovation*, *1*(1), 59–74.

Tatnall, C., & Tatnall, A. (2007). Using Educational Management Systems to Enhance Teaching and Learning in the Classroom: an Investigative Study. In Tatnall, A., Okamoto, T., & Visscher, A. J. (Eds.), *Knowledge Management for Educational Innovation* (pp. 75–82). New York: Springer. doi:10.1007/978-0-387-69312-5_10

von Lubitz, D., & Wickramasinghe, N. (2006). Creating Germane Knowledge in Dynamic Environments. *Intl. J. Innovation and Learning*, *3*(3), 326–347. doi:10.1504/IJIL.2006.009226

Wan Ismail, W. K., & Abd Majid, R. (2007). Framework of the culture of innovation: a revisit. *Journal Kemanusiaan*, *9*, 38–39.

Wickramasinghe, N. (2003). Do We Practise What We Preach: Are Knowledge Management Systems in Practice Truly Reflective of Knowledge Management Systems in Theory? *Business Process Management Journal*, *9*(3), 295–316. doi:10.1108/14637150310477902

Wickramasinghe, N. (2006). Knowledge Creation: A meta-Framework. *International J. Innovation and Learning*, *3*(5), 558–573.

Wickramasinghe, N., & von Lubitz, D. (2007). *Knowledge-Based Enterprise: Theories and Fundamentals*. Hershey, PA: IGI Global.

This work was previously published in International Journal of Actor-Network Theory and Technological Innovation, Volume 2, Issue 4, edited by Arthur Tatnall, pp. 30-42, copyright 2010 by IGI Publishing (an imprint of IGI Global).

Chapter 16
Aspects of e-Learning in a University

Karen Manning
Victoria University, Australia

Lily Wong
Victoria University, Australia

Arthur Tatnall
Victoria University, Australia

ABSTRACT

Most universities make use of e-learning facilities to manage and deliver on-line learning. Many universities have adopted an approach to teaching and the delivery of course content that combines traditional face-to-face delivery with online teaching resources: a blended learning approach. Many factors act to determine how online learning is adopted, accepted, and the balance between online and face-to-face delivery is formed. In this paper, the authors suggest that educational technology adoption decisions are made at three levels: strategic decisions are made by the university to implement a particular package, and then individual academics made adoption decisions regarding those aspects of the package they will use in their teaching and how they will use them. They also make a decision on the balance they will have between on-line and face-to-face teaching. This article questions how decisions are made to adopt one e-learning package rather than another. The authors then examine how individual academics relate to this technology once it is adopted and make use of it to deliver some or all of their teaching and determine the appropriate blend.

DOI: 10.4018/978-1-4666-1559-5.ch016

E-LEARNING TECHNOLOGIES IN A UNIVERSITY

Garrison and Vaughan (2008) have identified three major changes that have recently occurred in higher education around the world:

- Unprecedented advances in communication technology
- New challenges within institutions resulting in less contact time with academic staff
- Recognition that traditional methods are unable to address the need for higher-order learning experiences and outcomes demanded by a changing knowledge and communication-based society.

A university in Melbourne, in common with many other universities around the world, is making good use of various aspects of e-learning. By its nature, e-learning involves interactions of technology and people and so actor-network theory provides an appropriate frame for investigating its use. This paper examines several uses of e-learning technologies and the politics of their use at this university.

Some years ago the university took a strategic decision to adopt WebCT as its primary e-Learning platform, and undertook a number of strategies to encourage use of this technology. As most academics will know, the WebCT e-learning platform offers facilities for the management of e-learning including discussion boards, results/mark book, an e-mail system, live chat, and support for student downloading of content including documents and PowerPoint presentations. At this university, the extent to which each of these facilities have been adopted and used varies considerably from one course to another.

Recently, a meeting of interested academic staff at the university were told that the company that supplies the WebCT product, Blackboard Learning Systems Inc, had indicated that they would soon withdraw support for this product in favour of Blackboard, their main product, and that this would require the university to decide whether to move to Blackboard or to adopt an open source e-learning product such as Moodle. Another strategic decision was thus required, but while the decision to purchase and implement a particular e-learning product by the university would be a strategic one, this decision would not necessarily determine the extent to which each individual academic would make use of it in their teaching. In this university, while there is a general policy requiring academics to make some use of WebCT, decisions on how to make use of it in their own teaching subjects had been left largely up to the lecturer co-ordinating each subject. So, while the overall adoption decision by the university should be considered in terms of strategy, individual adoption decisions to use some aspects of the package but not others are best considered thought the lens of innovation adoption. Adoption, implementation and use of an appropriate e-learning package can thus be looked at as involving a series of decisions made at two different levels: the university level and that of the individual academic.

1. The initial strategic decision by the university to adopt WebCT as an e-learning platform should be considered in terms of strategic decision making.
2. Decisions by individual academic staff on how to use e-learning in their teaching, or whether they will adopt it as an e-learning environment at all should be considered in terms of innovation adoption.
3. The university's decision to be made in adopting a new e-learning platform to replace WebCT is clearly a strategic one.
4. The decision by academic staff on how they will use this new e-learning platform, how they will balance the blend between on-line and face-to-face teaching, or whether they will adopt it at all, is an innovation adoption decision.

This article investigates the strategies and innovation factors behind all these adoption decisions –strategic decisions made by the university administration and adoption decisions made by individual academic staff members.

STRATEGIC ADOPTION DECISIONS

At the conceptual level strategic management is a process for co-ordinating decision making in what may be large, diversified organisations (Tatnall & Manning, in press). Hanson et al. (2008) describe strategic management as the process of making and implementing strategic decisions. In this approach tactics and strategy are often distinguished: tactics being seen as short term adaptive actions while strategic decisions determine the overall direction of the organisation. The problem is that strategic decisions are made at all levels of the organisation and not always recognised as significant at that time (Boxall & Purcell, 2007). In other words, a decision can be either a planned activity or a series of events, which lead to a desirable objective. Deliberative strategy is consciously formulated while emergent strategy results from incremental decisions emergent through networks of actors (Latour, 1996). The fact that many organisations do not systematically plan, or fail to implement plans leads to the adaptive type of models. Often strategies are formulated but not implemented because these cut across organisation units, information is inadequate and the control imposed by planning actually inhibits innovation and decision making. This leads to an understanding that the notion of strategy is not neutral. How it is defined and used in an organisation will impact on the conceptualisation of technological innovation in this organisation (Tatnall & Manning, in press).

The university has experienced significant internal change over the last few years with the notions of systematic strategic planning driving such changes. There is no doubt this approach has been driven by top management, with a mission for the whole organisation and plans for each business unit, and shared functions linked to this strategic plan. However, despite the range of plans a decision to adopt a particular innovation is not straightforward. In our investigation to date it has been quite difficult to pinpoint when and how the decision will actually be made. In this case a number of decisions will probably come together to make 'the decision' on the adoption of a particular e-learning technology. The quality of the decision making is particularly important in this case because of the longer term educational and financial implications for the university. Poorly researched decisions presented as rational and ordered often mean that the organisation suffers, and in this case large diverse institutional decision making can be affected by the behaviour of the participants in many ways as they may preserve, delay, stop a decision or cover up any inconsistencies. Here it is difficult to tease out the decision making knowledge and power-related decision making as the decision making process seems so unclear. It is important to note that the actual users of the system are not well represented in the decision making process. This approach of collecting together a particular grouping of people who in this case are from the corporate level of the organisation rather than the academic users of the system, assumes they can correctly forecast and interpret the changes for all levels, however people perceive these decisions in terms of the organisation and operation beliefs they come from (Tatnall & Manning, in press). The problem in large, diversified organisations such as this university is that strategic leaders may not provide sufficient control to co-ordinate decision making or comprehend the entire strategic variable simultaneously. Over 20 years ago Quinn (1988) argued there are both cognitive and process limits to managers' ability to cope with these variables simultaneously.

The decision to adopt a new e-learning environment will result more from an incremental series of decision with the construction of limited representation of decision makers from the corporate level structure to make the decision, with time imperatives imposed by the expiry of contractual arrangements and the inattention to the earlier technology problem decision. This is a non-routine decision and an important one where the key players are looking to see what the powerful are giving out about how they should act, and they are trying to do what they think is expected of them. It seems clear this big decision has been avoided for as long as possible. Senior management is now trying to involve a particular constructed group of decision makers so that if the decision goes badly the blame can be passed off or shared around. It is a culture of sidestepping decisions and trying to avoid being seen to make a mistake. It is certainly not about the users' needs or knowledge given they are largely excluded from the decision making process (Tatnall & Manning, in press).

E-LEARNING IN A FIRST YEAR ACCOUNTING SUBJECT

In the Faculty of Business at this university the first-year core accounting subject: *Accounting for Decision Making* is compulsory for all students undertaking a Bachelor of Business degree, and enrols around 1,000 students each semester. This is a very diverse group comprising accounting and non-accounting students from a broad spectrum of business degrees which range from music industry management through to marketing and information systems (Wong & Tatnall, 2010). It has been acknowledged (McInnis, James, & Mc Naught, 1995) that age, gender, country of birth, language spoken at home, socio-economic background and ethnicity contribute to shaping student expectations of university study, and affect their adjustment to being university students, and ultimately their overall teaching and learning experience (Wong & Tatnall, 2009). The co-ordinator of this subject has been keen to consider the *balance* between online and face-to-face teaching in this large first-year business subject. One of the university's key policies has been to use make use of technology, along side of traditional face-to-face approaches, in the teaching and learning process in an effort to enhance the quality of the learning experienced by its students. This policy is, of course, not unique and the trend toward blended learning is emerging as a prominent method of delivery in higher education around the world (Bonk & Graham, 2006).

The students taking this subject have had very different experiences in studying accounting, if they have previously studied it at all, and their perceptions about this subject are quite varied. Negative attitudes towards accounting are not unusual among introductory accounting students (Mladenovic, 2000) and earlier studies suggest that changes in accounting education should begin with the very first subject in accounting as it not only sets the tone, but also provides the foundation for further interest in accounting studies (Mintz & Cherry, 1993; Wong & Tatnall, 2009). It is therefore very important that the teaching material used in this subject is designed and developed with an understanding of these differences so that it meets the varying needs of its students (Wong & Tatnall, 2010).

WebCT was initially introduced into the first-year accounting subject in 2006, with a basic level of online teaching resources provided to students. Over the following semesters, additional resources have been developed, including video, audio-visual, text, images and animations to support student learning. In first semester 2009 recorded lectures were made available to students via WebCT and online tutorials are now also being introduced. WebCT's communication tools which include discussion boards and a chat function enable students to regularly interact with each other as well as their tutor or lecturer. Various assessment tasks can also be undertaken online and statistical details provided by this learning system enable the monitoring of student performance (Wong

& Tatnall, 2009). These changes have led to the emergence of blended learning which, according to Bonk and Graham (2006) "is part of the ongoing convergence of two archetypal learning environments": the traditional face-to-face and the computer-mediated learning environment. In the past these had remained quite separate. Bonk and Graham (2006) go on to suggest that: "Whilst it is acknowledged that it is impossible to predict what the future holds, there is some certainty that the trend toward blended learning systems will increase".

VIDEO SCREEN CAPTURE TO PROVIDE ASSESSMENT FEEDBACK

Another e-learning technology being used in the university is video screen capture as a technique for providing formative student feedback to assignments in a postgraduate Information Systems subject (Deal & Tatnall, 2010). This technology, still in the early stages of its use, was seen to offer significant advantages over more conventional approaches to providing student feedback.

Careful planning is necessary to use video marking successfully, and this includes selecting which assessment tasks are appropriate, what tools should be used, what submission formats are appropriate and the logistics required. For the technology to be successfully adopted and used, however, it was necessary to gain the co-operation of a number of different actors including: the subject lecturer, the students, the computer software (Centra Virtual Classroom and Camtasia Studio), the computer screens, university information technology infrastructure, university information technology services and university administration. Fortunately this was forthcoming as all the human actors were keen to give it a try and the technology (so far at least) has not presented too many difficulties.

INNOVATION AND CHANGE: ADOPTION OF INNOVATIONS

Just because a new e-learning system has been built and made available does not mean that it can automatically be assumed that organisations or individuals will want to adopt or to use it. Even if an organisation does adopt a new innovation, it also cannot be assumed that its employees will want to use it, and even if they have no choice and are made to use it, that they will get the most out of it. Making any sort of change to the way things are done is always complex and can be quite difficult to achieve successfully. The successful adoption of any new technological innovation is often in doubt if people who might be prepared to support the innovator cannot be convinced to do so. To investigate the adoption of new ideas or technologies it is useful to follow one of the theories of technological innovation (Al-Hajri & Tatnall, 2007). A number of approaches exist to modelling how technological innovation takes place, including the Theory of Reasoned Action (Ajzen & Fishbein, 1980), the Theory of Planned Behaviour (Ajzen, 1991), the Technology Acceptance Model (Davis, 1986), Diffusion of Innovations (Rogers, 1995, 2003) and Innovation Translation (Callon, 1986; Latour, 1996). In particular, both the Diffusion of Innovations and the Technology Acceptance Model (TAM) are very well known and widely used approaches to theorising technological innovation. One important difference between some of these theories though is the degree to which the adoption decision is seen as completely rational, and whether provision is made for partial adoption (Tatnall, 2009). In this article we will make use of Innovation Translation informed by Actor-Network Theory.

ACTORS, NETWORKS AND E-LEARNING

A simple investigation quickly shows that a large number of different entities have an effect on the adoption of e-learning technologies and in determining how much online and how much face-to-face teaching to include in a university subject like this one. Furthermore, not all of these entities, or actors, are *human* as the technology itself has an important determining effect (Tummons, 2009). Is it easy to use? What functions does it offer? How much does it cost? Other *non-human* actors include university policy, computer labs and infrastructure. Actor-network theory (ANT) declares that the world is full of hybrid entities (Latour, 1993) containing both human and non-human elements, and was developed to analyse situations like this one where separation of these elements is difficult (Callon, 1999; Tatnall, 2009; Tatnall & Gilding, 1999). It is difficult, for example, to differentiate a computer program's technical aspects from the influence exerted by the socio-cultural background of the software development team (Cusumano & Selby, 1997; Sahay, 1997).

The first step in an actor-network analysis is to identify the actors involved. Law (1987) describes an actor as any human or non-human entity that is able to make its presence *individually felt* by other actors. The actors involved in selection, adoption and use of e-learning technologies at this university and in this particular subject include: the Bachelor of Business Course Co-ordinator, the *Accounting for Decision Making* Subject Co-ordinator, Subject Lecturers, Subject Tutors, Sessional (Contract) Tutors, other lecturers, the Faculty Dean and the University Administration, the Head of School of Accounting, University Policy, University Infrastructure, Technical Staff from Information Technology Services, students, computers, screens, computer laboratories, e-learning infrastructure (including remote access), competing technologies and the WebCT/ Blackboard e-learning environment itself. Each of these actors has a potential influence on how or whether the adoption occurs and the balance between an online and a face-to-face approach. Latour (1996) speaks of "chains of translation" and suggests that the innovation moves only if it interests one group of actors or another, and Callon et al. (1983) suggest that translation involves all the strategies that an actor goes through to identify other actors and to work with or against them in order to achieve the adoption.

E-LEARNING INNOVATION ADOPTION DECISIONS

We have already discussed how the strategic adoption decisions will probably be made at the university level, and the actors involved in these. Another factor that comes into these decisions, however, is pressure from some individual academics even though they are not officially represented in the decision making process. At the university there are a number of academics who strongly believe in the benefits of open source software and so would favour a decision to adopt Moodle, while there are others who prefer the idea of sticking with the 'tried and true' commercial product of a large company. If these people feel strongly enough about this matter and have problematised (Callon, 1986) the use of an e-learning environment in their own way then they will certainly apply pressure to the decision makers to try to enrol them (Callon, 1986) into making the 'right' decision.

The first step in an actor-network analysis of the decisions by individual academics to adopt some, or all, of the e-learning package features is to identify the actors involved in this event. Firstly consider the university hierarchy. If course or subject co-ordinators, or the Faculty Dean, expresses a view on this then it must be taken into account, but this much is obvious. Not so obvious is the influence of some of the non-human actors. If the e-learning infrastructure requires too much effort to come to grips with, or the e-learning interface is too off-putting or non-intuitive then adoption becomes less likely. Even if the package is adopted, however, how can partial adoption be explained? The less than friendly interface of WebCT has been one reason for only partial adoption of this package, and there are other alternatives to the e-mail it offers. The in-built testing/marking facilities are of interest to some academics but not to others and so these may or may not be adopted as they will fit less well with their problematisation of what an e-learning environment should be about. On a human level, many of us prefer human-to-human interactions and are reluctant to use technology in this way for teaching and learning. There is then also the concern that students will no longer bother to come to lectures. All of this means that many academics will translate the e-learning package into something that suits their own needs.

DETERMINING THE BALANCE OF E-LEARNING AND FACE-TO-FACE TEACHING IN AN ACCOUNTING SUBJECT

In considering how academics determine the balance in e-learning we will make use of Callon's (1986) four "moments" in the process of translation: Problematisation, Interessement, Enrolment and Mobilisation. Getting the views of the human actors just involves talking to them, but not so obvious is the influence of some of the non-human actors that must be obtained by other means (Wong & Tatnall, 2010).

Problematisation

WebCT, the e-learning package itself, is a non-human actor, designed with the express purpose of providing an online learning environment. Its problematisation of this issue would be that it can provide an efficient means of delivering teaching materials whilst enhancing student accessibility. From this perspective it might ask: "Why would you want to use anything else? Why do you need to think about face-to-face teaching at all when WebCT can do everything you need?" Other non-human actors include the computers, screens, computer laboratories and Internet services. As with WebCT, these facilities and services were purchased with the prime purpose of providing appropriate infrastructure for the teaching function, therefore their problematisation is similar to that of WebCT. Similarly Information Technology Services, whose responsibility is to manage the computing infrastructure in the university, view it as their duty to make the technology work and not to argue about whether or not it should be used. Perhaps the most important human actor who has the highest level of interest and commitment to this subject, the actor that Law (1987) calls the "Heterogeneous Engineer", is the Accounting subject co-ordinator. The problematisation proposed by this individual is a simple one: the combination of online and face-to-face teaching must provide the best possible learning experience for the students, whatever that may be.

The teaching responsibilities of this large subject are shared between about 12 teaching staff, the majority of whom are part-time. This is a diverse group who vary in age, experience and teaching styles. They also share different views of using technology in their teaching, with many of the lecturers and tutors having mixed views on the optimal balance. Some are insistent in retaining as much as possible of the traditional modes of delivery and others are more willing to experiment with more innovative techniques such as recorded lectures and online tutorials. The majority of students are less than 20 years of age and there is much pressure from this section of the student population to incorporate the latest technology to enhance their learning. Recent subject evaluations have shown that student perceptions of this subject have improved with the increased availability of online teaching resources. The student and teaching staff problematisations are therefore also quite varied.

University colleagues who lecture in subjects other than first year accounting also have their own views on the balance of online versus face-to-face teaching, but the importance of these views depends on how close is their relationship with those teaching the accounting subject. In some cases where the relationship and respect is quite close, these views will have a significant effect on the problematisations of the subject lecturers. With a strong academic and research background in technology and education, the Head of the School of Accounting was very keen for all his teaching staff to incorporate greater use of technology to support learning. His problematisation is one of the value of this approach in contrast to traditional methods. The views of the university hierarchy, which in many ways, can be thought of as a "black box" (Callon, 1986), are a little harder to ascertain. University policy problematises use of technology as an important tool in delivery of learning, but the extent to which all parts of the university agree with this is unclear. In many ways, one of the most important actors is represented by the students enrolled in this subject. Does their gender, age, ethnicity, socio-economic background or part-time or full-time enrolment status affect their views on online versus face-to-face teaching? One can strongly suspect that it does, but this is at present not completely clear (Wong & Tatnall, 2010).

Interessement

The "Heterogeneous Engineer", being the Subject Co-ordinator, is perhaps the most important actor at this stage of adoption where there is a need to work with the other actors to persuade them to agree to the proposed problematisation. This persuasion involves discussions with the subject lecturers, getting feedback from the students and working along with university administration to best determine how to make the balance more appropriate between online and traditional methods of subject delivery so that it is conducive to good learning practices. One problem to overcome here is some aspects of the e-learning package. If it requires too much effort to come to grips with, or the e-learning interface is too off-putting or non-intuitive then adoption becomes less likely. The designers of the WebCT platform have worked over successive versions to offer an interessement here by making the package more intuitive and easier to use. The heterogeneous engineer, subject lecturers and tutors can also offer an interessement to the students by helping them become more familiar with the software. Subject lecturers, in particular, have been instructed by the Heterogeneous Engineer to demonstrate the various functions of WebCT during their teaching sessions so that students can maximise the benefits available from using this e-learning package (Wong & Tatnall, 2010).

Enrolment

All going well, enrolment should then follow through a process of "coercion, seduction, or consent" (Grint & Woolgar, 1997) leading to the establishment of a solid, stable network of alliances. Exactly when enrolment should be considered to have been achieved is questionable when talking about a balance between two approaches. We will say that the actors are enrolled when the "optimum" balance, whatever that might be, between online and face-to-face teaching has been reached. Research on student motivation by de Lange et al. (2003) identified that "the challenge for educators is to develop strategies that ensure any novelty effect does not wear off with an end result of technology impeding learning". As a compulsory first-year subject, there is continual pressure on the heterogeneous engineer/subject co-ordinator to keep abreast of the latest technological advancements and to incorporate these where possible to enhance the student learning experience.

Mobilisation

Finally, mobilisation occurs when a consensus has been reached and that the optimum balance between online and traditional approaches to teaching and learning has been achieved, and this is then conveyed to others. This has not happened as yet.

CONCLUSION

Adoption, implementation and use of technology, such as an e-learning system, in a large organisation such as a university has both strategic and individual adoption aspects. In this article we have argued that the initial decision by the university to invest in the technology is a strategic one, best considered in terms of strategic decision making theory, while the decisions regarding individual subjects and made by individual academics to ignore or to use the technology, and to determine the appropriate blend of on-line versus face-to-face teaching can be analysed using one of the models of innovation adoption – we have used innovation translation as it gives adequate weight to all human and also technology (non-human) factors. One of the issues brought out by an ANT investigation is the effect that force of personality and presence has in a teaching and learning environment and how this might contrast with the effect of the technology on the final outcome. It is clear that the level and quality of interaction between student and lecturer may have a significant impact on student learning and satisfaction. Feedback from a recent student survey conducted on the use of technology used in this first-year accounting subject seems to support this and many students believe that the personal interaction added value to their learning experience (Wong, 2010).

REFERENCES

Ajzen, I. (1991). The Theory of Planned Behavior. *Organizational Behavior and Human Decision Processes*, *50*(2), 179–211. doi:10.1016/0749-5978(91)90020-T

Ajzen, I., & Fishbein, M. (1980). *Understanding Attitudes and Predicting Social Behavior*. Englewood Cliffs, NJ: Prentice-Hall.

Al-Hajri, S., & Tatnall, A. (2007, June 4-6). *Internet Technology in Omani Banks – a Case of Adoption at a Slower Rate.* Paper presented at the 20th Bled e-Conference - eMergence: Merging and Emerging Technologies, Processes and Institutions, Bled, Slovenia.

Bonk, C. J., & Graham, C. R. (2006). *The Handbook of Blended Learning - Global Perspectives, Local Designs*. San Francisco: Pfeiffer.

Boxall, P., & Purcell, J. (2007). *Strategy and Human Resource Management* (2nd ed.). London: Palgrave McMillan.

Callon, M. (1986). Some Elements of a Sociology of Translation: Domestication of the Scallops and the Fishermen of St Brieuc Bay. In Law, J. (Ed.), *Power, Action & Belief. A New Sociology of Knowledge?* (pp. 196–229). London: Routledge & Kegan Paul.

Callon, M. (1999). Actor-Network Theory - The Market Test. In Law, J., & Hassard, J. (Eds.), *Actor Network Theory and After* (pp. 181–195). Oxford, UK: Blackwell Publishers.

Callon, M., Courtial, J. P., Turner, W. A., & Bauin, S. (1983). From Translations to Problematic Networks: An Introduction to Co-Word Analysis. *Social Sciences Information. Information Sur les Sciences Sociales*, *22*(2), 191–235. doi:10.1177/053901883022002003

Cusumano, M. A., & Selby, R. W. (1997). How Microsoft Builds Software. *Communications of the ACM*, *40*(6), 53–61. doi:10.1145/255656.255698

Davis, F. (1986). *A Technology Acceptance Model for Empirically Testing New End-User Information Systems: Theory and Results*. Boston: MIT.

de Lange, P., Suwardy, T., & Mavondo, F. (2003). Integrating A Virtual Learning Environment into an Introductory Accounting Course: Determinants Of Student Motivation. *Accounting Education*, *12*(1), 1–14. doi:10.1080/0963928032000064567

Deal, D., & Tatnall, A. (2010). *Using Video Screen Capture to Provide Assessment Feedback for Information Systems Students.* Paper presented at the Computer Science Education: Innovation and Technology: CSEIT 2010, Phuket, Thailand.

Garrison, D. R., & Vaughan, N. D. (2008). *Blended Learning in Higher Education - Framework, Principles and Guidelines*. San Francisco: Jossey-Bass.

Grint, K., & Woolgar, S. (1997). *The Machine at Work - Technology, Work and Organisation*. Cambridge, UK: Polity Press.

Hanson, D., Dowling, P. J., Hitt, M. A., Ireland, R. D., & Hoskisson, R. E. (Eds.). (2008). *Strategic Management: Competitiveness & Globalisation* (3rd ed.). Cengage Learning.

Latour, B. (1993). *We Have Never Been Modern* (Porter, C., Trans.). Cambridge, MA: Harvester University Press.

Latour, B. (1996). *Aramis or the Love of Technology*. Cambridge, MA: Harvard University Press.

Law, J. (1987). Technology and Heterogeneous Engineering: The Case of Portuguese Expansion. In Bijker, W. E., Hughes, T. P., & Pinch, T. J. (Eds.), *The Social Construction of Technological Systems: New Directions in the Sociology and History of Technology* (pp. 111–134). Cambridge, MA: MIT Press.

McInnis, C., James, R., & McNaught, C. (1995). *First Year on Campus - Diversity in the Initial Experience of Australian Undergraduates*. Melbourne, Australia: Centre for the Study of Higher Education,University of Melbourne.

Mintz, S., & Cherry, A. A. (1993). The Introductory Accounting Courses: Educating Majors And Nonmajors. *Journal of Education for Business*, *68*(5), 276–280. doi:10.1080/08832323.1993.10117627

Mladenovic, R. (2000). An Investigation into Ways of Challenging Introductory Accounting Student's Negative Perceptions of Accounting. *Accounting Education*, *9*(2), 135–155. doi:10.1080/09639280010000147

Quinn, R. E. (1988). *Beyond Rational Management*. San Francisco: Jossey-Bass.

Rogers, E. M. (1995). *Diffusion of Innovations* (4th ed.). New York: The Free Press.

Rogers, E. M. (2003). *Diffusion of Innovations* (5th ed.). New York: The Free Press.

Sahay, S. (1997). Implementation of Information Technology: A Space-Time Perspective. *Organization Studies*, *18*(2), 229–260. doi:10.1177/017084069701800203

Tatnall, A. (2009). Information Systems, Technology Adoption and Innovation Translation. *International Journal of Actor-Network Theory and Technological Innovation*, *1*(1), 59–74.

Tatnall, A., & Gilding, A. (1999). *Actor-Network Theory and Information Systems Research.* Paper presented at the 10th Australasian Conference on Information Systems (ACIS), Wellington, Australia.

Tatnall, A., & Manning, K. (in press). Innovation or Renovation? The Management of Strategic and Adoption Decisions within a University. In Tatnall, A., Visscher, A. J., & Kereteletswe, O. C. (Eds.), *Information Technology and the Management of Quality Education*. Heidelberg, Germany: Springer.

Tummons, J. (2009). Higher Education in Further Education in England: An Actor-Network Ethnography. *International Journal of Actor-Network Theory and Technological Innovation*, *1*(3), 55–69.

Wong, L. (2010). *The E-Learning Experience - Its Impact on Student Engagement and Learning Outcomes*. Paper presented at the Business & Economics Society International Conference.

Wong, L., & Tatnall, A. (2009). The Need to Balance the Blend: Online versus Face-to-Face Teaching in an Introductory Accounting Subject. *Journal of Issues in Informing Science and Information Technology*, *6*, 309–322.

Wong, L., & Tatnall, A. (2010). Factors Determining the Balance between Online and Face-to-Face Teaching: an Analysis using Actor-Network Theory. *Interdisciplinary Journal of Information, Knowledge and Management*, *5*, 167–176.

This work was previously published in International Journal of Actor-Network Theory and Technological Innovation, Volume 2, Issue 4, edited by Arthur Tatnall, pp. 43-52, copyright 2010 by IGI Publishing (an imprint of IGI Global).

Compilation of References

(2000). Knowledge management and new organizational form. InMalhotra, Y. (Ed.), *Knowledge Management and Virtual Organizations*. Hershey, PA: IGI Global.

Abowd, G., & Mynatt, E. (2000). Charting past, present, and future research in ubiquitous computing. *ACM Transactions on Computer-Human Interaction*, *7*(1), 29–58. doi:10.1145/344949.344988

Adriaans, P., & Zantinge, D. (1996). *Data Mining*. Reading, MA: Addison-Wesley.

Aenestad, M., & Hanseth, O. (2000). *Implementing open network technologies in complex work practices. A case from telemedicine.* Paper presented at the IFIP WG 8.2 International Conference. The Social and Organizational Perspective on Research and Practice in Information Technology, Aalborg, Denmark.

Ahmed, P. K. (1998). Culture and climate for innovation. *European Journal of Innovation Management*, *1*(1), 30–43. doi:10.1108/14601069810199131

Ajzen, I. (1991). The Theory of Planned Behavior. *Organizational Behavior and Human Decision Processes*, *50*(2), 179–211. doi:10.1016/0749-5978(91)90020-T

Ajzen, I., & Fishbein, M. (1980). *Understanding Attitudes and Predicting Social Behavior*. Englewood Cliffs, NJ: Prentice-Hall.

Akrich, M. (1992). The de-scription of technical objects. In W. E. Bijker & J. Law (Eds.), *Shaping technology / building society: studies in sociotechnical change* (pp. 205-224). Cambridge Ma: The MIT Press.

Akrich, M., & Latour, B. (1992). A summary of a convenient vocabulary for the semiotics of human and non-human assemblies. In W. E. Bijker & J. Law (Eds.), *Shaping technology / building society: studies in sociotechnical change* (pp. 259-264). Cambridge, Ma: The MIT Press.

Akrich, M., Callon, M., & Latour, B. (2006). *Sociologie de la traduction: textes fondateurs*. Paris: Mines Paris, les Presses, Sciences sociales.

Akrich, M. (1992). The description of technical objects. In Bijker, W. E., & Law, J. (Eds.), *Shaping Technology/ Building Society: Studies in Sociotechnical Change* (pp. 205–224). Cambridge, MA: MIT Press.

Akrich, M. (1992). The de-scription of technical objects. In Bijker, W., & Law, J. (Eds.), *Shaping technology/building society: Studies in sociotechnical change*. Cambridge, MA: MIT Press.

Akrich, M., Callon, M., & Latour, B. (2002). The Key to Success in Innovation Part II: The Art of Choosing Good Spokespersons. *International Journal of Innovation Management*, *6*(2), 207–225. doi:10.1142/S1363919602000562

Alavi, M., & Leidner, D. (2001). Review: Knowledge Management And Knowledge Management Systems: Conceptual Foundations And Research Issues. *Management Information Systems Quarterly*, *25*(1), 107–136. doi:10.2307/3250961

Al-Hajri, S., & Tatnall, A. (2007, June 4-6). *Internet Technology in Omani Banks – a Case of Adoption at a Slower Rate.* Paper presented at the 20th Bled e-Conference - eMergence: Merging and Emerging Technologies, Processes and Institutions, Bled, Slovenia.

American Heritage. (2002). *The Making of The Mouse*. Retrieved from http://www.americanheritage.com/articles/magazine/it/2002/3/2002_3_48.shtml

Anderson, A. (1999, March 20). Beware the F Word, Unless You Know What it Means. *New Scientist, 3*.

Andersson, M., & Lindgren, R. (2005). The mobile-stationary divide in ubiquitous computing environemnts: Lessons from the transport industry. *Information Systems Management, 22*(4), 65–79. doi:10.1201/1078.10580530/45520.22.4.20050901/90031.7

Armour, F., Kaisler, S., & Bitner, J. (2007). Enterprise Architecture: Challenges and Implementations. In *Proceedings of the 40th Hawaii International Conference on System Sciences* (pp. 217-217).

Avgerou, C. (2002). *Information Systems and Global Diversity*. Oxford, UK: Oxford University Press.

Avital, M., & Germonprez, M. (2003, October 23-26). *Ubiquitous computing: Surfing the trend in a balanced act.* Paper presented at the Workshop on ubiquitous computing, Cleveland, OH.

BAA. (2006). ABB provides turnkey robotic solution in £650k Lander Automotive project. Retrieved from http://www.abb.co.uk/cawp/seitp202/91DE58BEDD547C3CC12571E000533F56.aspx

Bakos, J. Y., & Treacy, M. E. (1986). Information technology and corporate strategy: a research perspective. *MIS Quarterly, 10*(2), 107–119. doi:10.2307/249029

Bali, R. K., Wickramasinghe, N., & Lehaney, B. (2009). *Knowledge Management Primer*. New York: Routledge.

Bannon, L. J. (1997). Dwelling in the "Great Divide": The case of HCI and CSCW. In Bowker, G. C., & Star, S. L. (Eds.), *Social Science, Technical Systems, and Co-operative Work* (pp. 355–377). Mahwaw, NJ: Lawrence Erlbaum Associates.

Barad, K. (2003). Posthumanist Performativity: Toward an Understanding of How Matter Comes to Matter. *Signs: Journal of Women in Culture and Society, 28*(3), 801–831. doi:10.1086/345321

Bardini, T. (1996). *Changement et Réseaux Socio-Techniques: De l'inscription à l'affordance, Réseaux (No. 76)*. CENT.

Barley, S. R. (1986). Technology as an occasion for structuring: evidence from observations of CT scanners and the social order of radiology departments. *Administrative Science Quarterly, 31*(1), 78–108. doi:10.2307/2392767

Barthes, R. (1985). *Éléments de sémiologie*. Éditions du Seuil.

Basden, A. (2008). *Philosophical Frameworks for Understanding Information Systems*. Hershey, PA: IGI Global.

BBC. (2008). *E-mail Error Ends Up on Road Sign*. Retrieved February 24, 2010, from http://news.bbc.co.uk/2/hi/uk_news/wales/7702913.stm

Becerra-Fernandez, I., & Sabherwal, R. (2001). Organizational Knowledge Management: A contingency Perspective. *Journal of Management Information Systems, 18*(1), 23–55.

Bendoly, E. (2003). Theory and Support for Process Frameworks of Knowledge Discovery and Data Mining from ERP Systems. *Information & Management, 40*, 639–647. doi:10.1016/S0378-7206(02)00093-9

Bhattacherjee, A. (2001). An empirical analysis of the antecedents of electronic commerce service continuance. *Decision Support Systems, 32*, 201–214. doi:10.1016/S0167-9236(01)00111-7

Bielenia-Grajewska, M. (2009). Actor-Network Theory in Intercultural Communication – Translation through the Prism of Innovation, Technology, Networks and Semiotics. *International Journal of Actor-Network Theory and Technological Innovation, 1*(4), 39–49.

Bitner, M. J., Ostrom, A. L., & Meuter, M. L. (2002). Implementing Successful Self-Service Technology. *The Academy of Management Executive, 16*(4), 96–108.

Björk, B.-C., Roosr, A., et al. (2008). *Global annual volume of peer reviewed scholarly articles and the share available via different open access options.* Paper presented at the Openness in Digital Publishing: Awareness, Discovery and Access - Proceedings of the 12th International Conference on Electronic Publishing (ELPUB2008), Toronto, Canada.

Bloomfield, B., & Vurdubakis, T. (1997). Paper traces: inscribing organization and information technology. In B. Bloomfield, R. Coombs, D. Knights, & D. Littler (Eds.), *Information Technology and Organization*. Oxford: Oxford University Press.

Bloomfield, B. P. (1991). The role of information systems in the UK national health service: Action at a distance and the fetish of calculation. *Social Studies of Science*, *21*(4), 701–734. doi:10.1177/030631291021004004

Boar, B. H. (1998). *Information Technology Strategy as Commitment*. RCG Information Technology. Available: http://www.rcgit.com/Default.aspx. Accessed 02 December 2004

Boland, R. J. (1985). Phenomenology: A Preferred Approach to Research in Information Systems. In E. Mumford, R. Hirschheim, G. Fitzgerald, & T. Wood Harper (Eds.), *Research Methods in Information Systems*. Amsterdam: NorthHolland.

Boland, R. J. (2000). The Limits of Language in Doing Systems Work. In Baskerville, R., Stage, J., & DeGross, J. I. (Eds.), *Organizational and Social Perspectives on Information Technology* (pp. 47–60). Boston: Kluwer Academic.

Bonk, C. J., & Graham, C. R. (2006). *The Handbook of Blended Learning - Global Perspectives, Local Designs*. San Francisco: Pfeiffer.

Boucaut, R. (2001). Understanding workplace bullying: A Practical Application of Giddens' Structurational Theory. *International Education Journal*, *2*(4), 65–73.

Boudourides, M. A. (2001, November 1-3). *Networks, Fluids, Chaos*. Paper presented at the International Conference on Spacing and Timing: Rethinking Globalization & Standardization, Palermo, Italy. Retrieved from http://www.math.upatras.gr/~mboudour/

Bourdieu, P. (1972). *Outline of a Theory of Practice*. Cambridge, UK: Cambridge University Press.

Bowker, G., & Star, S. L. (1994). Knowledge and Infrastructure in international information management: Problems of classification and coding. In L. Bud-Frierman (Ed.), *Information acumen: The understanding and use of knowledge in modern business* (pp. 187-216). London: Routledge.

Bowker, G., & Star, S. L. (1996). How things (actor-net) work: Classification, magic and the ubiquity of standards. *Available at,* http://weber.ucsd.edu/~gbowker/actnet.html.

Boxall, P., & Purcell, J. (2007). *Strategy and Human Resource Management* (2nd ed.). London: Palgrave McMillan.

Boyd, J. R. (Col USAF). (1976). Destruction and Creation. In R Coram (Ed.), *Boyd*. New York: Little, Brown & Co.

Broadbent, M., Weill, M., & Clair, D. (1995). *The role of information technology infrastructure in business process redesign*. Unpublished manuscript, Center for information systems research, Sloan School of Management.

Broadbent, M., Weill, M., & St. Clair, D. (1999). The Implications of Information Technology Infrastructure for Business Process Redesign. *MIS Quarterly*, *23*(2). doi:10.2307/249750

Broadbent, M., & Weill, P. (1999). The implication of information technology Infrastructure for business process redesign. *MIS Quarterly*, *23*(3).

Brooks, L., & Atkinson, C. (2003). STRUCTURANTION in Research and Practice: Representing Actor Networks, Their Structurated Orders and Translations. In B. Kaplan, D. Truex, D. Wastell, T. Wood-Harper, & J. I. DeGross (Eds.), *Information Systems Research: Relevant Theory and Informed Practice* (pp. 389-409). Boston: Kluwer Academic Publishers.

Brooks, F. (1975). *The Mythical Man-Month*. Reading, MA: Addison-Wesley.

Brown, J. S., & Duguid, P. (1991). Organizational learning and communities-of-practice: Toward a unified view of working, learning, and innovation. *Organization Science*, *2*(1), 40–57. doi:10.1287/orsc.2.1.40

Brusoni, S., Prencipe, A., & Pavitt, K. (2001). Knowledge specialization, organizational coupling, and the boundaries of the firm: why do firms know more than they make? *Administrative Science Quarterly*, *46*(4), 597–621. doi:10.2307/3094825

Budapest Open Access Initiative. (2002). *Budapest Open Access Initiative*. Retrieved April 7, 2006 from http://www.soros.org/openaccess/

Burgess, S. (2002). Information Technology in Small Business: Issues and Challenges. In S. Burgess (Ed.), *Information Technology and Small Business: Issues and Challenges* (pp. 1-17). Hershey, Pennsylvania, USA: IGI Global.

Burgess, S., & Trethowan, P. (2002). *GPs and their Web sites in Australia: Doctors as Small Businesses*. IS OneWorld, Las Vegas.

Butler, J. (1994). Rapid Application Development in Action–Managing System Development. *Applied Computer Research, 14*(5), 6–8.

Butler, T. (1998). Towards a Hermeneutic Method for Interpretive Research in Information Systems. *Journal of Information Technology, 13*, 285–300. doi:10.1057/jit.1998.7

Butler, T. (2003). An institutional perspective on developing and implementing intranet-and Internet based information systems. *Information Systems Journal, 13*, 209–231. doi:10.1046/j.1365-2575.2003.00151.x

Cabena, P., Hadjinian, P., Stadler, R., Verhees, J., & Zanasi, A. (1998). *Discovering Data Mining from Concept to Implementation*. Upper Saddle River, NJ: Prentice Hall.

Cagan, J., & Vogel, C. M. (2001). *Creating Breakthrough Products: Innovation from Product Planning to Program Approval*. Upper Saddle River, NJ: FT Press.

Caillé, A. (2001). Une politique de la nature sans politique. *Ecologisme, naturalisme et constructivisme, 17*.

Callon, M. (1986). Some Elements of a Sociology of Translation: Domestication of the Scallops and the Fishermen of St Brieuc Bay. Power, Action & Belief. A New Sociology of Knowledge? *Law, J. London*, 196-229.

Callon, M. (1986a). The Sociology of an Actor-Network: The Case of the Electric Vehicle. In M. Callon, J. Law, & A. Rip (Eds.), *Mapping the Dynamics of Science and Technology* (pp. 19-34). London, Macmillan Press.

Callon, M. (1987). Society in the Making: The Study of Technology as a Tool for Sociological Analysis. In W. E. Bijker, T. P. Hughes, & T. J. Pinch (Eds.), *The Social Construction of Technological Systems. New Directions in the Sociology and History of Technology.* Cambridge, MA: MIT press.

Callon, M. (1991). Réseaux technico-économiques et irréversibilités. In R. Chavance, B. Godard, & Olivier (Eds.), *Les Figures de l'irréversibilité en économie*. Paris: Editions de l'Ecole des Hautes Etudes en Sciences Sociales.

Callon, M. (1991). Techno-Economic Networks and Irreversibility. In J. Law (Ed.), *A Sociology of Monsters. Essays on Power, Technology and Domination* (pp. 132-164). London, Routledge.

Callon, M. (1993). Variety and Irreversibility in Networks of Technique Conception and Adoption. In D. Foray & C. Freemann (Eds.), *Technology and the Wealth of Nations: Dynamics of Constructed Advantage* (pp. 232-268). London, New York: Pinter.

Callon, M. (1999). Actor-Network Theory - The Market Test. Actor-network Theory and After. *Law, J. and Hassard, J*, 181-195.

Callon, M., & Latour, B. (1981). Unscrewing the Big Leviathan: How Actors Macro-Structure Reality and How Sociologist Help Them To Do So. In K. Knorr-Cetina & A. V. Cicouvel (Eds.), *Advances in Social Theory and Methodology: Towards an Integration of Micro and Macro-Sociology* (pp. 277-303). Boston, MA; London: Routledge.

Callon, M., & Law, J. (1989). On the Construction of Sociotechnical Networks: Content and Context Revisited. *Knowledge and Society: Studies in the Sociology of Science Past and Present* (Vol. 8) (pp. 57-83).

Callon, M. (1986). Eléments pour une sociologie de la traduction. La domestication des coquilles Saint-Jacques et des marins-pêcheurs dans la baie de Saint-Brieuc. *L'Annee Sociologique, 36*, 169–208.

Callon, M. (1986). Some Elements of a Sociology of Translation: Domestication of the Scallops and the Fishermen of St Brieuc Bay. In Law, J. (Ed.), *Power, Action & Belief. A New Sociology of Knowledge?* (pp. 196–229). London: Routledge & Kegan Paul.

Callon, M. (1986a). On the Methods of Long Distance Control: Vessels, Navigation and the Portuguese Route to India. In Law, J. (Ed.), *Power, Action and Belief: A New Sociology of Knowledge?* (pp. 234–263).

Callon, M. (1986b). The Sociology of an Actor-Network: The Case of the Electric Vehicle. In Callon, M., Law, J., & Rip, A. (Eds.), *Mapping the Dynamics of Science and Technology: Sociology of Science in the Real World* (pp. 19–34). London: Macmillan.

Callon, M. (1987). Society in the Making: the Study of Technology as a Tool for Sociological Analysis. In Bijker, W. E., Hughes, T. P., & Pinch, T. J. (Eds.), *The Social Construction of Technical Systems: New Directions in the Sociology and History of Technology* (pp. 83–103). Cambridge, MA: MIT Press.

Callon, M. (1991). Techno-economic networks and irreversibility. In Law, J. (Ed.), *A sociology of monsters. Essays on power, technology and domination* (pp. 132–164). London: Routledge.

Callon, M. (1994). *L'innovation technologique et ses mytes*. Gérer & Comprendre.

Callon, M. (1999). Actor-Network Theory - The Market Test. In Law, J., & Hassard, J. (Eds.), *Actor Network Theory and After* (pp. 181–195). Oxford, UK: Blackwell Publishers.

Callon, M., Courtial, J. P., Turner, W. A., & Bauin, S. (1983). From Translations to Problematic Networks: An Introduction to Co-Word Analysis. *Social Sciences Information. Information Sur les Sciences Sociales*, *22*(2), 191–235. doi:10.1177/053901883022002003

Callon, M., & Latour, B. (1981). Unscrewing the Big Leviathan: how actors macro-structure reality and how sociologists help them to do so. In Knorr-Cetina, K., & Cicourel, A. V. (Eds.), *Advances in social theory and methodology. Toward an integration of micro and macro-sociologies* (pp. 277–303). London: Routledge & Kegan Paul.

Callon, M., & Law, J. (1995). Agency and the hybrid collectif. *The South Atlantic Quarterly*, *94*(2).

Castells, M. (2000). *The Information Age: Economy, Society and Culture - The Rise of the Network Society* (2nd ed., *Vol. 1*). Malden, MA: Blackwell Publishing.

Castells, M., Fernández Ardèvol, M., Qiu, J. L., & Sey, A. (2007). *Mobile Communication and Society: A Global Perspective*. London: The MIT Press.

Cats-Baril, W., & Thompson, R. (1997). *Information Technology and Management*. Chicago: Irwin Press.

Cazal, D. (2007). *Traductions De La Traduction et Acteur-Réseau: Sciences, Sciences, Sociales et Sciences en Gestion* ? De Lille: IAE.

Cecez-Kecmanovic, D., & Nagm, F. (2009). Have you Taken your Guys on the Journey? An ANT Account of Information Systems Project Evaluation. *International Journal of Actor-Network Theory and Technological Innovation*, *1*(1), 1–22.

Chae, B. (2003, October 24-26). *Ubiquitous computing for mundane knowledge management: Hopes, challenges and questions.* Paper presented at the Workshop on Ubiquitous computing environment, Cleveland, OH.

ChipIdea. (2008). *MIPS-Chipidea merger's goal: 'virtual' SoCs'*. Retrieved from http://www.design-reuse.com/news/16608/mips-chipidea-merger-goal-virtual-socs.html

Ciborra, C. U. (2004). *Digital Technologies and the Duality of Risk*. Retrieved from http://www.lse.ac.uk/collections/CARR/pdf/Disspaper27.pdf

Ciborra, C. U. (Ed.). (2000). *From Control to Drift*. Oxford: Oxford University Press.

Ciborra, C. U., & Failla, A. (2000). Infrastructure as a process: the case of CRM in IBM. In C. U. Ciborra (Ed.), *From Control to Drift: the Dynamics of Corporate Information Infrastructures* (pp. 105-124). Oxford: Oxford University Press.

Clarke, R., & Kingsley, D. (2008). ePublishing's Impacts on Journals and Journal Articles. *Journal of Internet Commerce*, *7*(1), 120–151. doi:10.1080/15332860802004410

Connell, J. L., & Shafer, L. B. (1989). *Structured Rapid Prototyping*. Yourdon Press.

Cook, M. A. (1996). *Building enterprise information architectures: reengineering information systems*. Upper Saddle River, NJ: Prentice-Hall.

Cordella, A., & Shaikh, M. (2003). *Actor Network Theory and After: What's new for Information Systems research* Paper presented at the European Conference on Information systems, ECIS, Naples, Italy.

Cordella, A. (2006). Transaction costs and information systems: does IT add up? *Journal of Information Technology*, *21*(3), 195–202. doi:10.1057/palgrave.jit.2000066

Curley, K. F., & Pyburn, P. J. (1982). "Intellectual" Technologies: The key to Improving White-Collar Productivity. *Sloan Management Review*, *24*, 31–39.

Cusumano, M. A., & Selby, R. W. (1997). How Microsoft Builds Software. *Communications of the ACM, 40*(6), 53–61. doi:10.1145/255656.255698

Daft, R. L. (2007). *Organization Theory and Design* (9th ed.). Mason, OH: Thomson South-Western.

Dahlbom, B. (2000). Postface: from infrastructure to networking. In C. U. Ciborra (Ed.), *From Control to Drift*. Oxford: Oxford University Press.

Dahlbom, B., & Mathiassen, L. (1993). *Computer in Context*. Cambridge, Massachusetts: Blackwell.

Dahlbom, B. (1997). The new informatics. *Scandinavian Journal of information. System, 8*(2).

Dahlbom, B., & Mathiassen, L. (1993). *Computers in Context: The Philosophy and Practice of Systems Design*. Cambridge, MA: Blackwell Publishers Inc.

Dale, K. (2005). Building a social materiality: spatial and embodied politics in organizational control. *Organization, 12*(5), 649. doi:10.1177/1350508405055940

Darke, P., Shanks, G., & Broadbent, M. (1998). Successfully Completing Case Study Research: Combining Rigor, Relevance and Pragmatism. *Information Systems Journal, 8*, 273–289. doi:10.1046/j.1365-2575.1998.00040.x

Darroch, J., & McNaughton, R. B. (2002). Examining the link between knowledge management practices and types of innovation. *Journal of Intellectual Capital, 3*(3), 210–222. doi:10.1108/14691930210435570

Dasgupta, M., & Gupta, R. K. (2009). Innovation in Organizations: A Review of the Role of Organizational Learning and Knowledge Management. *Global Business Review, 10*(2), 203–224. doi:10.1177/097215090901000205

Davenport, T. H., & Prusak, L. (1998). *Working Knowledge*. Boston: Harvard Business School Press.

Davis, F. D. (1986). *A Technology Acceptance Model for Empirically Testing New End-User Information Systems: Theory and Results*. Boston, MIT. Doctor of Philosophy.

Davis, G. B. (2003, October 24-26). *Affordances of ubiquitous computing and productivity in knowledge work*. Paper presented at the Workshop on ubiquitous computing, Cleveland, OH.

Davis, F. (1986). *A Technology Acceptance Model for Empirically Testing New End-User Information Systems: Theory and Results*. Boston: MIT.

Davis, F. D. (1989). Perceived Usefulness, Perceived Ease of Use, and User Acceptance of Information Technology. *MIS Quarterly, 13*(3), 318–340. doi:10.2307/249008

de Lange, P., Suwardy, T., & Mavondo, F. (2003). Integrating A Virtual Learning Environment into an Introductory Accounting Course: Determinants Of Student Motivation. *Accounting Education, 12*(1), 1–14. doi:10.1080/09639 28032000064567

Deal, D., & Tatnall, A. (2010). *Using Video Screen Capture to Provide Assessment Feedback for Information Systems Students*. Paper presented at the Computer Science Education: Innovation and Technology: CSEIT 2010, Phuket, Thailand.

Deering, P., & Tatnall, A. (2008). Adoption of ICT in an Australian Rural Division of General Practice. In N. Wickramasinghe & E. Geisler (Eds.), *Encyclopaedia of Healthcare Information Systems, 1*, 23-29. Hershey, PA: IGI Global.

Degenne, A., & Forsé, M. (1994). *Les réseaux sociaux*. France: Armand Collin.

Delone, W. H., & McLean, E. R. (1992). Information systems success: The quest for the dependant variable. *Information Systems Research, 3*(1), 60–95. doi:10.1287/isre.3.1.60

DeLone, W., & McLean, E. (1992). Information Systems Success: The Quest for the Dependent Variable. *Information Systems Research, 3*(1). doi:10.1287/isre.3.1.60

DeLone, W., & McLean, E. (2003). The DeLone and McLean Model of Information Systems Success: A Ten-year Update. *Journal of Management Information Systems, 19*(4).

Dey, A. K. (2001). Understanding and Using Context. *Personal and Ubiquitous Computing, 5*(1), 4–7. doi:10.1007/s007790170019

Dey, A. K., Abowd, G., & Salber, D. (2001). A conceptual framework and a toolkit for supporting the rapid prototyping of context-aware applications. *Human-Computer Interaction, 16*, 97–166. doi:10.1207/S15327051HCI16234_02

Dodier, N. (1995). *Les Hommes et les Machines. La conscience collective dans les sociétés techniques* (pp. 30–31). Paris: Métailié.

Doolin, B. (1998). Information Technology as Disciplinary Technology: Being Critical in Interpretive Research on Information Systems. *Journal of Information Technology*, *14*(4), 301–311. doi:10.1057/jit.1998.8

Dosse, F. (1995). *L'empire du sens, La Découverte*. Rééd: En poche.

Dutta, A., & Roy, R. (2004). A Process Oriented Framework for Justifying IT Projects in eBusiness Environments. *International Journal of Electronic Commerce*, *9*(1), 49–68.

Eco, U. (1976). *A Theory of Semiotics*. Bloomington: Indiana University Press.

Edwards, P. N. (2003). Infrastructure and Modernity: Force, Time, and Social Organization in the History of Sociotechnical Systems. In T. J. Misa (Eds.), *Modernity and Technology*. Cambridge, MA: MIT Press.

Electronic News Weekly. (2009). *Synopsys pays $22m for MIPS analogue business group*. Retrieved from http://www.electronicsweekly.com/Articles/2009/05/11/46047/synopsys-pays-22m-for-mips-analogue-business-group.htm

Everitt, P., & Tatnall, A. (2003). *Investigating the Adoption and Use of Information Technology by General Practitioners in Rural Australia and Why This is Less Than it Might Be*. ACIS 2003, Perth, ACIS.

Faraj, S., Kwon, D., & Watts, S. (2004). Contested artifact: technology sensemaking, actor networks, and the shaping of the Web browser. *Information Technology & People*, *17*(2), 186–209. doi:10.1108/09593840410542501

Figueiredo, J. (2004). *Abordagem sócio-técnica ao desenvolvimento de sistemas de informação inter-institucionais, IST* (Sociotechnical approaches to the design and development of inter-institutional information systems).

Fleisch, E. (2002). Von der Vernetzung von Unternehmen zur Vernetzung von Dingen. In M. T. Schögel & T. Belz (Eds.), *Roadm@p to E-business* (pp. 124-136). St Gallen: Thexis.

Flichy, P. (2007). *Understanding technological innovation: a socio-technical approach*. Cheltenham, UK: Edward Elgar Publishing.

Fomin, V. (2003). *The role of standards in information infrastructure development, revisited.* Paper presented at the Standard Making: A Critical Research Frontier for Information Systems MISQ Special Issue Workshop, Seattle.

Ford, R. M., & Coulston, C. (2007). *Design for Electrical and Computer Engineers: Theory, Concepts, and Practice*. New York: McGraw-Hill.

Forsé, M. (2005). Rôle spécifique et croissance du capital social. *Sociologie et Politique Sociales*, *8*(1), 101–125.

Fortunati, L. (2005). Mobile Telephone and the Presentation of Self. In Ling, R., & Pedersen, P. E. (Eds.), *Mobile Communications: Re-negotiation of the Social Sphere* (pp. 203–218). London: Springer.

Franklin, U. (1990). *The Real World of Technology*. Montreal, Quebec: CNC.

Fred. (1997). *Interview on Programming Curricula at RMIT*. Melbourne, Australia: RMIT.

Fred. (1998). *Interview on Programming Curricula at RMIT*. Melbourne, Australia: RMIT.

Galison, P. (1997). *Image and Logic: A Material Culture of Microphysics*. Chicago: University of Chicago Press.

Garcia, A. C. (2006). Workplace studies and technological change. *Annual Review of Information Science & Technology*, *40*, 393–437. doi:10.1002/aris.1440400117

Garfield, M. J. (2005). Acceptance of ubiquitous computing. *Information Systems Management*, *22*(4), 24–31. doi:10.1201/1078.10580530/45520.22.4.20050901/90027.3

Garfinkel, H. (1967). *Studies in Ethnomethodology*. Englewood Cliffs: Prentice-Hall.

Garfinkel, H. (2002). *Ethnomethodology's Program: Working out Durkheim's Aphorism. Lanham: Rowman & Littlefield* (Rawls, A. W., Ed.).

Garfinkel, H. (2007). Lebenswelt origins of the sciences: Working out Durkheim's aphorism. *Human Studies*, *30*(1), 9–56. doi:10.1007/s10746-007-9046-9

Garrison, D. R., & Vaughan, N. D. (2008). *Blended Learning in Higher Education - Framework, Principles and Guidelines*. San Francisco: Jossey-Bass.

Gergen, K. J. (2002). The Challenge of Absent Presence. In Katz, J. E., & Aakhus, M. A. (Eds.), *Perpetual Contact: Mobile Communication, Private Talk, Public Performance* (pp. 227–241). Cambridge, UK: Cambridge University Press. doi:10.1017/CBO9780511489471.018

Gershman, A., & Fano, A. (2005). Examples of commercial applications of ubiquitous computing. *Communications of the ACM*, *48*(3), 71. doi:10.1145/1047671.1047711

Gerson, E. M., & Star, S. L. (1986). Analyzing Due Process in the Workplace. *ACM Transactions on Office Information Systems*, *4*, 257–270. doi:10.1145/214427.214431

Gibson, S. (1998). Evangelizing about Enterprise Architecture. *PC Week*, *15*(38), 78.

Giddens, A. (1984). *The constitution of society: outline of the theory of structuration*. Cambridge Cambridgeshire: Polity Press.

Giddens, A. (1984). *The Constitution of Society: Outline of the Theory of Structuration*. Cambridge, UK: Polity Press.

Giles, C. L., & Purao, S. (2003, October 23-26). *The role of search in ubiquitous computing.* Paper presented at the Workshop on ubiquitous computing, Cleveland, OH.

Goldense, B. L. (1994). Rapid Product Development Metrics. *World Class Design to Manufacture*, *1*(1), 21–28. doi:10.1108/09642369210049924

Gonçalves, F. A., & Figueiredo, J. (2010). How to recognize an Immutable Mobile when you find one - translations on innovation and design. *International Journal of Actor Network Theory and Technological Innovation (IJANTTI)*.

Gonçalves, A., & Figueiredo, J. (2007). Organizing Competences: Actor-Network Theory in Virtual Settings. *International Journal of Networking and Virtual Organisations*, *6*(1), 23–35.

GPCG. (2001). *Measuring IT Use in Australian General Practice. Brisbane, General Practice Computing Group.* University of Queensland.

GPSRG. (1998). *Changing the Future Through Partnerships. Canberra, Commonwealth Department of Health and Family Services.* General Practice Strategy Review Group.

Grint, K., & Woolgar, S. (1995). On Some failures of nerve in the construction of feminist analyses of technology. *Science, Technology & Human Values*, *20*(3), 286–310. doi:10.1177/016224399502000302

Grint, K., & Woolgar, S. (1997). *The Machine at Work - Technology, Work and Organisation*. Cambridge, MA: Polity Press.

Grudin, J. (1990). The computer reaches out: The historical continuity of interface design. In *Proceedings of the SIGCHI Conference on Human Factors in Computing Systems: Empowering People (CHI'90)* (pp. 261-268). New York: ACM.

Grudin, J. (2003, October 23-26). *Implications of technology use throughout organizations.* Paper presented at the Workshop on ubiquitous computing, Cleveland, OH.

Grudin, J. (2001). Desituating action: Digital representation of context. *Human-Computer Interaction*, *16*, 269–286. doi:10.1207/S15327051HCI16234_10

Guide, P. M. B. O. K. (2004). *A Guide to the Project Management Body of Knowledge* (3rd ed.).

Gummerus, J., Liljander, V., Pura, M., & van Riel, A. (2004). Customer loyalty to content based Web sites: The case of an online health-care service. *Journal of Services Marketing*, *18*(2), 175–186. doi:10.1108/08876040410536486

Haddon, L. (2005). Research Questions for the Evolving Communications Landscape. In Ling, R., & Pedersen, P. E. (Eds.), *Mobile Communications: Re-negotiation of the Social Space* (pp. 7–23). London: Springer Verlag.

Hammer, M., & Champy, J. (1993). *Reengineering the corporation: a manifesto for business revolution* (1st ed.). New York, NY: HarperBusiness.

Hannemeyr, G. (2003). The Internet as Hyperbole: A Critical Examination of Adoption Rates. *The Information Society*, *19*, 111–121. doi:10.1080/01972240309459

Hanseth, O. (1996). *Information technology as Infrastructure.* Unpublished Ph.D Thesis, School of Economics and Commercial Law, Goteborg University, Goteborg.

Hanseth, O. (2000). Infrastructures: From Systems to Infrastructures. In K. Braa, C. Sørensen & B. Dahlbom (Eds.), *Planet Internet.* Lund, Sweden: Studentlitteratur.

Hanseth, O. (2004b). *From systems and tools to networks and infrastructures - from design to cultivation. Towards a theory of ICT solutions and its design methodology implications.* Unpublished manuscript.

Hanseth, O., & Braa, K. (1998). *Technology as a Traitor: Emergent SAP Infrastructure in a Global Organisation.* Paper presented at the Proceedings of the Nineteenth International Conference on Information systems, ICIS'98, Helsinki.

Hanseth, O., & Braa, K. (2000). Who is in control? Designers, managers – or technology? In C. U. Ciborra (Ed.), *From Control to Drift: The Dynamics of Corporate Information Infrastructures.* Oxford: Oxford University Press.

Hanseth, O., & Monteiro, E. (2002). *Understanding Information Infrastructure*: Manuscript.

Hanseth, O., Monteiro, E., & Hatling, M. (1996b). Inscribing behaviour in information infrastructure standards. *Accounting, Management and Information System.*

Hanseth, O. (2004a). Actor network theory and information systems: What's so special. *Information Technology & People, 17*(2), 116–123. doi:10.1108/09593840410542466

Hanseth, O., & Aanestad, M. (2004). Actor-network theory and information systems: What's so special? *Information Technology & People, 17*(2), 116–123. doi:10.1108/09593840410542466

Hanseth, O., Aanestad, M., & Berg, M. (2004). Guest Editors' Introduction: Actor-Network Theory and Information Systems. What's so Special? *Information Technology & People, 17*(2), 116–123. doi:10.1108/09593840410542466

Hanseth, O., Aanestad, M., & Berg, M. (2004). Guest editors' introduction – Actor-network theory and information systems. What's so special? *Information Technology & People, 17*(2), 116–123. doi:10.1108/09593840410542466

Hanseth, O., & Braa, K. (2001). Hunting for the treasure at the end of the rainbow. Standardizing corporate IT infrastructure. *Computer Supported Cooperative Work (CSCW). The Journal of Collaborative Computing, 10*(3-4), 261–292. doi:10.1023/A:1012637309336

Hanseth, O., & Monteiro, E. (1996). Developing Information Infrastructure: The tension between standardization and flexibility. *Science, Technology & Human Values, 21*(4), 407–426. doi:10.1177/016224399602100402

Hanseth, O., & Monteiro, E. (1997). Inscribing Behaviour in Information Infrastructure Standards. *Accounting. Management & Information Technology, 7*(4), 183–211. doi:10.1016/S0959-8022(97)00008-8

Hanseth, O., Monteiro, E., & Hatling, M. (1996a). Developing information infrastructure: The tension between standardization and flexibility. *Science, Technology & Human Values, 21*(4), 407–426. doi:10.1177/016224399602100402

Hanson, D., Dowling, P. J., Hitt, M. A., Ireland, R. D., & Hoskisson, R. E. (Eds.). (2008). *Strategic Management: Competitiveness & Globalisation* (3rd ed.). Cengage Learning.

Harnad, S. (1999). Free at Last: The Future of Peer-Reviewed Journals. *D-Lib Magazine, 5*(12). Retrieved from http://www.dlib.org/dlib/december99/12harnad.html.

Haythornwaite, C. (2005). *Social networks and Internet connectivity effects.* Information, Communicaion & Society, 8(2), 125-147Latour, B. (1984). *The Pasteurization of France: Irréductions.* Cambridge, MA: Harvard

Heath, C., & Luff, P. (2000). *Technology in Action.* Cambridge, UK: Cambridge University Press. doi:10.1017/CBO9780511489839

Heidegger, M. (1977). *The Question Concerning Technology, and Other Essays* (Lovitt, W., Trans.). New York: Harper Torchbooks.

Henderson, J., Britt, H., & Miller, G. (2006). Extent and utilisation of computerisation in Australian general practice. *The Medical Journal of Australia, 185*(2), 84–87.

Henfridsson, O., & Lindgren, R. (2005). Multi-contextuality in ubiquitous computing: Investigating the car case through action research. *Information and Organization, 15*, 95–124. doi:10.1016/j.infoandorg.2005.02.009

Hewitt, C. (1986). Offices are Open Systems. *ACM Transactions on Office Information Systems, 4*(3), 271–287. doi:10.1145/214427.214432

Holmström, J., & Robey, D. (2005). Understanding IT's organizational consequences: An actor network approach. In Czarniawska, B., & Hernes, T. (Eds.), *Actor-Network Theory and Organizing* (pp. 165–187). Stockholm, Sweden: Liber.

Hosein, I. (2003). A Research Note on Capturing Technology: Toward Moments of Interest. In Whitley, E. A., Wynn, E. H., Myers, M. D., & DeGross, J. I. (Eds.), *Global and Organizational Discourse about Information Technology* (pp. 133–154). Boston: Kluwer Academic Publishers.

Høstaker, R. (2002, October 10-13). *Latour – Semiotics and science studies*. Paper presented at the Annual Meeting in the Society for Literature and Science, Pasadena, CA. Retrieved from http://ansatte.hil.no/rohar/artiklar/latourggreimas.htm

Hughes, T. P. (1993). The Evolution of Large Technological Systems. In T. P. Bijker, T. P. Hughes & T. J. Pinch (Eds.), *The social construction of technological systems: New directions in the sociology and history of technology*. Cambridge: MIT Press

Hughes, T. P. (1986). The Seamless Web: Technology, Science, Etcetera, Etcetera. *Social Studies of Science, 16*(2), 281–292. doi:10.1177/0306312786016002004

Husserl, E. (1938, 1970). *The Crisis of European Sciences and Transcendental Phenomenology.* Evanston: Northwestern University Press.

Hutchins, E. (1995). *Cognition in the Wild.* Cambridge, MA: MIT Press.

Iberomoldes. (2008). *Based on personal communication of the CEO, Mr. Henrique Neto.*

Introna, L. D. (2007). Maintaining the Reversibility of Foldings: Making the Ethics (Politics) of Information Technology Visible. *Ethics and Information Technology, 9*(1), 11–25. doi:10.1007/s10676-006-9133-z

Introna, L. D., & Whitley, E. A. (1999). Limiting the Web: The politics of search engines. *IEEE Computer, 33*(1), 54–62.

Iyamu, T. (2009). The Factors affecting Institutionalisation of Enterprise Architecture in the Organisation. In *Proceedings of the 11th IEEE Conference on Commerce and Enterprise Computing* (pp. 221-225). Washington, DC: IEEE Computer Society.

Iyamu, T., & Dewald, R. (2010). The use of Structuration and Actor Network Theory for analysis: A case study of a financial institution in South Africa. *International Journal of Actor-Network Theory and Technological Innovation, 2*(1), 1–26.

James. (1997). *Interview on Programming Curricula at RMIT*. Melbourne, Australia: RMIT.

Johnson, W. (2009). *Pick, Universe, Unidata Resources*. Retrieved from http://knol.google.com/k/pick-universe-unidata-resources#

Jones, M. (1999). Structuration Theory. In W. L. Currie & R. D. Galliers (Eds.), *Rethinking Management Information Systems* (pp. 103-134). UK: Oxford University Press.

Jones, M. (2000). The moving finger: The use of theory. In Baskerville, R., Stage, J., & DeGross, J. (Eds.), *Organizational and social perspectives on information technology* (pp. 1975–1999). Boston: Kluwer Academic Publishers.

Jonsson, K., Westergren, U. H., & Holmström, J. (2008). Technologies for value creation: an exploration of remote diagnostics systems in the manufacturing industry. *Information Systems Journal, 18*(3), 227–245. doi:10.1111/j.1365-2575.2007.00267.x

Juliff, P. (1992). *Interview on Business Computing Curriculum*. Melbourne, Australia: RMIT.

Kallinikos, J. (2002). *Re-opening the Black Box of Technology.* Paper presented at the EGOS 2002, Barcelona.

Kallinikos, J. (2006). *The Consequences of Information: Institutional Implications of Technological Change*. Cheltenham: Edward Elgar.

Kappelman, L. A. (2002). We've Only Just Begun to Use IT Wisely. *Management Information Systems Quarterly, 887*, 116.

Kautz, K., & McMaster, T. (1994). Introducing structured methods: An undelivered promise? - A case study. *Scandinavian Journal of Information Systems*, *6*(2), 59–78.

Keen, P. W. (1991). *Shaping the future: Business Redesign through information technologies* Boston: Harvard Business School Press.

Kennan, M. A. (2008). *Reassembling scholarly publishing: open access, institutional repositories and the process of change.* Unpublished doctoral thesis, The University of New South Wales, Sydney, Australia. Retrieved from: http://unsworks.unsw.edu.au/vital/access/manager/Repository/unsworks:3488

Klein, H. K., & Myers, M. D. (1999). A set of principles for conducting and evaluating interpretive field studies in information systems. *MIS Quarterly*, *23*(1), 67–93. doi:10.2307/249410

Klein, H., & Myers, M. (1999). A set of principles for conducting and evaluating interpretive field studies in Information Systems. *Management Information Systems Quarterly*, *23*(1), 67–93. doi:10.2307/249410

Kling, R. (2000). Learning About Information Technologies and Social Change: The Contribution of Social Informatics. *The Information Society*, *16*(3), 217–232. doi:10.1080/01972240050133661doi:10.1080/01972240050133661

Kling, R., & Callahan, E. (2003). Electronic journals, the Internet and scholarly communication. [ARIST]. *Annual Review of Information Science & Technology*, *37*, 127–178. doi:10.1002/aris.1440370105

Knorr-Cetina, K. D. (1988). The Micro-social Order: Towards a Reconception. In Fielding, N. G. (Ed.), *Action and Structure: Research Methods and Social Theory* (pp. 21–53). London: Sage Publications.

Kuschel, J., & Ljungberg, F. (2004, September 6-10). *Decentralized Remote Diagnostics: A Study of Diagnostics in the Marine Industry.* Paper presented at the 18th British HCI Group Annual Conference, Leeds, UK.

Kwon, T. H., & Zmud, R. W. (1987). Unifying the fragmented models of information systems implementation. In Boland, R. J., & Hirscheim, R. A. (Eds.), *Critical Issues in Information Systems Research*. New York: John Wiley & Sons.

Laing, A., Hogg, G., & Winkleman, D. (2004). Health Care and the Information Revolution: reconfiguring the healthcare service encounter. *Health Services Management Research*, *17*(3), 188–199. doi:10.1258/0951484041485584

Lampe, M., Strassner, M., & Fleisch, E. (2004, March 14-17). A ubiquitous computing environment for aircraft maintenance. In *Proceedings of the Proceedings of the 2004 ACM Symposium on Applied computing*, Nicosia, Cyprus.

Lang, J. R., & Collen, A. (2005). Evaluating Personal Health Care and Health Promotion Web Sites. *Methods of Information in Medicine*, *44*, 328–333.

Lanzara, G. F. (1999). Designing Systems In-Action: between transient constructs and permanent structures. Copenhagen: Keynote Speech, European Confrence of Information Systems.

Latour, (1996). Social Theory and the Study of Computerised Work Sites, In W. J. Orlikowski, G. Walsham, M. R. Jones, & J. I. DeGross, (Eds.), *Information Technology and Changes in Organizational Work* (pp. 295-307). London: Chapman & Hall.

Latour, B. (1986). The Powers of Association. In J. Law (Ed.), *Power, Action and Belief. A New Sociology of Knowledge? Sociological Review monograph* (pp. 264-280). London, Routledge & Kegan Paul.

Latour, B. (1987). *Science in Action: How to Follow Scientists and Engineers Through Society*. Milton Keynes: Open University Press.

Latour, B. (1996). *Aramis or the Love of Technology*. Cambridge, MA: Harvard University Press.

Latour, B. (1998). On Recalling ANT. J. Law & J. Hassard (Eds.), *Actor Network Theory and After*. London: Blackwell.

Latour, B. (1999a). On Recalling ANT. In J. Law & J. Hassard (Eds.), *Actor Network Theory and After* (pp. 15-25). Oxford: Blackwell Publishers / The Sociological Review.

Latour, B. (1999b). *Pandora's hope*. Cambridge, Massachusetts: Harvard University Press.

Latour, B. (2001). Réponse aux objections. *Ecologisme, naturalisme et constructivisme, 17*.

Latour, B. (2004). Comment finir une thèse en sociologie? Petit dialogue entre un étudiant et un professeur (quelque peu socratique). *Une théorie sociologique générale est-elle pensable, 24*. Latour, B. (2007). Changer de société, refaire de la sociologie. Paris: La Découverte/Poche.

Latour, B. (2008). The Metaphorical/Literal Divide. *Arch Literary Journal*. Retrieved from http://archjournal.wustl.edu/interviews/latour/interview.htm

Latour, B. (1985). Les "Vues" de L'Esprit. Une Introduction à L'Anthropologie des Sciences et des Techniques. *Culture Technique, 14*, 5–29.

Latour, B. (1986). The Power of Association. In Law, J. (Ed.), *Power, Action and Belief*. London: Routledge & Kegan Paul.

Latour, B. (1986). The Powers of Association. *The Sociological Review, 32*.

Latour, B. (1987). *Science in action*. Cambridge, MA: Harvard University Press.

Latour, B. (1987). *Science in Action: How to Follow Scientists and Engineers through Society*. Cambridge, MA: Harvard University Press.

Latour, B. (1988). *Irréductions, published with The Pasteurisation of France*. Cambridge, MA: Harvard University Press.

Latour, B. (1990). Drawing Things Together. In Lynch, M., & Woolgar, S. (Eds.), *Representation in Scientific Practice* (pp. 19–68). Cambridge, MA: MIT Press.

Latour, B. (1991). *Nous n'avons jamais été modernes: essai d'anthropologie symétrique* (p. 167). Paris: Découverte & Syros.

Latour, B. (1991a). Technology is Society made durable. In Law, J. (Ed.), *A Sociology of Monsters: essays on power, technology and domination*. London: Routledge.

Latour, B. (1991b). *Nous n'avons jamais été modernes: essai d'anthropologie symétrique* (p. 167). Paris: La Découverte & Syros.

Latour, B. (1992). Where Are the Missing Masses? The Sociology of a Few Mundane Artifacts. In Wiebe, E., Bijker, E., & Law, J. (Eds.), *Shaping Technology/Building Society: Studies in Sociotechnical Change* (pp. 225–258). Cambridge, MA: MIT Press.

Latour, B. (1993). *Petites leçons de sociologie des sciences, III. Les Tribulations de L'Image Scientifique*. Paris: La Découverte.

Latour, B. (1993). *We Have Never Been Modern* (Porter, C., Trans.). Cambridge, MA: Harvester University Press.

Latour, B. (1993). *We Have Never Been Modern*. UK: Hemel Hempstead.

Latour, B. (1993a). Les Tribulations de L'Image Scientifique, Le «pédofil» de Boa Vista – montage photo-philosophique. In *Petites leçons de sociologie des sciences* (pp. 213–219). Paris: Éditions La Découverte.

Latour, B. (1994). *Nous n'avons jamais été modernes. Essai d'anthropologie symétrique*. La Découverte.

Latour, B. (1995). *Le métier de chercheur – Regard d'un anthropologue*. Paris: INRA.

Latour, B. (1996). *Aramis or the Love of Technology*. Cambridge, MA: Harvard University Press.

Latour, B. (1996). Social Theory and the Study of Computerised Work Sites. In Orlikowski, W. J., Walsham, G., Jones, M. R., & DeGross, J. I. (Eds.), *Information Technology and Changes in Organizational Work* (pp. 295–307). London: Chapman & Hall.

Latour, B. (1999a). On Recalling ANT. In Law, J., & Hassard, J. (Eds.), *Actor Network Theory and After* (pp. 15–25). Oxford, UK: Blackwell Publishers.

Latour, B. (1999b). *Pandora's Hope: Essays on the Reality of Science Studies*. Cambridge, MA: Harvard University Press.

Latour, B. (2002). Morality and Technology: The End of the Means. *Theory, Culture & Society, 19*(5/6), 247–260. doi:10.1177/026327602761899246

Latour, B. (2003). The promises of constructivism. In Ihde, D., & Selinger, E. (Eds.), *Chasing Technoscience: Matrix of Materiality*. Bloomington, IN: Indiana University Press.

Latour, B. (2004). Why Has Critique Run out of Steam? From Matters of Fact to Matters of Concern. *Critical Inquiry, 30*(2), 25–248. Retrieved from http://www.bruno-latour.fr/articles/article/089.html. doi:10.1086/421123

Latour, B. (2007). *Reassembling the Social An Introduction to Actor-Network-Theory*. Oxford, UK: Oxford University Press.

Latour, B., Mauguin, P., & Teil, G. (1992). A Note on Socio-Technical Graphs. *Social Studies of Science*, *22*(1), 33–57. doi:10.1177/030631279202200100 2

Latour, B., & Woolgar, S. (1986). *Laboratory Life: The Construction of Scientific Facts*. Princeton, NJ: Princeton University Press.

Law, J. (1986). On the methods of long distance control: vessels, navigation, and the Portuguese route to India, Power, Action and Belief. In J. Law (Ed.), *A New Sociology of Knowledge*. London: Routledge. Retrieved from http:// www.comp.lancs.ac.uk/sociology /papers/law-methods-of-long-distance-control.pdf

Law, J. (1987, 1990). Technology and Heterogeneous Engineering: The Case of Portuguese Expansion. In W. E. Bijker, T. P. Hughes, & T. J. Pinch (Eds.), *The Social Construction of Technological Systems: New Directions in the Sociology and History of Technology* (pp. 111-134). Cambridge, MA: MIT Press.

Law, J. (1990). Technology and heterogeneous engineering: The case of Portuguese expansion. In W. E. Bijker, T. P. Hughes & T. J. Pinch (Eds.), *The social construction of technological systems: New directions in the sociology and history of technology* (pp. 111-134). Cambridge, Mass. and London: MIT Press.

Law, J. (1991). Monsters, Machines and Sociotechnical Relations. In J. Law (Ed.), *A Sociology of Monsters: Essays on Power, Technology and Domination* (pp. 1-23). London: Routledge.

Law, J. (1992). *Notes on the Theory of the Actor Network: Ordering, Strategy, and Heterogeneity*. Retrieved from http://www.lancs.ac.uk/fss/sociology/papers/law-notes-on-ant.pdf

Law, J. (1999). After ANT: complexity, naming and topology. In J. Law & J. Hassard (Eds.), *Actor Network Theory and After* (pp. 1-14). Oxford: Blackwell Publishers / The Sociological Review.

Law, J., & Mol, A. (2003). *Situating Technoscience: an Inquiry into Spatialities*. Lancaster, UK: Lancaster University. Retrieved from http://www.comp.lancs.ac.uk/sociology/papers/Law-Mol-Situating-Technoscience.pdf

Law, J. (1987). On the methods of long-distance control: Vessels, navigation and the Portuguese route to India. In Law, J. (Ed.), *Power, action and belief: A new sociology of knowledge* (pp. 234–263). London: Routledge & Kegan Paul.

Law, J. (1987). Technology and Heterogeneous Engineering: The Case of Portuguese Expansion. In Bijker, W. E., Hughes, T. P., & Pinch, T. J. (Eds.), *the Social Construction of Technological Systems: New Directions in the Sociology and History of Technology* (pp. 111–134). Cambridge, MA: MIT Press.

Law, J. (1991). Introduction: monsters, machines and sociotechnical relations. In Law, J. (Ed.), *A Sociology of Monsters: Essays on Power, Technology and Domination*. London: Routledge.

Law, J. (1992). Notes on The Theory of the Actor Network: Ordering, Strategy and Heterogeneity. *Systems Practice*, *5*(4). doi:10.1007/BF01059830

Law, J. (1992). Notes on the theory of the actor-network: ordering, strategy, and heterogeneity. *Systems Practice*, *5*(4), 79–393. doi:10.1007/BF01059830

Law, J. (1994). *Organizing Modernity*. Oxford, UK: Blackwell Publishing.

Law, J. (2004). *After Method: Mess in Social Science Research*. London: Routledge.

Law, J., & Callon, M. (1988). Engineering and Sociology in a Military Aircraft Project: A Network Analysis of Technological Change. *Social Problems*, *35*(3), 284–297. doi:10.1525/sp.1988.35.3.03a00060

Law, J., & Callon, M. (1992). The Life and Death of an Aircraft: A Network Analysis of Technical Change. In Bijker, W. E., & Law, J. (Eds.), *Shaping Technology/ Building Society: Studies in Sociotechnical Change*. Cambridge, MA: The MIT Press.

Law, J., & Hassard, E. (Eds.). (1999). *Actor Network Theory and After*. Oxford, UK: Blackwell.

Law, L. (1986). On the Methods of Long Distance Control: Vessels, Navigation and the Portuguese Route to India. In Law, J. (Ed.), *Power, Action and Belief: A New Sociology of Knowledge* (pp. 234–263).

Lee, A. S. (1999). Researching MIS. In W. L. Currie & R. D. Galliers (Eds.), *Rethinking Management Information Systems*. Oxford: Oxford University Press.

Lee, A. S., Liebenau, J., & De Gross, J. I. (Eds.). (1997). *Information Systems and Qualitative Research*. London: Chapman and Hall.

Lee, A. S. (1994). Electronic Mail as a Medium for Rich Communication: An Empirical Investigation Using Hermeneutic Interpretation. *MIS Quarterly*, *19*(2), 143–157. doi:10.2307/249762

Lee, A. S. (2001). Editorial. *MIS Quarterly*, *25*(1).

Lincoln, Y. S., & Guba, E. G. (1985). *Naturalistic Inquiry*. Beverly Hills: Sage Publications.

Lucas, H. C. (1981). *Implementation: Key to Successful Information Systems*. New York: Columbia University Press.

Lynch, C. A., & Lippincott, J. K. (2005). Institutional repository deployment in the United States as of early 2005. *D-Lib Magazine*, *11*(9). Retrieved from http://webdoc.sub.gwdg.de/edoc/aw/d-lib/dlib/september05/lynch/09lynch.html. doi:10.1045/september2005-lynch

Lynch, M. (1993). *Scientific Practice & Ordinary Action: Ethnomethodology and Social Studies of Science*. Cambridge, UK: Cambridge University Press.

Lynch, M. (2007). Law courts as perspicuous sites for ethnomethodological investigations. In Hester, S., & Francis, D. (Eds.), *Orders of Ordinary Action: Respecifying Sociological Knowledge* (pp. 107–120). Aldershot, UK: Ashgate.

Lynn, J., & Jay, A. (1984). *The Complete Yes Minister - The Diaries of a Cabinet Minister*. London: British Broadcasting Corporation.

Lyytinen, K., & Hirscheim, R. (1987). Information system failures: A survey and classification of the empirical literature. *Oxford Survey in Information Technology*, *4*, 257–309.

Lyytinen, K., & Yoo, Y. (2002a). Issues and challenges in ubiquitous computing. *Communications of the ACM*, *45*(12), 63–65.

Lyytinen, K., & Yoo, Y. (2002b). Research commentary: The next wave of nomadic computing. *Information Systems Research*, *13*(4), 377–388. doi:10.1287/isre.13.4.377.75

Macintosh Mouse. (2002). Retrieved from http://library.stanford.edu/mac/mouse.html

MacKenzie, D. A. (1996). Negotiating arithmetic, constructing proof. In *Knowing Machines: Essays on Technical Change* (pp. 165–183). Cambridge, MA: MIT Press.

MacKenzie, D. A. (2001). *Mechanizing Proof: Computing, Risk, and Trust*. Cambridge, MA: MIT Press.

Mahoney, M. S. (2005). The histories of computing(s). *Interdisciplinary Science Reviews*, *30*(2), 119–135. doi:10.1179/030801805X25927

Mähring, M., Holmström, J., Keil, M., & Montealegre, R. (2004). Trojan actor-networks and swift translation: Bringing actor-network theory to IT project escalation studies. *Information Technology & People*, *17*(2), 210–238. doi:10.1108/09593840410542510

Markus, L. (2001). Toward a Theory of Knowledge Reuse: Types of Knowledge Reuse Situations and Factors in Reuse Success. *Journal of Management Information Systems*, *18*(1), 57–93.

Markus, M. L., & Pfeffer, J. (1983). Power and the design and implementation of accounting and control systems. *Accounting, Organizations and Society*, *8*(2), 205–218. doi:10.1016/0361-3682(83)90028-4

Markus, M. L., & Robey, D. (1988). Information Technology and Organizational Change: Causal Structure in theory and Research. *Management Science*, *34*(5). doi:10.1287/mnsc.34.5.583

Martin, J. (1991). *Rapid Application Development*. New York: Macmillan Publishing Company.

Maude, T., & Willis, G. (1991). *Rapid Prototyping, The Management of Software Risk*. Pitman.

McDowell, C. S. (2007). Evaluating Institutional Repository Deployment in American Academe Since Early 2005 Repositories by the Numbers, Part 2. *D-Lib Magazine*, *13*(9-10). Retrieved from http://dlib.org/dlib/september07/mcdowell/09mcdowell.html.

McInnis, C., James, R., & McNaught, C. (1995). *First Year on Campus - Diversity in the Initial Experience of Australian Undergraduates*. Melbourne, Australia: Centre for the Study of Higher Education,University of Melbourne.

Medovich, M. (2003, October 23-26). *Pervasive computing and pervasive economies in the 21st century.* Paper presented at the Workshop on ubiquitous computing, Cleveland, OH.

Meuter, M. L., Ostrom, A. L., Roundtree, R. I., & Bitner, M. J. (2000). Self-Service Technologies: Understanding Customer Satisfaction with Technology-Based Encounters. *Journal of Marketing*, *64*, 50–64. doi:10.1509/jmkg.64.3.50.18024

Mintzberg, H. (1983). *Power In and Around Organizations*. London: Prentice-Hall.

Mintz, S., & Cherry, A. A. (1993). The Introductory Accounting Courses: Educating Majors And Nonmajors. *Journal of Education for Business*, *68*(5), 276–280. doi:10.1080/08832323.1993.10117627

Mladenovic, R. (2000). An Investigation into Ways of Challenging Introductory Accounting Student's Negative Perceptions of Accounting. *Accounting Education*, *9*(2), 135–155. doi:10.1080/09639280010000147

Mol, A. (2002). *The Body Multiple: Ontology in Medical Practice*. London: Duke University Press.

Mol, A., & Law, J. (1994). Regions, Networks and Fluids: Anaemia and Social Topology. *Social Studies of Science*, *24*(4), 641–671. doi:10.1177/030631279402400402

Monteiro, & Hanseth, O. (1996). Social Shaping of Information Infrastructure: On Being Specific about the Technology, In W. J. Orlikowski, G. Walsham, M. R. Jones & J. I. DeGross, (Eds.), *Information Technology and Changes in Organizational Work* (pp. 325-343). London: Chapman and Hall.

Monteiro, E. (2000). Actor-Network Theory and Information Infrastructure. In C. U. Ciborra, K. Braa, & A. C ordella (Eds.), *From Control to drift: the dynamics of corporate information infrastructures* (pp. 71-83). Oxford, UK: Oxford University Press.

Monteiro, E., & Hanseth, O. (1995). Social shaping of information infrastructure: on being specific about the technology. In W. J. Orlikowski, J. Walsham, M. R. Jones & J. I. De Gross (Eds.), *Information Technology and Changes in Organizational Work* (pp. 325-343). London: Chapman a& Hall.

Monteiro, E., & Hanseth, O. (1996). Social shaping of Information Infrastructure: on being specific about technology. In W. J. Orlikowski, G. Walsham, R. Jones & J. I. De Gross (Eds.), *Information technology and changes in organizational work*. London: Chapman & Hall.

Monteiro, E., & Hanseth, O. (1996). Social Shaping of Information Infrastructure: On Being Specific about the Technology. In Orlikowski, W. J., Walsham, G., Jones, M. R., & DeGross, J. I. (Eds.), *Information Technology and Changes in Organizational Work* (pp. 325–343). London: Chapman and Hall.

Mort, M., May, C. R., & Williams, T. (2003). Remote Doctors and Absent Patients: Acting at a Distance in Telemedicine? *Science, Technology & Human Values*, *28*(2), 274–295. doi:10.1177/0162243902250907

Moser, I., & Law, J. (2006). Fluid or Flows? Information and qualculation in medical practice. *Information Technology & People*, *19*(1), 55–73. doi:10.1108/09593840610649961

Mott, K. (2001). GP Corporatisation - The Consumer Perspective. *The Medical Journal of Australia*, *175*, 75–76.

Mouse, M. (2002). Retrieved from http://www.stanfordalumni.org/news/magazine/2002/marapr/features/mouse.html

Muhr, T., & Friese, S. (2004). *User's Manual for ATLAS. ti 5.0* (2nd ed.). Berlin: Scientific Software Development.

Murray-Smith, S., & Dare, A. J. (1987). *The Tech: a centenary history of the Royal Melbourne Institute of Technology*. Melbourne, Australia: Hyland House.

Musso, P. (2003). *Réseaux et Société*. Paris: PUF.

Myers, M. D. (1994). A disaster for everyone to see: An interpretive analysis of a failed IS project. *Accounting. Management & Information Technology*, *4*(4), 185–201. doi:10.1016/0959-8022(94)90022-1

Myers, M. D., & Avison, D. (2002). An Introduction to Qualitative Research in Information Systems. In Myers, M. D., & Avison, D. (Eds.), *Qualitative Research in Information Systems: A Reader* (pp. 3–12). London: Sage publications.

Naidoo, R., & Leonard, A. (2007). Perceived usefulness, service quality and loyalty incentives: Effects on electronic service continuance. *South African Journal of Business Management*, *38*(3), 39–48.

Naidoo, R., & Leonard, A. (2009). Tracing the many translations of a Web-based IT artefact. In Cunha, M. M., Oliveira, E., Tavares, A., & Ferreira, L. (Eds.), *Handbook of Research on Social Dimensions of Semantic Technologies and Web Services*. Portugal: Polytechnic Institute of Cavado and Ave.

Newell, S., Robertson, M., Scarbrough, H., & Swan, J. (2002). *Managing Knowledge Work*. New York: Palgrave.

Ngwenyama, O. K. (1998). Groupware, social action and organizational emergence: on the process dynamics of computer mediated distributed work. *Accounting, Management and Information Technologies,* (8), 127-146.

NHIMAC. (1999). *Health On-Line: A Health Information Action Plan for Australia.* Canberra, NHIMAC.

Nonaka, I. (1994). A dynamic theory of organizational knowledge creation. *Organization Science*, *5*, 14–37. doi:10.1287/orsc.5.1.14

Nonaka, I., & Nishiguchi, T. (2001). *Knowledge Emergence*. Oxford, UK: Oxford University Press.

OED. (2001). *Oxford English Dictionary*. Retrieved from www.oed.com.

Olsson, C.-M., & Henfridsson, O. (2005). Designing context-aware interaction: An action research study. In Sorensen, C., Yoo, Y., Lyytinen, K., & DeGross, J. I. (Eds.), *Designing ubiquitous information environments: Socio-technical issues and challenges*. New York: Springer. doi:10.1007/0-387-28918-6_18

Open Access and Research Conference. (2008). *The Brisbane Declaration.* Retrieved from http://www.oaklaw.qut.edu.au/files/Brisbane.Declaration.pdf

Orlikowski, W. (1993). CASE tools as organisational change: Investigating incremental and radical changes in systems development. *MIS Quarterly*, *17*(3), 1–28. doi:10.2307/249774doi:10.2307/249774

Orlikowski, W., & Robey, D. (1991). Information Technology and the Structuring of Organizations. *Information Systems Research*, *2*(2), 143–169. doi:10.1287/isre.2.2.143doi:10.1287/isre.2.2.143

Orlikowski, W. J. (1992). The duality of technology: Rethinking the concept of technology in organizations. *Information Systems Research*, *3*(3).

Orlikowski, W. J. (2000). Using Technology and Constituting Structures: A Practice Lens for Studying Technology in Organizations. *Organization Science*, *11*(4), 404–428. doi:10.1287/orsc.11.4.404.14600

Orlikowski, W. J. (2007). Sociomaterial practices: Exploring technology at work. *Organization Studies*, *28*(9), 1435–1448. doi:10.1177/0170840607081138

Orlikowski, W. J. (2010). The Sociomateriality of Organisational Life: Considering Technology in Management Research. *Cambridge Journal of Economics*, *34*(1), 125–141. doi:10.1093/cje/bep058

Orlikowski, W. J., & Barley, R. B. (2001). Technology and Institutions: What can research on information technology and research on organization learn from each other? *MIS Quarterly*, *25*(2), 145–165. doi:10.2307/3250927

Orlikowski, W. J., & Iacono, C. S. (2001). Desperately Seeking the "IT" in IT Research - A Call to Theorizing the IT Artifact. *Information Systems Research*, *12*(2), 121–134. doi:10.1287/isre.12.2.121.9700

Orlikowski, W. J., & Iacono, S. (2001). Research commentary: desperately seeking the "IT" in IT research - a call for theorizing the IT artifact. *Information Systems Research*, *10*(2).

Orlikowski, W. J., & Robey, D. (1991). Information technology and the structuring of the organizations. *Information Systems Research*, *2*(2). doi:10.1287/isre.2.2.143

Orlikowski, W. J., & Scott, S. V. (2008). Sociomateriality: Challenging the Separation of Technology, Work and Organization. *The Academy of Management Annals*, *2*(1), 433–474. doi:10.1080/19416520802211644

Orlikowski, W. J., & Scott, S. V. (2008). *The entangling of technology and work in organizations (Tech. Rep.)*. London: London School of Economics and Political Science.

Pandya, A., & Dholakia, N. (2005). B2C Failures: Towards an Innovation Theory Framework. *Journal of Electronic Commerce in Organizations*, *3*(2), 68–81.

Parasuraman, A., & Zinkhan, G. M. (2002). Marketing to and Serving Customers Through the Internet: An Overview and Research Agenda. *Journal of the Academy of Marketing Science*, *30*(4), 286–295. doi:10.1177/009207002236906

Paul. (1997). *Interview on Programming and Curriculum at RMIT*. Melbourne, Australia: RMIT.

Payette, S., & Lagoze, C. (1998). Flexible and Extensible Digital Object and Repository Architecture (FEDORA). In *Proceedings of the Second European Conference on Research and Advanced Technology for Digital Libraries* (LNCS 1513), Heraklion, Crete, Greece.

Peppard, J. (2001). Bridging the gap between the IS organization and the rest of the business: plotting a route. *Information Systems Journal*, *11*(3), 249–270. doi:10.1046/j.1365-2575.2001.00105.x

Pepper, S. C. (1948). *World Hypotheses: A Study in Evidence*. Berkley, CA: University California Press.

Pettigrew, A. M., Woodman, R. W., & Cameron, K. S. (2001). Studying organizational change and development: Challenges for future research. *Academy of Management Journal*, *44*(4), 697–713. doi:10.2307/3069411

Polyani, M. (1958). *Personal knowledge: towards a post-critical philosophy*. Chicago: Chicago University Press.

Polyani, M. (1966). *The Tacit Dimension*. London: Routledge & Kegan Paul.

Porsander, L. (2005). My Name is Lifebuoy: An Actor-Network Emerging from Action-net. In Czarniawska, B., & Hernes, T. (Eds.), *Actor-Network Theory and Organizing* (pp. 14–30). Copenhagen, Denmark: Copenhagen Business School Press.

Porter, M. E. (2008). The five competitive forces that shape strategy. *Harvard Business Review*, *86*(1), 78–93.

Pouloudi, A., & Whitley, E. A. (2000). Representing human and non-human stakeholders: on speaking with authority. In Baskerville, R., Stage, J., & DeGross, J. I. (Eds.), *Organizational and Social Perspectives on Information Technology* (pp. 339–354). Boston: Kluwer Academic.

Pressman, R. S. (1997). *Software Engineering a practitioners approach* (4th ed.). New York: McGraw Hill.

Quattrone, P., & Hopper, T. (2006). What is IT? SAP, Accounting, and Visibility in a Multinational Organisation. *Information and Organization*, (16): 212–250. doi:10.1016/j.infoandorg.2006.06.001

Quéau, P. (1989). *Metaxu, Champ Vallon, et Le Virtuel*. France: Champ Vallon.

Quinn, R. E. (1988). *Beyond Rational Management*. San Francisco: Jossey-Bass.

Randall, D., Harper, R., & Rouncefield, M. (2007). *Fieldwork for Design: Theory and Practice*. London: Springer.

Rawls, A. W. (2008). Harold Garfinkel, ethnomethodology and workplace studies. *Organization Studies*, *29*(5), 701–732. doi:10.1177/0170840608088768

Reilley, J. P., & Carmel, E. (1995). Does RAD Live Up to the Hype? *IEEE Software*, 24–26. doi:10.1109/52.406752

RMIT. (1995). *Teaching and Learning at RMIT: philosophy and principles*. Melbourne, Australia: RMIT.

RMIT. (1998, December). About RMIT University. *About RMIT*. Retrieved from http://www.rmit.edu.au/About/

Robertson, N., & Shaw, R. (2005). Conceptualizing the Influence of the Self-Service Technology Context on Consumer Voice. *Services Marketing Quarterly*, *27*(2), 33–50. doi:10.1300/J396v27n02_03

Rogers, E. M. (2003). *Diffusion of Innovations* (5th ed.). New York: The Free Press.

Rose, R. (1998). Evaluating the contribution of Structuration Theory to the Information Systems discipline. In *Proceedings of the 6th European Conference on Information Systems (ECIS), Aix-en-Provence*, France.

Ross, J. W., Weill, P., & Robertson, D. (2006). *Enterprise Architecture as a Strategy: Creating Foundation for Business Execution*. Boston: Harvard Business School Press.

Sabherwal, R., & Robey, D. (1993). An empirical taxonomy of implementation processes based on sequence of events in information systems development. *Organization Science*, *4*(4), 548–576. doi:10.1287/orsc.4.4.548

Sahay, S. (1997). Implementation of Information Technology: A Space-Time Perspective. *Organization Studies*, *18*(2), 229–260. doi:10.1177/017084069701800203

Sahay, S., & Robey, D. (1996). Organizational Context, Social Interpretation, and the Implementation and Consequences of Geographic Information Systems. *Accounting. Management & Information Technology*, *6*(4), 255–282. doi:10.1016/S0959-8022(96)90016-8

Sangiovanni-Vincentelli, A. (2003). *The Tides of EDA, IEEE CS, CASS*. Retrieved from http://embedded.eecs.berkeley.edu/research/hsc/class/papers/d6sang.lo.pdf

Schekkerman, J. (2004). *How to survive in the jungle of Enterprise Architecture Frameworks*. Victoria, Australia: Trafford.

Schilit, B. N. (1995). *System architecture for context-aware mobile computing*. New York: Columbia University.

Schneider, A., & Ingram, H. (2007, August 29-September 2). *Ways of Knowing: Implications for Public Policy*. Paper presented at the annual meeting of the American Political Science Association, Chicago, IL.

Schultze, U., & Leidner, D. (2002). Studying Knowledge Management In Information Systems Research: Discourses and Theoretical Assumptions. *Management Information Systems Quarterly*, *26*(3), 212–242. doi:10.2307/4132331

Schultze, U., & Orlikowski, W. (2004). A practice perspective on technology-mediated network relations: The use of Internet-based self-serve technologies. *Information Systems Research*, *15*(1), 87–106. doi:10.1287/isre.1030.0016

Sculley, J., & Byrne, J. A. (1989). *Odyssey: Pepsi to Apple*. London: Fontana.

Serres, A. (2000). *Aux sources d'Internet: exploration du processus d'émergence d'une infrastructure informationnelle*. Description des trajectoires des acteurs et actants, des filières et des réseaux constitutifs de la naissance d'ARPANET. Problèmes critiques et épistémologiques posés par l'histoire des innovations, Rennes.

Serres, M. (1992). *Eclaircissements* (Bourin, F., Ed.).

Sfez, L. (1990). *Critique de la communication* (2nd ed.). Paris: Le seuil.

Shapin, S. (1984). Pump and circumstance: Robert Boyle's literary technology. *Social Studies of Science*, *14*, 481–520. doi:10.1177/030631284014004001

Shapin, S. (1996). *The Scientific Revolution*. Chicago: University of Chicago Press.

Shapin, S., & Schaffer, S. (1985). *Leviathan and the Air-Pump: Hobbes, Boyle, and the Experimental Life*. Princeton, NJ: Princeton University Press.

Shelley, M. (1818). *Frankenstein, or the Modern Prometheus*. London: Penguin Classics.

Silverman, D. (1993). *Interpreting qualitative data: methods for analysing talk, text and interaction*. London: Sage.

Singleton, V., & Michael, M. (1993). Actor-Networks and Ambivalence: General Practitioners in the UK Cervical Screening Programme. *Social Studies of Science*, *23*(2), 227–264. doi:10.1177/030631293023002001

Smith, M. F. (1991). *Software Prototyping, Adoption, Practice and Management*. New York: McGraw-Hill.

Spewak, S. H. (1992). *Enterprise Architecture Planning: Developing a Blueprint for Data, Applications and Technology*. New York: John Wiley & Sons Inc.

Star, S. (2002). Got Infrastructure? How Standards, Categories and Other Aspects of Infrastructure Influence Communication. The 2nd Social Study of IT: LSE workshop on ICT and Globalization.

Star, S. L., & Griesemer, J. R. (1989). Institutional Ecology, 'Translations' and Boundary Objects: Amateurs and Professionals in Berkeley's Museum of Vertebrate Zoology. *Social Studies of Science*, *19*, 387–420. doi:10.1177/030631289019003001

Star, S., & Ruhleder, k. (1996). Steps toward an Ecology of Infrastructure: Design, Access for Large Information Space. *Information Systems Research*, *7*(1), 111–134. doi:10.1287/isre.7.1.111

Stephen. (1997). *Interview on Business Computing Curriculum at RMIT*. Melbourne, Australia: RMIT.

Straub, W. D., & Wetherbe, C. J. (1989). Information Technologies for the 1990s: And Organisational Impact Perspective. *Communications of the ACM*, *32*(11). doi:10.1145/68814.68818doi:10.1145/68814.68818

Sturgeon, T. J. (2001). *How Do We Define Value Chains and Production Networks*? Retrieved from www.inti.gov.ar/cadenasdevalor/Sturgeon.pdf

Sturgeon, T. J. (2006). *Conceptualizing Integrative Trade: The Global Value Chains Framework*. Retrieved from www.dfait-maeci.gc.ca/eet/research/TPR_2006/Chapter_3_Sturgeon-en.pdf

Suchman, L. (1987). *Plan and situated actions: the problem of human machine communication*. Cambridge: Cambridge University Press.

Suchman, L. (2007). *Human-Machine Re-configurations: Plans and Situated Actions* (2nd ed.). Cambridge, UK: Cambridge University Press.

Swan, A., & Carr, L. (2008). Institutions, Their Repositories and the Web. *Serials Review*, *34*(1), 31–35. doi:10.1016/j.serrev.2007.12.006

Swanson, E. B. (1988). *Information System Implementation: Bridging the Gap between Design and Utilisation*. Irwin, Canada: Homewood.

Swanson, E. B., & Ramiller, N. C. (2004). Innovating mindfully with information technology. *Management Information Systems Quarterly*, *28*(4), 553–583.

Tapscott, D., & Caston, A. (1993). *Paradigm shift: The new promise of information technology*. New York: McGraw-Hill.

Tatnall, A. (2007). *Innovation Translation in a University Curriculum*. Melbourne: Heidelberg Press.

Tatnall, A., & Davey, B. (2001). How Visual Basic Entered the Curriculum at an Australian University: An Account Informed by Innovation Translation. In *Challenges to Informing Clients: A Transdisciplinary Approach (Informing Science 2001)*, Krakow, Poland, Informing Science.

Tatnall, A., & Gilding, A. (1999). *Actor-Network Theory and Information Systems Research*. Paper presented at the 10th Australasian Conference on Information Systems (ACIS), Wellington, New Zealand.

Tatnall, A. (2000). *Innovation and change in the information systems curriculum in an Australian University: A socio-technical perspective*. Queensland, Australia: Central Queensland University.

Tatnall, A. (2001, June). How Visual Basic Entered the Curriculum at an Australian University: An Account Informed by Innovation Translation. *Informing Science*, 510–517.

Tatnall, A. (2005). Real-Life Learning, What is Meant by 'Real. In Weert, T. v., & Tatnall, A. (Eds.), *Information and Communication Technologies and Real-Life Learning - New Education for the Knowledge Society* (pp. 143–150). New York: Springer. doi:10.1007/0-387-25997-X_16

Tatnall, A. (2007). *Innovation Translation in a University Curriculum*. Melbourne, Australia: Heidelberg Press.

Tatnall, A. (2009). Information Systems, Technology Adoption and Innovation Translation. *International Journal of Actor-Network Theory and Technological Innovation*, *1*(1), 59–74.

Tatnall, A. (2009b). Innovation Translation and Innovation Diffusion: A Comparison of Two Different Approaches to Theorising Technological Innovation. *International Journal of Actor-Network Theory and Technological Innovation*, *1*(2), 67–74.

Tatnall, A., & Manning, K. (in press). Innovation or Renovation? The Management of Strategic and Adoption Decisions within a University. In Tatnall, A., Visscher, A. J., & Kereteletswe, O. C. (Eds.), *Information Technology and the Management of Quality Education*. Heidelberg, Germany: Springer.

Tatnall, C., & Tatnall, A. (2007). Using Educational Management Systems to Enhance Teaching and Learning in the Classroom: an Investigative Study. In Tatnall, A., Okamoto, T., & Visscher, A. J. (Eds.), *Knowledge Management for Educational Innovation* (pp. 75–82). New York: Springer. doi:10.1007/978-0-387-69312-5_10

Teil, G., & Latour, B. (1995). The Hume machine: can association networks do more than formal rules? *SEHR*, *4*(2). Retrieved from http://www.stanford.edu/group/SHR/4-2/text/teil-latour.html

Telegraph.co.uk. (2010). *Car Alarms Are "Most Irritating Piece of Technology Ever Invented", Poll Finds.* Retrieved January 12, 2010, from http://www.telegraph.co.uk/technology/news/6950876/Car-alarms-are-most-irritating-piece-of-technology-ever-invented-poll-finds.html ten Have, P. (2007). Ethnomethodology. In C. Seale, G. Gobo, J. F. Gubrium, & D. Silverman (Eds.), *Qualitative Research Practice* (Concise paperback ed., pp. 139-152). London: Sage Publications.

Thompson, J. D. (1967). *Organizations in action; social science bases of administrative theory.* New York: McGraw-Hill.

Times Asia, E. E. (2007). *MIPS boosts analog IP line with Chipidea acquisition.* Retrieved from http://www.eetasia.com/ART_8800477579_480100_NT_8dd61497.HTM

Times, E. E. (2007). *MIPS-Chipidea merger's goal: 'virtual' SoCs.* Retrieved from http://www.eetimes.com/showArticle.jhtml?articleID=201803503

Timmermans, S., & Berg, M. (1997). Standardization in action: Achieving universalism and localisation through medical protocols. *Social Studies of Science, 27*(1), 111–134.

Toffler, A. (1971). *Future Shock.* London: Pan.

Tolmie, P., Grasso, A., O'Neill, J., & Castellani, S. (2004, September 7-10). *Supporting remote problem-solving with ubiquitous computing: Research policies and objectives.* Paper presented at the Ubicomp Conference, Giving help at a distance workshop, Nottingham, UK.

Treloar, A. (2005). *ARROW Targets: Institutional Repositories, Open-Source, and Web Services.* Paper presented at the AusWeb05 the Eleventh Australasian World Wide Web Conference. Retrieved September 13, 2005 from http://ausweb.scu.edu.au/aw05/papers/refereed/treloar/

Tschabitscher, H. (2010). *How Many Email Users Are There?* Retrieved February 16, 2010, from http://email.about.com/od/emailtrivia/f/how_many_email.htm

Tummons, J. (2009). Higher Education in Further Education in England: An Actor-Network Ethnography. *International Journal of Actor-Network Theory and Technological Innovation, 1*(3), 55–69.

Tuomi, I. (2009). *The Future of Semiconductor Intellectual Property Architectural Blocks in Europe.* Retrieved from http://ipts.jrc.ec.europa.eu/publications/pub.cfm?id=2799

Van Orsdel, L. C., & Born, K. (2008, April 14). Periodicals Price Survey 2008: Embracing openness. *Library Journal.* Retrieved from http://www.libraryjournal.com/article/CA6547086.html

Vidgen, R., & McMaster, T. (1996). *Black boxes, non-human stakeholders and the translation of IT through mediation.* Paper presented at the IFIP WG8.2 Working Conference on Information Technology and Changes in Organizational Work, Cambridge, UK.

von Lubitz, D., & Wickramasinghe, N. (2006). Creating Germane Knowledge in Dynamic Environments. [IJIL]. *Intl. J. Innovation and Learning, 3*(3), 326–347. doi:10.1504/IJIL.2006.009226

Walsham, G. (1993). *Interpreting Information Systems in Organizations.* New York: John Wiley.

Walsham, G. (1995). The Emergence of Interpretivism in IS Research. *Information Systems Research, 6*(4), 376–394. doi:10.1287/isre.6.4.376doi:10.1287/isre.6.4.376

Walsham, G. (1997). Actor Network Theory and IS Research: Current Status and Future Prospects. InA. S. Lee, J. Liebenau, & J. I. DeGross, (Eds.), Information Systems and Qualitative Research. London: Chapman & Hall.

Walsham, G. (1997). Actor-Network Theory and IS research: Current status and future prospects. In A. S. Lee, J. Liebenau & J. I. DeGross (Eds.), *Information systems and qualitative research* (pp. 466-480). London: Chapman and Hall.

Walsham, G. (1993). *Interpreting information systems in organizations.* Chichester, UK: John Wiley & Sons.

Walsham, G. (1995). Interpretive case studies in IS research: nature and method. *European Journal of Information Systems, 4,* 74–81. doi:10.1057/ejis.1995.9

Walsham, G. (1997). Actor Network Theory and IS Research: Current Status and Future Prospects. In Lee, A. S., Liebenau, J., & DeGross, J. I. (Eds.), *Information Systems and Qualitative Research.* London: Chapman & Hall.

Walsham, G. (1997). Actor-network theory and IS research: Current status amd future prospects. In Lee, A. S., Liebenau, J., & DeGross, J. (Eds.), *Information systems and qualitative research* (pp. 466–480). New York: Chapman & Hall.

Walsham, G. (2001). *Making a World of difference: IT in a Global context*. Chichester, UK: John Wiley & Sons.

Walsham, G., & Sahay, S. (1999). GIS for district-level administration in India: Problems and opportunities. *Management Information Systems Quarterly*, *23*, 39–66. doi:10.2307/249409

Wan Ismail, W. K., & Abd Majid, R. (2007). Framework of the culture of innovation: a revisit. *Journal Kemanusiaan*, *9*, 38–39.

Weill, P., & Broadbent, M. (1998). *Leveraging the new infrastructure: how market leaders capitalize on information technology*. Boston, Mass.: Harvard Business School Press.

Wellman, B., Quan-Haase, A., Boase, J., Chen, W., Hampton, K., & Isla de Díaz, I. (2003). The Social Affordances of the Internet for Networked Individualism. *Journal of Computer-Mediated Communication*, *8*(3).

Wells, M. (1976). *Computing Systems Hardware (Cambridge Computer Science Texts - 6)*. Cambridge, UK: Cambridge University Press.

Whittle, A., & Spicer, A. (2008). Is Actor Network Theory Critique? *Organization Studies*, *29*(4), 611–629. doi:10.1177/0170840607082223

Wickramasinghe, N. (2003). Do We Practise What We Preach: Are Knowledge Management Systems in Practice Truly Reflective of Knowledge Management Systems in Theory? *Business Process Management Journal*, *9*(3), 295–316. doi:10.1108/14637150310477902

Wickramasinghe, N. (2006). Knowledge Creation: A meta-Framework. *International J. Innovation and Learning*, *3*(5), 558–573.

Wickramasinghe, N., & Goldberg. (2007). Adaptive Mapping to Realisation Methodology (AMR) to facilitate Mobile Initiatives in Healthcare. *International Journal of Mobile Communications*, *5*(3), 300–318. doi:10.1504/IJMC.2007.012396

Wickramasinghe, N., Bali, K. R., & Goldberg, S. (2009). The S'ANT Approach to Facilitate a Superior Chronic Disease Self-Management Model. *International Journal of Actor-Network Theory and Technological Innovation*, *1*(4), 15–26.

Wickramasinghe, N., Tumu, S., Bali, R. K., & Tatnall, A. (2007). Using actor-network theory (ANT) as an analytical tool in order to effect superior PACS implementation. *International Journal of Networking and Virtual Organisations*, *4*(3), 257–279. doi:10.1504/IJNVO.2007.015164

Wickramasinghe, N., & von Lubitz, D. (2007). *Knowledge-Based Enterprise: Theories and Fundamentals*. Hershey, PA: IGI Global.

Williams, M. (1922). *The Velveteen Rabbit, or How Toys Become Real*. London: Heinemann.

Willinsky, J. (2006). *The Access Principle: The Case for Open Access to Research and Scholarship*. Retrieved from http://mitpress.mit.edu/catalog/item/default.asp?ttype=2&tid=10611

Wong, L. (2010). *The E-Learning Experience - Its Impact on Student Engagement and Learning Outcomes*. Paper presented at the Business & Economics Society International Conference.

Wong, L., & Tatnall, A. (2009). The Need to Balance the Blend: Online versus Face-to-Face Teaching in an Introductory Accounting Subject. [IISIT]. *Journal of Issues in Informing Science and Information Technology*, *6*, 309–322.

Wong, L., & Tatnall, A. (2010). Factors Determining the Balance between Online and Face-to-Face Teaching: an Analysis using Actor-Network Theory. *Interdisciplinary Journal of Information. Knowledge and Management*, *5*, 167–176.

Woo, J. (2006). *A Short History of the Development Of Ultrasound In Obstetrics And Gynaecology.* Retrieved from http://www.ob-ultrasound.net/history1.html

Woodward, J. (1965). *Industrial organization: theory and practice*. London, New York: Oxford University Press.

Woolgar, S. (2005). Mobile Back to Front: Uncertainty and Danger in Theory-Technology Relation. In Ling, R., & Pedersen, P. E. (Eds.), *Mobile Communications: Renegotiation of the Social Sphere*. London: Springer Verlag.

Yates, J. (2005). *Structuring the Information Age: Life Insurance and Technology in the Twentieth Century*. Baltimore: Johns Hopkins University Press.

Yin, R. K. (1994). *Case Study Research, Design and Methods*. Newbury Park: Sage Publications.

Yin, R. K. (1994). *Case Study Research, Design and Methods* (2nd ed.). Newbury Park, CA: Sage Publications.

Yin, R. K. (1999b). Enhancing the Quality of Case Studies in Health Services Research. *Health Services Research*, *34*(1), 1209–1218.

Zachman, J. A. (1996). Enterprise Architecture: The View Beyond 2000. In *Proceedings of 7th International Users Group Conference for Warehouse Repository Architecture Development*.

Zeithaml, V. A., Parasuraman, A., & Malhotra, A. (2002). Service Quality Delivery Through Web Sites: A Critical Review of Extant Knowledge. *Journal of the Academy of Marketing Science*, *30*(4), 362–375. doi:10.1177/009207002236911

Zuboff, S. (1988). *In the Age of the Smart Machine*. New York: Basic Books, Inc.

Zuboff, S. (1982). New Worlds of Computer-mediated Work. *Harvard Business Review*, *60*(5), 142–152.

About the Contributors

Arthur Tatnall is an Associate Professor in the School of Management and Information Systems at Victoria University in Melbourne, Australia. In his PhD he used actor-network theory to investigate adoption of Visual Basic in the curriculum of an Australian university. Arthur's research interests include technological innovation, history of technology, project management, information systems curriculum, information technology in educational management and electronic business. Much of his research is based on the use of actor-network theory. Arthur is a Fellow of the Australian Computer Society and active in the International Federation for Information Processing (IFIP) as Chair of IFIP WG9.7 – *History of Computing*, Chair of IFIP WG3.4 – *ICT in Professional and Vocational Education* and a member of IFIP WG3.7 – *Information Technology in Educational Management.*

* * *

Antonio Díaz Andrade is a Senior Lecturer in Business Information Systems at Auckland University of Technology (AUT), New Zealand. Before joining AUT in 2009, Antonio was a Lecturer at The University of Auckland, where he obtained his PhD in Management Science and Information Systems in 2007. His thesis, *Interaction between Existing Social Networks and Information and Communication Technology Tools: Evidence from Rural Andes*, was nominated for the Best Doctoral Thesis Award. Antonio started his academic career at Universidad ESAN, Peru in 2000 after having spent 15 years in the Peruvian Air Force. His work has been published in a number of international refereed journals, books and conference proceedings in the information systems field.

Rajeev K. Bali is a Reader in Healthcare Knowledge Management at Coventry University (UK). His main research interests lie in clinical and healthcare knowledge management (from both technical and organisational perspectives). He founded and leads the Knowledge Management for Healthcare (KARMAH) research subgroup (working under BIOCORE). He is well published in peer-reviewed journals and conferences and has been invited to deliver presentations and speeches in the USA, Canada, Singapore and Finland among other countries. He serves on various editorial boards and conference committees and is a regular international invited speaker.

Stephen Burgess has research and teaching interests that include the use of ICTs in small businesses (particularly in the tourism field), the strategic use of ICTs, medical informatics and B2C electronic commerce. He has received a number of competitive research grants in these areas. He has completed several studies related to website features in small businesses and how well websites function over time.

He has authored/ edited three books and special editions of journals in topics related to the use of ICTs in small business and been track chair at the international ISOneWorld, IRMA, Conf-IRM and ACIS conferences in related areas.

Dubravka Cecez-Kecmanovic (dubravka@unsw.edu.au) is a Professor of Information Systems in the School of Information Systems, Technology and Management at the Australian School of Business, University of New South Wales (UNSW), Sydney, Australia. Her research has spanned a wide domain from technological design and applications of formal logics in information systems, to studies of social systems of information and government information systems, to ethnographies of electronically mediated work and electronic collaboration, to exploring social theoretic foundations of Information Systems (IS). She has published in the top IS journals such as *Journal of Information Systems, International Journal of Global Information Technology Management, Information Technology and People, Decision Support Systems, Journal of Information Technology, International Journal of Actor Network Theory and Technological Innovation*, and others. She has made a particular contribution to the critical research approach to IS development, deployment, and use in organisations and society.

Fletcher T. H. Cole is currently Visiting Fellow in the School of Information Systems, Technology and Management at the University of New South Wales, Sydney, Australia. His research background is in information management and organization studies. Fletcher's current research is on the anthropological and language aspects of information-related technologies, especially focusing on fundamental issues in data management practice. He has taught widely on various aspects of information systems analysis & design, information science, the management of information services, business communication, professional practice and ethics.

Antonio Cordella is Lecturer in Information Systems at the London School of Economics and Political Science. His research interests cover the areas of e-Government actor-network theory, and the Social Studies of Information Systems. He has published numerous journal papers, book chapters, and conference papers on the impact of Information and communication technologies on public and private organisations.

Patricia Deering has a long term interest in the theories addressing adoption of innovation and she has researched across education and health. Based on her experience in applying actor network theory through research, Patricia is currently employed by the Victorian Department of Human Services in health workforce restructure. This employment reflects her driving interest in innovation and reform, particularly in seeking explanations for the macro and micro socio-technical relationships involved in the contemporary workplace - including the workforce area of general practice. Patricia has recently been applying Actor Network Theory to an evaluation of innovation pilot projects which sought to explore role redesign in the health workforce.

José Figueiredo is a Professor at the Engineering and Management Department of the Technical University of Lisbon (IST) and a Researcher at CEG-IST, Engineering and Management Research Center (IST). He has a PhD in Industrial Engineering and Management with the research 'Sociotechnical approaches to inter-institutional Information Systems Design', from the Technical University of Lisbon

(IST); an MBA in Information Management at UCP (Portuguese Catholic University–Lisbon); and an Engineering Degree in Electronics and Digital Systems (Technical University of Lisbon, IST). He was instrumental in the start-up of two small companies: one in the computer systems domain (design and development of controlling devices), the other in the internet arena (portal development and workflow systems).

Fernando Abreu Gonçalves is a Professor at ISCAL (IPL), Accounting and Administration Institute in Lisbon, and a Researcher at CEG-IST, Engineering and Management Research Center (IST). He has an MSc in 'Critical Success Factors in Engineering Services'; an MBA in Information Management from UCP (Portuguese Catholic University–Lisbon); and an Engineering degree in Chemistry (IST, Technical University of Lisbon). He has more then 30 years of experience in engineering and information systems in private Portuguese companies in the sectors of railways, petrochemicals and engineering consulting.

Jonny Holmström is a professor of Informatics at Umeå University, Sweden. His research interests include IT's organizational consequences, digital innovation, and open innovation methods for university-industry collaboration. Holmström's larger research program has examined how organizations innovate with IT, and he is currently investigating how organizations in the process industry sector can develop sustainable competitive advantages through mindful use of IT, and how media organizations make use of a heterogeneous media portfolio.

Tiko Iyamu (PhD) is an Associate Professor of information systems and currently the Head of Department, Informatics at Tshwane University of Technology. He also serves as an Extraordinaire Professor at the Department of Computer Science, University of the Western Cape, both of South Africa. Before taken fulltime appointment in academic, he heard several positions in both government and corporate. They include Chief Architect at the City of Cape Town and Head of Architecture and Governance at MWEB (a telecommunication company), South Africa. Research interests include Mobile Computing, Enterprise Architecture and Information Technology Strategy. His interests are on Actor Network Theory (ANT) and Structuration Theory (ST). Iyamu is author of numerous peer-reviewed journal and conference proceeding articles. The most recent articles include The Impact of non-Technical Factors on Information Technology Strategy and E-business; Strategic Approach used for the Implementation of Enterprise Architecture; and The Impact of Network of People in the Computing Environment.

Katrin Jonsson is a PhD student at the Department of Informatics, Umeå University. Her research is situated within the domains of IT-enabled services and their role in organizational contexts. She is currently completing her thesis focused on remote diagnostics services in industrial organizations.

Mary Anne Kennan (mkennan@csu.edu.au) is a Senior Lecturer in the School of Information Studies at Charles Sturt University. While completing her PhD at UNSW she worked as a facilitator in the MBT program at UNSW, a lecturer at UTS and a tutor and research associate at UNSW. Her research interests lie in the areas of open access, e-participation and education for information. She has published in both the information systems and information science literature. Prior to coming to academia she worked for 25 years in libraries and the information world, in management and information technology.

Kalle Lyytinen is Iris S. Wolstein Professor Case Western Reserve University, U.S.A., adjunct professor at University of Jyvaskyla, Finland, and visiting professor at University of Loughborough U.K. He is currently involved in research projects that look at the IT-induced radical innovation in software development, IT innovation in architecture, engineering and construction industry, requirements discovery and modeling for large-scale systems, implementation processes of ERP, and the adoption of broadband wireless services in the U.K., South Korea and the U.S. He serves currently on the editorial boards of several leading information systems and requirements engineering journals including Journal of AIS (Editor-in-Chief), Journal of Strategic Information Systems, Information & Organization, Requirements Engineering Journal, Information Systems Journal, Scandinavian Journal of Information Systems, and Information Technology and People, among others.

Thavandren R. Naidoo (Rennie) is a part-time Senior Lecturer in Information Systems at the University of the Witwatersrand, Johannesburg, South Africa. Prior to joining Wits, he worked for 15 years in various management and consulting positions, largely focusing on the design and implementation of IT systems such as ERP, BI and E-Commerce applications. He also consults and runs specialist courses on business analysis and business case writing. His current teaching includes the Honours Capstone Systems Development Project focusing on Project Management and Business Systems Analysis and Design, and to Masters Students an Introduction to Philosophy in Information Systems, Research Methods, and Structuration and Actor-Network Theory. His research interests is in applying a practice lens using social theories such as actor-network theory and structuration to better understand general IS management, IS implementation, IS decision-making and IS education challenges. He holds a BCom, double BCom(Hons), a Postgraduate diploma in Marketing, a MCom(IS) as well as a PhD (IT). Rennie is also a member of the IT Governance Institute (ITGI), the Project Management Institute, and the International Institute of Business Analysis (IIBA).

Agneta Nilsson is a senior lecturer at Umeå University and Gothenburg University. Her research interests focus on organizing and managing IT enabled change processes in organizational contexts. She is particularly interested in the interplay between technical and non-technical design decisions, and implications for work and organizations. She holds a PhD in Informatics from Gothenburg University.

Dewald Roode (PhD) is a visiting professor in the Department of Information Systems at the University of Cape Town, and Cape Peninsula University of Technology. His research interests include the sociotechno divide in society, ICT and socio-economic development, strategic planning for information systems and the impact of ICT on organizations. His work has been published in many journals and conference proceedings such as *Information Technology and People*, *Studies in Communications Sciences*, *Journal of Education for MIS*, *IEEE Transactions on Software Engineering*, *SA Computer Journal* and *SA Journal for Economic and Management Sciences*. He received a best paper award at ECIS 2004. He completed a six year term in 2007 as chair of IFIP's Technical Committee 8 on Information Systems, and was a member of the Steering Committee of IFIP's World Information Technology Forum in Lithuania in 2003 and in Botswana in 2005.

Jim Underwood (Jim.Underwood@uts.edu.au) is a Senior Lecturer in Information Systems at the University of Technology, Sydney. He was previously at Canberra CAE and, a long time ago, in several IT consulting companies. His interests include the politics of information systems development, the dynamics of learning, and the meaning of knowledge and self in a virtual society. He has also recently published on cultural issues in e-commerce and IT for indigenous people. These are approached through the philosophical lenses of Foucault, Latour and Deleuze (amongst others). He has a PhD in Information Systems, a BSc in Pure Mathematics and Diplomas in Administration, Recreation Planning, and Teaching LOTE.

Nilmini Wickramasinghe received her PhD from Case Western Reserve University, USA and currently is the Epworth Chair in Health Information Management and a professor at RMIT University, Australia. She researches and teaches within the information systems domain with a special focus on IS/IT solutions to effect superior, patient centric healthcare delivery. She has collaborated with leading scholars at various premier healthcare organizations throughout US and Europe. She is well published with more than 200 referred scholarly articles, 10 books, numerous book chapters, an encyclopaedia and a well established funded research track record. In addition, Prof. Wickramasinghe is the editor-in-chief of two scholarly journals: International Journal of Networking and Virtual Organisations (IJNVO – www.inderscience.com/ijnvo) and International Journal of Biomedical Engineering and Technology (IJBET- www.inderscience.com/ijbet).

Nisrine Zammar was born in 1984 in Beirut – Lebanon where I grew up. In 2005, I earned my Bachelor's degree in Publicity Information and Documentation from the Lebanese University of Beirut after which I joined the University of Haute Bretagne – Rennes 2 and obtained my Master degree in Information and Communication Science in 2007. Today, I am in my third year of doctorate, (Rennes 2) working on the Social Network Services and the new communication practices and challenges. I am also teaching the Information and Communication Science at the same University and I am member of the CERSIC-ERELLIF laboratory. I have participated to an International seminar last year, at Rennes 2, and got published in the acts of the seminar. I am certainly looking for more … mainly spreading knowledge and fighting ignorance.

Index

H

I

J

K

M

N

O

P